William Augustus Henderson

How to Cook, Carve and Eat

Or, Wholesome Food, and How to Prepare it for the Table

William Augustus Henderson

How to Cook, Carve and Eat
Or, Wholesome Food, and How to Prepare it for the Table

ISBN/EAN: 9783744786546

Printed in Europe, USA, Canada, Australia, Japan

Cover: Foto ©Andreas Hilbeck / pixelio.de

Turkey
Pidgeon
Fowl
Woodcock
Rabbit
Partridge
Goose
Duck
Hare

HOW TO

COOK, CARVE AND EAT;

OR,

WHOLESOME FOOD,

AND

HOW TO PREPARE IT FOR THE TABLE.

BEING A COMPLETE

TREATISE ON THE ART OF COOKING EVERY VARIETY OF FOOD IN COMMON USE IN A PALATABLE AND DIGESTIBLE MANNER AT A REASONABLE COST.

TO WHICH IS ADDED

A Chapter on the Art of Carving,

AND

TWO HUNDRED OF THE MOST VALUABLE AND POPULAR RECEIPTS KNOWN FOR DOMESTIC PURPOSES.

THE WHOLE

FORMING A HISTORY OF DOMESTIC KNOWLEDGE AND USEFUL ECONOMY.

BY W. A. HENDERSON.

Illustrated with Steel Engravings.

NEW YORK:
LEAVITT & ALLEN BRO'S, PUBLISHERS,
No. 8 HOWARD STREET.

ADVERTISEMENT.

As there is scarce an individual who is not aware of the comfort resulting from a regular and cleanly meal, it may appear to many labour lost, to write a preface to a work which is designed to teach us how to prepare such a repast.

But, in the daily progress of life, we may often discover an amiable and accomplished woman, who possesses a general knowledge, with the exception of domestic cookery, which, I must be suffered to remark, is a subject of infinitely greater importance to her than superficial acquirements, whether we consider her as a daughter, wife, or mother. Indeed, she can never be properly the mistress of a family, unless she makes herself acquainted with its interior economy.

Exclusive of the necessity of such knowledge, it is surprising, how much such a woman, possessed of it may save in the yearly expenditure of her family, which, in the present times, is an object of material importance to all persons of moderate incomes, for whom this book is peculiarly adapted, combining economy and gentility in its receipts and directions.

GENERAL DIRECTIONS

FOR THE

MANAGEMENT OF A FAMILY.

ALL persons should endeavour to discharge the duties of the station they may fill, so as to claim the respect of their compeers; and afford a beneficial example to the younger branches of society: to such as are desirous of respect, this mode of conduct is a matter of necessity, the neglect of which no excuse can extenuate.

The accomplishments proper for the female character, are not so seriously attended to as formerly, when all persons, whatever might be their rank, were studious to render themselves useful. Yet domestic occupations should never for one moment be neglected, as such neglect must produce misery, and may, perhaps, ultimately terminate in *ruin*. At no very distant period, ladies knew but little beyond their own family concerns; now, alas! there are few things of which they know so little. Viewed either way, this is running into extremes, which should be carefully avoided, because elegant acquirements may, with some little care, be easily united with useful knowledge, and without which they become ridiculous. That this may be done, we have numerous examples, even in the most elevated ranks of society, in which the mistress of a family, possessed of every possible feminine accomplishment, may be frequently seen superintending her family arrangements, investigating her accounts, instructing her servants, and keeping within the bounds of her husband's income; by such means, reflecting credit on him, as well as herself.

If such minute attention to domestic concerns reflects honour upon females of elevated rank, at the same time that it is useful to them, how much more therefore must it be beneficial to such as possess contracted incomes, and who can only support an elegant, nay even a neat appearance, by exerting the most rigid economy, and attentively directing their efforts to the proper management of their domestic affairs.

Females should be early taught to prefer the society of their homes, to engage themselves in domestic duties, and to avoid every species of idle vanity, to which thousands of them owe their ruin; and, above all things, to consider their parents as their best friends, who are interested only in their welfare; then indeed we might hope to see all as it should be, and to have daily evidence of real comfort and happiness. Were females thus instructed, they would soon learn to discriminate between the solid enjoyments of domestic peace, and the fleeting phantoms of delusive pleasure.

It is natural to imagine, that when a female marries, she does so from a principal of love. It must surely, therefore, be admitted, that her duties then become still more seriously important, because her station is more responsible than it previously was. She will then have to superintend the affairs of the man with whose destiny she has united her own; the domestic part of which falls particularly within the sphere of her management, and the duties of which she ought actively to execute, and at the same time to support as neat and elegant an appearance as is consistent with prudent economy; without which even princely fortunes must fail; in which case, her husband will soon discover her merits, and place a proper value on the treasure he possesses.

A person who desires to please, will seldom fail to do so. This conviction should of itself be sufficient to stimulate to the attempt, as domestic knowledge in a female is of more real importance than vain acquirements, not that accomplishments, when properly directed, are incompatible with domestic duties; on the contrary, they become intimately combined with them, because they add to the rational enjoyments of that home which should ever be the centre of attraction to the husband, to her children, and others connected with it; and this is what an ignorant, unsocial, and unaccomplished woman can never render it. It is the abuse of things from which alone mischief can originate, not from the temperate use of them.

The domestic arrangements of a family belonging entirely to the female, the table, of course, becomes entitled to no small share of her attention in respect to its expenditure, appearance, and general supplies.

Taste and judgment are highly requisite in this department, because the credit of keeping a good and respectable table depends not (as of old) on the vast quantity of articles with which it is covered, but the neatness, propriety, and cleanliness, in which the whole is served up, which alone can confer real credit on her who directs the preparation.

Dinner parties are very expensive, and certainly fall very heavy on persons whose incomes are moderate; such persons, therefore, should not support a custom productive of unpleasant consequences, by lending it the sanction of their example. But if it is found requisite occasionally to give dinners, it should be done in a liberal and genteel manner, otherwise it is far better to decline it altogether

Dinners are not so sumptuous now as they formerly were, which may be accounted for from the increased price of provisions; in consequence of which, persons who possess a moderate property are compelled to be as economical as possible, in order to support that genteel appearance necessary for the promotion of comfort.

Yet a certain degree of caution is requisite in providing even a family dinner, as a casual visiter may unexpectedly enter, whose company cannot be avoided, and every man feels his consequence hurt, should such a visiter chance to drop in to a dinner not sufficiently good or abundant; a table should therefore be furnished according to the income and rank of its master; thus I would not have a tradesman emulate the expenditure and appearance of a noble, nor a noble of royalty. A good plain dinner, of which there should be sufficient, with clean linen and decent attendance, will obviate every difficulty; and the entrance of an unexpected visiter will occasion no additional trouble, and all uneasy sensations on account of the appearance of the dinner, will be banished from the breasts of the master and mistress, by which harmony and enjoyment will of course ensue.

This mode of providing a table may be extended to every class of society, where each individual should have a table provided according to the fortune which must pay for it, and such an arrangement will meet with the respect and approbation of all serious persons.

Carving also, though seldom attended to, merits attention; for, without a due knowledge of it, the honours of a table cannot be performed with propriety, or without considerable pain. It also makes a great difference in the daily consumption of a family. I therefore recommend my readers to study this useful branch of domestic knowledge, which can be attained only by constant practice, as written instructions can merely point out the way which practice must render perfect, and without which no person can preside with honour at the head of a table.

Where there are young persons in a family, it would greatly improve them, were they made to take the head of the table, under the superintendence of their parents, by whose salutary directions they would soon discharge the duty thus thrown upon them with equal ease and grace, and learn more in one month's practical employment, than they would in twelve months' observation. This would also prepare them to discharge their duties in a proper manner, when they become mistresses themselves. For my own part, I can imagine nothing more disagreeable than to behold a person at the head of a well-furnished table, presiding only to haggle and spoil the finest articles of provision, by which great waste is occasioned, and, we may add, some disgust, because many delicate persons, when helped in a clumsy manner, absolutely loathe the provisions (however good) thus set before them.

Every lady who fills the situation of a mistress of a family, will, I am confident, upon mature reflection, be convinced, that much depends on the vigilance of her conduct, as far as respects good management and domestic economy; the most trifling events should claim her notice, for the keen eye of a superior can alone restrain servants and dependants within proper bounds, and prevent that waste which would otherwise ensue. This is a line of conduct which the present price of every article of life renders still more imperative. No female should ever harbour a moment's doubt respecting her power to conduct and manage a family, even if previously unused to it, as many of her senior friends will freely give her their advice, and a short practical experience will soon render her able to estimate the best mode of management, and also teach her how to keep her family expenditure agreeable to her income, and how to lay out her money to the greatest advantage. To execute this in a proper manner, a strict account of the yearly income set apart for domestic expenses, should be carefully taken; and that it may not be ignorantly exceeded, a minute account of the daily expenditure should be invariably made out, by which a regular habit of prudent economy will be obtained: and should the expenses of one week then exceed their bounds, it must be made up by retrenching on those of the following weeks. For where persons depend for their support and comfort on the skill and active exertions of a father, much also depends on the mother, who, should she be a bad manager, will soon undo all that her husband has done; but should she understand her duties, prosperity will smile upon the family, and perhaps fortune may be ultimately secured.

To prevent useless trouble in the household accounts, a Family Book-keeper should be purchased, when the sums laid out will only require to be noted down, as the various articles are printed, with a column for every day in the year, by which means the exact expenditure is always ascertained for any period in a few minutes.

Persons who possess the means, should always pay for every article in ready money, the benefit of which they will very soon experience; and tradesmen will be careful to supply such valuable customers with the best of their goods. They are also willing to sell their goods cheaper for money than on credit, consequently, by properly attending to this circumstance, a considerable saving may be made in the course of a year. I would also recommend my readers never to change their trades-people without some serious cause that regular and early hours in a family is of serious importance to every branch of it, as far as relates to comfort, and it should be remembered that servants have feelings equally with ourselves.

It is prudent and economical to have a sufficient quantity of household articles and culinary utensils. The stock should invariably be well kept up, and to do this effectually, requires some consideration.

The best, and indeed only regular method of doing this, is to keep a correct account of these, as well as different articles of household furniture, linen, plate, china, &c. &c. and the various articles should be occasionally examined, and every article replaced as soon as broken.

Much time will also be saved, if every article is kept in its proper place, clean; and remember every thing should be mended the moment it is injured, and *never applied to any other use than that for which it was originally designed*, by which mode of management any thing will last much longer than it otherwise would do.

What an active person may perform in the course of one year by a punctual attendance to regular hours, and a persevering industry, would, if calculated, astonish a common observer by its extent and utility. In respect to servants, a mistress should be extremely careful whom she hires, and be particular in procuring a good character from the persons with whom they have previously resided. It is also the solemn duty of a mistress, to be just in giving a character to such servants as leave her, because a servant's whole dependance rests entirely on the possession of a good character; destitute of which, inevitable ruin must follow. This is a duty, the breach of which nothing can extenuate; for by giving an undeserved bad character to a good servant, through caprice, eternal infamy must be reflected on the person who does so. Faithful, honest servants should be treated with respect and kindness, and when an occasion offers, they should be duly rewarded, which will create emulation in others; but never more kept than sufficient.

Should you deal on credit, a book should be kept, in which every article, with its weight and price, should be inserted the instant it is received, which will prevent imposition, and also serve as a reference.

In a well regulated family, every article should be kept in constant readiness, such as broken sugar, pounded spices, &c. by which much trouble will be prevented when such articles are wanted for immediate use. Servants should also be required to pay the same attention in waiting on the family, when alone, as they do when there is company: this will soon become a regular habit, and visiters will occasion but little additional trouble, while every thing will appear to go on smoothly.

HOW TO COOK.

CHAPTER I.

SOUPS *and* BROTHS.

AS a proper mode is the first and most judicious step that can be taken in the display of any subject, so we shall commence our work with a particular description of the manner of making all kinds of Soups and Broths, those articles in the *Art of Cookery* being, at most entertainments, whether of a public or private nature, first brought upon the table.

To acquire reputation, and give satisfaction to those for whom any kind of provision is dressed, the first grand consideration of the cook should be a particular attachment to cleanliness, and this more immediately in the proper care of all vessels wherein such provision is to be dressed. They must be kept properly tinned, and, as soon as possible after being used, well cleaned, and placed, with their covers on, in some situation adapted for the purpose. Previous to their being again used, examine them very strictly, and be careful that they are totally free from any kind of grease, or any particles of sand, which will be too apt to secrete themselves in unobserved cavities of the vessels. To avoid this, rub the palm of your hand all round, with the ends of your fingers in the cavities, and if any sand is left, it will stick to the flesh, which will naturally draw it out. After this, wipe it all round with a clean cloth, and you may be pretty well satisfied it is thoroughly cleansed for use. The pains you have taken in this first degree of care will be amply repaid by the articles you cook being, if properly managed according to the rules here laid down, brought to table in the highest state of perfection.

As a necessary prelude to the making of soups and broths, we shall introduce a few general observations; which we recommend as deserving the particular notice and attention of the cook.

When you make any kinds of soups, more especially portable, vermicelli, or brown gravy soup, or, indeed, any other that hath roots or herbs in it, always observe to lay the meat at the bottom of your pan, with a good lump of butter. Cut the herbs and roots small, lay them over the meat, cover it close, and set it over a slow fire: this will draw all the virtue out of the roots or herbs, turn it to a good gravy, and give the soup a different flavour from what it would have on putting the water in at first. As soon as you find the gravy is nearly dried up, then fill the saucepan with water, and when it begins to boil skim off the fat, and pursue the directions given for the soup intended to be made. In making peas soup observe, that if they are old, you must use soft water; but if green, hard or spring water, as it will greatly contribute to the preservation of their colour. One principal thing to be observed in making all kinds of soup is, that no one ingredient is more powerful in the taste than another, but that all are as nearly as possible equal, and that the soup be relished in proportion to the purpose for which it is designed.

Vermicelli Soup.

TAKE a knuckle of veal and a scrag of mutton, from each of which cut the flesh into small pieces about the size of walnuts, and mix them together, with five or six thin slices of lean ham. Put into the bottom of your pan about four ounces of butter, and then your meat; to which add three or four blades of mace, two or three carrots, two parsnips, two large onions, with a clove stuck on both sides of each, cut in four or five heads of celery washed clean, a bunch of sweet herbs, eight or ten morels, and an anchovy. When your articles are thus prepared and mixed together in the pan, cover it very close, and set it over a slow fire, without any water, till the gravy is drawn out of the meat. When this is done, pour it out into a pot or large basin; then let the meat brown, (taking care that it does not burn,) and put into the saucepan four quarts of water. Let the whole boil gently till it is wasted to three pints, then strain it, and mix with it the first gravy drawn from the meat. Set it on the fire, and add two ounces of vermicelli, a nice head of celery cut small, chyan pepper and salt to your taste, and let the whole boil about six minutes. Lay a small French roll in the soup dish, pour the soup upon it, strew some of the vermicelli on the surface, and then serve it to table.

Vermicelli Soup White.

WASH your vermicelli in boiling water, and leave it to drain on a sieve that it may not lump: boil it with some good gravy soup; and the moment before serving it up, put in a cullis a-la-reine, or the yolks of some eggs beat up with cream or milk. It must not boil after the eggs are in, or else it will curdle.

Soup a-la-Reine.

TAKE a knuckle of veal, and three or four pounds of lean beef, to which put in six quarts of water, with a little salt. When it boils take off the scum quite clean, then put in six large onions, two carrots, a head or two of celery, a parsnip, one leek, and a little thyme. Let the whole stew together till the meat is quite boiled down, then strain it through a hair sieve, and after it has stood about half an hour, skim it well, and clear it off gently from the settlings into a clean pan. Boil half a pint of cream, and pour it on the crumb of a small loaf till the whole is soaked in. Take half a pound of almonds, blanch and beat them as fine as possible, putting in now and then a little cream to prevent them from oiling. Then take the yolks of six hard eggs, beat them with a loaf soaked in the cream, and mix the whole together. Put your broth in again into the saucepan, and when hot pour it to your almonds. Strain it through a fine hair sieve, rubbing it with a spoon till all the virtue and flavour are extracted. Put the whole into the saucepan, adding a little more cream to make it white. Set it over the fire, keep stirring it till it boils, and skim off the froth as it rises. In the meantime soak the tops of two French rolls in melted butter in a stew-pan till they are crisp, but not brown; then take them out of the butter, and lay them in a plate before the fire. After remaining there a short time put them at the bottom of the tureen, pouring to them a small quantity of the soup. When your soup has been thoroughly skimmed from froth, and is just ready to boil, then take it off, pour it into the tureen, and serve it hot to table. In making this soup, particular care must be taken that no fat be on the surface of the broth at the time it is poured upon the almonds, otherwise the whole will be spoiled.

Soup Cressy.

Cut a pound of lean ham into small bits, and put at the bottom of a stew-pan, with a French roll cut in slices, and laid on the top. Take two dozen heads of celery cut small, six onions, two turnips, one carrot, six cloves, four blades of mace, and two bunches of water cresses. Put them all in a stew-pan, with a pint of good broth. Cover them close, and let them sweat gently for about twenty minutes, after which fill it up with veal broth, and stew it four hours. When this is done, strain it through a fine sieve or cloth, and put it again into the saucepan, seasoning it with salt and a little chyan pepper. As soon as it is simmered up, pour it into the tureen, putting in some French roll toasted hard.

Transparent Soup.

Cut off the meat from a leg of veal as clean as you can, after which break the bone in small pieces. Put the meat into a large jug, with the bones at top, and add to it a bunch of sweet herbs, a quarter of an ounce of mace, half a pound of blanched almonds, and pour in four quarts of boiling water. Set it over a slow fire, close covered, and let it stand all night. The next day take it out of the jug, put it into a clean saucepan, and let it boil slowly till it is reduced to two quarts. During the time it boils be particularly careful to take off all the scum and fat. Strain it into a large bowl, and when you think the meat is perfectly settled at the bottom, so that no sediment can intermix with the soup, put it into a clean saucepan, and intermix it with three or four ounces of boiled rice, or two ounces of vermicelli, which you like best. When it has boiled about a quarter of an hour, pour it into the tureen, and serve it to table.

Almond Soup.

TAKE a quart of almonds, and beat them in a marble mortar, with the yolks of six hard eggs, till they become a fine paste. Mix them by degrees with two quarts of new milk, a quart of cream, and a quarter of a pound of double refined sugar, beat fine, and stir the whole well together. When it is properly mixed, set it over a slow fire, and keep it stirring quick till you find it of a good thickness: then take it off, pour it into your dish, and serve it up. The principal care to be observed in making this soup is to prevent its curdling, which can only be done by keeping it constantly stirring till it boils.

Soup Santé, or Gravy Soup.

TAKE a pound and a half of lean ham cut in slices, and put them in the bottom of the stew-pan, with about two ounces of butter under them. Over the ham, put three ounces of lean beef, and over the beef the same quantity of veal. Put in six onions cut in slices, two carrots, and two turnips sliced, two heads of celery, a bunch of sweet herbs, six cloves, and two blades of mace. Let there be a little water at the bottom, and when you have gently drawn it till it sticks, put in a gallon of boiling water. Let it stew gently for two hours; season with salt and chyan pepper, and strain it clear off. Having ready a carrot cut in thin pieces about two inches in length, a turnip, two heads of leeks, two of celery, two of endive cut across, two cabbage lettuces cut in the same manner, with a little sorrel and chervil. Put these into a stew-pan, and sweat them over the fire for about fifteen minutes; then put them into your soup. Set the whole over the fire, and let it boil gently about a quarter of an hour: then pour it into your tureen, with the crust of a French roll on the top, and send it to table.

Soup and Bouille.

TAKE about five pounds of brisket of beef, roll it up as tight as you can, and fasten it with a piece of tape. Put it into the stew-pan, with four pounds of the leg of mutton piece of beef, and about two gallons of water. When it boils, take off the scum quite clean, and put in one large onion, two or three carrots, two turnips, a leek, two heads of celery, six or seven cloves, and some whole pepper. Stew the whole very gently, close covered, for six or seven hours. About an hour before dinner strain the soup quite clear from the meat. Have ready boiled carrots cut into small pieces with a carrot cutter, turnips cut in balls, spinach, a little chervil and sorrel, two heads of endive, and one or two of celery cut into pieces. Put these into a tureen, with a French roll dried after the crumb is taken out. Pour the soup to these boiling hot, and add a little salt and chyan pepper. Take the tape from the beef, or bouille, and place it in a dish by itself, with mashed turnips and sliced carrots, each in a separate small dish, and in this manner serve up the whole.

Ox Cheek Soup.

BREAK the bones of the cheek, and after having washed it thoroughly clean, put it into a large stew-pan, with about two ounces of butter at the bottom, and lay the fleshy side of the cheek downwards. Add to it about half a pound of lean ham, cut in slices

Peas Soup in the Common Way.

PUT a quart of split peas into four quarts of water, with some beef bones, or a little lean bacon. Add one head of celery cut small, with three or four turnips. Let it boil gently till it is reduced to two quarts, and then work it through a fine sieve with a wooden spoon. Mix a little flour and water well together, and boil them in the soup. Add another head of celery, with chyan pepper and salt to your taste. Cut a slice of bread in dice, fry them a light brown, and put them into your dish; after which pour in the soup, and serve it up.

White Peas Soup.

TAKE four or five pounds of lean beef, and put it into six quarts of water with a little salt. When it boils skim it clean, and put in two carrots, three whole onions, a little thyme, and two heads of celery. When you have done this, put in three quarts of peas, and boil them with the meat till the latter is quite tender: then strain the soup through a hair sieve, at the same time rubbing the pulp of the peas so as to extract all their virtue. Split three coss lettuces into four quarters each, and cut them about four inches in length, with a little mint shredded small: then put half a pound of butter in a stew-pan that will hold your soup, and put the lettuce and mint into the butter, with a leek sliced very thin. Stew them a quarter of an hour, shaking them about often; and after adding a little of the soup, stew them a quarter of an hour longer: then put in your soup, and as much thick cream as will make it white: keep stirring it till it boils, fry a French roll in butter a little crisp, put it in the bottom of the tureen, pour the soup over, and serve it up.

Green Peas Soup.

CUT a knuckle of veal into thin slices, with one pound of lean ham. Lay them at the bottom of a soup-pot with the veal uppermost. Then put in six onions cut in slices, with two or three turnips, two carrots, three heads of celery cut very small, a little thyme, four cloves, and four blades of mace. Put a little water at the bottom, cover the pot close, and draw it gently, taking particular care the meat does not stick to the pot. When it is properly drawn, put in six quarts of boiling water, and let it stew gently four hours, skimming it well during the time. Take two quarts of peas, and stew them in some of the liquor till tender; then strain them off and beat them fine, put the liquor in, and mix them up. Take a tammy, or fine cloth, and rub them through till you have rubbed all the pulp out, and then put your soup in a clean pot, with half a pint of spinach juice, and boil it up for about a quarter of an hour: season with salt and a little [illegible]. If you think your soup not thick enough, take the crumb of a French roll, and boil it in a little of the soup, beat it in a mortar, and rub it through your tammy, or cloth, then put it into your soup, and boil it up. Pour the soup into the tureen, with half a pint of young peas and mint, stewed in fresh butter; then serve it up.

Onion Soup.

TAKE eight or ten large Spanish onions, and boil them in milk and water till they become quite soft, changing your milk and water three times while the onions are boiling. When they are quite soft rub them through a hair sieve. Cut an old fowl into pieces, and boil it for gravy, with one blade of mace. Then strain it, and having poured the gravy on the pulp of the onions, boil it gently, with the crumb of a stale penny loaf grated into half a pint of cream, and season it to your taste with salt and chyan pepper. When you serve it up, grate a crust of brown bread round the edge of the dish. It will contribute much to the delicacy of the flavour, if you add a little stewed spinach, or a few heads of asparagus.

Milk Soup.

BOIL a pint of milk with a little salt, and if you please sugar; arrange some sliced bread in a dish, pour over part of your milk to soak it, and keep it hot upon your stove, taking care that it does not burn. When you are ready to serve your soup, beat up the yolks of five or six eggs, and add them to the rest of the milk. Stir it over the fire till it thickens, and then take it off for fear it should curdle.

Milk Soup. Another Way.

TAKE two quarts of new milk, and put into it two sticks of cinnamon, two bay leaves, a small quantity of basket salt, and a little sugar. While these are heating, blanch half a pound of sweet almonds, and beat them up to a paste in a marble mortar. Mix some milk with them by a little at a time, and while they are heating, grate some lemon-peel with the almonds, and a little of the juice; after which strain it through a coarse sieve; mix all together, and let it boil up. Cut some slices of French bread, and dry them before the fire; soak them a little in the milk, lay them at the bottom of the tureen, pour in the soup, and serve it up.

Milk Soup, with Onions.

TAKE a dozen of onions, and set them over a stove till they are done without being coloured. Then boil some milk, add to it the onions, and season it with salt alone. Put some button onions to scald, then pass them in butter, and when tender add it to the soup, and serve it up.

Rice Soup.

PUT a pound of rice and a little cinnamon into two quarts of water. Cover it close, and let it simmer very gently till the rice is quite tender. Take out the cinnamon, then sweeten it to your palate; grate into it half a nutmeg, and let it stand till it is cold. Then beat up the yolks of three eggs, with half a pint of white wine; mix them well together, and stir them into the rice. Set the whole over a slow fire, and keep stirring it all the time, lest it should curdle. When it is of a good thickness, and boils, take it up, and keep stirring it till you pour it into your dish.

Rice Soup, or Potage du Ris.

TAKE a handful of rice, or more, according to the quantity of soup you make; wash it well in warm water, rubbing it in your hands, and let it stand two hours and a half or three hours over a slow fire, with good beef and veal gravy: when it is done, season it to your palate, and serve it up.

Scotch Barley Broth.

TAKE a leg of beef cut into pieces, and boil it in three gallons of water, with a sliced carrot and a crust of bread. Let it continue boiling till reduced to one half. Then strain it off, and put it again into the pot, with half a pound of barley, four or five heads of [illegible] cut small, a bunch of sweet herbs, a large onion, a little parsley chopped small, and a few marigolds. When this has been boiled an hour, put in a large fowl, and let it continue boiling till the broth is quite good. Season it with salt to your taste, take out the onion and sweet herbs, and send it to table with the fowl in the middle. The fowl may be used or omitted, according to your own discretion, as the broth will be exceeding good without it.

Instead of a leg of beef, some make this broth with a sheep's head, which must be chopped all to pieces. Others use thick flank of beef, in which case six pounds must be boiled in six quarts of water. Put in the barley with the meat, and boil it very gently for an hour, keeping it clear from scum. Then put in the before-mentioned ingredients, with turnips and carrots clean scraped and pared, and cut into small pieces. Boil all together softly till you find the broth very good, and season it to your palate. Then take it up, pour the broth into your dish or tureen, put the beef in the middle, with carrots and turnips round the dish, and send it hot to table. This is a very comfortable repast, more particularly in cold and severe weather.

Soup Lorraine.

TAKE a pound of almonds, blanch them, and beat them in a fine mortar, with a very little water to keep them from oiling. Then take all the white part of a large roasted fowl, with the yolks of four poached eggs, and pound all together as fine as possible. Take three quarts of strong veal broth, let it be very white, and all the fat clean skimmed off. Pour it into a stew-pan with the other ingredients, and mix them well together. Boil them gently over a slow fire, and mince the white part of another fowl very fine. Season it with pepper, salt, nutmeg, and a little beaten mace. Put in a bit of butter about the size of an egg, with a spoonful or two of the soup strained, and set it over the fire to be quite hot. Cut two French rolls into thin slices, and set them before the fire to crisp. Then take one of the hollow loaves which are made for oysters, and fill it with the minced fowl: close the roll as neat as possible, and keep it hot. Strain the soup through a very fine sieve into a clean saucepan, and let it stew till it is of the thickness of cream. Put the crisped bread into the dish or tureen, pour the soup over it, place the roll with the minced meat in the middle, and serve it up.

Soup Maigre.

Put half a pound of butter into a deep stew-pan, shake it about, and let it stand till it has done making a noise; then throw in six middle-sized onions, peeled and cut small, and shake them about. Take a bunch of celery, clean washed and picked, cut it into pieces about half an inch in length; a large handful of spinach clean washed and picked, a good lettuce (if it can be got) cut small, and a bundle of parsley chopped fine. Shake all these well together in the pan for a quarter of an hour, and then strew in a little flour: stir all together in the stew-pan, and put in two quarts of water. Throw in a handful of hard dry crust, with about a quarter of an ounce of ground pepper, and three blades of mace beat fine. Stir all together, and let it boil gently for about half an hour: then take it off, beat up the yolks of two eggs, and stir them in with one spoonful of vinegar. Pour the whole into a soup dish, and send it to table. If the season of the year will admit, pot with an old fowl, and four or five slices of lean ham. Let these stew without any liquor over a very slow fire, but be careful they do not burn to the pot. As soon as you find the meat begins to stick to the bottom, stir it about, and put in some good beef broth clear of all the fat: then put in some turnips, carrots, and celery cut small, a bunch of sweet herbs, and a bay leaf; then add some more clear broth, and let it stew about an hour. While this is doing, take a cow heel, split it, and set it on to boil in some of the same broth. When it is very tender take it off, and set on a stew-pan with some crusts of bread, and some more broth, and let it soak eight or ten minutes. When the soup is stewed till it tastes rich, lay the crusts in a tureen, and the two halves of the cow heel upon them. Then pour in the soup, season it to your palate, and serve it to table.

White Soup.

TAKE a knuckle of veal, a large fowl, and a pound of lean bacon: put these into a saucepan with six quarts of water: add half a pound of rice, two anchovies, a few peppercorns, a bundle of sweet herbs, two or three onions, and three or four heads of celery cut in slices. Stew them all together, till the soup is as strong as you would have it, and then strain it through a hair sieve into a clean earthen pan. Let it stand all night, and the next day take off the scum very clean, and pour the liquor into a stew-pan. Put in half a pound of sweet almonds beat fine, boil it for about a quarter of an hour, and strain it through a lawn sieve. Then put in a pint of cream, with the yolk of an egg, stir all together, let it boil a few minutes, then pour it into your tureen, and serve it up.

Gravy Soup.

TAKE a shin of beef, with the bone well chopped, and put it into your saucepan with six quarts of water, a pint of peas, and six onions. Set it over the fire, and let it boil gently till the juices of the meat are drawn out: then strain the liquor through a sieve, and stew-pan with some stewed celery and fried bread. When it is near boiling, pour it into your tureen, and serve it up hot.

Cray Fish Soup.

Boil an hundred fresh cray fish, as also a fine lobster, and pick the meat clean out of each. Pound the shells of both in a mortar till they are very fine, and boil them in four quarts of water with four pounds of mutton, a pint of green split peas nicely picked and washed, a large turnip, a carrot, an onion, mace, cloves, an anchovy, a little thyme, pepper, and salt. Stew them on a slow fire till all the goodness is out of the mutton and shells: then strain it through a sieve, and put in the meat of your cray fish and lobster, but let them be cut into very small pieces, with the red coral of the lobster, if it has any. Boil it half an hour, and just before you serve it up, add a little butter melted thick and smooth: stir it round when you put it in, and let it simmer very gently about ten minutes. Fry a French roll nice and brown, lay it in the middle of the dish, pour the soup on it, and serve it up hot.

Eel Soup.

Take a pound of eels, which will make a pint of good soup, or any greater weight, in proportion to the quantity of soup you intend to make. To every pound of eels put a quart of water, a crust of bread, two or three blades of mace, a little whole pepper, an onion, and a bunch of sweet herbs. Cover them close, and let them boil till half the liquor is wasted: then strain it, and toast some bread; cut it small, lay the bread in your dish, and pour in the soup. This soup is very balsamic, and particularly nutritious to weak constitutions.

Oyster Soup.

Take a pound of skate, four or five flounders, and two eels: cut them into pieces, just cover them with water, and season with mace, an onion stuck with cloves, a head of celery, two parsley roots sliced, some pepper and salt, and a bunch of sweet herbs. Cover them down close, and after they have simmered about an hour and a half, strain the liquor clear off, and put it into a clean saucepan. In the mean time take a quart of oysters, bearded, and beat them in a mortar with the yolks of six eggs boiled hard. Season it with pepper, salt, and grated nutmeg; and when the liquor boils put all into it. Let the whole boil till it becomes of the thickness of cream, then take it off, pour it into your tureen, and serve it to table.

Mutton Broth.

TAKE a neck of mutton about six pounds, cut it in two, boil the scrag part in a gallon of water, skim it well, and then put in a small bundle of sweet herbs, an onion, and a good crust of bread. When the scrag has boiled about an hour, put in the other part of the mutton, and about a quarter of an hour before the meat is done, put in a turnip or two, some dried marigolds, a few chives, with parsley chopped small, and season it with salt. You may at first put in a quarter of a pound of barley or rice, which both thickens and contributes a grateful flavour. Some like it thickened with oatmeal, and some with bread; and, instead of sweet herbs and onions, season it with mace: but this is a mere fancy, and determined by the different palates of different people. If you boil turnips as sauce to the meat, let it be done by themselves, otherwise the flavour, by being too powerful, will injure the broth.

Beef Broth.

TAKE a leg of beef with the bone well cracked, wash it thoroughly clean, and put it into your pot with a gallon of water. Scum it well, and put in two or three blades of mace, a small bunch of parsley, and a large crust of bread. Let it boil till the beef and sinews are quite tender. Cut some toasted bread and put into your tureen, then lay in the meat, and pour the soup all over

Beef Drink.

TAKE a pound and a half of lean beef, cut it into small pieces, and put it into a gallon of water, with the under crust of a penny loaf, and a little salt. Let it boil till it is reduced to two quarts, then strain it off, and it will be very good drink.—Observe, when you first put the meat into the water, that it is clear of all skin and fat.

Strong Beef Broth to keep.

TAKE part of a leg of beef, and the scrag end of a neck of mutton. Break the bones well of each, and put to it as much water as will cover it, with a little salt. When it boils skim it clean, and put to it a large onion stuck with cloves, a bunch of sweet herbs, some pepper, and a nutmeg quartered. Let these boil till the virtues of the mace are drawn out, then strain the soup through a fine sieve, and keep it for use.

Veal Broth.

STEW a knuckle of veal in about a gallon of water, put in two ounces of rice or vermicelli, a little salt, and a blade of mace. When the meat is thoroughly boiled, and the liquor reduced to about one half, it will be very good and fit for use.

Chicken Broth.

SKIN a large old fowl, cut off the fat, break the fowl to pieces, and put it into two quarts of water, with a good crust of bread, and a blade of mace. Let it boil gently five or six hours: then pour off all the liquor, put a quart more of boiling water to it, and cover it close; let it boil softly till it is good, then strain it off, and season it with a little salt. In the meantime boil a chicken, and save the liquor; and when the flesh is eat, take the bones, break them, and put them in the liquor in which you boiled the chicken, with a blade of mace, and a crust of bread. When the juice of the bones is extracted, strain it off, mix it with the other liquor, and send it to table.

Spring Broth.

TAKE a crust of bread, and about a quarter of a pound of fresh butter; put them into a soup-pot or stew-pan, with a good quantity of herbs, as bear, sorrel, chervil, lettuce, leeks, and purslain, all washed clean, and coarsely chopped. Put to them a quart of water, and let them stew till it is reduced to one half, when it will be fit for use. This is an excellent purifier of the blood.

Plum Porridge to keep.

TAKE a leg and shin of beef, put them into eight gallons of water, and boil them till the meat is quite tender. When the broth is strong, strain it off, shake out the meat, and put the broth again into the pot. Slice six penny loaves thin, cutting off the tops and bottoms, put some of the liquor to them, cover them over, and let them soak for a quarter of an hour: then boil and strain it, and put it into your pot. When the whole has boiled a short time, put in five pounds of stewed raisins of the sun, and two pounds of prunes. After it has boiled a quarter of an hour, put in five pounds of currants clean washed and picked. Let these boil till they swell, and then put in three quarters of an ounce of mace, half an ounce of cloves, and two nutmegs, all beat fine. Before you put these into the pot, mix them with a little cold liquor, and put them in but a short time before the whole is done. When you take off the pot, put in three pounds of sugar, a little salt, a quart of sack, a quart of claret, and the juice of two or three lemons. If you think proper, instead of bread, you may thicken it with sago. Pour your porridge into earthen pans, and keep it for use.

Mock Turtle Soup.

SCALD a calf's head with the skin on, and take off the horny part, which must be cut into pieces about two inches square. Let these be well washed and cleaned, then dry them in a cloth, and put them into a stew-pan, with four quarts of water made as follows:

Take six or seven pounds of beef, a calf's foot, a shank of ham, an onion, two carrots, a turnip, a head of celery, some cloves and whole pepper, a bunch of sweet herbs, a little lemon-peel, and a few truffles. Put these into eight quarts of water, and let it stew gently till the broth is reduced one half; then strain it off, and put it into the stew-pan, with the horny parts of the calf's head. Add some knotted marjorum, a little savory, thyme, and parsley, all chopped small together, with some cloves and mace pounded, a little chyan pepper, some green onions, a shalot cut fine, a few chopped mushrooms, and half a pint of Madeira wine. Stew all these together gently till the soup is reduced to two quarts; then heat a little broth, mix some flour smooth in it, with the yolks of two eggs, and keep it stirring over a gentle fire till it is near boiling. Add this to the soup, keeping it stirring as you pour it in, and let them all stew together for another hour. When you take it off the fire, squeeze in the juice of half a lemon, and half an orange, and throw in some boiled force-meat balls. Pour the whole into your tureen, and serve it up hot to table. This is a rich soup, and to most palates deliciously gratifying.

Portable Soup.

THIS soup (which is particularly calculated for the use and convenience of travellers, from its not receiving any injury by time,) must be made in the following manner. Cut into small pieces three large legs of veal, one of beef, and the lean part of a ham. Put a quarter of a pound of butter at the bottom of a large caldron, then lay in the meat and bones, with four ounces of anchovies, and two ounces of mace. Cut off the green leaves of five or six heads of celery, wash the heads quite clean, cut them small, put them in with three large carrots cut thin, cover the caldron quite close, and set it over a moderate fire. When you find the gravy begins to draw, keep taking it up till you have got it all out; then put water in to cover the meat; set it on the fire again, and let it boil gently for four hours; then strain it through a hair sieve into a clean pan, till it is reduced to one part out of three. Strain the gravy you draw from the meat into the pan, and let it boil gently till you find it of a glutinous consistence, observing to keep skimming off the fat clean as it rises. You must take particular care, when it is nearly enough, that it does not burn. Season it to your taste with chyan pepper, and pour it on flat earthen dishes a quarter of an inch thick. Let it stand till the next day, and then cut it out by round tins a little larger than a crown piece. Lay the cakes in dishes, and set them in the sun to dry, to facilitate which turn them often. When the cakes are dry, put them into a tin box, with a piece of clean white paper between each, and keep them in a dry place. If made in frosty weather, it will be sooner formed in its proper solidity This soup is not only particularly useful to travellers, but it is also exceeding convenient to be kept in private families; for by putting one of the cakes into a saucepan, with about a pint of water, and a little salt, a basin of good broth may be had in a few minutes. There is also another great convenience in it; that by boiling a small quantity of water with one of the cakes, it will make an excellent gravy for roast turkeys and fowls.

CHAPTER II.

BOILING IN GENERAL.

SECT. I.

BUTCHER'S MEAT.

AS a necessary prelude to the directions given under this head, we shall make a few necessary and general observations. All meat should be boiled as slow as possible, but in plenty of water, which will make it rise and look plump. Be careful to keep it clear from scum, and let your pot be close covered. If you boil it fast, the outside will be hardened before the inside is warm, and the meat will be disagreeably discoloured. A leg of veal of twelve pounds weight, will take three hours and a half boiling; and the slower it boils the whiter and plumper it will be.

With respect to mutton and beef, if they are rather under done, they may be ate without being either disagreeable or unwholesome; but lamb, pork, and veal, should be thoroughly done, otherwise, they will be obnoxious to the sight, and consequently ungrateful to the palate. A leg of pork will take half an hour's more boiling than a leg of veal of the same weight; but in general, when you boil beef and mutton, you may allow as many quarters of an hour as the meat weighs pounds. To put in the meat when the water is cold must be allowed to be the best method, as thereby the middle gets warm before the outside becomes hardened. Three quarters of an hour will boil a leg of lamb four pounds and a half weight. From these general directions, it would be unnecessary to describe the usual mode of boiling the common joints of either mutton or beef. We shall therefore proceed to those articles which require more particular notice.

To dress a Calf's Head, one half boiled, the other baked.

After having well cleansed the head, parboil one half, beat up the yolk of an egg, and rub it over the head with a feather; then strew over it a seasoning of pepper, salt, thyme, parsley chopped small, shred lemon-peel, grated bread, and a little nutmeg; stick bits of butter over it, and send it to the oven. Boil the other half white in a cloth, and put them both into a dish. Boil the brains in a piece of clean cloth, with a very little parsley, and a leaf or two of sage. When they are boiled chop them small, and warm them up in a saucepan, with a bit of butter, and a little pepper and salt. Lay the tongue, boiled and peeled, in the middle of a small dish, and the brains round it; have in another dish, bacon or pickled pork; and in a third, greens and carrots.

Grass Lamb.

Whatever the number of pounds is that the joint weighs, so many quarters of an hour must it boil. When done, serve it up with spinach, carrots, cabbage, or brocoli.

A Ham.

Put your ham into a copper of cold water, and when it boils take care that it boils slowly. A ham of twenty pounds weight will take four hours and a half boiling; and so in proportion for one of a larger or smaller size. An old and large ham will require sixteen hours soaking in a large tub of soft water; but a green one does not require any soaking. Be sure, while your ham is boiling, to keep the water clear from scum. When you take it up, pull off the skin, and rub it all over with an egg, strew on crumbs of bread, baste it with a little butter, and set it to the fire till it is of a light brown.

Another Way of boiling a Ham.

With respect to its being an old ham, or a green one, observe the before-mentioned directions. Pare it round and underneath, taking care no rusty part is left. Put it into a pan or pot that will properly contain it, cover it with water, and put in a few cloves, thyme, and laurel leaves. Let it boil on a slow fire about five hours, and then add a glass of brandy, and a pint of red wine: finish boiling in the same manner. If it is to be served up hot, take off the skin, and throw it over with crumbs of bread, a little parsley finely chopped, and a few bits of butter, and give it a good colour either in the oven, or with a salamander. If it is to be kept cold, it will be better to let the skin remain, as it will be a means of preserving its juices.

Ham a-la-Braise.

PARE your ham round and underneath, taking care no rusty part is left; cover it well with meat under and over, with roots and spices, filling it up with water. The gravy that comes from the ham being excellent for all kinds of brown sauces.

Tongues.

IF it be a dried tongue, steep it all night in water; but if it be a pickled one, only wash it well from the brine. Let it boil moderately three hours. If it is to be eat hot, stick it with cloves, rub it over with the yolk of an egg, strew crumbled bread over it, and, when done, baste it with butter, and set it before the fire till it becomes of a light brown. Dish it up with a little brown gravy, or red wine sauce, and lay slices of currant jelly round the dish.

Neat's Tongue, with Parsley.

BOIL it a quarter of an hour, then take it out, and lard it; put it in again to boil with any meat you have going on; when it is done, take the skin off, cut almost half through the middle lengthwise, that it may open in two parts, without the pieces coming apart, and serve it up with some gravy, pepper, and parsley shred fine. If you wish you may add a dash of lemon-juice.

Leg of Mutton, with Cauliflowers and Spinach.

TAKE a leg of mutton, cut venison fashion, and boil it in a cloth. Boil two fine cauliflowers in milk and water, pull them into sprigs, and stew them with butter, pepper, salt, and a little milk: stew some spinach in a saucepan, and put to it a quarter of a pint of gravy, with a piece of butter, and a little flour. When all is done, put the mutton in the middle of the dish, the spinach round it, and the cauliflower over all. The butter the cauliflower was stewed in must be poured over it, and it must be made to appear like smooth cream.

Lamb's Head.

WASH the head very clean, take the black part from the eyes, and the gall from the liver. Lay the head in warm water; boil the lights, heart, and part of the liver. Chop and flour them, and toss them up in a saucepan with some gravy, catchup, and a little pepper, salt, lemon-juice, and a spoonful of cream. Boil the head very white, lay it in the middle of the dish, and the mince-meat round it. Place the other parts of the liver fried, with some very small bits of bacon on the mince-meat, and the brains fried in little cakes and laid on the rim of the dish, with some crisped parsley put between. Pour a little melted butter over the head, and garnish with lemon.

Or you may dress it thus:

BOIL the head and pluck tender, but do not let the liver be too much done. Take the head up, hack it cross and cross with a knife, grate some nutmeg over it, and lay it in a dish before a good fire. Then grate some crumbs of bread, some sweet herbs rubbed, a little lemon-peel chopped fine, a very little pepper and salt, and baste it with a little butter; then throw a little flour over it, and just as it is done do the same, baste and dredge it. Take half the liver, the heart, the lights, and tongue, chop them very small, with about a gill of gravy or water. First shake some flour over the meat, and stir it together, then put in the gravy or water a good piece of butter rolled in a little flour, a little pepper and salt, and what runs from the head in the dish. Simmer all together a few minutes, and add half a spoonful of vinegar; pour it into your dish, lay the head in the middle of the mince-meat, have ready the other half of the liver cut thin with some slices of bacon broiled, and lay round the head. Garnish with lemon.

Leg of Lamb boiled, and Loin fried.

Cut your leg from the loin, and boil it three quarters of an hour. Cut the loin in handsome steaks, beat them with a cleaver, and fry them a good brown. Then stew them a little in strong gravy. Put your leg on the dish, and lay your steaks round it. Pour on your gravy, lay round lumps of staved spinach and crisped parsley on every steak. Send it to table with gooseberry sauce in a boat, and garnish with lemon.

A Haunch or Neck of Venison.

As a necessary preparation for either of these joints, let it lie in salt for a week; then boil it in a cloth well floured, and allow a quarter of an hour's boiling for every pound it weighs. For sauce, boil some cauliflowers, pulled into little sprigs, in some milk and water, with some fine white cabbage, and turnips cut in dice: add some beet-root cut into narrow pieces about an inch and a half long, and half an inch thick. After your cabbage is boiled, beat it up in a saucepan with a piece of butter and salt. When your meat is done, and laid in the dish, put the cabbage next the cauliflower, and then the turnips. Place the beet-root here and there, according to your fancy: and have a little melted butter in a cup, in case it should be wanted. This dish is not only excellent in its quality, but particularly pleasing in its appearance. If any is left, it will eat well the next day, hashed with gravy and sweet sauce.

Pickled Pork.

After washing and scraping it perfectly clean, put it into the pot with the water cold, and when the rind feels tender, it is enough. The general sauce is greens, among the variety of which you are to make choice to your own direction.

Pig's Pettitoes.

Boil the feet till they are quite tender, but take up the heart, liver, and lights, when they have boiled ten minutes, and shred them small. Then take out the feet and split them: thicken your gravy with flour and butter, and put in your mince-meat, a spoonful of white wine, a slice of lemon, a little salt, and give it a gentle boil. Beat the yolk of an egg: put to it two spoonsful of cream, and a little grated nutmeg. Then put in the pettitoes, and shake it over the fire till it is quite hot, but do not let it boil. Put sippets into the dish, pour over the whole, and garnish with sliced lemon.

SECT. II.

BOILING POULTRY.

Turkeys.

A Turkey should not be dressed till three or four days after being killed, as it will otherwise not boil white, neither will it eat tender. When you have plucked it, draw it at the rump, cut off the legs, put the ends of the thighs into the body, and tie them with a string. Having cut off the head and neck, grate a penny loaf, chop fine about a score of oysters, shred a little lemon-peel, and put in a sufficient quantity of salt, pepper, and nutmeg. Mix these up into a light forcemeat, with a quarter of a pound of butter, three eggs, and a spoonful or two of cream. Stuff the craw of the turkey with one part of this composition: the other must be made into balls, and boiled. When you have sewed up the turkey, and dredged it with flour, put it into a kettle of cold water; cover it close, set it over the fire, and when the scum begins to rise, take it clean off, and then cover the kettle close. If a young one of a moderate size, let it boil very slowly for half an hour: then take off your kettle, and let it stand for some tim close covered, when the steam being confined, will sufficiently do it. When you dish it up, pour a little of your oyster sauce over it, lay the force-meat balls round it, and serve it up with the rest of the sauce in a boat. Garnish your dish with barberries and lemon.

The best sauces for a boiled turkey are, good oyster and celery sauce. Make the oyster sauce thus: Take a pint of oysters, strain the liquor from them, and beard and wash them in cold water. Pour the liquor clear off into a stew-pan, and put in the oysters with a blade of mace, some butter rolled with flour, and a quarter of a lemon. When they boil up, put in half a pint of cream, and boil the whole gently together. Take the lemon and mace out: squeeze the juice of the lemon into the sauce, and serve it up in your boats or basins. Make the celery sauce thus: Cut the white part of the celery into pieces about an inch in length, and boil it in some water till it is tender. Then take half a pint of veal broth and a blade of mace, and thicken it with a little flour and butter; add half a pint of cream, and boil them gently together. Put in your celery, and when it boils, pour them into your boats

Chickens.

After you have drawn them, lay them in skimmed milk for two hours, and truss them. When you have properly singed, and dusted them with flour, cover them close in cold water, and set them over a slow fire. Having taken off the scum, and boiled them slowly five or six minutes, take them off the fire, and keep them close covered for half an hour in the water, which will do them sufficiently, and make them plump and white. Before you dish them, set them on the fire to heat then drain them and pour over them white sauce, which you must have made ready in the following manner:

Take the heads and necks of the chickens, with a small bit of scrag of veal, or any scraps of mutton you may have by you, and put them into a saucepan, with a blade or two of mace, and a few black peppercorns, an anchovy, a head of celery, a slice of the end of a lemon, and a bunch of sweet herbs. Put to these a quart of water, cover it close, and let it boil till it is reduced to half a pint. Then strain it, and thicken it with a quarter of a pound of butter mixed with flour, and boil it five or six minutes. Then put in two spoonsful of mushrooms, and mix the yolks of two eggs with a tea-cup full of cream, and a little nutmeg grated. Put in your sauce, and keep shaking it over the fire till it is near boiling; then pour it into your boats, and serve it up with your chickens.

Fowls.

After having drawn your fowls, which you must be particularly careful in doing, cut off the head, neck, and legs. Skewer them with the ends of their legs in their bodies, and tie them round with a string. Singe and dust them well with flour, put them into cold water, cover the kettle close, and set it on the fire; but take it off as soon as the scum begins to rise. Cover them close again, and let them boil gently twenty minutes: then take them off, and the heat of the water will do them sufficiently. Melted butter with parsley shred fine is the usual sauce, but you may serve them up with the like sauce as before directed for chickens.

Rabbits or Ducks.

Boil your duck or rabbit in a good deal of water, and when the scum rises take it clean off. A duck will take about twenty minutes, and a rabbit half an hour. Melted butter and parsley is frequently used as sauce for rabbits; but if you prefer onion sauce, which will do for either, make it thus: Peel your onions, and throw them into water as you peel them; then cut them into thin slices, boil them in milk and water, and scum the liquor. About half an hour will boil them. When they are sufficiently boiled, put them into a clean sieve to drain: chop them, and rub them through a cullender; then put them into a saucepan, and shake a little flour, with two or three spoonsful of cream, and a good piece of butter. Stew them all together till they are thick and fine; lay the duck or rabbit in a dish, and pour the sauce all over. If a rabbit, you must pluck out the jaw-bones, and stick one in each eye, the small end inwards

Another sauce for a boiled duck may be made thus: Take a large onion, a handful of parsley clean washed and picked, and a lettuce: cut the onion small, chop the parsley fine, and put them into a quarter of a pint of good gravy, with a spoonful of lemon-juice, and a little pepper and salt. When they have stewed together half an hour, add two spoonsful of red wine. Lay the duck in your dish, and pour the sauce over it.

Pigeons.

WHEN you draw your pigeons, be careful to take out the craw as clean as possible. Wash them in several waters, and having cut off the pinions turn their legs under their wings. Let them boil very slowly a quarter of an hour, and they will be sufficiently done. Dish them up, and pour over them good melted butter; lay round the dish a little brocoli, and serve them up with melted butter and parsley in boats. They should be boiled by themselves, and may be eaten with bacon, greens, spinach, or asparagus.

Geese.

SINGE a goose, and pour over it a quart of boiling milk. Let it continue in the milk all night, then take it out, and dry it well with a cloth. Cut an onion very small with some sage, put them into the goose, sew it up at the neck and vent, and hang it up by the legs till the next day: then put it into a pot of cold water, cover it close, and let it boil gently for an hour. Serve it up with onion sauce.

Partridges.

BOIL them quick in a good deal of water, and fifteen minutes will be sufficient. For sauce, take a quarter of a pint of cream, and a bit of fresh butter about the size of a walnut. Stir it one way till it is melted, and then pour it over the birds.

Pheasants.

THESE must be likewise boiled in plenty of water. If it be a small one, half an hour will be sufficient, but if a large one, three quarters. For sauce, stew some heads of celery cut very fine, thickened with cream, and a small piece of butter rolled in flour, and season with salt to your palate. When your bird is done, pour the sauce over it, and garnish the dish with thin slices of lemon.

Snipes or Woodcocks.

SNIPES or Woodcocks must be boiled in good strong broth, or beef gravy, which you must make as follows: Cut a pound of lean beef into small pieces, and put it into four quarts of water, with an onion, a bundle of sweet herbs, a blade or two of mace, six cloves, and some whole pepper. Cover it close, let it boil till it is half wasted, then strain it off, and put the gravy into a saucepan, with salt enough to season it. Draw the birds clean, but take particular care of the guts. Put the birds into the gravy, cover them close, and ten minutes will boil them. In the meantime cut the guts and liver small, then take a little of the gravy the birds are boiling in, and stew the guts in it with a blade of mace. Take about as much of the crumb of bread as the inside of a roll, and rub or grate it very small into a clean cloth, then put into a pan with some butter, and fry it till crisp, and of a fine light brown colour. When your birds are ready, take about half a pint of the liquor they were boiled in, and add to the guts two spoonsful of red wine, and a piece of butter about the size of a walnut, rolled in flour. Set them on the fire, and shake your saucepan often, (but by no means stir it with a spoon,) till the butter is melted; then put in the fried crumbs, give the saucepan another shake, take up your birds, lay them in the dish, and pour your sauce over them Garnish with sliced lemon.

SECT. III.

BOILING FISH.

Turbot.

When you have thoroughly washed and cleansed your fish, rub some allegar over it, which will greatly contribute to its firmness. Put it in your fish-plate with the belly upwards, and fasten a cloth tight over it to prevent its breaking. Let it boil gently in hard water, with plenty of salt and vinegar, and scum it well, to prevent the skin being discoloured. Be sure not to put in your fish till the water boils, and when it is enough, take it up, and drain it. Remove the cloth carefully, and slip the fish very cautiously on the dish, for fear of breaking it. Lay over it oyster-patties, or fried oysters. Put your lobster or gravy sauce into boats, and garnish with crisped parsley and pickles.

Another Way to dress a Turbot.

Put into the bottom of your stew-pan some thyme, parsley, sweet herbs, and an onion sliced. Then lay in your fish, and strew over it the like quantity of the same herbs, with some chives and sweet basil. Cover the fish with an equal quantity of white wine and the best vinegar. Strew in a little bay salt with some whole pepper. Set the stew-pan over a gentle fire, and gradually increase the heat till it is enough; when done, take it off the fire, but let the fish remain in the liquor, till you have made your sauce as follows: Set a saucepan over the fire, with a pound of butter, two anchovies split, boned, and washed, two large spoonsful of capers, cut small, some chives whole, a little pepper and salt, some nutmeg grated, a little flour, a spoonful of vinegar, and a little water.—Keep shaking it round for some time, and then put on the fish to make it quite hot. When both are done, put the turbot into a dish, pour some of the sauce over it, and the remainder into a boat. Garnish the dish with horse-radish.

Turbot en Maigre.

PUT into your stew-pan a pint of water, a good bit of salt, some garlic, onions, all sorts of sweet herbs, and cloves; boil the whole half an hour over a slow fire Let it settle. Pour it off clear, and strain it through a sieve; then put in twice as much milk as brine, and put the fish in it over a slow fire, letting it simmer only. When your turbot is done, you may serve it with any one of the following sauces: Ragout of egg balls, ragout of oysters, or truffles, or mushroom, or a sauce hachée.

Salmon.

THIS is so substantial a fish, that it requires to be well boiled. A piece not very thick will take half an hour Boil horse-radish in the water. For sauce, melt some butter plain, and some other with anchovy. Garnish with horse-radish and sliced lemon.

To dress a whole Salmon for a large Company.

WHEN the salmon is scalded and gutted, take off the head and tail, cut the body through into slices an inch and a half thick, and throw them into a large pan of pump water. When they are all put in, sprinkle a handful of bay salt upon the water, stir it about, and then take out the fish. Set on a large deep stew-pan, boil the head and tail, but do not split the head, and put in some salt. When they have boiled ten minutes, skim the water very clean, and put in the slices. When they are boiled enough, take them out, lay the head and tail in a dish, and the slices round. Serve it up with plain melted butter and anchovy sauce. Garnish with horse-radish, mixed with the slices.

Cod's Head.

TAKE out the gills and the blood, wash the whole very clean, rub over it a little salt, and a glass of allegar, and lay on your fish plate. When the water boils, throw in a good handful of salt, with a glass of allegar. Then put in the fish, and let it boil gently half an hour (if it s a large one, three quarters.) Take it up very carefully, and strip the skin clean off, set it before a brisk fire, dredge it all over with flour. and baste it well with butter. When the froth begins to rise, throw over it some very fine white bread crumbs, and continue basting it to make it froth well. When it is of a fine light brown, dish it up, and garnish it with lemon cut in slices, scraped horse-radish, barberries, a few small fish fried and laid round it, or fried oysters. Cut the row and liver in slices, and lay it over a little of the lumpy part of the lobster out of the sauce, which you must make as follows: Take a good lobster, and stick a skewer in the vent of the tail to keep out the water. Throw into the water a handful of salt, and when it boils, put in the lobster, which will be done in half an hour. If it has spawn, pick them off, and pound them very fine in the mortar. Put them into half a pound of good melted butter: then take the meat out of your lobster, break it in bits, and put that in likewise, with a large spoonful of lemon-pickle, the same of walnut catchup, a slice of lemon, one or two slices of horse-radish, and a small quantity of beaten mace; season it to your taste with salt and chyan pepper. Boil them one minute, then take out the horse-radish and lemon, pour it into your sauce-boat, and serve it up with your fish.—If lobsters cannot be procured, you may make use of oysters or shrimps the same way; and if you cannot get any kind of shell fish, you may then add to the butter two anchovies cut small, a spoonful of walnut liquor, and an onion stuck with cloves.

Whole Cod.

Put a large quantity of water into your fish-kettle, which must be of a proper size for the cod, with a quarter of a pint of vinegar, a handful of salt, and half a stick of horse-radish. Let these boil together for some time, and then put in the fish. When it is done enough (which will be known by feeling the fins, and the look of the fish) lay it to drain, put it in a hot fish-plate, and then in a warm dish, with the liver cut in half, and laid on each side. Serve it up with shrimp or oyster-sauce, and garnish with scraped horse-radish.

Salt Cod.

STEEP your salt fish in water all night, with a glass of vinegar thrown into it, with which take out the salt; and make it as mild as fresh fish. The next day boil it, and when it is enough, separate it in flakes into your dish. Then pour egg-sauce over it, or parsnips boiled and beat fine with butter and cream. As it will soon grow cold, send it to table on a water plate.

Cod Sounds.

BOIL your sounds well, but be careful they are not done too much. Take them up, and let them stand till they are quite cold. Then make a forcemeat of chopped oysters, crumbs of bread, a lump of butter, the yolks of two eggs, nutmeg, pepper, and salt, and fill your sounds with it. Skewer them in the shape of a turkey, and lard them down each side, as you would the breast of a turkey. Dust them well with flour, and put them before the fire in a tin oven to roast. Baste them well with butter, and when enough, pour on them oyster-sauce, and garnish with barberries. This is a pretty side-dish for a large table; or very proper in the time of Lent.

Soles.

TAKE a pair of soles, skin and gut them. Then wash them thoroughly clean, and lay them in vinegar, salt and water, for two hours; then dry them in a cloth, put them into a stew-pan with a pint of white wine, a bunch of sweet herbs, an onion stuck with six cloves, some whole pepper, and a little salt. Cover them quite close, and when enough, take them up, lay them in your dish, strain the liquor, and thicken it with butter and flour. Pour the sauce over, and garnish with scraped horse-radish and lemon. You may add prawns, shrimps, or muscles to your sauce, according to the fancy of those for whom you provide. This is a very good method; but to make a variety, you may dress them as follows:

Take two or three pair of middling sized soles, skin, gut, and wash them in spring water. Then put them on a dish, and pour half a pint of white wine over them, turn them two or three times in it, and then pour it away. Cut off the heads and tails of the soles, and set on a stew-pan with a little rich fish broth; put in an onion cut in pieces, a bunch of sweet herbs, pepper, salt, and a blade of mace. When these boil, put in the soles, and with them half a lemon cut in slices with the peel on. Let them simmer slowly for some time, then take out the sweet herbs, and put in a pint of strong white wine, and a piece of butter rolled in flour. Let them all simmer together till the soles are enough. While the fish are doing, put in half a pint of veal gravy, and a quarter of a pint of essence of ham, let it boil a little, then take up the soles, and pour this over them. Serve up sauce as before directed, and garnish your dish with sliced lemon and horse-radish.

Trout.

Boil them in vinegar, water, and salt, with a piece of horse-radish; and serve them up with anchovy-sauce and plain butter.

Pike.

When you have taken out the gills and guts, and thoroughly washed it, make a good forcemeat of chopped oysters, the crumb of half a penny loaf, a little lemon-peel shred fine, a lump of butter, the yolks of two eggs, a few sweet herbs, and season them to your taste with salt, pepper, and nutmeg. Mix all these well together, and put them into the belly of the fish, which must be sewed up, and skewered round. Boil it in hard water with a little salt, and a tea-cup full of vinegar put into the pan. As soon as the water boils, put in the fish, (but not before,) and if it is of a middling size, it will be done in half an hour. Serve it up with oyster-sauce in a boat, having first poured a little on the fish. Garnish with pickled barberries.

Carp.

When you kill your carp, save all the blood, and have ready some nice gravy, made of beef and mutton, seasoned with pepper, salt, mace, and onion. Before you put in your fish, strain it off, and boil your carp before you put it into the gravy. Set it on a slow fire about a quarter of an hou, and thicken the sauce with a large piece of butter rolled in flour; or you may make your sauce thus: take the liver of the carp clean from the guts, three anchovies, a little parsley, thyme, and an onion. Chop these small together, and take half a pint of Rhenish wine, four spoonsful of vinegar, and the blood of the carp. When all these are stewed gently together, put it to the carp, which must first be boiled in water with a little salt and a pint of wine: but take care not to do it too much after the carp is put into the sauce.

Mullets.

These must be boiled in salt and water. When they are enough, pour away part of the water, and put to the rest a pint of red wine, some salt and vinegar, two onions sliced, with a bunch of sweet herbs, some nutmeg, beaten mace, and the juice of a lemon. Boil these well together, with two or three anchovies. Then put in the fish, and when they have simmered in it some time, put them into a dish, and strain the sauce over them. You may add shrimp or oyster-sauce according to your discretion.

Mackarel.

Gut and wash them clean, then dry them in a cloth, and rub them gently over with vinegar. Lay them strait on your fish plate, and be very careful in handling them, as they are so tender a fish that they will easily break. When the water boils, put them into your fish-pan with a little salt, and let them boil gently about a quarter of an hour. When you take them up, drain them well, and put the water that runs from them into a sauce-pan with one large spoonful of catchup, a blade or two of mace, an anchovy, and a slice of lemon. Let these all boil together about a quarter of an hour, then strain it through a hair sieve, and thicken it with flour and butter. Put this sauce in one boat, and melted butter and parsley in another. Dish up your fish with their tails in the middle; and garnish with scraped horse-radish and barberries. Mackarel may be served with melted butter and a little fennel, cut fine, mixed with scalded gooseberries; also with sweet herbs, cut fine, in melted butter, with a little anchovy essence.

Mackarel a-la Bourgeois.

SPLIT them open, put pepper, salt, mace, parsley, shalots, and bread crumbs, with some butter on them. You may either fry or send them to the oven. Serve them up with plain melted butter.

Herrings.

SCALE, gut, and wash them, then dry them thoroughly in a cloth, and rub them over with a little salt and vinegar. Skewer their tails in their mouths, and lay them on your fish plate. When the water boils, put them in, and about ten or twelve minutes will do them. After you have taken them up, let them drain properly, and then turn their heads into the middle of the dish. Serve them up with melted butter and parsley, and garnish with scraped horse-radish.

Flounders, Plaice, and Dabs.

As the similarity of these fish is so great, the method of dressing either must be the same. First cut off the fins, nick the brown side under the head, and take out the guts. Then dry them with a cloth, and boil them in salt and water. Serve them up with shrimp, cockle, or muscle sauce, and garnish with red cabbage.

Perch.

PUT your fish into the water when it boils, with some salt, an onion cut in slices, some parsley, and as much milk as will turn the water. When the fish is enough, put it into a soup-dish, and pour a little of the water with the parsley and onions over it. Serve it up with melted butter and parsley in a boat.

Eels.

After skinning, gutting, and properly washing them, cut off their heads, dry them, and twist them round on your fish plate. Boil them in salt and water, and serve them up with melted butter and parsley. If you only boil them in such a quantity of water as will just cover them, the liquor will be exceeding good, and very beneficial to weak or consumptive constitutions.

Sturgeon.

When you have cleaned your fish properly, prepare as much liquor as will boil it in the following manner To two quarts of water put a pint of vinegar, a stick of horse-radish, two or three bits of lemon-peel, some whole pepper, a bay-leaf, and a small quantity of salt. Boil your fish in this liquor, and when enough (which you will know by the flesh appearing likely to separate from the bones) take it up, and have ready the following sauce: Melt a pound of butter, dissolve an anchovy in it, put in a blade or two of mace, bruise the body of a crab in the butter, a few shrimps or cray-fish, a little catchup, and a little lemon-juice. When it boils, take up the sturgeon, drain it well, lay it in your dish, and serve it up with the sauce poured into boats. Garnish with fried oysters, sliced lemon, and scraped horse-radish.

Turtles.

These animals not only furnish the most delicious repast to the epicure, but to all those who can obtain so luxurious a gratification. They are of various sizes, and that the reader may be informed how to dress them, we shall here confine ourselves to one of about eighty pounds weight. Take the turtle out of the water the night before you intend to dress it. In the morning cut its throat, or the head off, and let it bleed for some time. Then cut off the fins; scald, scale, and trim them and the head, and raise the callipee, which is the belly or under shell: clean it well, leaving to it as much meat as you conveniently can. Take from the back shell all the meat and entrails, except the monsieur, which is the fat, and looks green: this must also be baked with the shell. Wash all clean with salt and water, and cut it into pieces of a moderate size. Take it from the bones, and put them with the fins and head into a soup-pot, with a gallon of water, some salt, and two blades of mace. When it boils, skim it clean, and put in it a bunch of thyme, parsley, savory, and young onions, and your veal part, except about one pound and a half, which must be made forcemeat of, as for Scotch collops, adding a little chyan pepper. When the veal is boiled in the soup about an hour, take it out, cut it into pieces, and put to the other part. The guts, which are considered as the best part, must be split open, scraped, and made clean, and cut into pieces about two inches long. Scald and skin the paunch or maw, and cut it like the other parts: mix them with the guts and other parts, except the liver, and add half a pound of fresh butter, a few shalots, a bunch of thyme, parsley, and a little savory, seasoned with salt, white pepper, mace, three or four cloves beaten, and a little chyan pepper. Stew them about half an hour over a good charcoal fire, and put in half a pint of Madeira wine, with as much of the broth as will cover it, and let it stew till tender, which will take about four or five hours. When it is nearly enough, skim it, thicken it with flour, and some veal broth, and make it about the thickness of a fricasee. Let your forcemeat balls be fried about the size of a walnut, and stewed about half an hour with the rest. If there are any eggs, let them be boiled and cleaned: but if none, get twelve or fourteen yolks of hard eggs. Then put the stew (which is the callipash) into the shell with the eggs, and either make use of a salamander, or put it into the oven to bake. Slash the callipee in several places, put some butter to it, and season it moderately with chyan and white pepper, salt, beaten mace, chopped thyme, parsley, and young onions. Put a piece on each slash, and some over the whole, and a dust of flour: then bake it in a brisk oven, in a tin or iron dripping-pan. The back shell, which is called the callipash, must be seasoned like the callipee, and baked in a dripping-pan, set upright, with four brick-bats, or any thing of that kind. An hour and a half will bake it, which must be done before the stew be put in. The fins, when boiled very tender, must be taken out of the soup, and put into a stew-pan, with some good veal gravy, not high coloured, a little Madeira wine, seasoned and thickened as the callipash, and served in a dish by itself. The lights, heart, and liver, may be done the same way, but a little higher seasoned; or the lights and heart may be stewed with the callipash, and taken out before you put it into the shell, with a little of the sauce, adding a little more seasoning; but dish it by itself. The veal part may be made fricandos, or Scotch collops. The liver should never be stewed with the callipash, but dressed by itself in any manner you like; except you separate the lights and heart from the callipash, and serve them together in one dish. Be careful to strain the soup, and serve it in a tureen, or large china bowl. The different dishes may be placed on the table as follows: The callipee at the head, the callipash at the bottom, and the lights, soup, fins, &c. in the centre.—The fins kept in the liquor will eat well when cold.

Court Bouillon for all kinds of fresh Fish.

Put into your fish kettle, which must be according to the size of your fish, some water, a quart of white wine, a bit of butter, salt, pepper, a faggot of sweet herbs, some stewed onions and carrots: boil your fish in this liquor.

CHAPTER III.

ROASTING IN GENERAL.

SECT. I

BUTCHER'S MEAT.

THE first consideration of the cook in roasting must be to regulate the strength of her fire in proportion to the article she has to dress. If it is a small or thin joint, the fire must be brisk, that it may be done quick; but if a large one, a substantial fire must be made, in order that it may gradually receive the heat, and by stirring up the fire, when it begins to burn up, and keeping the bottom clear, the meat must be roasted as it ought to be, and with little trouble to the cook. Never put salt on your meat before you lay it to the fire, as it will be apt to draw out the gravy. In roasting *Beef*, if it be a large piece, skewer a sheet of writing paper over the fat, and baste it well while roasting. When it is near enough, which you will know by the smoke drawing to the fire, take off the paper, then baste it well and dredge it with flour to make it frothy. *Mutton* and *Lamb* must be roasted with a clear quick fire. *Veal* requires particular care, and must be done of a fine light brown colour. If it is a fillet or loin, put paper over the fat, in the same manner as you do beef. At first let it be some distance from the fire, and baste it with butter: but when it is got thoroughly warm put it nearer, and when nearly done, dredge it with flour. If a breast, put the caul over it, with the sweetbread skewered on the back, and, when sufficiently done, take off the caul and dredge it with flour. *Pork* well as *Veal* should be well done, otherwise it will nauseate: but mutton and beef, if a little underdone, may be dispensed with. *Wild Fowls* must be roasted with a clear, brisk fire, and when they are frothy, and of a light brown colour, they are enough. Great care must be taken not to overdo them as the loss of gravy will produce a want of the flavour. *Tame fowls* require more roasting, and must be often basted, in order to keep up a strong froth, which will make them look well when brought to table. *Pigs* and *Geese* must be done with a quick fire, turned quick, and frequently basted. *Hares* and *Rabbits* require time and care, otherwise the body will be done too much, and the ends too little. In roasting any article, always allow longer time for it in frosty than in mild weather, and take particular care that your spits are thoroughly clean before you put on your meat, as nothing is more disagreeable than the mark of it left in the flesh.

Having laid before the cook these necessary and general observations in roasting, we shall now proceed to give directions for dressing the respective articles under this head; beginning with

Beef.

The first steps to be taken in roasting Beef we have already noticed in the foregoing observations. It remains, therefore, only to say, that the time each joint will take doing must be proportioned to its weight. If a piece of ten pounds, it will take an hour and a half at a good fire. Twenty pounds weight, if a thick piece, will take three hours, but if thin, half an hour less; and so on in proportion to the weight. When done, take it up, and put it into your dish. Serve it with potatoes, horse-radish, and pickles for sauce, and garnish the rim of the dish with horse-radish scraped very fine.

Mutton and Lamb.

Mutton and Lamb must be roasted with a quick clear fire. Baste it as soon as you lay it down, sprinkle on a little salt, and when near done, dredge it with flour. A leg of mutton of six pounds will take an hour and a quarter, and one of twelve two hours; a breast half an hour at a quick fire: a neck an hour, and a shoulder much about the same time as a leg. In dressing the loin, the chine (which is the two loins) and the saddle (which is the two necks and part of the shoulders cut together) you must raise the skin, and skewer it on, and when near done, take off the skin, and baste it to froth it up. Send some good plain gravy up with it.

Haunch of Mutton dressed like Venison.

Take a hind-quarter of fine mutton, stale killed, and cut the leg like a haunch. Lay it in a pan with the back downwards, pour in a bottle of red wine, and let the meat soak in it twenty-four hours. Before you spit it, let it be covered with clean paper and paste as you do venison, in order to preserve the fat. Roast it before a quick fire, and keep basting with butter mixed with some of the liquor in which it was soaked. When done, serve it up with some good rich gravy in one boat, and sweet sauce in another. It will take about three hours roasting.

A Fore-quarter of House Lamb.

A small fore-quarter of house-lamb will take an hour and a half roasting; a leg three quarters of an hour. When it is done, and put into the dish, cut off the shoulder, and pepper and salt the ribs. Serve it up with salad, broccoli, potatoes, or mint sauce.

Tongues or Udders.

Parboil the tongue before you put it down to roast: stick eight or ten cloves about it, baste it with butter, and serve it up with some gravy and sweet-meat sauce. An udder may be roasted after the same manner. You may also lard the tongue nicely, but take care that the fire does not burn the larding.

Veal.

If your fire is good, veal will take about a quarter of an hour to each pound in roasting. The fat of the loin and fillet must be covered with paper, as we have before observed. The fillet and shoulder must be stuffed with the following savoury composition: a quarter of a pound of suet chopped fine, parsley and sweet herbs chopped, grated bread, and lemon peel; pepper, salt, and a little nutmeg, and the yolk of an egg. Work these all well together, and stuff them into your veal as secure as you can, that it may not fall out while roasting. The breast must be roasted with the caul on till it is near enough; then take it off, and flour and baste the meat. When you have taken it up, and put it into your dish, pour a little melted butter over it, and serve it up with any of the following sauces; potatoes, brocoli, cucumbers stewed, French beans, peas, cauliflowers, celery stewed. Remember in dressing any joint of veal that it is well done, but at the same time let it not be too much. If it is not done enough it will be too disgustful to enjoy, and if too much, the juices will be lost, and the flesh eat tasteless.

Pork.

PORK, like veal, must be well done. If it is a loin, take a sharp penknife, and cut the skin across, which will not only make the joint more convenient to carve, but will also make the rind or crackling more pleasant to eat. A leg of pork must be scored in the same manner as the loin; if not particularly objected to, stuff the knuckle part with sage and onion chopped fine, with pepper and salt: or cut a hole under the twist, put the seasoning there, and fasten it with a skewer. Roast it crisp, as it will make the crackling, of which most people are fond, eat the better. If you want a *Spring*, (which is not very common, though, at the same time, if young, will eat exceeding well,) cut off the shank, or knuckle, sprinkle sage and onion over it, roll it round, and tie it with a string. About two hours will do it. The *Spare-rib* should be basted with a little bit of butter, a very little dust of flour, and some dried sage shred small. The principal sauces for any kind of roast pork are, potatoes, mustard, and apple sauce, the latter of which you must make thus. Pare, core, and slice some apples, and put them into a sauce-pan with a little water, to prevent their burning, and throw in a bit of lemon-peel. When they are enough, take out the peel, bruise the apples, and add a piece of butter and a little sugar. When you have worked the whole together very fine, set it on the fire till it is quite hot, then put it into your basin, and serve it up with the meat. If it is a leg of pork, have a little drawn gravy ready against it is done, and pour it into the dish when you serve it up. The best way of dressing *Pork Griskin* is to roast it, baste it with a little butter and sage, and a little pepper and salt. The only article used as sauce for this is mustard.

Sucking Pigs

WHEN your pig is properly prepared for dressing, put into the belly of it a little sage shredded fine, with some salt, a tea-spoonful of black pepper, and a crust of brown bread. Then spit it, sew up the belly, and lay it down to a brisk clear fire, with a pig-plate hung in the middle to prevent the body part being done before the extremities. As soon as it is warm, put a piece of butter into a cloth, and frequently rub the pig with it while roasting. When it becomes of a fine brown, and the steam draws to the fire, rub it quite dry with a clean cloth, and then with a bit of cold butter, which will help to crisp it. Having taken it up, and put it into your dish, cut off the head with a sharp knife, and take off the collar, the ears, and the jaw-bone. Split the jaw in two, and when you have cut the pig down the back, which must be done before you draw out the spit, lay the two sides with the back part to each other, a jaw on each side, and an ear on each shoulder, and the collar on the shoulder. Have ready your sauce, which you must make in the following manner: Having chopped the brains, put them in a saucepan, with a tea-spoonful of white gravy, the gravy that runs out of the pig, (which you must be careful to save, by putting a basin or pan in the dripping-pan under the pig as soon as the gravy begins to run,) and a small piece of anchovy. Add to these half a pound of butter, and as much flour as will thicken the gravy.

a slice of lemon, a spoonful of white wine, some caper liquor, and a little salt. Shake it over the fire till it is quite hot, then pour it into your dish with the pig, and serve it up. You may likewise boil a few currants, and send them in a tea-saucer, with a glass of currant jelly in the middle.

As there may sometimes be a necessity for the cook's killing the pig herself, it may not be improper to inform her in that case how to proceed. Stick the pig just above the breast-bone, and let the knife touch its heart, otherwise it will be a long time dying. As soon as it is dead, put it into cold water for a few minutes, and rub it over with a little rosin beat exceeding fine, or instead of that use its own blood, which will nearly answer the same purpose. Let it lie half a minute in a pail of scalding water, then take it out, lay it upon a clean table, and strip off all the hairs as fast as possible ; but if they do not come clean off, put it into the hot water again, and when it is perfectly clean off, wash it in warm water, and then in two or three cold waters, that, when dressed, it may not taste of the rosin. Take off the four feet at the first joints, slit it down the belly, and take out all the entrails. Put the heart, liver, lights, and pettitoes together ; wash the pig well in cold water, and having perfectly dried it with a cloth, hang it up. When you dress it, proceed as before directed.

Calf's Head.

When you have thoroughly washed, and cleansed it from the slime, take out the bones, and dry it well in a cloth. Make a seasoning of beaten mace, pepper, salt, nutmeg, and cloves, some bacon cut very small, and some grated bread. Strew this over the head, roll it up, skewer it, and tie it with tape. While roasting, baste it with butter, and when done, having previously made a rich veal gravy, thickened with butter rolled in flour, pour it over, and serve it to table. Some like mushroom sauce, in which case make it as follows: Clean and wash a quart of fresh mushrooms, cut them into pieces, and put them into a stew-pan.

with a little salt, a blade of mace, and a little butter. Stew them gently for half an hour, and then add a pint of cream, and the yolks of two eggs beaten up fine. keep stirring it till it boils, then pour it into a boat, and serve it up with the head. This is an excellent sauce for fowls or turkeys.

Ham, or Gammon of Bacon.

WHICHEVER you dress of these, take off the skin or rind, and lay the meat in luke-warm water for two or three hours. Then put it into a pan, pour over it a quart of Canary wine, and let it soak about half an hour. When you have spitted it, put a sheet of clean paper over the fat side, pour the Canary, in which it was soaked, into the dripping-pan, and baste the meat with it all the time it is roasting. When it is enough, take off the paper, and dredge it well with crumbled bread and parsley shred fine. Make the fire brisk, and brown it well. If you serve it up hot, garnish with raspings of bread; but if cold for a second course, garnish with green parsley.

SECT. II.

ROASTING POULTRY.

Turkeys.

WHEN your Turkey is properly trussed for dressing, stuff it with the following ingredients: Take four ounces of butter, or chopped suet, some grated bread, a little lemon peel, parsley, and sweet herbs chopped together, pepper, salt, and nutmeg, a little cream, and the yolks of two or three eggs; work these all well together, and fill the craw with it. Let your fire be very brisk, and when you put it down paper the breast, and let it continue on till near done; then take it off, dredge it with flour, and keep basting it till it is done. If it is a large turkey, serve it up with gravy alone, or brown celery, or mushroom sauce. If it is a turkey-poult, serve it up with gravy and bread sauce, the latter of which make thus: Cut the crumby part of a penny loaf into thin slices, put it into a saucepan with cold water, a few pepper corns, a little salt, and an onion: boil it till the bread is quite soft, and then beat it very fine: put it into a quarter of a pound of butter, with two spoonsful of thick cream, and when it boils up, pour it into a basin, or boat, and serve it up with the turkey. A middling sized turkey will take more than an hour, a small one three quarters of an hour, and a very large one an hour and a half. In dressing these, as well as fowls, always let your fire be clear and brisk.

Fowls.

WHEN your fowls are laid to the fire, singe them, then baste them with butter, and dredge over some flour. When the smoke begins to draw to the fire, baste and dredge them again: let the fire be brisk, and send them to table with a good froth. The proper sauces for roast fowls are, gravy, egg, mushroom, or celery-sauce, the latter of which make thus: Wash and pare a large bunch of celery very clean, cut it into thin bits, and boil it gently in a little water till it is tender: then add a little beaten mace, nutmeg, pepper, and salt, and thicken it with a large piece of butter rolled in flour: then give it a boil, and serve it up in a boat. To the water in which you boil the celery put a half pint of cream, which will make it very rich and substantial. This is an excellent sauce, not only for fowls but also for partridges, or any other game of the same kind.

Chickens.

BE particularly careful in drawing your chickens, which done, cut off their claws, and truss them for dressing. Put them down to a good fire, and singe, dust, and baste them with butter. When they are enough, froth them, and lay them in your dish. Serve them up with parsley and butter poured over them, and gravy and mushroom sauce in boats. A large chicken will take half an hour, a small one twenty minutes.

Green Geese.

WHEN the goose is properly cleaned, and ready for dressing, put into the body a large lump of butter, then spit it, and lay it down to a brisk clear fire. Singe it, dredge it with flour, and as soon as it begins to receive the heat of the fire, baste it well with butter, which will occasion the flesh to rise, and make it look well. When you think it near enough, dredge it again with flour; and baste it till the froth rises, and it is of a clear light brown. When done, take it up, and put it into your dish, having ready the following sauce: Melt some butter, and put it into a spoonful of sorrel juice, a little sugar, and a few scalded gooseberries. Pour it into your sauce-boat, and send it up hot with the goose to table. You may likewise add gravy and apple-sauce, and garnish your dish with a crust of bread grated very fine.

A Stubble Goose

TAKE two onions, with a few leaves of sage washed clean, and chop them as fine as possible. Mix with them a large piece of butter, some salt, and pepper. Put this into the body of the goose, then tie both ends, and put it down to the fire to roast. Singe and dredge it with flour, and when it is thoroughly hot, baste it with fresh butter. When near done dredge it again, and keep basting it till the froth rises, and the steam draws to the fire, then take it up, and put it into your dish, pour a little boiling hot water over it, and serve it up with good gravy-sauce in one boat, apple-sauce in another, and mustard.

Ducks.

YOU must prepare them for the spit in the same manner you do geese, by putting into the body some sage and onion chopped fine, with pepper and salt. When you lay them down, singe, dust, and baste them with butter, and a good fire will roast them in about twenty minutes. Before you take them up, dust them with flour, and give them another basting with butter to make them froth and look brown. Your gravy must be made of the gizzard and pinions, with an onion, a tea-spoonful of lemon-pickle, a few grains of pepper, a large blade of mace, and a tea-spoonful of catsup. When they are thoroughly stewed, strain off the gravy, put some into the dish with the ducks, and the remainder in a boat or basin. Wild ducks must be done in the same manner.

Pigeons.

After you have drawn your Pigeons, and taken the craws clean out, wash them in several waters. When you have dried them, roll a good lump of butter in some chopped parsley, and season it with pepper and salt. Put this into your pigeons, then spit, dust with flour, and baste them. When enough, serve them up with parsley and butter for sauce, and, if in season, garnish your dish with bunches of asparagus. A good fire will roast them in twenty minutes.

Larks.

Take a dozen of Larks, put them on a skewer, and tie both ends of the skewer to the spit. Dredge and baste them, and in about ten or twelve minutes they will be done. Make your sauce thus: take the crumb of half a penny loaf, shred it very fine, and put it into a stew-pan or frying pan, with a piece of butter about the size of a walnut. Shake it over a gentle fire till it is of a light brown, then lay it between your birds on your plate or dish, and pour a little melted butter over them.

Rabbits.

When you have cased your rabbits, skewer their heads upon their backs, their fore legs into their ribs, and the hind legs double. Take the crumb of half a penny loaf, a little parsley, thyme, sweet-marjorum, and lemon-peel. Shred all these fine, and season them with pepper, salt, and nutmeg. Mix them up into a light stuffing with two eggs, a little cream, and a quarter of a pound of butter. Put this into their bellies, sew them up, and dredge and baste them well with butter. When done, take them up, chop the livers after boiling, and lay them in lumps round the edge of your dish. Serve them up with parsley and butter for sauce.

To roast a rabbit hare fashion, you must lard it with bacon, and baste it in the same manner you do a hare, directions for which you will find in the next section. If you lard it, make gravy sauce; if not, white sauce will be most proper.

SECT. III.

ROASTING GAME.

Pheasants and Partridges.

THE same methods are to be taken in dressing either of these birds. When you have spitted and laid them down, dust them with flour, and baste them often with fresh butter, keeping them at a good distance from the fire. About half an hour will roast them. Make your gravy of a scrag of mutton, and put into the sauce-pan with it a tea-spoonful of lemon-pickle, a large spoonful of catsup, and the same of browning.* Strain it, and put a little into the dish with the birds. Serve them up with the remainder in one ba-

---

*As we shall have frequent occasion to mention the article BROWNING, it will be necessary here to give proper directions how to make it.—Beat small four ounces of treble refined sugar, and put it into a frying pan with one ounce of butter.—Set it over a clear fire, and mix it well together. When it begins to be frothy by the sugar dissolving, hold it higher over the fire, and have ready a pint of red wine. When the sugar and butter is of a deep brown, pour in a little of the wine, and stir it well together; then add more wine, and keep stirring it all the time. Put in half an ounce of Jamaica pepper, six cloves, four shalots peeled, two or three blades of mace, three spoonsful of catsup, a little salt, and a rind of one lemon. Boil them slowly about ten minutes, and then pour it into a basin. When cold, take off the scum very clean, and bottle it up for use.

sin, and bread sauce in another. By way of ornament fix one of the principal feathers of the pheasant in its tail.

Woodcocks or Snipes.

These birds are so peculiar from all others, that they must never be drawn. When you have spitted them, take the round of a threepenny loaf, and toast it nice and brown; then lay it in a dish, under the birds, and when you put them to the fire, baste them with a little butter, and let the trail or gut drop on the toast. When they are done, put the toast in a dish, and lay the birds on it. Pour about a quarter of a pint of gravy into the dish, and set it over a lamp or chafing-dish for three or four minutes, and then take it hot to table. A woodcock will take about twenty minutes roasting, and a snipe fifteen.

Hares.

When your hare is cased and properly trussed for dressing, make a stuffing thus: Take a large slice of bread, and crumble it very fine, put to it a quarter of a pound of beef marrow, or suet, the like quantity of butter, the liver boiled and shred fine, a sprig or two of winter savory, a bit of lemon-peel, an anchovy, a little chyan pepper, and half a nutmeg grated. Mix these well together with a glass of red wine and two eggs, put it into the belly of the hare and sew it up. When you have spitted it, and laid it before the fire, put into your dripping-pan a quart of milk, and keep basting your hare with it till there is little left. When it is nearly done, dredge it with flour, and baste it with butter till it is properly frothed. If it is a small hare it will take about an hour and a half; and if a large one two hours. When done, put it into your dish, and serve it up with plenty of good rich gravy, and some currant-jelly warmed in a cup; or red wine and sugar done to a syrup thus: Take a pint of red wine, put it into a quarter of a pound of sugar, set it over a slow fire, and let it simmer for a quarter of an hour: then take it off, and pour it into your sauce-boat or basin.

6

Venison.

TAKE a haunch of venison, and when you have spitted it, rub some butter all over it. Take four sheets of clean paper, well buttered, two of which put on the haunch. Then make a paste with some flour, a little butter and water: roll it out half as big as your haunch, and put it over the fat part; cover this with the other two sheets of paper, and tie them fast with packthread. Lay it to a brisk fire, and baste it well all the time it is roasting. When it is near done, take off both paper and paste, dredge it well with flour, and baste it with butter. As soon as it becomes of a light brown, take it up, and serve it to table with brown gravy, currant-jelly, or the syrup mentioned in the preceding article for a hare. A haunch will take about three hours roasting.

SECT. IV.

ROASTING FISH.

To roast Sturgeon.

PUT a piece of butter rolled in flour into a stew-pan, with salt, pepper, parsley, onions, sweet herbs, cloves, half a pint of water, and a little vinegar. Stir it over the fire, and when it is luke-warm take it off, and put your sturgeon in to steep. When it has taken the flavour of the herbs, roast it, and serve it up with any vege table sauce you think fit.

Roasted en Gras.

LARD it with fat bacon, roast it, and serve it with a ragout of truffles, morels, mushrooms, veal, sweet bread, &c.

Lobsters.

WHEN you have half boiled your lobster take it out of the water, rub it well with butter, and lay it before the fire: continue basting it with butter till it has a fine froth, and the shells look of a dark brown. Then put it into your dish, and serve it up with plain melted butter in a sauce-boat.

CHAPTER IV.

BAKING.

SECT. I.

BUTCHER'S MEAT.

THE only method to be observed previous to this mode of cookery, is to have the pans, or whatever vessels you send your provisions in to the oven, perfectly clean, so that the care you have taken in preparing the article may not be injured from neglect in cleanliness.

Rump of Beef a-la-Braise.

CUT out the bone quite clean, then beat the flesh well with a rolling-pin, and lard it with a piece of bacon cut out of the back. Season your bacon with pepper, salt, and cloves, and lard across the meat, that it may cut handsomer. Season the meat with pepper, salt, and cloves; put it into an earthen pot with all the broken bones, half a pound of butter, some bay leaves, whole pepper, one or two shalots, and some sweet herbs. Let the top of the pan be covered quite close, then put it into the oven, and it will be done in about six hours. When enough, skim off the fat clean, put the meat into a dish, and serve it up with a good ragout of mushrooms, truffles, force-meat-balls, and yelks of eggs. Let the gravy which comes from the beef be added, nicely seasoned, to those ingredients.

Calf's Head.

WHEN you have properly cleansed the head, put it into a large earthen dish, or pan, and rub the inside with butter. Put some long iron skewers across the top of the dish, and lay the head on them. Grate some nutmeg all over the head, with a few sweet herbs shred small, some crumbs of bread, and a little lemon-peel cut fine. Then flour it all over, stick pieces of butter in the eyes, and on different parts of the head, and send it to the oven. You may throw a little pepper and salt over it, and put into the dish a bunch of sweet herbs, an onion, a blade of mace, some whole pepper, two cloves, and a pint of water, and boil the brains with some sage. When the head is enough, lay it on a dish, and put it before the fire to keep warm; then stir all together in the dish, and put it into a saucepan, and when it is quite hot strain it off, and pour it into the saucepan again. Put in a piece of butter rolled in flour, the sage and brains chopped fine, a spoonful of catsup, and two of red wine. Boil them well together, pour the whole over the head in a dish, and send it to table.

Pigs.

LAY your pig into a dish well buttered, flour it all over, rub some butter on the pig, and send it to the oven. When you think it is enough, take it out, rub it over with a buttered cloth, and put it into the oven again till it is dry: then take it out, lay it in a dish, and cut it up. Skim off the fat from the dish it was baked in, and some good gravy will remain at the bottom. Put this to a little veal gravy, with a piece of butter rolled in flour, and boil it up with the brains; then pour it into a dish, and mix it well with the sage that comes out of the belly of the pig. Serve it up hot to table with apple-sauce and mustard.

A Bullock's or Calf's Heart.

TAKE some crumbs of bread, chopped suet, (or a bit of butter,) parsley chopped, sweet marjorum, lemon-peel grated, pepper, salt, and nutmeg, with the yolk of an egg; mix these all well together, stuff the heart with it, and send it to the oven. When done, serve it up with gravy, melted butter, and currant jelly in boats. The same methods are to be used whether you bake or roast it; but if care is taken, baking it is the best way, as it will be more regularly done than it can be by roasting.

SECT. II.

BAKING FISH.

Cod's Head.

WHEN it is thoroughly cleansed and washed, lay it in the dish, which you must first rub round with butter. Put in a bunch of sweet herbs, an onion stuck with cloves, three or four blades of mace, some black and white pepper, a nutmeg bruised, a little lemon-peel, a piece of horse-radish, and a quart of water. Dust the head with flour, grate a little nutmeg over it, stick bits of butter on various parts, and sprinkle raspings all over it, and send it to the oven. When done, take the head out of the dish, and put it into that it is to be served up in. Set the dish over boiling water, and cover it close to prevent its getting cold. In the mean time, as expeditiously as you can, pour all the liquor out of the dish in which it was baked into a saucepan, and let it boil three or four minutes: then strain it, and put to it a gill of red wine, two spoonsful of catsup, a pint of shrimps, half a pint of oysters, a spoonful of mushroom pickle, and a quartern of butter rolled in flour. Stir all well together, and let it boil till it is thick; then strain it, and pour it into the dish. Have ready some toasted bread cut three corner ways, and fried crisp. Stick some pieces of toast about the head and mouth, and lay the remainder round the head. Garnish your dish with crisped parsley, lemon notched, and scraped horse-radish. This method is equally good for roasting.

Salmon

TAKE a piece of salmon, of five or six pounds weight, (or larger according to your company,) and cut it into slices about an inch thick, after which make a forcemeat thus: Take some of the flesh of the salmon, and the same quantity of the meat of an eel.

with a few mushrooms. Season it with pepper, salt, nutmeg, and cloves, and beat all together till it is very fine. Boil the crumb of a roll in milk, and beat it up with four eggs till it is thick; then let it cool, add four more raw eggs to it, and mix the whole well together. Take the skin from the salmon, and lay the slices in a dish. Cover every slice with the forcemeat, pour some melted butter over them, with a few crumbs of bread, and place oysters round the dish. Put it into the oven, and when it is of a fine brown, pour over a little melted butter with some red wine boiled in it, and the juice of a lemon, and serve it up hot to table

Carp.

TAKE a brace of carp, and having greased the pan, in which they are to be baked, with butter, put them into it. Let it be of such a size as will hold them at full length, otherwise they will be apt to break. When you have put them into the pan, season them with a little black and white pepper, mace, cloves, nutmeg, a bunch of sweet herbs, an onion, and an anchovy: then pour in a bottle of white wine, cover them close, and put them into the oven. If of a large size they will take an hour baking; but if small, a less time will do. When enough, take them out of the pan, and lay them in a dish. Set it over boiling water to keep it hot, and cover it close. Pour all the liquor in which they were baked into a saucepan; let it boil a minute or two, strain it, and add half a pound of butter rolled in flour. Keep stirring it all the time it is boiling; squeeze in the juice of half a lemon, and put in a proper quantity of salt, observing to skim all the fat off the liquor. Pour the sauce over the fish, lay the roes round them, and garnish with lemon.

Eels and Lampreys.

CUT off their heads, gut them, and take out the blood from the bone as clean as possible. Make a forcemeat of shrimps or oysters chopped small, half a penny loaf crumbled, a little lemon-peel shred fine, the yolks of two eggs, and a little salt, pepper, and nutmeg. Put this into the bellies of the fish, sew them up, and turn them round on the dish. Put flour and butter over them, pour a little water into the dish, and bake them in a moderate oven. When done, take the gravy from under them, and skim off the fat, strain it through a hair sieve, and add one tea-spoonful of lemon-pickle, two of browning, a large spoonful of walnut catsup, a glass of white wine, an anchovy, and a slice of lemon. Let it boil ten minutes, and thicken it with butter and flour. Garnish with lemon and crisped parsley.

Herrings

SCALE, wash, and dry them well in a cloth, then lay them on a board, and take a little black pepper, a few cloves, and plenty of salt; mix them together, and rub the fish all over with it. Lay them straight in a pot, cover them over with vinegar, put in a few bay-leaves, tie a strong paper over the top, and bake them in a moderate oven. They may be eat either hot or cold; and if you use the best vinegar, they will keep good for two or three months.

Sprats may be done in the same manner, and either of them will furnish an occasional and pleasing relish.

Turbot.

TAKE a dish about the size of the turbot, rub butter thick all over it, throw on a little salt, a little beaten pepper, half a large nutmeg, and some parsley chopped fine. Pour in a pint of white wine, cut off the head and tail, and lay the turbot in the dish: pour another pint of white wine all over, grate the other half of the nutmeg over it, a little pepper, some salt, and chopped parsley. Lay a piece of butter here and there all over, then strew it with flour and crumbs of bread, Being thus prepared, send it to the oven, and let it be done of a fine brown colour. When you take it out, or have it home, put the turbot into the dish in which you mean to serve it up, then stir the sauce in the dish it was baked in, pour it into a saucepan, shake in a little flour, let it boil, and then stir in a piece of butter with two spoonsful of catsup. When the whole boils, pour it into basins, and serve it up with the fish. Garnish your dish with lemons: and you may add what other sauce you fancy, as shrimps, anchovies, mushrooms, &c.

Pike, with forcemeat.

Prepare your pike thus:—Gut it, without cutting it open, and take care it is well cleaned. Cut a notch down the back from head to tail, turn it round, and fasten the tail in the mouth. Make your forcemeat thus: Take the udder of a leg of veal, or the kidney part of a loin of lamb, some fat bacon cut in dice, the spawn or melt of the fish, some green onions, a mushroom or two, or truffles, parsley and salt, and a little nutmeg and pepper: add a bit of butter to fry it: chop it all well, with the crumb of a French roll soaked in cream or milk. Pound all together in a large mortar, with three or four eggs; try if it is seasoned to your mind, fill the belly of your fish with it, close up that part which was cut in the back, and make it nice and even. Then take two or three eggs, beat them up, daub the fish well over with it, and strew on some crumbs of bread. Put it in a gentle oven, and proportion the time according to the size of your fish. When done use the following sauce: take two or three ladles of good gravy, and add to it three large spoonsful of whole capers, some parsley chopped fine, the juice of two lemons, and a little minced shalot. Pour this into a boat or basin, and serve it up hot with your fish. Garnish with fried parsley. A piper may be baked the same as the pike.

Mackarel.

Cut their heads off, wash and dry them in a cloth, cut them open, rub the bone with a little bay-salt, beat fine: take some mace, black and white pepper, and a few cloves, all beat fine; lay them in a long pan, and between every layer of fish put two or three bay leaves, and cover them with vinegar. Tie writing paper over them first, and then thick brown paper doubled. They must be put into a very slow oven, and will take a long time doing. When they are enough, uncover them, and let them stand till they are cold, then pour away all the vinegar they are boiled in, cover them with some more vinegar, and put in an onion stuck with cloves. Send them to a very slow oven again, and let them stand two hours. When completely done, put them aside, and they will keep good a considerable time. When you take them out, let it be with a slice, as your hands will be apt to break and spoil them. They make a most excellent occasional repast.

CHAPTER V

BROILING.

IN this mode of cooking, three things are to be prin cipally observed. First, that your gridiron is tho roughly clean, and your fire quite clear. Secondly, that you turn your meat quick and often while broiling, as it will be a means of preserving the juices. And, thirdly, to have your dish placed on a chafing-dish of hot coals, that by putting one piece after another into it as they are done, the whole may be taken quite hot to table.

SECT. I.

BUTCHER'S MEAT *and* POULTRY.

Beef Steaks.

LET your steaks be cut off the rump of beef about half an inch thick; take care to have your fire clear, and rub your gridiron well with beef suet. When it is hot lay on your steaks: let them broil till the side next the fire is brown; then turn them, and when the other side is brown, lay them on a hot dish, with a slice of butter between each steak: sprinkle a little pepper and salt over them, and let them stand two or three minutes; in the mean time slice a shalot as thin as possible into a spoonful of water: lay on your steaks again, and keep turning them till they are enough; then put them on your dish, pour the shalot and water over them, and send them to table. Add for sauce horse-radish and pickles. Garnish with scraped horse-radish.

Mutton Steaks.

Cut your steaks about half an inch thick, and if it be the loin, take off the skin with a part of the fat. When your gridiron is hot, rub it with fresh suet, lay on your steaks, and keep turning them as quick as possible: if you do not take great care, the fat that drops from them into the fire will smoke and spoil them: but this may be in a great measure prevented, by placing your gridiron on a slant. When enough put them into a hot dish, rub them well with butter, slice a shalot very thin into a spoonful of water, and pour it on them, with a spoonful of catsup. Serve them up hot, with scraped horse-radish and pickles.

Pork Chops.

In broiling these the same rules are to be observed as those given for mutton chops, except with this difference, that they require more doing. When they are enough, put a little good gravy to them: and in order to give them an agreeable flavour, strew over a little sage shred very fine. The only sauce is mustard.

Ox Palates.

Prepare your palates for broiling thus: having peeled them, put into a stew-pan a little butter rolled in flour, salt, and pepper, two shalots, a clove of garlic, two cloves, parsley, a laurel leaf, thyme, and as much milk as will simmer your palates till tender. When this is done, take them out, and rub over them the yolks of eggs with bread crumbs; then put them on your gridiron, broil them slowly, and when enough serve them up with sharp sauce.

Chickens.

SPLIT your chickens down the back, season them with pepper and salt, and lay them on the gridiron over a clear fire, and at a great distance. Let the insides continue next the fire till they are nearly half done; then turn them, taking care that the fleshy sides do not burn, and let them broil till they are of a fine brown. Have ready good gravy sauce, with some mushrooms, and garnish them with lemon and the livers broiled; the gizzards cut, slashed, and broiled, with pepper and salt. Or you may make the following sauce: take a handful of sorrel, and dip it in boiling water; then drain it, and have ready half a pint of good gravy; a shalot shred small, and some parsley boiled very green; thicken it with a piece of butter rolled in flour, and add a glass of red wine; then lay your sorrel in heaps round the chickens, and pour the sauce over them. Garnish with sliced lemon.

Pigeons.

PIGEONS may be broiled either whole or slit, and must be done very slowly over a clear fire. If you broil them whole, take some parsley shred fine, a piece of butter as big as a walnut, with a little pepper and salt, and put into their bellies, tying both ends with a bit of coarse thread. If you split them, season the inside with pepper and salt; and when done, serve them up with parsley and butter poured over them. They will be quicker done by being slit: but the best method is to broil them whole.

SECT. II.

BROILING FISH.

Fresh Salmon.

Cut some slices from a fresh salmon, and wipe them clean and dry; then melt some butter smooth and fine, with a little flour and basket salt. Put the pieces of salmon into it, and roll them about, that they may be covered all over with butter. Then lay them on a nice clean gridiron, and broil them over a clear but slow fire. While the salmon is broiling make your sauce thus: take two anchovies, wash, bone, and cut them into small pieces, and cut a leek into three or four long pieces. Set on a saucepan with some butter and a little flour, put in the anchovies and leek, with some capers cut small, some pepper and salt, and a little nutmeg; add to them some warm water, and two spoonsful of vinegar, shaking the saucepan till it boils; and then keep it on the simmer till you are ready for it. When the salmon is done on one side, turn it on the other till it is quite enough; then take the leek out of the sauce, pour it into a dish, and lay the broiled salmon upon it. Garnish with lemons cut in quarters.

Dried Salmon.

Lay your dried salmon in soak for two or three hours, then lay it on the gridiron, and shake over it a little pepper. It will take but a short time, and when done serve it up with melted butter.

Cod.

Cut the cod into slices about two inches thick, and dry and flour them well. Make a good clear fire, rub the gridiron with a piece of chalk, and set it high from the fire Then put in your slices of fish, turn them often, and let them brown till they are of a fine brown colour. Great care must be taken in turning them that they do not break. When done serve them up with lobster and shrimp sauce.

Crimped Cod.

TAKE a gallon of spring water, put it into a saucepan over the fire, and throw in a handful of salt. Boil 't up several times, and keep it clean scummed. When t is well cleared from the scum, take a middling sized cod, as fresh as possible, and put it into some fresh pump water. Let it lie a few minutes, and then cut t into slices about two inches thick. Throw these into the boiling brine, and let them boil briskly a few minutes. Then take the slices out with great care that they may not break, and put them on a sieve to drain. When they are well dried, flour them, and lay them at a distance upon a very good fire to broil. When enough serve them up with lobster, shrimp, or oyster sauce.

Cod Sounds.

LAY them a few minutes in hot water; then take them out, rub them well with salt, and take off the skin and black dirt, that they may look white. After this put them into water, and give them a boil, then take them out, flour them well, strew on some pepper and salt, and lay them on the gridiron. When enough lay them on your dish, and pour over them melted butter and mustard.

Trout.

WHEN you have properly cleansed your fish, and made it thoroughly dry with a cloth, tie it round with packthread from head to tail, in order to preserve its shape entire. Then melt some butter, with a good deal of basket salt, and pour it all over the trout till it is perfectly covered: after lying in it a minute or two, take it out, and put it on the gridiron over a clear fire, that it may do gradually. For sauce wash and bone an anchovy, and cut it very small; chop a large spoonful of capers: melt some butter, with a little flour, pepper, salt and nutmeg, and put it into the anchovy and capers, with half a spoonful of vinegar. When the trout is done lay it in a warm dish, pour your sauce boiling hot over it, and send it to table

Mackarel.

WASH them clean, cut off their heads, and take out the roes at the neck end. Boil the roes in a little water; then bruise them with a spoon, beat up the yolk of an egg, with a little nutmeg; a little lemon-peel cut fine, some thyme, parsley boiled and chopped fine, a little salt and pepper, and a few crumbs of bread. Mix these well together, and put it into the bellies of the fish; then flour them well, and broil them nicely. Let your sauce be melted butter, with a little catsup or walnut pickle.

Mackarel a-la-Maitre d'Hotel.

BROIL your Mackarel whole: the sauce is sweet herbs, chopped fine, in melted butter.

Haddocks and Whitings.

WHEN you have gutted and clean washed them, dry them well in a cloth, and rub a little vinegar over them, which will prevent the skin from breaking. Having done this, dredge them well with flour, and before you put them on, rub the gridiron well with beef suet. Let your gridiron be very hot when you lay your fish on, otherwise they will stick to it, and the fish be broke in turning. While they are broiling, turn them two or three times, and when enough serve them up with plain melted butter, or shrimp sauce.

Another, and indeed a very excellent method of broiling these fish is thus: when you have cleaned and dried them as before-mentioned, put them into a tin oven, and set them before a quick fire. As soon as the skins begin to rise, take them from the fire, and having beat up an egg, rub it over them with a feather. Sprinkle a few crumbs of bread over them, dredge them well with flour, and rub your gridiron, when hot, with suet or butter. Lay on your fish, and when you have turned them, rub over a little butter, and keep turning them till they are done, which will be known by their appearing of a nice brown colour; when done, serve them up either with shrimp sauce, or plain melted butter, and garnish with melted butter or red cabbage

Eels.

HAVING skinned, cleansed, and dried your eels, rub them with the yolk of an egg; strew over them some crumbs of bread, chopped parsley and sage, and season them with pepper and salt. Baste them well with butter, and then put them on the gridiron over a clear fire. When done, serve them up with melted butter and parsley.

Eels pitch-cocked.

TAKE a large eel, and scour it well with salt, to clean off the slime; then slit it down the back, take out the bone, and cut it into three or four pieces. Take the yolk of an egg, and put it over the inside, sprinkle on crumbs of bread with some sweet herbs and parsley chopped very fine, a little nutmeg grated, and some pepper and salt mixed together. Then put it on a gridiron over a clear fire, broil it of a fine light brown, and when enough, serve it up with anchovy sauce, and parsley and butter. Garnish with raw parsley and horse-radish.

Another method of pitch-cocking eels is, when you have gutted, cleansed, and properly dried them, sprinkle them with pepper, salt, and a little dried sage, turn them backward and forward, and skewer them. Rub your gridiron with beef suet, broil them a good brown, and when done, put them into your dish, and serve them up with plain melted butter for sauce. Garnish your dish with fried parsley.

Herrings.

SCALE, gut, and cut off their heads; wash them clean, and dry them in a cloth; then dust them well with flour, and broil them. Take the heads, mash them, and boil them in small beer or ale, with a little whole pepper and onion. When it is boiled a quarter of an hour strain it off, thicken it with butter and flour, and a good deal of mustard. Lay the herrings, when done, in a plate or dish, pour the sauce into a boat, and serve them up.

CHAPTER VI.

FRYING

SECT. I.

BUTCHER'S MEAT.

Venison.

CUT your meat into slices, and make gravy of the bones. Fry it of a nice brown, and when done take it up, and keep it hot before the fire. Then put some butter, well rolled in flour, into the pan, and keep stirring it till it is quite thick and brown; but be careful that it does not burn. Stir in half a pound of fine sugar beat to powder, put in the gravy made from the bones, and some red wine. Make it the thickness of a fine cream; squeeze in the juice of a lemon, warm the venison in it, put it in the dish, and pour the sauce over it.

Veal Cutlets.

CUT your veal into slices of a moderate thickness, dip them in the yolk of eggs beat up fine, and strew over them crumbs of bread, a few sweet herbs, some lemon-peel, and a little grated nutmeg. Then put them into your pan, and fry them with fresh butter. While they are frying, make a little good gravy, and when the meat is done, take it out, and lay it in a dish before the fire. Shake a little flour into the pan, and stir it round; put in the gravy, with the juice of a lemon, stir the whole well together, and pour it over the cutlets. Garnish your dish with sliced lemon.

Neck or Loin of Lamb.

Cut your lamb into chops, rub both sides with the yolk of an egg, and sprinkle over them some crumbs of bread, mixed with a little parsley, thyme, marjorum, winter savory, and a little lemon-peel, all chopped very fine. Fry them in butter till they are of a nice light brown, then put them into your dish, and garnish with crisped parsley. Or you may dress them thus:

Put your steaks into the pan with half a pint of ale, and a little seasoning, and cover them close. When enough take them out of the pan, lay them in a plate before the fire to keep hot, and pour all out of the pan into a basin: then put in half a pint of white wine, a few capers, the yolks of two eggs beat fine, with a little nutmeg and salt; add to this the liquor they were fried in, and keep stirring it one way all the time till it is thick; then put in the chops, keep shaking the pan for a minute or two, lay the chops in the dish, and pour the sauce over them. Garnish with crisped parsley and lemon.

Sweetbreads.

Cut them into long slices, beat up the yolk of an egg, and rub it over them with a feather. Make a seasoning of pepper, salt, and grated bread, strew this over them, and fry them in butter. Serve them up with melted butter and catsup, and garnish with crisped parsley, and very small thin slices of toasted bacon.

Calf's Brains.

Cut the brains into four pieces, and soak them in broth and white wine, with two slices of lemon put into it, a little pepper and salt, thyme, laurel, cloves, parsley, and shalots. When they have remained in this about half an hour take them out, and soak them in batter made of white wine, a little oil, and a little salt, and fry them of a fine colour. You may likewise strew over them crumbs of bread mixed with the yolks of eggs. Serve them up with plain melted butter, and garnish with parsley.

Beef Steaks.

FRY your steaks over a brisk fire, with a little butter in the pan, and when they are of a nice light brown take them out, and put them in a dish before the fire. Then take half a pint of hot gravy, and put it into the pan with a little pepper and salt, and two or three shalots chopped fine. Boil them up in the pan for two or three minutes, and then pour the whole over the steaks. Garnish with scraped horse-radish.

Ox Tongues.

WHEN you have boiled the tongue till it is tender, cut it into slices, and season them with a little nutmeg, cinnamon, and sugar. Then beat up the yolk of an egg with a little lemon-juice, and rub it over the slices with a feather. Make some butter boiling hot in the frying-pan, and then put in the slices. When done serve them up with melted butter, sugar, and white wine, all well mixed together.

Ox Feet, or Cow-Heel.

SPLIT the feet asunder, then take out all the bones, and put the meat into the frying-pan with some butter. When it has fried a few minutes, put in some mint and parsley shred small, a little salt and some beaten butter. Add likewise the yolks of two eggs beat fine, half a pint of gravy, the juice of a lemon or orange, and a little nutmeg. When the foot is done, take it out, put it into your dish, and pour the sauce over it.

Tripe.

CUT your tripe into pieces about three inches square, dip them in some small beer batter, or yolks of eggs, and have a good quantity of mutton or beef dripping in your pan. Fry it till it is of a nice light brown, then take it out, let it drain for a minute, put it into your dish, and serve it up with plain melted butter in a boat, and mustard.

Sausages.

THE mode of frying sausages is so simple, and generally known, that it needs no description. However, we shall notice one way of which the cook may not be informed. Take six apples, and slice four of them as thick as a crown piece: cut the other two into quarters, and take the cores clean out. Fry the slices with the sausages till they are of a nice light brown colour. When done put the sausages into the middle of the dish, and the apples round them. Garnish with the apples quartered.

Chickens.

CUT your chickens into quarters, and rub them with the yolk of an egg; then strew on some crumbs of bread, with pepper, salt, grated nutmeg, and lemon-peel, and chopped parsley. Fry them in butter and when done put them into your dish before the fire For sauce thicken some gravy with a little flour, and put into it a small quantity of chyan pepper, some mushroom powder or catsup, and a little lemon-juice. When it is properly heated, pour it over the chickens, and serve it up.

Artichoke Bottoms.

BLANCH them in water, then flour them, and fry them in fresh butter. Lay them in your dish, and pour melted butter over them for sauce. Or you may put a little red wine into the butter, and season with nutmeg, pepper, and salt.

Celery.

TAKE six or eight heads of fresh celery, and cut off the green tops with the outside stalks. Wash them well and have the roots clean. Have ready a pint of white wine, the yolks of three eggs beat fine, and a little salt and nutmeg. Mix all well together with flour, and make it into a batter, then dip every head into it, put them into a pan, and fry them with butter. When enough lay them in your dish, and pour melted butter over them for sauce.

Potatoes

CUT your potatoes into thin slices, and fry them in butter till they are nicely brown. Then lay them in a dish or plate, and pour melted butter over them for sauce.

Potatoes are likewise fried by the French in batter, and served up with powdered sugar thrown over them. You must fry all your batter in sweet oil or hog's lard. Any kind of fruit may be fried in the same manner, and served up as a corner dish in the second course.

SECT. II.

FRYING FISH.

As a necessary prelude to our directions for frying fish, it may not be improper to make the few following general observations: When you fry any kind of fish, first dry them in a cloth, and then flour them. Put into your frying-pan plenty of dripping or hog's lard, and let it boil before you put it into a dish. When they are properly fried, lay them in a dish, or hair sieve, to drain. If you fry parsley, be sure to pick it very cautiously, wash it well, dip it into cold water, and throw it into a pan of boiling fat. This will make it very crisp, and of a fine green, provided you do not let it remain too long in the pan; but this you may prevent by its appearance while doing.

Turbot.

HAVING properly cleansed your fish (which in this mode of dressing must be small) and thoroughly dried it, strew on some flour, and put it into your pan, with a sufficient quantity of hot lard to cover it. When it is fried nice and brown, take it carefully out, and thoroughly drain the fat from it. In the meantime clean the pan, put into it as much claret and white wine as will nearly cover the fish, with an anchovy, salt, nutmeg, and a little ginger. Put in the turbot, and let it remain in the liquor till it is half wasted; then take it out, and put in a piece of butter rolled in flour, and a minced lemon. Let them simmer together till of a proper thickness, then rub a hot dish with a piece of shalot, lay the turbot in the dish, pour over the sauce, and serve it up. You may likewise add plain melted butter in a basin.

Carp.

AFTER having cleansed your fish, lay them in a cloth to dry, then flour them, put them into the pan, and fry them of a light brown. Take some crusts of bread, cut them three corner ways, and fry them with the roes of the fish. When your fish are nicely fried, lay them on a coarse cloth to drain, and prepare anchovy sauce with the juice of a lemon. Lay your carp in the dish, with the roes on each side, and garnish with the fried crust, and slices of lemon.

Tench.

SPLIT the fish along the backs, and raise the flesh from the bone: then cut the skin across at the head and tail, strip it clean off, and take out the bone. Having thus prepared them for frying, take one of them, and mince the flesh very small, with mushrooms, chives, and parsley chopped fine; a little salt, pepper, beaten mace, nutmeg, and a few savory herbs. Mix these well together, then pound them in a mortar and crumbs of bread soaked in cream, the yolks of three or four eggs, and a piece of butter; and with this composition stuff your fish. Put clarified butter into your pan, set it over the fire, and when it is hot strew some flour on your fish, and put them in one by one. When they have fried till they are of a nice brown colour, take them up, and lay them in a coarse cloth before the fire to keep hot. Then pour all the fat out of the pan, put in a quarter of a pound of butter, and shake in some flour. Keep it sirring with a spoon till the butter is a little brown, and then put in half a pint of white wine. Stir them together, and put in half a pint of boiling water, an onion shred with cloves, a bunch of sweet herbs, and two blades of mace. Cover these close, and let them stew as gently as you can for a quarter of an hour, then strain off the liquor, and put them into the pan again, adding two spoonsful of catsup, an ounce of truffles or morels boiled tender in half a pint of water, a few mushrooms, and half a pint of oysters, washed clean in their own liquor. When your sauce is properly heated, and has a good flavour, put in your tench, and let them lay in it till they are thoroughly hot; then take them out, lay them in your dish, and pour the sauce over them. Garnish with sliced lemon. The same methods may be used in frying of carp.

Soles.

TAKE off the skin, rub the fish over with the yolk of an egg, and strew on some crumbs of bread. Fry them in hog's lard over a brisk fire, till they are of a fine light brown. Then take them up, drain them, put them into your dish, and serve them up with plain melted butter in a boat. Garnish with green pickles.

Smelts.

BE careful to take away the gills, but leave in the roes. After you have washed them, dry them well in a cloth, then beat up an egg very fine, rub it over them with a feather, and strew on crumbs of bread. Fry them in hogs lard over a brisk fire, and put them in when the fat is boiling hot. When they are done of a fine brown, take them out, and drain the fat from them, and when you dish them up, put a basin with the bottom upwards, into the middle of your dish, and lay the tails of your fish on the side of it. Garnish with fried parsley.

Eels.

AFTER having properly cleaned them, and taken off the heads, cut them into pieces, season them with pepper and salt, strew on some flour, and fry them till they are of a fine brown colour. Drain them properly before you lay them in the dish. Serve them up with melted butter and the juice of a lemon squeezed into it. Garnish with crisped parsley.

Lampreys.

WHEN you cut them open to clean them, be careful to save the blood, and wash them thoroughly clean in warm water. Fry them in clean dripping, and when nearly enough, put out the fat, put a little white wine, and give the pan a shake round. Throw a little pepper, with some sweet herbs, a few capers, a piece of butter rolled in flour, and the blood you saved from the fish. Cover the pan close, and shake it often. When they are enough, take them out, strain the sauce, put it into the pan again, and give it a quick boil. Squeeze in the juice of a lemon, stir all together, and when it is just upon the boil, pour it over the fish, and serve it up. Garnish with sliced lemon.

Mullets.

SCORE the fish across the back, and dip them in melted butter. Fry them in butter clarified, and when enough, lay them on a warm dish. Serve them up with plain melted butter or anchovy sauce.

Herrings.

FIRST scrape off all the scales, then wash them dry them well in a cloth, and dredge them with flour. Fry them in butter over a brisk fire, and when done, set their tails up one against another in the middle of the dish. Fry a large handful of parsley crisp, take it out before it loses its colour; lay it round the fish, and serve them up with melted butter, parsley, and mustard.

Oysters.

THE largest oysters you can get should be chosen for frying. When you have properly cleaned and rinsed them, strew over them a little grated nutmeg, a blade of mace pounded, a spoonful of flour, and a little salt. Dip your oysters singly into this, and fry them in hog's lard till they are of a nice brown colour. Then take them out of the pan, pour them into your dish, and pour over them a little melted butter, with crumbs of bread mixed.

CHAPTER VII.

STEWING.

SECT. I.

BUTCHER'S MEAT.

Fillet of Veal.

TAKE the fillet of a cow calf, stuff it well under the udder, and at the bone end quite through to the shank. Put it into the oven, with a pint of water under it, till it is of a fine brown; then put it into a stew-pan, with three pints of gravy. Stew it till it is tender, and then put a few morels, truffles, a tea-spoonful of lemon-pickle, a large one of browning, one of catsup, and a little chyan pepper. Thicken it with a lump of butter rolled in flour. Take out your veal and put it into your dish, then strain the gravy, pour it over, and lay round forcemeat balls. Garnish with sliced lemon and pickles.

Breast of Veal.

PUT a breast of veal into the stew-pan, with a little broth, a glass of white wine, a bunch of sweet herbs, a few mushrooms, two or three onions, with some pepper and salt. Stew it over a gentle fire till it is tender; and when done strain and scum the sauce. Garnish with forcemeat balls.

Knuckle of Veal.

LAY at the bottom of your saucepan four wooden skewers cross ways, then put in the veal, with two or three blades of mace, a little whole pepper, a piece of thyme, a small onion, a crust of bread, and two quarts of water. Cover it down close, make it boil, and then only let it simmer for two hours. When enough, take it up, put it into your dish, and strain the liquor over it. Garnish with lemon.

Neck of Veal.

LARD it with large pieces of bacon rolled in pepper and shalots and spices. Put it into your stew-pan with about three pints of broth, two onions, a laurel leaf, and a little brandy. Let it simmer gently till it is tender, then put it into your dish, take the scum clean off the liquor, and then pour it on the meat.

Calf's Head.

AFTER having properly cleaned the head, put it into cold water, and let it lie for an hour: then carefully take out the brains, the tongue, the eyes, and the bones. Then take a pound of veal, and a pound of beef suet, a very little thyme, a good deal of lemon-peel minced, a nutmeg grated, and two anchovies: chop all very fine, then grate two stale rolls, and mix the whole together with the yolks of four eggs: save enough of this to make about twenty balls. Take half a pint of fresh mushrooms, clean peeled and washed, the yolks of six eggs, beat fine, half a pint of oysters clean washed, or pickled cockles; mix these all together, after first stewing your oysters. Put the forcemeat into the head and close it, tie it tight with packthread, and put it into a deep stew-pan, with two quarts of gravy and a blade or two of mace. Cover it close, and let it stew two hours. In the meantime, beat up the brains with some lemon-peel cut fine, a little parsley chopped, half a nutmeg grated, and the yolk of an egg. Have some dripping boiling, and fry half the brains in little cakes; fry all the forcemeat balls, and keep them both hot by the fire. Take half an ounce of truffles and morels, then strain the gravy the head was stewed in, and put the truffles and morels to it, with a few mushrooms. Boil all together, then put in the rest of the brains, stew them together for a minute or two, pour the whole over the head, and lay the cakes of fried brains and forcemeat balls round it. Garnish with lemons. For a small family, the half of a head may be done equally fine, only propeily proportioning the quantity of the respective articles.—A lamb's head must be done in the very same manner.

Calf's Liver.

LARD the liver, and put it into a stew-pan, with some salt, whole pepper, a bunch of sweet herbs, an onion, and a blade of mace. Let it stew till tender, then take it up, and cover it to keep hot. Strain the liquor it was stewed in, scum off all the fat, thicken it with a piece of butter rolled in flour, and pour it over the liver.

Rump of Beef.

HALF roast your beef, then put it into a stew-pan, with two quarts of water, and one of red wine, two or three blades of mace, a shalot, one spoonful of lemon-pickle, two of walnut catsup, and the same of browning. Put in chyan pepper and salt to your taste. Cover it close, and let it stew over a gentle fire for two hours; then take up your beef, and lay it in a deep dish, scum off the fat, and strain the gravy: put in an ounce of morels, and half a pint of mushrooms; thicken your gravy, and pour it over the beef. Garnish with force-meat balls and horse-radish.

Beef Steaks.

PEPPER and salt your steaks, and lay them in a stew-pan. Put in half a pint of water, a blade or two of mace, an anchovy, a small bunch of herbs, a piece of butter rolled in flour, a glass of white wine, and an onion. Cover the whole close, and let it stew till the steaks are tender; then take them out, strew some flour over them, fry them in fresh butter till they are of a nice brown, and then pour off all the fat. Strain the sauce they were stewed in, pour it into the pan, and toss it up all together ti l the sauce is quite hot and thick. Then lay your eaks in the dish, pour the sauce over them, and garnish with horse-radish and pickles.

Beef Gobbets.

TAKE any piece of beef, except the leg, cut it into small pieces, and put them into a stew-pan. Cover them with water, and when they have stewed an hour, put in a little mace, cloves, and whole pepper, tied loosely in a muslin rag, with some celery cut small. Then add some salt, turnips and carrots pared and cut in slices, a little parsley, a bunch of sweet herbs, a large crust of bread, and an ounce either of barley or rice Cover it close, and let it stew till it is tender. Then take out the herbs, spices, and bread, and have ready a French roll nicely toasted and cut into four parts. Put these into your dish, pour in the meat and sauce, and send it hot to table.

Neat's Tongue.

Put the tongue into your stew-pan with a sufficient quantity of water to cover it. When it has stewed about two hours, take it out, peel it, and put it in again, with a pint of strong gravy, half a pint of white wine, a bunch of sweet herbs, a little pepper and salt some mace, cloves, and whole pepper, tied in a muslin rag; add likewise a spoonful of capers chopped fine, some turnips and carrots sliced, and a piece of butter rolled in flour. Let the whole stew together very gently for two hours. then take out the spice and sweet herbs, put the tongue into your dish, strain the sauce, pour it over, and serve it up.

To dress Ox Palates.

Having cleansed and boiled your palates, take off the skin, and pick out all that part that is black, and cut them in bits: turn some onions a few times over the fire with a bit of butter, and when it is half done put it in the palates. Moisten your ragout with some good broth, and a little cullis; season it to your taste, and add a bunch of sweet herbs: when it is well skimmed, and the sauce of a proper consistence, put in a little mustard, and serve it up.

Ox Palates forced.

Stew your palates whole with forcemeat rolled up; when done, cut them in half: serve them up with a good sauce of truffles.

To marinade Ox Palates.

HAVING boiled some palates in water till tender, cut them in pieces of what shape you please, and steep them two or three hours in some vinegar, with salt, pepper, a clove of garlic, a little flour and butter, a laurel leaf, and three cloves. The whole marinade must be made luke-warm, then take them out, dry, flour and fry them, and serve them up with fried parsley.

SECT. II.

STEWING POULTRY, &c.

Turkey en Pain.

TAKE a fine turkey, bone it, and put into the carcase a ragout composed of large livers, mushrooms, and streaked bacon, all cut in small dice, and mingled with salt, fine spices, and shred parsley and onions Sew the turkey up, but take care to shape it nicely; then put a thin slice of bacon upon the breast, and wrap it in a cloth. Stew it in a pot, but not too large a one, with good broth, a glass of white wine, and a bunch of sweet herbs; when it is done, strain the liquor the turkey was done in into a stew-pan, after having taken off the fat; reduce it to a sauce, adding a spoonful of cullis; then unwrap your turkey, take off the bacon, dry away the grease, and serve it up with the sauce.

Fowls.

PURSUE the same method, at first, in stewing fowls as you do turkeys; that is to say, put skewers crossways at the bottom of your stew-pan. When you have laid in your fowl, put to it a quart of gravy, a bunch of celery clean washed and cut very small, with two or three blades of mace. Let it stew gently till the liquor is reduced to a quantity only sufficient for sauce; then add a large piece of butter rolled in flour, two spoonsful of red wine, the same quantity of catsup, with pepper and salt to season it. Lay your fowl in the dish, pour the sauce over it, and send it to table

Chickens.

HALF boil them in as much water as will just cover them, then take them out, cut them up, and take out the breast bones. Put them into your stew-pan with the liquor, and add a blade of mace and a little salt. Cover the pan close, and set it over a slow fire. Let it stew till the chickens are enough, then put the whole into your dish, and serve it to table.

Goose Giblets.

PUT them into scalding water, by which you will be enabled to make them properly clean. When this is done, cut the neck into four pieces, the pinions in two, and slice the gizzard. Put them into your stew-pan with two quarts of water, or, if you have it, mutton broth, with some sweet herbs, an anchovy, a few peppercorns, three or four cloves, a spoonful of catsup, and an onion. When the giblets are tender, put in a spoonful of good cream, thicken it with flour and butter, then pour the whole into a soup-dish, with sippets of bread at the bottom, and serve it up.

Ducks.

TAKE two ducks, properly picked and drawn, dust them with flour, and set them before the fire to brown. Then put them into a stew-pan, with a quart of water, a pint of red wine, a spoonful of walnut catsup, the same of browning, an anchovy, half a lemon, a clove of garlic, a bunch of sweet herbs, with chyan pepper and salt to your taste. Let them stew gently for half an hour, or till you find them tender; then lay them on a dish, and keep them hot. Skim off the fat from the liquor in which they were stewed, strain it through a hair sieve, add to it a few morels and truffles, boil it quick till reduced to little more than half a pint, then pour it over your ducks, and serve them up.

Duck with green Peas.

Put into your stew-pan a piece of fresh butter, and set it on the fire; then put in your duck, and turn it in the pan two or three minutes: take out the fat, but let the duck remain. Put to it a pint of good gravy, a pint of peas, two lettuces cut small, a bunch of sweet-herbs, and a little pepper and salt. Cover them close, and let them stew for half an hour, now and then shaking the pan. When they are just done, grate in a little nutmeg, with a small quantity of beaten mace, and thicken it either with a piece of butter rolled in flour, or the yolk of an egg beat up with two or three spoonsful of cream. Shake it all together for two or three minutes, then take out the sweet herbs, lay the duck in the dish, and pour the sauce over it. Garnish with boiled mint chopped very fine.

Pigeons.

Put into the bodies of your pigeons a seasoning made with pepper and salt, a few cloves and mace, some sweet herbs, and a piece of butter rolled in flour. Tie up the necks and vents, and half roast them. Then put them into a stew-pan, with a quart of good gravy, a little white wine, a few peppercorns, three or four blades of mace, a bit of lemon, a bunch of sweet herbs, and a small onion. Stew them gently till they are enough: then take the pigeons out, and strain the liquor through a sieve: scum it and thicken it in your stew-pan with a piece of butter rolled in flour: then put in the pigeons with some pickled mushrooms; stew it about five minutes; put the pigeons into a dish, and pour the sauce over them.

Pheasants.

Put into your stew-pan with the pheasant as much veal broth as will cover it, and let it stew till there is just enough liquor left for sauce. Then scum it, and put in artichoke bottoms parboiled, a little beaten mace, a glass of wine, and some pepper and salt. If it is not sufficiently substantial, thicken it with a piece of butter rolled in flour, and squeeze in a little lemon-juice. Then take up the pheasant, pour the sauce over it, and put forcemeat balls into the dish.

Partridges.

TRUSS your partridges in the same manner as for roasting, stuff the craws, and lard them down each side of the breast; then roll a lump of butter in pepper, and salt, and beaten mace, and put into the bellies, Sew up the vents, and then put them into a stew-pan with a quart of good gravy, a spoonful of Madeira wine, the same of catsup, a tea-spoonful of lemon-pickle, half the quantity of mushroom powder, one anchovy, half a lemon, and a sprig of sweet marjorum. Cover the pan close, and stew them half an hour · then take them out and thicken the gravy. Boil it a little, and pour it over the partridges, and lay round them artichoke bottoms boiled and cut in quarters, and the yolks of four hard eggs. Woodcocks must be stewed in the same manner.

Cucumbers.

PARE twelve middle sized cucumbers, slice them about the thickness of half a crown, and lay them in a coarse cloth to drain. When quite dry, flour them, and fry them in fresh butter till they are brown; then take them out with an egg-slice, and lay them on a plate before the fire. Take a large cucumber, cut a long piece out of the side, and scoop out all the pulp. Have ready some onions nicely fried, fill the cucumber with these, and season with pepper and salt: then put in the piece that was cut out, and tie it round with packthread. Flour it, and fry it till it is brown; then take it out of the pan, and keep it hot. Let the pan remain on the fire, and while you are putting in a little flour with one hand, keep stirring it with the other. —When it is thick, put in two or three spoonsful of water, half a pint of white or red wine, and two spoonsful of catsup. Stir them together, and add three blades of mace, four cloves, half a nutmeg grated, and a little pepper and salt, all beat fine together. Stir it into the saucepan, and then throw in your cucumbers. Let them stew for two or three minutes, then lay the whole cucumber in the middle of your dish, having first untied it, the rest round it, and pour the sauce all over. Garnish the dish with fried onions.

Peas and Lettuce.

PUT a quart of green peas, and two large lettuces washed clean, and cut small across, into a stew-pan, with a quart of gravy, and stew them till they are tender. Put in a piece of butter rolled in flour, and season with pepper and salt. When of a proper thickness, dish them up, and send them to table. Instead of butter you may thicken them with the yolks of four eggs, and if you put two or three thin rashers of lean ham at the bottom of the stew-pan, it will give the whole a very fine flavour.

SECT. III.

STEWING FISH.

Carp and Tench.

HAVING scaled and gutted your fish, wash them thoroughly clean, dry them with a cloth. Then put them into a stew-pan, with a quart of water, the same quantity of red wine, a large spoonful of lemon-pickle, another of browning, a little mushroom-powder, chyan pepper, a large onion stuck with cloves, and a stick of horse-radish. (If carp, add the blood, which you must be careful to save when you kill them.) Cover your pan close to keep in the steam; and let them stew gently over a slow fire till your gravy is reduced to just enough to cover them. Then take the fish out, and put them into the dish you intend for table. Set the gravy again on the fire, and thicken it with a large lump of butter rolled in flour: boil it a little, and then strain it over your fish. Garnish with pickled mushrooms, scraped horse-radish, and the roes of the fish, some of them fried and cut into small pieces, and the rest boiled. Just before you send it up, squeeze into the sauce the juice of a lemon.

Barbel.

TAKE a large barbel, scale, gut, and wash it in vinegar and salt, and afterwards in clear water. Then put it into a stew-pan, with a sufficiency of eel broth to cover it, and add some cloves, a bunch of sweet herbs, and a bit of cinnamon. Let them stew gently till the fish is done, then take it out, thicken the sauce with butter and flour, pour it over the fish, and serve it up.

Small Barbel.

THE small barbel is stewed like a carp, and when large may be done on the gridiron, served up with a white sauce.

Trout.

MAKE a stuffing with grated bread, a piece of butter, chopped parsley, lemon-peel grated, pepper, salt, nutmeg, savory herbs, and the yolk of an egg, all well mixed together. Fill the belly of your fish with this, and then put it into a stew-pan with a quart of good boiled gravy, half a pint of Madeira wine, an onion, a little whole pepper, a few cloves, and a piece of lemon-peel. Stew it very gently over a slow fire, and when done, take out the fish, and add to the sauce a little flour mixed in some cream, a little catsup, and the juice of a lemon. Let it just boil up, then strain it over your fish, and serve it up.

Pike.

MAKE a browning with butter and flour, and put it into your stew-pan with a pint of red wine, a faggot, four cloves, a dozen of small onions half boiled, with some pepper and salt. Cut your pike into pieces, put it in, and let it stew very gently. When done, take it out, and add to the sauce two anchovies and a spoonful of capers chopped fine. Boil it for a minute or two, and then pour it over the fish. Garnish with bread nicely fried, and cut three-corner ways.

A Fricandeau of Pike.

CUT a pike into slices, according to its size; after having scaled, gutted, and washed it, lard all the upper part with bacon cut small, and put it into a stew-pan with a glass of white wine, some good broth, a bunch of sweet herbs, and some fillet of veal cut into small dice: when it is stewed, and the sauce strained off, glaze it like other fricandeaus. It may also be fricaseed like chickens (as a side dish); or you may stew it, and serve it up with a white sauce.

Cod.

CUT some slices of cod, as for boiling, and season them with grated nutmeg, pepper, salt, and sweet herbs. Put them into a stew-pan with half a pint of white wine and a quarter of a pint of water. Cover them close, and let them simmer for five or six minutes. Then squeeze in the juice of a lemon, and add a few oysters with their liquor strained, a piece of butter rolled in flour, and a blade or two of mace. Let them stew very gently, and frequently shake the pan to prevent its burning. When the fish is done, take out the onion and sweet herbs, lay the cod in a warm dish, and strain the sauce over it.

Soles, Plaice, and Flounders.

THE same methods must be taken for stewing either of these kinds of fish. Half fry them in butter, then take them out of the pan, and put to the butter a quart of water, two anchovies, and an onion sliced. When they have boiled slowly for about a quarter of an hour, put your fish in again, and let them stew gently about twenty minutes; then take out the fish, and thicken the sauce with butter and flour. Give the whole a gentle boil, then strain it through a hair-sieve over the fish, and serve them up with oyster, cockle, or shrimp sauce.

Lampreys and Eels.

HAVING skinned, gutted, and thoroughly washed your fish, season them with salt, pepper, a little lemon peel shred fine, mace, cloves, and nutmeg. Put some thin slices of butter into your stew-pan, and having rolled your fish round, put them in, with half a pint of good gravy, a gill of white wine, a bunch of marjorum, winter savory, thyme, and an onion sliced. Let them stew over a gentle fire, and keep turning them till they are tender. Then take them out, and put an anchovy into the sauce. Thicken it with the yolk of an egg beat very fine, or a piece of butter rolled in flour. When it boils, pour it over the fish, and serve them to table.

Prawns, Shrimps, and Cray-fish.

TAKE about two quarts of either of these fish, and pick out the tails. Put the bodies into your stew-pan, with about a pint of white wine (or water with a spoonful of vinegar) and a blade of mace. Stew these a quarter of an hour, then stir them together, and strain them. Having done this, wash out your pan, and put into it the strained liquor and tails. Grate into it a small nutmeg, put in a little salt, a quarter of a pound of butter rolled in flour, and shake it all together. Cut a thin slice of bread round a quartern loaf, toast it brown on both sides, cut it into six pieces, lay it close together in the bottom of your dish, pour your fish and sauce hot over it, and send it hot to table. If cray-fish, garnish the dish with some of their biggest claws laid thick round.

Oysters.

STRAIN the liquor of your oysters, and put it into your saucepan with a little beaten mace, and thicken it with flour and butter. Boil this three or four minutes, then toast a slice of bread, cut it in three-cornered pieces, and lay them round the dish into which you intend to put the oysters. Then put into the pan a spoonful of cream with your oysters, shake them round, and let them stew till they are quite hot, but be careful they do not boil. Pour them into a deep plate or soup-dish, and serve them up. Most kinds of hell-fish may be stewed in the same manner.

Oysters scollop'd.

WASH them thoroughly clean in their own liquor, and then put them into your scollop shells; strew over them a few crumbs of bread. Lay a slice of butter on the first you put in, then more oysters, and bread and butter successively till the shell is full. Put them into a Dutch oven to brown, and serve them up hot in the shells.

Muscles.

WASH them very clean in several waters, then put them into a stew-pan, and cover them close. Let them stew till the shells open, and then pick out the fish clean, one by one. Look under the tongue to see if there be a crab, and if you find one, throw that muscle away. You will likewise find a little tough article under the tongue, which you must pick off. Having thus properly cleansed them, put them into a sauce-pan, and to a quart of muscles, put half a pint of the liquor strained through a sieve: add a few blades of mace, a small piece of butter rolled in flour, and let them stew gently. Lay some toasted bread in the dish, and when the muscles are done, pour them on it, and serve them up.

CHAPTER VIII.

HASHING AND MINCING.

SECT. I.

BUTCHER'S MEAT.

Calf's Head.

AS a *whole* calf's head is rather too large for the consumption of most families at one time, and as we mean to confine our receipts within such compass as may with equal convenience and pleasure suit all, so we shall here give directions for only hashing *one-half*, observing that should there be occasion for doing the whole, it is only doubling the ingredients here given for a part.

Wash the head as clean as possible, and then boil it a quarter of an hour. When cold, cut the meat, as also the tongue, into thin broad slices, and put them into a stewing-pan, with a quart of good gravy. When it has stewed three quarters of an hour, put in an anchovy, a little beaten mace, chyan pepper, two spoonsful of lemon-pickle, the same quantity of walnut catsup, half an ounce of truffles and morels, a slice or two of lemon, some sweet herbs, and a glass of white wine. Mix a quarter of a pound of butter with some flour, and put it in a few minutes before the meat is done. In the mean time put the brains into hot water, and beat them fine in a basin; then add two eggs, a spoonful of flour, a bit of lemon-peel shred fine, and a little parsley, thyme, and sage chopped small. Beat them all well together, and strew in a little pepper and salt; then drop them in little cakes into a pan with boiling lard; fry them of a light brown, and lay them on a sieve to drain. Take your hash out of your pan with a fish slice, and lay it in your dish. Strain your gravy over it, and lay upon it a few mushrooms, forcemeat balls, the yolks of two eggs boiled hard, and the brain cakes. Garnish with sliced lemon and pickles. If the company is so large that there should be a necessity for dressing the whole head, in order to make a pleasing variety, do the other half thus: When it is parboiled, hack it cross and cross with a knife, and grate some nutmeg all over it. Take the yolks of two eggs, a little salt and pepper, a few sweet-herbs, some crumbs of bread, and a little lemon-peel chopped very fine. Strew this over the head, and then put it into a deep dish before a good fire. Baste it with butter, and keep the dish turning till all parts are equally brown. Then take it up, and lay it on your hash. Blanch the half of the tongue, and lay it on a soup plate; boil the brains with a little sage and parsley, chop them fine, and mix them with some melted butter, and a spoonful of cream, make it quite hot, then pour it over the tongue, and serve it up with the head. The mode of doing this half is usually termed *grilling*

Veal Minced.

First cut your veal into thin slices, and then into small bits. Put it into a saucepan with half a pint of gravy, a little pepper and salt, a slice of lemon, a good piece of butter rolled in flour, a tea-spoonful of lemon-pickle, and a large spoonful of cream.—Keep shaking t over the fire till it boils, have sippets of bread ready in the dish, and then pour the whole over them. Garnish with sliced lemon.

Mutton Hashed.

Cut your meat into small pieces, as thin as possible; then boil the bones with an onion, a few sweet herbs, a blade of mace, a very little whole pepper, a little salt, and a piece of crust toasted very crisp. Let it boil till there is just enough for sauce; then strain it, and put it into a saucepan, with a piece of butter rolled in flour; then put in the meat, and when it is very hot it is enough. Season with pepper and salt. Have ready some thin bread toasted brown and cut three corner ways, lay them in the dish, and pour over the hash. Garnish with pickles and horse-radish

---

SECT. II.

HASHING POULTRY *and* GAME.

Turkeys.

Cut the flesh into pieces, and take off all the skin, otherwise it will give the gravy a greasy disagreeable taste. Put it into a stew-pan with a pint of gravy, a tea-spoonful of lemon-pickle, a slice of the end of a lemon, and a little beaten mace. Let it boil about six or seven minutes, and then put it into your dish. Thicken your gravy with flour and butter, mix the yolks of two eggs with a spoonful of thick cream, put it into your gravy, and shake it over the fire till it is quite hot, but do not let it boil; then strain it, and pour it over your turkey. Lay sippets round, serve it up, and garnish with lemon and parsley.

Or you may do it thus·

CUT the remains of a roasted turkey into pieces, and put them into a stew-pan with a glass of white wine, chopped parsley, shalots, mushrooms, truffles, salt, and pepper, and about half a pint of broth. Let it boil half an hour, which will be sufficient to do it; then add a pounded anchovy and a squeeze of lemon. Scum the fat clear from the sauce, then pour the whole into your dish over sippets made of toasted bread cut thin. Garnish with sliced lemon.

Fowls.

CUT up your fowl as for eating, then put it into a stew-pan with half a pint of gravy, a tea-spoonful of lemon-pickle, a little catsup and a slice of lemon. Thicken it with flour and butter; and just before you dish it up, put in a spoonful of good cream. Lay sippets in the dish, and pour the hash over them.

Chickens.

CUT a cold chicken into pieces, and if you have no gravy, make a little with the long bones, onion, spice, &c. Flour the chicken, and put into the gravy, with white pepper, salt, nutmeg, and grated lemon. When it boils, stir in an egg, and mix it with a little cream. As soon as it is thoroughly hot, squeeze in a little lemon-juice, then put the whole into a dish, strew over it some crumbs of bread, brown them with a salamander, and then serve it up hot to table.

Partridges or Woodcocks.

HAVING cut it up in the usua' manner as when first brought to the table, work the entrails very fine with the back of a spoon, put in a spoonful of red wine, the same of water, and half a spoonful of vinegar; cut an onion in slices, and put it into rings; roll a little butter in flour, put them all into your pan, and shake it over the fire till it boils; then put in your bird, and when it is thoroughly hot, lay it in your dish, with sippets round it. Strain the sauce over the bird, and lay the onions in rings. This will make a delicate dish for two people either for dinner or supper; and where there is a large company is an ornamental addition to other articles provided.

Wild Ducks.

CUT up your duck in the usual manner, then put it into a pan, with a spoonful of good gravy, the same of red wine, and an onion sliced exceeding thin. When it has boiled two or three minutes, lay the duck in the dish, and pour the gravy over it. You may add a tea-spoonful of caper liquor, or a little browning.

Hares.

CUT your hare into small pieces, and if you have any of the pudding left, rub it small, and put to it a gill of red wine, the same quantity of water, half an anchovy chopped fine, an onion stuck with four cloves, and a quarter of a pound of butter rolled in flour. Put these all together into a saucepan, and set it over a slow fire, shaking it at times that the whole may be equally heated. When it is thoroughly hot (for you must not let any kind of hash boil, as it will harden the meat) take out the onion, lay sippets in and round the dish, pour in your hash, and serve it hot to table.

Hare Jugged.

AFTER you have cut your hare into small pieces, lard them here and there with very thin slips of bacon; season them with a little pepper and salt, and put them into an earthen jug, with a blade or two of mace, an onion stuck with cloves, and a bunch of sweet herbs. Cover the jug close, that the steam may be retained: set it in a pot of boiling water, and about three hours will do it. Then turn it out of the jug into the dish, take out the onion and sweet herbs, and send it hot to table. With respect to the larding, it may be used or omitted, at your own discretion. Garnish with sliced lemon.

Venison.

CUT your venison into very thin slices, and put it into a stewing-pan, with a large glass of red wine, a spoonful of catsup, the same of browning, an onion stuck with cloves, and half an anchovy chopped fine. When it boils, put in your venison, and let it remain till it is thoroughly heated. Then pour the whole together into a soup dish, with sippets underneath. Garnish with red cabbage or current-jelly.

CHAPTER IX.

FRICASSEEING.

SECT. I.

BUTCHER'S MEAT, POULTRY, &c.

Neat's Tongue.

HAVING boiled the tongue till it is tender, take it up, peel it, and cut it into slices. Put them into a frying-pan with a proper quantity of butter, and let them fry till they are brown. Then pour the butter clean out of the pan, and put in some good gravy, with a bunch of sweet herbs, an onion, some pepper and salt, a blade or two of mace, and a gill of wine. When they have all simmered together about half an hour, take out the slices of tongue, strain the gravy, and put all again into the pan, with the yolks of two eggs beat fine, a little nutmeg grated, and a small piece of butter rolled in flour. Shake the whole well together, and when it has simmered for about five minutes, put the tongue into your dish, pour over the sauce, and serve it to table.

Sweetbreads White.

THESE must be likewise first scalded, and then cut into long slices; when done, thicken some veal gravy with a piece of butter rolled in flour, a little cream some grated lemon-peel and nutmeg, white pepper, salt, and a little mushroom powder. When these have stewed together about ten minutes, put in the sweet-breads, shake the pan, and let them simmer; then squeeze in a little lemon-juice, pour the whole into your dish, and serve it up.

Calf's Feet a-la-Carmagot.

PARBOIL them, then take out the long bones, split them, and put them into a stew-pan, with some veal gravy, and a glass of white wine. Add likewise the yolks of two or three eggs beat up with a little cream, grated nutmeg, salt, and a piece of butter. Stir it till it is of a good thickness; and when the whole has gently simmered for about ten minutes, put the feet into your dish, and pour the sauce over them. Garnish with sliced lemon.

Tripe.

CUT your tripe into pieces, about two inches square, and put them into your stew-pan, with as much white wine as will half cover them, a little white pepper, sliced ginger, a blade of mace, a bunch of sweet herbs, and an onion. When it has stewed a quarter of an hour, (which will be sufficient time to do it,) take out the herbs and onion, and put a little shred parsley, the juice of a lemon, half an anchovy cut small, a cup full of cream, and either the yolk of an egg, or a piece of butter. Season it to your taste; and when you dish it up, garnish with lemon.

Chickens.

SKIN your chickens, and then cut them into small pieces, after which wash them with warm water, and thoroughly dry them with a cloth. Season them with salt and pepper, and put them into a stew-pan with a little water, a large piece of butter, a bunch of thyme, and sweet-marjorum, an onion stuck with cloves, a little lemon-pickle, a glass of wine, an anchovy, a little mace and nutmeg. When the chickens have stewed till they are tender, take them up, and lay them in your dish. Thicken your gravy with butter rolled in flour, and then strain it. Beat up the yolks of three eggs, and mix them with a gill of rich cream; put this into your gravy, and shake it over the fire till it is quite hot, but do not suffer it to boil. Pour this over your chickens, and serve them up. Garnish with sliced lemon.

Rabbits White.

To fricasee rabbits white, you must cut them up as for eating, and then put them into a stew-pan, with a pint of veal gravy, a little beaten mace, a slice of lemon, an anchovy, a tea-spoonful of lemon pickle, a little chyan pepper and salt. Let them stew over a gentle fire till they are enough, then take them out, and lay them in your dish. Thicken the gravy with butter and flour; then strain it, and add the yolks of two eggs, mixed with a gill of thick cream, and a little grated nutmeg. Stir these well together, and when it begins to simmer, pour it quite hot over your rabbits, and serve them to table.

Rabbits Brown.

Cut them into pieces as before directed, and fry them in butter of a light brown. Then put them into a stew-pan, with a pint of water, a slice of lemon, an anchovy, a large spoonful of browning, the same of catsup, a tea-spoonful of lemon-pickle, and a little chyan pepper and salt. Stew them over a slow fire till they are enough, then thicken your gravy with butter and flour, and strain it. Dish up your rabbits, and pour the gravy over them. Garnish with sliced lemon.

SECT. II.

FRICASEEING FISH, &c.

Cod Sounds.

Having properly cleaned them, cut them into small pieces, boil them in milk and water, and then set them to drain. Then put them into a clean saucepan, and season them with beaten mace, grated nutmeg, and a little pepper and salt. Add to them a cup full of cream, with a good piece of butter rolled in flour, and keep shaking the whole till it is thoroughly hot, and of a good thickness. Then pour all into your dish, and serve it up, with a sliced lemon for garnish.

Soles.

When you have skinned, gutted, and thoroughly washed them, cut off their heads, and dry the fish in a cloth. Then cut the flesh very carefully from the bones and fins on both sides: cut it first long-ways, and then across, in such divisions that each fish may make eight pieces. Put the heads and bones into a stew-pan, with a pint of water, a bunch of sweet herbs, an onion, a little whole pepper, two or three blades of mace, a small piece of lemon-peel, a little salt, and a crust of bread. Cover it close, and let it boil till it is half wasted: then strain it through a fine sieve, and put it into a stew-pan with your fish. Add to them half a pint of white wine, a little parsley chopped fine, a few mushrooms cut small, a little grated nutmeg, and a piece of butter rolled in flour. Set altogether over a slow fire, and keep shaking the pan till the fish are enough: then dish them up with the gravy, and serve them to table. Garnish with lemon.

Eels.

Skin three or four large eels, and notch them from end to end. Cut them into four or five pieces each, and lay them in some spring water for half an hour to crimp: then dry them in a cloth, and put them into your pan, with a piece of fresh butter, a green onion or two, and a little chopped parsley. Set the pan on the fire, and shake them about for a few minutes: then put in about a pint of white wine, and as much good broth with pepper, salt, and a blade of mace. Stew all together about half an hour: and then add the yolks of four or five eggs beat smooth, and a little grated nutmeg, and chopped parsley. Stir the whole well together, and let it simmer four or five minutes, then squeeze in the juice of a lemon, give the whole a good shake, pour it into your dish, and serve it up hot. Garnish with lemon.

Tench are exceeding fine dressed in the same manner.

Flounders.

TAKE a sharp knife, and carefully raise the flesh on both sides from head to tail; then take the bone clear out, and cut the flesh into pieces in the same manner as directed for soles, only let the pieces of each consist of six instead of eight. Dry your fish well, then sprinkle them with salt, dredge them with flour, and fry them in a pan of hot beef dripping, so that the fish may be crisp. When so done, take them out of the pan, drain the fat from them, and set them before the fire to keep warm. Then clean the pan, and put into it some minced oysters, with their liquor clean strained, some white wine, a little grated nutmeg, and three anchovies. Stew these together a few minutes, and then put in your fish, with about a quarter of a pound of fresh butter. Shake them well together, and, when quite hot, dish up your fish with the sauce, and serve them to table. Garnish with yolks of eggs, boiled hard and minced, and sliced lemon. You may fricasee salmon, or any other firm fish, in the same manner.

Skate or Thornback.

THESE must be prepared for dressing in the same manner as directed for soles and flounders; after which put them into your stew-pan. To one pound of the fish put a quarter of a pint of water, a little beaten mace, and grated nutmeg, a small bunch of sweet herbs, and a little salt. Cover it close, and let it boil about a quarter of an hour. Then take out the sweet herbs, put in a quarter of a pint of good cream, a piece of butter, the size of a walnut, rolled in flour, and a glass of white wine. Keep shaking the pan all the time one way till your fricasee is thick and smooth; then dish it up, and garnish with lemon.

Oysters.

Put a little butter into your stew-pan, with a slice of ham, a faggot of parsley and sweet herbs, and an onion stuck with two cloves. Let them stew over a slow fire a few minutes, and then add a little flour, some good broth, and a piece of lemon-peel; then put in your oysters, and let them simmer till they are thoroughly hot. Thicken with the yolks of two eggs, a little cream, and a bit of good butter, take out the ham, faggot, onion, and lemon-peel, and add the squeeze of a lemon. Give the whole a shake in the pan, and when it simmers put it into your dish, and serve it up.

Eggs.

Boil your eggs hard, and take out some of the yolks whole; then cut the rest in quarters, yolks and whites together. Set on some gravy with a little shred thyme and parsley in it, and let it boil about a minute. Then put in your eggs, with a little grated nutmeg, and shake them up with a piece of butter till it is of a proper thickness. Pour it into your dish, and serve it up.

Eggs with Onions and Mushrooms.

When you have boiled the eggs hard take out the yolks whole, and cut the whites in slips, with some onions and mushrooms. Fry the onions and mushrooms, throw in the whites, and turn them about a little. If there is any fat, pour it off. Flour the onions, &c. and put to them a little good gravy. Boil this up, then put in the yolks, and add a little pepper and salt. Let the whole simmer for about a minute, and then dish it up.

Mushrooms.

If your mushrooms are very small (such as are usually termed buttons) you must only wipe them with a flannel; but if large peel them, scrape the insides, and throw them into some salt and water. After lying some time, take them out and boil them in water with some salt in it; and when they are tender, put in a little shred parsley, an onion stuck with cloves, and a glass of wine. Shake them up with a good piece of butter rolled in flour, and put in three spoonsful of thick cream, and a little nutmeg cut in pieces. When the whole has stood two or three minutes, take out the onion and nutmeg, then pour the mushrooms with their sauce into your dish, and serve them to table.

Skirrits.

WASH them thoroughly clean, and when you have boiled them till they are tender, skin the roots, and cut them into slices. Have ready a little cream, a piece of butter rolled in flour, the yolk of an egg beaten fine, a little grated nutmeg, two or three spoonsful of white wine, with a very little salt, and stir all together. Put your roots into the dish, and pour the sauce over them.

Artichoke Bottoms.

THESE may be fricaseed either dried or pickled. If dried, lay them in warm water for three or four hours, shifting the water two or three times. Having done this, put some cream into your saucepan, with a large piece of fresh butter, and stir them together one way till the butter is melted. Then put in the artichokes, and when they are hot dish them up.

CHAPTER X.

RAGOOS.

SECT. I.

BUTCHER'S MEAT.

Breast of Veal.

HALF roast it, then take out the bones, and put the meat into a stew-pan, with a quart of veal gravy an ounce of morels, and the same quantity of truffles

When the meat has stewed till it is tender, and just before you thicken the gravy, put in a few oysters, some pickled mushrooms, and pickled cucumbers, all cut in small square pieces, and the yolks of four eggs boiled hard. In the meantime, cut your sweetbread into pieces, and fry it of a light brown. When the veal is properly stewed, dish it up, and pour the gravy hot upon it. Lay your sweetbread, morels, truffles, and eggs round it, and garnish with pickled barberries. In placing this dish on the table, if the company is large, and the provisional entertainment designed to be set out in taste, if for supper, it must be placed at the bottom of the table, but if for dinner, either on the top or on one side. It may likewise be stewed tender, and served with a white sauce of young peas or button mushrooms.

Neck of Veal.

Cut your veal into steaks, and flatten them with a rolling-pin; then season them with salt, pepper, cloves, and mace: lard them with bacon strewed with lemon-peel and thyme, and dip them in the yolks of eggs. Having done this, make up a sheet of strong cap-paper at the four corners in the shape of a dripping-pan, butter it all over, as also the gridiron, and set over a charcoal fire, put in your meat, and let it do leisurely, keep turning it often, and baste it well in order to keep in the gravy. When it is enough have ready half a pint of strong gravy, season it high, and put into it mushrooms and pickles, forcemeat balls dipped in the yolks of eggs, oysters stewed and fried, to lay round and at the top of your dish, and then serve it up. If for white ragoo, put in a gill of white wine, with the yolks of two eggs beat up with two or three spoonsful of cream; but if a brown ragoo, put in red wine.

Sweetbreads Brown.

First scald your sweetbreads, and then cut them into slices. Beat up the yolk of an egg very fine, with a little flour, pepper, salt, and nutmeg. Dip your slices of sweetbread into this, and fry them of a nice light brown. Then thicken a little good gravy with some flour; boil it well, and add catsup or mushroom powder, a little juice of a lemon, and chyan pepper. Put your sweetbreads into this; and when they have stewed in it about five minutes, put the whole into your dish, and seve it up. Garnish with sliced lemon.

Calf's Feet.

AFTER boiling the feet, take out the bones, cut the meat into slices, and brown them in a frying-pan: then put them into some good beef gravy, with morels, truffles, pickled mushrooms, and the yolks of four eggs boiled hard, some salt, and a little butter rolled in flour. Let them stew together about five minutes, and then put all into your dish. Garnish with sliced lemon.

Pig's Feet and Ears.

FIRST boil them till they are tender, then cut the ears into long narrow slices, and split the feet down the middle. Put into a stew-pan about half a pint of beef gravy, a tea-spoonful of lemon-pickle, a large one of catsup, the same of browning, and a little salt. Thicken these with a piece of butter rolled in flour, and let the feet and ears be yolked over with egg, then roll them in bread-crumbs and seasoning; let the feet be nicely browned with a salamander, or fried: then let them boil gently, and, when enough, lay the feet in the middle of the dish, and the ears round them. Then strain your gravy, pour it over them, and garnish with curled parsley.

A Fore-quarter of House Lamb.

TAKE off the knuckle-bone, and then with a sharp knife cut off the skin. Lard it well with bacon, and fry it of a nice light brown. Then put it into a stew-pan, and just cover it over with mutton gravy, a bunch of sweet herbs, some pepper, salt, beaten mace, and a little whole pepper. Cover it close, and let it stew half an hour. Then pour out the liquor, and take care to keep the lamb hot. Strain off the gravy, and have ready half a pint of oysters fried brown. Pour all the fat from them, and put them into the gravy, with two spoonsful of red wine, a few mushrooms, and a bit of butter rolled in flour. Boil all together, with the juice of half a lemon. Lay the lamb in the dish, pour the sauce over it, and send it to table.

Beef.

TAKE any piece of beef that has got some fat to it, cut the meat clean from the bones, strew some flour over it, and fry it in a large stew-pan with butter till it is of a nice brown: then cover it in the pan with gravy made in the following manner: take about a pound of coarse beef, half a pound of veal cut small, a bunch of sweet herbs, an onion, some whole black and white pepper, two or three blades of mace, four or five cloves, a piece of carrot, a slice of lean bacon steeped in vinegar, and a crust of bread toasted brown. Add to these a quart of wine, and let it boil till it is half wasted. In the meantime pour a quart of boiling water into the stew-pan, cover it close, and let it stew gently. As soon as the gravy is done, strain it, and pour it into the stew-pan with the beef. Then take an ounce of truffles and morels cut small, with some fresh or dried mushrooms, and two spoonsful of catsup. Cover it close, and let it stew till the sauce is thick and rich. Have ready some artichoke bottoms quartered, and a few pickled mushrooms. Boil the whole together, and when your meat is tender, and the sauce rich, lay the meat in a dish, pour the sauce over it, and serve it hot to table.

Mutton.

CUT some thin slices, the right way of the grain, off a fine leg of mutton, and pare off all the skin and fat. Then put a piece of butter into your stew-pan, and shake some flour over it: add to these two or three slices of lemon, with half an onion cut very small, a bunch of sweet herbs, and a blade of mace. Put your meat with these into the pan, stir them together for five or six minutes, and then put in half a pint of gravy, with an anchovy minced small, and a piece of bu ter rolled in flour. Stir the whole well together, and when it has stewed about ten minutes, dish it up, and serve it to table. Garnish with pickles and sliced lemon.

SECT. II.

RAGOOS *of* POULTRY, VEGETABLES, &c.

A Goose.

SKIN your goose, dip it into boiling water, and break the breast-bone, so that it may lay quite flat. Season it with pepper and salt, and a little mace beaten to powder; lard it, and then flour it all over. Having done this, take about a pound of beef suet, and put into your stew-pan, and when melted, boiling hot, put in the goose. As soon as you find the goose brown all over, put in a quart of beef gravy boiling hot, a bunch of sweet herbs and a blade of mace, a few cloves, some whole pepper, two or three small onions, and a bay-leaf. Cover the pan quite close, and let it stew gently over a slow fire. If the goose is small, it will be done in an hour, but if large, an hour and a half. Make a ragoo for it in the following manner: Cut some turnips and carrots into small pieces, with three or four onions sliced, boil all enough, put them, with half a pint of rich beef gravy, into a saucepan, with some pepper, salt, and a piece of butter rolled in flour. Let them stew about a quarter of an hour. When the goose is done, take it out of the stew-pan, drain the liquor it was stewed in well from it, put it into a dish, and pour the ragoo over it.

Livers of Poultry.

TAKE the liver of a turkey, and the livers of six fowls, and put them into cold water. When they have laid in it some time, take them out, and put the fowls' livers into a saucepan, with a quarter of a pint of gravy, a spoonful of mushrooms either pickled or fresh, the same quantity of catsup, and a piece of butter rolled in flour. Season them to your taste with pepper and salt, and let them stew gently about ten minutes. In the meantime, broil the turkey's liver nicely, and lay it in the middle, with the stewed livers round it. Pour the sauce over all, and garnish with lemon.

Oysters.

When the oysters are opened, save as much of the liquor as you can, and strain it through a sieve; wash your oysters clean in warm water, and then make a batter as follows: Beat up the yolks of two eggs with half a nutmeg grated, cut a little lemon-peel small, a good deal of parsley, and add a spoonful of the juice of spinach, two spoonsful of cream or milk, and beat the whole up with flour till it is a thick batter. Having prepared this, put a piece of fresh butter into a stew-pan, and when it is thoroughly hot, dip your oysters one by one into the batter, then roll them in crumbs of bread grated fine, and fry them quick and brown, which done, take them out of the pan, and set them before the fire. Have ready a quart of chesnuts, shelled and skinned, and fry them in the batter. When enough, take them up, pour the fat out of the pan, shake a little flour all over the pan, and rub a piece of butter all round with a spoon. Then put in the oyster-liquor, three or four blades of mace, the chesnuts, and half a pint of white wine. Let them boil, and have ready the yolks of two eggs beat up, with four spoonsful of cream. Stir all well together, and when it is thick and fine, lay the oysters in the dish, and pour the ragoo over them. Garnish with chesnuts and lemon.

Muscles.

Put your muscles into a saucepan, and let them stew till they are open. Then take them out of the shells, and save the liquor. Put into your stew-pan a bit of butter, a few mushrooms chopped, a little parsley and grated lemon-peel. Stir these together, and then put in some gravy, with pepper and salt; thicken it with a little flour, boil it up, put in the muscles with their liquor, and let them be hot: then pour them into your dish, and serve them up. There are some muscles of a pernicious quality, to know which, when you stew them, put a half-crown into the saucepan, and if it is discoloured, the muscles are not wholesome.

Mushrooms.

TAKE some large mushrooms, peel them, and cut the inside. Then broil them on a gridiron, and when the outside is brown, put them into a stew-pan, with a sufficient quantity of water to cover them. When they have stewed ten minutes, put to them a spoonful of white wine, the same of browning, and a little vinegar. Thicken it with butter and flour, give it a gentle boil, and serve it up with sippets round the dish.

Artichoke Bottoms.

SOAK them in warm water for two or three hours, changing the water. Then put them into the stew-pan with some good gravy, mushroom catsup or powder, and a little chyan pepper and salt. When they boil, thicken with a little flour, put them into your dish, pour the sauce over them, and serve them up hot to table.

Asparagus.

TAKE an hundred of grass, scrape them clean, and put them into cold water; then cut them as far as is good and green, and take two heads of endive, with a young lettuce, and an onion, and cut them all very small. Put a quarter of a pound of butter into your stew-pan, and when it is melted, put in the grass, with the other articles. Shake them about, and when they have stewed ten minutes, season them with a little pepper and salt, strew in a little flour, shake them about, and then pour in half a pint of gravy. Let them stew till the sauce is very good and thick, and then pour all into your dish. Garnish with a few of the small tops of the grass.

Cucumbers.

SLICE two cucumbers and two onions, and fry them together in a little butter. Then drain them in a sieve, and put them into a saucepan, with a gill of gravy, two spoonsful of white wine, and a blade of mace. When they have stewed five or six minutes, put in a piece of butter, about the size of a walnut, rolled in flour, a little salt and chyan pepper. Shake them well together till the whole is of a good thickness, then put them into your dish, and serve them up.

Cucumbers

May likewise be stewed with forcemeat. Cut your cucumbers into two or three pieces, according to the size, take all the inside out with a cutter, put in your forcemeat, then put some butter into your stew-pan along with the cucumbers: after they have stewed some time add some good gravy, a glass of white wine, and let them go on till tender; then strain off the gravy, season and thicken it with cullis. Put it into the dish with the cucumbers; the dish must be glazed.

Cauliflowers.

TAKE a large cauliflower, wash it thoroughly clean, and separate it into pieces, in the same manner you would do for pickling. Stew them in a nice brown cullis till they are tender. Season with pepper and salt, and put them into a dish with the sauce over them. Garnish with a few sprigs of the cauliflower nicely boiled.

French Beans.

TAKE a quarter of a peck of beans, string them clean, but do not split them. Cut them across in three parts, and lay them in salt and water. After remaining thus about a quarter of an hour, dry them well in a cloth, then put them into a pan, and when you have fried them of a nice brown colour, take them out, pour all the fat from the pan, and put into it a quarter of a pint of hot water. Stir it into the pan, by degrees.

and let it boil. Then take a quarter of a pound of fresh butter rolled in a little flour, two spoonsful of catsup, one of mushroom pickle, four of white wine, an onion stuck with six cloves, two or three blades of beaten mace, a little grated nutmeg, and a little pepper and salt. Stir it altogether for a few minutes, and then put in the beans. Shake the pan till the whole is well mixed together, then take out the onion, and pour all into your dish. Garnish with what most pleases your fancy; but pickles may be preferred. This makes a very pretty side dish.

Endive.

TAKE three heads of fine white endive, wash them thoroughly clean, and then put them into salt and water for three hours. Cut off the green heads of a hundred of asparagus, chop the rest small as far as it runs tender, and throw it likewise into salt and water. Then take a bunch of celery, wash and scrape it clean, and cut it into pieces about three inches long. Put it into a saucepan with a pint of water, three or four blades of mace, and some white pepper tied in a cloth. When it has stewed till it is quite tender, put in the asparagus, shake the saucepan, and let it simmer till the grass is enough. Take the three heads of endive out of the water, drain them, and leave the largest whole. Pull the others asunder, leaf by leaf, and put them into the stew-pan, with a pint of white wine. Cover the pan close, and let it boil till the endive is just enough. Then put in a quarter of a pound of butter rolled in flour, cover the pan again, and keep shaking it. When the endive is enough, take it up, and lay the whole head in the middle; then with a spoon take out the celery and grass, and lay them round it, and the other parts of the endive over that. Pour the liquor out of the saucepan into the stew pan, stir the whole together, and season it with salt. Have ready the yolks of two eggs, beat up with a quarter of a pint of cream, and a little grated nutmeg. Mix this with the sauce, keep stirring it one way till it is thick, then pour it over the ragoo, and serve it to table

Cabbage Force Maigre.

TAKE a ine white-heart cabbage, wash it clean, and boil it about five minutes. Then drain it, cut the stalk flat to stand in a dish, carefully open the leaves, and take out the inside, leaving the outside leaves whole. Cut what you take out very fine: then take the flesh of two or three flounders or plaice, and chop it with the cabbage, the yolks and whites of four eggs boiled hard, and a handful of picked parsley. Beat all together in a mortar with a quarter of a pound of melted butter. Then mix it up with the yolk of an egg, and a few crumbs of bread. Fill the cabbage with this, and tie it together: put it into a deep stew-pan, with half a pint of water, a quarter of a pound of butter rolled in a little flour, the yolks of four eggs boiled hard, an onion stuck with six cloves, some whole pepper and mace tied in a piece of muslin, half an ounce of truffles and morels, a spoonful of catsup, and a few pickled mushrooms. Cover it close, and let it simmer an hour. When it is done, take out the onion and spice, lay the cabbage in your dish, untie it, pour over the sauce, and serve it to table.

Asparagus forced in French Rolls.

CUT a piece out of the crust of the tops of three French rolls, and take out all the crumb: but be careful that the crusts fit again in the places from whence they were taken. Fry the rolls brown in fresh butter: then take a pint of cream, the yolks of six eggs well beat fine, and a little salt and nutmeg. Stir them together over a slow fire till it begins to be thick. Have ready an hundred of small grass boiled, and save tops enough to stick the rolls with. Cut the rest of the tops small, put them into the cream, and fill the loaves with them. Before you fry the rolls, make holes thick in the top crusts to stick the grass in, which will make it look as if it was growing. This makes a very handsome side dish at a second course.

Peas François.

SHELL a quart of peas, cut a large Spanish onion

small, and two cabbage or Silesia lettuces. Put them into a stew-pan, with half a pint of water, a little salt, pepper, mace, and nutmeg, all beaten. Cover them close, and let them stew a quarter of an hour. Then put in a quarter of a pound of fresh butter rolled in a little flour, a spoonful of catsup, and a piece of butter about the size of a nutmeg. Cover them close, and let it simmer a quarter of an hour, observing frequently to shake the pan. Have ready four artichoke bottoms fried, and cut in two, and when you pour the peas with their sauce into a dish, lay them round it. If you choose to make a pleasing addition, do a cabbage in the manner directed in the article *Cabbage Force-maigre*, and put in the middle of the dish.

CHAPTER XI.

GRAVIES, CULLISES, *and other* SAUCES.

IN the preceding chapters we have, where a proper opportunity offered, directed the necessary sauces to be made for each respective article; but as there are many others which are used for different purposes, and on various occasions, we shall place them in the present chapter, beginning with

Gravies.

To make beef gravy, take a piece of the chuck, or neck, and cut it into small pieces; then strew some flour over it, mix it well with the meat, and put it into the saucepan, with as much water as will cover it, an onion, a little allspice, a little pepper, and some salt. Cover it close, and when it boils take off the scum, then throw in a hard crust of bread, or some raspings, and let it stew till the gravy is rich and good, then strain it off, and pour it into your sauce boat.

A very rich Gravy.

TAKE a piece of lean beef, a piece of veal, and a piece of mutton, and cut them into small bits: then take a large saucepan with a cover, lay your beef at the bottom, then your mutton, then a very little piece of bacon, a slice or two of carrot, some mace, cloves, whole black and white pepper, a large onion cut in slices, a bundle of sweet herbs, and then lay on your veal. Cover it close, and set it over a slow fire for six or seven minutes, and shake the saucepan often. Then dust some flour into it, and pour in boiling water till the meat is something more than covered. Cover your saucepan close, and let it stew till it is rich and good. Then season it to your taste with salt, and strain it off. This gravy will be so good as to answer most purposes.

Brown Gravy.

PUT a piece of butter, about the size of a hen's egg, into a saucepan, and when it is melted shake in a little flour, and let it be brown. Then by degrees stir in the following ingredients: half a pint of water, and the same quantity of ale or small beer that is not bitter; an onion and a piece of lemon-peel cut small, three cloves, a blade of mace, some whole pepper, a spoonful of mushroom pickle, the same quantity of catsup, and an anchovy. Let the whole boil together a quarter of an hour, then strain it, and it will be good for sauce for various dishes.

Sauce Italian.

PUT a piece of fresh butter into your stew-pan, with some mushrooms, onions, parsley, and the half of a laurel leaf, all cut fine; turn the whole over the fire some time, and shake in a little flour; moisten it with a glass of white wine, as much good broth, adding salt, pepper, and a little mace beat fine. Let it boil half an hour; then skim away the fat, and serve it up. You may give it a fine flavour while boiling, by putting in a bunch of sweet herbs, but take them out before you serve the sauce.

Sauce Piquante.

PUT a bit of butter with two sliced onions into a stew-pan, a carrot, a parsnip, a little thyme, laurel, basil, two cloves, two shalots, a clove of garlic, and some parsley; turn the whole over the fire till it be well coloured; then shake in some flour, and moisten it with some broth and a spoonful of vinegar. Let it boil over a slow fire, and skim and strain it through a sieve. Season it with salt and pepper, and serve it with any dish you wish to be heightened.

Sauce Piquante, to serve cold.

CUT some salad herbs very fine, with half a clove of garlic, and two shalots: mix the whole with mustard, sweet oil, a dash of vinegar, some salt and pepper.

A Cullis for all sorts of Ragoos and rich Sauces.

TAKE about two pounds of leg of veal, and two slices of lean ham, and put them into a stew-pan, with two or three cloves, a little nutmeg, a blade of mace, some parsley roots, two carrots cut in pieces, some shalots, and two bay-leaves. Set them over a slow fire, cover them close, and let them do gently for half an hour, taking care they do not burn: then put in some beef broth, let it stew till it is as rich as required, and then strain it off for use.

A Family Cullis.

TAKE a piece of butter rolled in flour, and stir it in your stew-pan till your flour is of a fine yellow colour; then put in some thin broth, a little gravy, a glass of white wine, a bundle of parsley, thyme, laurel and sweet-basil, two cloves, a little nutmeg or mace, a few mushrooms, and pepper and salt. Let it stew an hour over a slow fire, then skim all the fat clean off, and strain it through a lawn sieve.

A White Cullis.

CUT a piece of veal into thin bits, and put it into a stew-pan, with two or three slices of lean ham, and two onions, each cut into four pieces; then put in some broth, and season with mushrooms, parsley, green onions, and cloves. Let it stew till the virtues of all are pretty well extracted, then take out all your meat and roots with a skimmer, put in a few crumbs of bread, and let it stew softly. Take the white part of a young fowl, and pound it in a mortar till it is very fine, put this into your cullis, but do not let it boil; if it does not appear sufficiently white, you must add two dozen of blanched almonds. When it has stewed till it is of a good rich taste, strain it off.

A Cullis for Fish.

BROIL a jack or pike till it is properly done, then take off the skin, and separate the flesh from the bones. Boil six eggs hard, and take out the yolks; blanch a few almonds, beat them to a paste in a mortar, and then add the yolks of the eggs: mix these well with butter, then put in the fish, and pound all together. Then take half a dozen of onions, and cut them into slices, two parsnips, and three carrots. Set on a stew-pan, put into it a piece of butter to brown, and when it boils put in the roots; turn them till they are brown, and then pour in a little broth to moisten them. When it has boiled a few minutes, strain it into another saucepan; then put in a whole leek, some parsley, sweet-basil, half a dozen cloves, some mushrooms and truffles, and a few crumbs of bread. When it has stewed gently a quarter of an hour, put in the fish, &c. from the mortar. Let the whole stew some time longer, but be careful it does not boil. When sufficiently done, strain it through a coarse sieve. This is a very proper sauce to thicken all made dishes.

Ham Sauce.

CUT some thin slices of the lean part of a dressed ham, and beat it with a rolling-pin to a mash. Put it into a saucepan, with a tea-cup full of gravy, and set it over a slow fire: but keep stirring it to prevent its sticking at the bottom. When it has been on some time, put in a bunch of sweet herbs, half a pint of beef gravy, and some pepper. Cover it close, let it stew over a gentle fire, and when it is quite done, strain it off. This is a very good sauce for any kind of veal.

Essence of Ham.

TAKE three or four pounds of lean ham, and cut it into pieces about an inch thick. Lay them in the bottom of a stew-pan, with slices of carrots, parsnips, and three or four onions cut thin. Let them stew till they stick to the pan, but do not let it burn. Then pour on some strong veal gravy by degrees, some fresh mushrooms cut in pieces, (but if not to be had, mushroom powder,) truffles and morels, cloves, basil, parsley, a crust of bread, and a leek. Cover it down close, and when it has simmered till it is of a good thickness and flavour, strain it off. If you have preserved the gravy from a dressed ham, you may use it with the before-mentioned ingredients, instead of the ham, which will make it equally good, but not quite so high flavoured.

A Sauce for Lamb.

TAKE a bit of butter, and mix it with shred parsley, shalots, and a little crumb of bread grated very fine. Put the whole into a stew-pan with a glass of good broth and as much white wine, and let it boil some little time. Season it with pepper and salt; and when you use it squeeze a lemon into it.

Sauce for any kind of Roast Meat.

TAKE an anchovy, wash it clean, and put to it a glass of red wine, some gravy, a shalot cut small, and a little juice of a lemon. Stew these together, strain it off, and mix it with the gravy that runs from the meat.

A White Sauce.

PUT some good meat broth into a stew-pan, with a good piece of crumb of bread, a bunch of parsley, shalots, thyme, laurel, basil, a clove, a little grated nutmeg, some whole mushrooms, a glass of white wine, salt, and pepper. Let the whole boil till half is consumed, then strain it through a sieve; and when you are ready to use it, put in the yolks of three eggs, beat up with some cream, and thicken it over the fire, taking care that the eggs do not curdle. This sauce may be used with all sorts of meat or fish that is done white.

Sauce for most kinds of Fish.

TAKE some mutton or veal gravy, and put to it a little of the liquor that drains from your fish. Put it into a saucepan, with an onion, an anchovy, a spoonful of catsup, and a glass of white wine. Thicken it with a lump of butter rolled in flour, and a spoonful of cream. If you have oysters, cockles, or shrimps, put them in after you take it off the fire, but it will be exceeding good without. If you have no cream, instead of white wine you must use red.

Sauce Nonparcil.

TAKE a turnip, carrot, and some mushrooms, cut them into a dish, and put them into a stew-pan with some butter. Let them go gently on till tender, then add some good gravy, a glass of white wine, some salt, mace, and pepper, with a few girkins and a dash of vinegar. Roll a little butter in flour to thicken your sauce. This sauce is very good for braised lamb.

Sauce a-la-Menehout.

PUT a little cullis into a stew-pan, with a piece of butter rolled in flour, salt and pepper, the yolks of two eggs, three or four shalots cut small, and thicken it over the fire. This sauce should be thick, and may be used with every dish that is done a-la-Saint Menehout. It is spread over the meat or fish, which is afterwards covered with grated bread, and browned with a hot salamander.

Egg Sauce.

BOIL two eggs till they are hard: first chop the whites, then the yolks, but neither of them very fine, and put them together. Then put them into a quarter of a pound of good melted butter, and stir them well together.

Bread Sauce

CUT a large piece of crumb from a stale loaf, and

put it into a saucepan, with half a pint of water, an onion, a blade of mace, and a few pepper-corns in a bit of cloth. Boil them a few minutes, then take out the onion and spice, mash the bread very smooth, and add to it a piece of butter and a little salt.

Anchovy Sauce.

TAKE an anchovy, and put into it half a pint of gravy, with a quarter of a pound of butter rolled in a little flour, and stir all together till it boils. You may add, at your discretion, a little lemon-juice, catsup, red wine or walnut liquor.

Shrimp Sauce.

WASH half a pint of shrimps very clean, and put them into a stew-pan, with a spoonful of anchovy liquor, and half a pound of butter melted thick. Boil it up for five minutes, and squeeze in half a lemon. Toss 't up, and pour it into your sauce-boat.

Oyster Sauce.

WHEN the oysters are opened, preserve the liquor, and strain it through a fine sieve. Wash the oysters very clean, and take off the beards. Put them into a stew-pan, and pour the liquor over them. Then add a large spoonful of anchovy liquor, half a lemon, two blades of mace, and thicken it with butter rolled in flour. Put in half a pound of butter, and boil it up till the butter is melted. Then take out the mace and lemon, and squeeze the lemon-juice into the sauce. Give it a boil, stirring it all the time, and put it into your sauce-boat.

To melt Butter.

KEEP a plated or tin saucepan for the purpose only of melting butter. Put a little water at the bottom, and a dust of flour. Shake them together, and cut the butter in slices. As it melts shake it one way; .et i' boil up, and it will be smooth and thick.

Caper Sauce.

TAKE some capers, chop half of them very fine, and put the rest in whole. Chop also some parsley, with a little grated bread, and some salt; put them into butter melted very smooth, let them boil up, and then pour it into your sauce-boat

Shalot Sauce.

CHOP five or six shalots very fine, put them into a saucepan with a gill of gravy, a spoonful of vinegar, and some pepper and salt. Stew them for a minute, and then pour them into your dish or sauce-boat.

Lemon Sauce for boiled Fowls.

TAKE a lemon and pare off the rind, then cut it into slices, take the kernels out, and cut it into small square bits; blanch the liver of the fowl, and chop it fine; mix the lemon and liver together in a boat, pour on some hot melted butter, and stir it up.

Gooseberry Sauce.

PUT some coddled gooseberries, a little juice of sorrel, and a little ginger, into some melted butter.

Fennel Sauce

BOIL a bunch of fennel and parsley, chop it very small, and stir it into some melted butter.

Mint Sauce.

WASH your mint perfectly clean from grit or dirt, then chop it very fine, and put to it vinegar and sugar.

A relishing Sauce.

PUT into a small stew-pan two slices of ham, a clove of garlic, a laurel leaf, and two sliced onions; let them heat, and then add a little broth, two spoonsful of cullis, and a spoonful of tarragon vinegar. Stew them an hour over a slow fire, then strain it through a sieve, and pour it into your sauce-boat.

To crisp Parsley.

WHEN you have picked and washed your parsley quite clean, put it into a Dutch oven, or on a sheet of paper. Set at a moderate distance from the fire, and keep turning it till it is quite crisp. Lay little bits of butter on it, but not to make it greasy. This is a much better method than that of frying.

Sauce for Wild Ducks, Teal, &c.

TAKE a proper quantity of veal gravy, with some pepper and salt; squeeze in the juice of two Seville oranges, and add a little red wine; let the red wine boil some time in the gravy.

Pontiff Sauce.

PUT two or three slices of lean veal, and the same of ham, into a stew-pan, with some sliced onions, carrot, parsley, and a head of celery. When brown, add a little white wine, some good broth, a clove of garlic, four shalots, two cloves, a little coriander, and two slices of lemon-peel. Boil it over a slow fire till the juices are extracted from the meat, then skim it, and strain it through a sieve. Just before you use it, add a little cullis with some parsley chopped very fine.

Aspic Sauce.

INFUSE chervil, tarragon, burnet, garden cress, and mint, into a little cullis for about half an hour; then strain it, and add a spoonful of garlic-vinegar, with a little pepper and salt.

Forcemeat Balls.

TAKE half a pound of veal and half a pound of suet cut fine, and beat them in a marble mortar or wooden bowl, shred a few sweet herbs fine, a little mace dried, a small nutmeg grated, a little lemon-peel cut very fine, some pepper and salt, and the yolks of two eggs. Mix all these well together, then roll some of it in small round balls, and some in long pieces. Roll them in flour, and fry them of a nice brown. If they are for the use of white sauce, instead of frying, put a little water into a saucepan, and when it boils, put them in, and a few minutes will do them.

Lemon Pickle.

TAKE about a score of lemons, grate off the out rinds very thin, and cut them into quarters, but leave the bottoms whole. Rub on them equally half a pound of bay-salt, and spread them on a large pewter dish. Either put them in a cool oven, or let them dry gradually by the fire, till the juice is all dried into the peels; then put them into a well glazed pitcher, with an ounce of mace, and half an ounce of cloves beat fine, an ounce of nutmeg cut into thin slices, four ounces of garlic peeled, half a pint of mustard-seed bruised a little, and tied in a muslin bag. Pour upon them two quarts of boiling white wine vinegar, close the pitcher well up, and let it stand five or six days by the fire. Shake it well up every day, then tie it close, and let it stand three months to take off the bitter. When you bottle it, put the pickle and lemon into a hair sieve, press them well to get out the liquor, and let it stand till another day: then pour off the fine, and bottle it. Let the other stand three or four days, and it will refine itself. Pour it off and bottle it, let it stand again, and bottle it till the whole is refined. It may be put into any white sauce and will not hurt the colour. It is very good for fish sauce and made dishes. One tea-spoonful is enough for white, and two for brown sauce for a fowl. It is a most useful pickle, and gives a pleasant flavour. Always put it in before you thicken the sauce, or put any cream in, lest the sharpness should make it curdle.

CHAPTER XII.

MADE DISHES.

SECT. I.

BUTCHER'S MEAT.

Bombarded Veal.

TAKE a fillet of veal, and having clean cut out the bone, make a forcemeat thus: take the crumb of a penny loaf, half a pound of fat bacon scraped, an anchovy, two or three sprigs of sweet marjcrum, a little lemon-peel, thyme, and parsley. Chop these well together, and season them to your taste with salt, chyan pepper, and a little grated nutmeg. Mix up all together w.th an egg and a little cream; and with this forcemeat fill up the place from whence the bone was taken. Then make cuts all round the fillet at about an inch distance from each other. Fill one nich with forcemeat, a second with spinach that has been well boiled and squeezed, and a third with crumbs of bread, chopped oysters, and beef marrow, and thus fill up the holes round the fillet; wrap the caul close round it, and put it into a deep pot, with a pint of water. Make a coarse paste to lay over it, in order to prevent the over giving it a disagreeable taste. When it is taken out of the oven, skim off the fat, and put the gravy into a stew-pan, with a spoonful of mushroom catsup, another of lemon-pickle, five boiled artichoke bottoms cut into quarters, two spoonsful of browning, and half an ounce of morels and truffles. Thicken it with butter rolled in flour, give it a gentle boil, put your veal into the dish, and pour your sauce over it.

Fricandeau of Veal.

Take the thick part of the leg of veal, shape it nicely oval, lard it well, and put it into boiling water. Let it boil up once, then take it out, and put into your stew-pan some slices of veal, roots, sweet herbs, with salt, pepper, and mace. Put in half a pint of gravy, then put in your fricandeau, covering it with some pepper and butter. Let it go gently on for three hours, then take it out and glaze it. You may serve it with sorrel sauce, which is almost always used, or glazed onions, or endive sauce. If the larded fricandeau lies a few hours in water, it will be a great deal the whiter.

Veal Olives.

Cut some large collops off a fillet of veal, and hack them well with the back of a knife. Spread very thinly forcemeat over each, then roll them up, and either toast or bake them. Make a ragoo of oysters or sweet-breads cut in square bits, a few mushrooms and morels, and lay them in the dish with rolls of veal. Put nice brown gravy into the dish, and send them up hot, with forcemeat balls round them. Garnish with lemon.

Grenadines of Veal.

THESE are done the same as the fricandeau, excepting that the veal is cut into slices. Three pieces make a dish; and they are served with the same sauces.

Veal Cutlets en Papilotes.

CUT them thin, and put them in square pieces of white paper, with salt, pepper, parsley, shalots, mushrooms, all shred fine, with butter; twist the paper round the cutlets; letting the end remain uncovered; rub the outside of the paper with butter; lay the cutlets upon the gridiron over a slow fire, with a sheet of buttered paper under them. Serve them in the papers.

Porcupine of a Breast of Veal.

TAKE a fine large breast of veal, bone it, and rub it over with the yolks of two eggs. Spread it on a table, and lay over it a little bacon cut as thin as possible, a handful of parsley shred fine, the yolks of five hard boiled eggs chopped small, a little lemon-peel cut fine, the crumb of a penny loaf steeped in cream, and season to your taste with salt, pepper, and nutmeg. Roll the breast of veal close, and skewer it up. Then cut some fat bacon, the lean of ham that has been a little boiled, and pickled cucumbers, about two inches long. Lard the veal with this in rows, first ham, then bacon, and then cucumbers, till you have larded every part of it. Put it into a deep earthen pot, with a pint of water, cover it close, and set it in a slow oven for two hours. When it comes from the oven, skim off the fat, and strain the gravy through a sieve into a stew-pan. Put into it a glass of white wine, a little lemon-pickle and caper liquor, and a spoonful of mushroom catsup. Thicken it with a little butter rolled in flour, lay your porcupine on the dish, and pour your sauce over it. Have ready a roll of forcemeat made thus: take the crumb of a penny loaf, half a pound of beef suet shred fine, the yolks of four eggs, and a few chopped oysters. Mix these well together, and season it to your taste with chyan pepper, salt, and nutmeg. Spread it on a veal caul, and having rolled it up close like a collared eel, bind it in a cloth, and boil it an hour. This done, cut it into four slices, lay one at each end and the others on the sides. Have ready your sweet-bread cut in slices and fried, and lay them round it with a few mushrooms. This makes a grand bottom dish at that time of the year when game is not to be had.

Fricandeau of Veal a-la-Bourgeois.

Cut some lean veal into thin slices, lard them with streaked bacon, and season them with pepper, salt, beaten mace, cloves, nutmeg, and chopped parsley. Put in the bottom of your stew-pan some slices of fat bacon, lay the veal upon them, cover the pan, and set it over the fire for eight or ten minutes, just to be hot and no more. Then with a brisk fire, brown your veal on both sides, and shake some flour over it. Pour in a quart of good broth or gravy, cover it close, and let it stew gently till it is enough. Then take out the slices of bacon, skim all the fat off clean, and beat up the yolks of three eggs, with some of the gravy. Mix all together, and keep it stirring one way till it is smooth and thick. Then take it up, lay your meat in the dish, pour the sauce over it, and garnish with lemon.

Calf's Head Surprise.

When you have properly cleansed it for dressing, scrape a pound of fat bacon very fine, take the crumbs of two penny loaves, a small nutmeg grated, and season it to your taste with salt, chyan pepper, and a little lemon-peel. Beat up the yolks of six eggs, and mix all together into a rich forcemeat. Put a little of it into the ears, and the rest into the head. Then put it into a deep pot, just wide enough to admit it, and put to it two quarts of water, half a pint of white wine, a blade or two of mace, a bundle of sweet herbs, an anchovy, two spoonsful of walnut and mushroom catsup, the same quantity of lemon-pickle, and a little salt and chyan pepper. Lay a coarse paste over it to keep in the steam, and put it for two hours and a half into a very quick oven. When you take it out, lay your head in a soup-dish, skim off the fat from the gravy, and strain it through a hair sieve into a stew pan. Thicken it with a lump of butter rolled in flour, and when it has boiled a few minutes, put in the yolks of six eggs well beaten, and mixed with half a pint of cream. Have ready boiled a few forcemeat balls, and half an ounce of truffles and morels, but do not stew them in the gravy. Pour the gravy over the head, and garnish with truffles and morels, forcemeat balls, barberries, and mushrooms. This makes an elegant top dish, and is not very expensive.

A Calf's Pluck.

ROAST the heart stuffed with suet, sweet herbs, and a little parsley, all chopped small, a few crumbs of bread, some pepper, salt, nutmeg, and a little lemon-peel, all mixed up with the yolk of an egg. Boil the lights with part of the liver, and when they are enough chop them very small, and put them into a saucepan with a piece of butter rolled in flour, some pepper and salt, and a little juice of lemon. Fry the other part of the liver with some thin slices of bacon. Lay the mince at the bottom of the dish, the heart in the middle, and the fried liver and bacon round, with some crisped parsley. Serve them up with plain melted butter in a sauce-boat.

Loin of Veal en Epigram.

ROAST a loin of veal properly for eating, then take it up, and carefully cut off the skin from the back part without breaking it. Cut out the lean part, but leave the ends whole, to contain the following mince-meat: mince all the veal very fine with the kidney part, put it into a little gravy, enough to moisten it with the gravy that comes from the loin Put in a little pepper and salt, some lemon-peel shred fine, the yolks of three eggs, and a spoonful of catsup. Thicken it with a little butter rolled in flour. Give it a shake or two over the fire, put it into the loin, and pull the skin gently over it. If the skin should not quite cover it, give the part wanting a brown with a hot iron, or put it into an oven for about a quarter of an hour. Send it up hot, and garnish with lemon and barberries.

Pillow of Veal.

HALF roast a neck or breast of veal, then cut it into six pieces, and season it with pepper, salt, and nutmeg. Take a pound of rice, and put it to a quart of broth, some mace, and a little salt. Stew it over a stove on a very slow fire till it is thick; but butter the bottom of the pan you do it in. Beat up the yolks of six eggs, and stir them into it. Then take a little round deep dish, butter it, and lay some of the rice at the bottom. Then lay the veal in a round heap, and cover it over all with rice. Rub it over with the yolks of eggs, and bake it an hour and a half. Then open the top, and pour in a pint of good rich gravy. Send it hot to table, and garnish with a Seville orange cut in quarters.

Shoulder of Veal a-la-Piedmontoise.

CUT the skin of a shoulder of veal, so that it may hang at one end: then lard the meat with bacon or ham, and season it with pepper, salt, mace, sweet herbs, parsley, and lemon-peel. Cover it again with the skin, stew it with gravy, and when it is tender take it up. Then take sorrel, some lettuce chopped small, and stew them in some butter with parsley, onions, and mushrooms. When the herbs are tender, put to them some of the liquor, some sweet-breads and bits of ham. Let all stew together a short time: then lift up the skin, lay the stewed herbs over and under, cover it again with the skin, moisten it with melted butter, strew over it crumbs of bread, and send it to the oven to brown. Serve it up hot with some good gravy in the dish.

Sweetbreads of Veal a-la-Dauphine.

TAKE three of the largest sweetbreads you can get, and open them in such a manner that you can stuff in forcemeat. Make your forcemeat with a large fowl: skin it, and pick off all the flesh. Then take half a pound of fat and lean bacon, cut it very fine, and beat them in a mortar. Season it with an anchovy, some nutmeg, a little lemon-peel, a very little thyme, and some parsley. Mix these up with the yolks of two eggs, fill your sweetbreads with it, and fasten them together with fine wooden skewers. Put layers of bacon at the bottom of a stew-pan, and season them with pepper, salt, mace, cloves, sweet herbs, and a large onion sliced. Lay upon these thin slices of veal, and then your sweet breads. Cover it close, let it stand eight or ten minutes over a slow fire, and then pour in a quart of boiling water or broth, and let it stew gently for two hours. Then take out the sweetbreads, keep them hot, strain the gravy, skim all the fat off, and boil it up till it is reduced to about half a pint. Then put in the sweetbreads, and let them stew two or three minutes in the gravy. Lay them in a dish, and pour the gravy over them. Garnish with lemon.

Sweetbreads en Gordineere.

PARBOIL three sweetbreads: then take a stew-pan, and put into it layers of bacon, or ham and veal; over which lay the sweetbreads, with the upper sides downwards. Put in a layer of veal and bacon over them, a pint of veal broth, and three or four blades of mace. Stew them gently three quarters of an hour; then take out the sweetbreads, strain the gravy through a sieve, and skim off the fat. Make an amulet of yolks of eggs, in the following manner: beat up four yolks of eggs, put two on a plate, and set them over a stew-pan of boiling water, with another plate over it, and it will be soon done. Put a little spinach juice into the other half, and serve it the same. Cut it out in sprigs of what form you please, put it over the sweetbreads in the dish, and keep them as hot as you can. Thicken the gravy with butter rolled in flour and two yolks of eggs beat up in a gill of cream. Put it over the fire, and keep stirring it one way till it is thick and smooth. Pour it over the sweetbreads, and send it to table. Garnish with lemon and beet-root.

Sweetbreads a-la-daub.

TAKE three of the largest and finest sweetbreads you can get, and put them for five minutes into a saucepan of boiling water. Then take them out, and when they are cold, lard them with small pieces of bacon. Put them into a stew-pan with some good veal gravy, a little lemon-juice, and a spoonful of browning. Stew them gently a quarter of an hour, and a little before they are ready thicken with flour and butter. Dish them up, and pour the gravy over them. Lay round them bunches of boiled celery, or oyster patties; and garnish with barberries or parsley.

Scotch Collops.

CUT your collops off the thick part of a leg of veal, about the size and thickness of a crown piece, and put a piece of butter browned into your frying-pan, then lay in your collops, and fry them over a quick fire. Shake and turn them, and keep them on a fine froth. When they are of a nice light brown take them out, put them into a pot, and set them before the fire to keep warm. Then put cold butter again into your pan, and fry the collops as before. When they are done, and properly brown, your the liquor from them into a stew-pan, and add to it half a pint of gravy, half a lem n, an anchovy, half an ounce of morels, a large spoonful of browning, the same of catsup, two spoons-full of lemon-pickle, and season it to your taste with salt and chyan pepper. Thicken it with butter and flour, let it boil five or six minutes, and then put in your collops, and shake them over the fire, but be careful not to let them boil. When they have simmered a little, take them out, and lay them in the dish. Then strain your gravy, and pour it hot on them. Lay on them forcemeat balls, and little slices of bacon curled roun' a skewer and boiled. Throw a few mushrooms over them, and garnish with barberries and lemon.

Beef Collops.

Take a large rump stake, or any piece of beef that is tender, and cut it into pieces in the form of Scotch collops, but larger. Hack them a little with a knife, then flour them, and having melted a little butter in your stew-pan, put in your collops, and fry them quick for about two minutes. Then put in a pint of gravy, a bit of butter rolled in flour, and season it with pepper and salt. Cut four pickled cucumbers into thin slices, a few capers, half a walnut, and a little onion shred fine. Put these into the pan, and having stewed the whole together about five minutes, put them all hot into your dish, and send them to table. Garnish with lemon.

Beef a-la-daub.

Take a rump of beef, and cut out the bone, or a part of the leg of mutton piece, or what is usually called the mouse-buttock, and cut some fat bacon into slices as long as the beef is thick, and about a quarter of an inch square. Take four blades of mace, double that number of cloves, a little allspice, and half a nutmeg grated fine. Chop a good handful of parsley, and some sweet-herbs of all sorts very fine, and season with salt and pepper. Roll the bacon in these, and then take a large larding-pin, and with it thrust the bacon through the beef. Having done this, put it into a stew-pan, with a quantity of brown gravy sufficient to cover it. Chop three blades of garlic very fine, and put in some fresh mushrooms, two large onions, and a carrot. Stew it gently for six hours, then take it out, strain off the gravy, and skim off all the fat. Put your meat and gravy into the pan again, and add to it a gill of white wine; and if you find it not sufficiently seasoned, add a little more pepper and salt. Stew it gently for half an hour more, and then add some artichoke bottoms, morels and truffles, some oysters, and a spoonful of vinegar. Then put the meat into a soup dish, and pour the sauce over it.

Beef Tremblent.

Take a brisket of beef, and tie up the fat end quite tight. Put it into a pot of water, and let it boil gently for six hours. Season the water with a little salt, a handful of allspice, two onions, two turnips, and a carrot. In the mean time, put a piece of butter into a stew-pan, and melt it, then put in two spoonsful of flour, and stir it till it is smooth. Put in a quart of gravy, a spoonful of catsup, the same of browning, a gill of white wine, and some turnips and carrots cut into small pieces. Stew them gently till the roots are tender, and season with pepper and salt. Skim the fat clean off, put the beef in the dish, and pour the sauce over it. Garnish with any kind of pickles.

Beef Kidneys a-la-Bourgeoise.

Cut them in thin slices, and set them over the fire, with a bit of butter, salt, pepper, parsley, onions, and a small clove of garlic; the whole shred small: when done, take them off the fire, but do not let them lie long, as they will become tough. Add a few drops of vinegar and a little cullis. Beef kidneys may also be served a-la-braise, with sauce piquante.

Beef a-la-mode.

The most proper parts for this purpose are a small buttock, a leg of mutton piece, a clod or part of a large buttock. Being furnished with your meat, take two dozen of cloves, as much mace, and half an ounce of allspice beat fine, chop a large handful of parsley, and all sorts of sweet herbs fine; cut some fat bacon as long as the beef is thick, and about a quarter of an inch square, and put it into the spice, &c. and into the beef the same. Then put the beef into a pot, and cover it with water. Chop four large onions very fine, and six cloves of garlic, six bay leaves, and a handful of champignons, or fresh mushrooms, put all into the pot, with a pint of porter or ale, and half a pint of red wine; put in some pepper and salt, some chyan pepper, a spoonful of vinegar, strew three handfuls of bread raspings, sifted fine, all over: cover the pot close, and stew it for six hours, or according to the size of the piece; if a large piece, eight hours. Then take the beef out, put it into a deep dish, and keep it hot over some boiling water; strain the gravy through a sieve, and pick out the champignons or mushrooms; skim all the fat off clean, put it into your pot again, and give it a boil up; if not seasoned enough, season it to your liking: then put the gravy into your beef, and send it hot to table. If you like it best cold, cut it in slices with the gravy over it, which will be a strong jelly.

Beef a-la-Royal.

Take all the bones out of a brisket of beef, and make holes in it about an inch from each other. Fill one hole with fat bacon, a second with chopped parsley, and a third with chopped oysters. Season these stuffings with pepper, salt, and nutmeg. When the beef is completely stuffed, put it into a pan, pour upon it a pint of wine boiling hot, dredge it well with flour, and send it to the oven. Let it remain there three hours, and when it is taken out, skim off all the fat, put the meat into your dish, and strain the gravy over it. Garnish with pickles.

Beef Olives.

Cut some steaks from a rump of beef about half an inch thick, as square as you can, and about ten inches long; then cut a piece of fat bacon as wide as the beef, and about three parts as long Put part of the yolk of an egg on the bacon. Lay some good savory force meat, on that some of the yolk of an egg on the force-meat, and then roll them up, and tie them round with a string in two places. Strew on some crumbs of bread, and over them some of the yolk of an egg. Then fry them brown in a large pan, with some beef dripping, and when they are done take them out, and lay them to drain. Melt some butter in a stew-pan, put in a spoonful of flour, and stir it well till it is smooth.—Then put in a pint of good gravy, with a gill of white wine, and then the olives, and let them stew an hour. Add some mushrooms, truffles, and morels, forcemeat balls, sweet-breads cut in small pieces, and some ox-palates. Squeeze in the juice of half a lemon, and season it with pepper and salt. Shake them up, and having carefully skimmed off the fat, lay your olives in the dish, and pour the gravy over them. Garnish with lemon and beet root.

Bouille Beef.

Put the thick end of a brisket of beef into a kettle and cover it with water. Let it boil fast for two hours, then stew it close by the fire side for six hours more, and fill up the kettle as the water decreases. Put in with the beef some turnips cut in little balls, some carrots, and some celery. About an hour before the meat is done, take out as much broth as will fill your soup dish, and boil in it for an hour, turnips and carrots cut in little round or square pieces, with some celery, and season it to your taste with salt and pepper. Serve it up in two dishes, the beef in one dish, and the soup in another. You may put pieces of fried bread in your soup, and boil in a few knots of greens; and when you would have your soup very rich add a pound or two of mutton chops to your broth when you take it from the beef, and let them stew in it for half an hour; but remember to take out the mutton before you serve the soup up.

Sirloin of Beef en Epigram.

Roast a sirloin of beef, and when it is done, take

it off the spit, carefully raise the skin, and draw it off. Then cut out the lean part of the beef, but observe not to touch either the ends or sides. Hash the meat in the following manner: cut it into pieces about the size of a crown piece, put half a pint of gravy into a stew-pan, an onion chopped fine, two spoonsful of catsup, some pepper and salt, six small pickled cucumbers cut in thin slices, and the gravy that comes from the beef, with a little butter rolled in flour. Put in the meat, and shake it up for five minutes. Then put it on the sirloins, draw the skin carefully over, and send it to table. Garnish with lemon and pickles.

The Inside of a Sirloin of Beef forced.

Lift up the fat of the inside, cut out the meat quite close to the bone, and chop it small. Take a pound of suet, and chop that small; then put to them some crumbs of bread, a little lemon-peel, thyme, pepper and salt, half a nutmeg grated, and two shalots chopped fine. Mix all together with a glass of red wine, and then put the meat into the place you took it from: cover it with the skin and fat, skewer it down with fine skewers, and cover it with paper. The paper must not be taken off till the meat is put on the dish, and your meat must be spitted before you take out the inside. Just before the meat is done, take a quarter of a pint of red wine, and two shalots shred small: boil them, and pour it into the dish, with the gravy that comes from the meat. Send it hot to table, and garnish with lemon.

The inside of a *rump of beef forced* must be done nearly in the same manner, only lift up the outside skin, take the middle of the meat, and proceed as before directed. Put it into the same place, and skewer it down close.

A Round of Beef forced.

Rub your meat first with common salt, then a little bay-salt, some salt petre, and coarse sugar. Let it lay a full week in this pickle, turning it every day. On the day it is to be dressed, wash and dry it, lard it a little, and make holes, which fill with bread crumbs, marrow, or suet, parsley, grated lemon-peel, sweet herbs, pepper, salt, nutmeg, and the yolk of an egg, made into stuffing. Bake it with a little water and some small beer, whole pepper, and an onion. When it comes from the oven, skim the fat clean off, put the meat into your dish, and pour the liquor over it. Instead of baking, you may boil it, but it must be done gradually over a slow fire. When cold, it makes a handsome side-board dish for a large company.

Beef Steaks rolled.

Take some beef steaks, and beat them with a cleaver till they are tender; make some forcemeat with a pound of veal beat fine in a mortar; the flesh of a fowl, half a pound of cold ham, or gammon of bacon, fat and lean; the kidney fat of a loin of veal, and a sweetbread, all cut very fine: some truffles and morels stewed, and then cut small two shalots, some parsley, and a little thyme, some lemon-peel, the yolks of four eggs, a nutmeg grated, and half a pint of cream. Mix all these together, and stir them over a slow fire for ten minutes. Put them upon the steaks, and roll them up; then skewer them tight, put them into the frying-pan, and fry them of a nice brown. Then take them from the fat, and put them into a stew-pan, with a pint of good drawn gravy, a spoonful of red wine, two of catsup, a few pickled mushrooms, and let them stew for a quarter of an hour. Take up the steaks, cut them into two, and lay the cut side uppermost. Garnish with lemon.

Beef Rump en Matelotte.

Take your beef rump and cut it in pieces; parboil them, and then boil them in some broth without any seasoning; when about half done, stir in a little butter with a spoonful of flour over the fire till brown, and moisten it with the broth of your rumps: then put your rumps in with a dozen of large parboiled onions, a glass of white wine, a bunch of parsley, a laurel leaf, with a bunch of sweet herbs, and pepper and salt. Let them stew till the rump and onions are done; then skim it well, and put an anchovy cut small and some capers cut into the sauce. Put the rump in the middle of the dish with the onions round it. A beef rump will take four hours doing.

Beef Escarlot.

THE proper piece of beef for this purpose is the brisket, which you must manage as follows: take half a pound of coarse sugar, two ounces of bay salt, and a pound of common salt. Mix these well together, rub the beef with it, put it into an earthen pan, and turn it every day. It may lie in this pickle a fortnight, then boil it, and serve it up with savoys; but it eats much better when cold, and cut into slices.

Tongue and Udder forced.

FIRST parboil them, then blanch the tongue, and stick it with cloves: then fill the udder with forcemeat made with veal. First wash the inside with the yolk of an egg, then put in the forcemeat, tie the ends close, and spit them, roast them, and baste them with butter. When they are done, put good gravy into the dish, sweet sauce into a cup, and serve them up.

Tripe a-la-Kilkenny.

TAKE a piece of double tripe, and cut it into square pieces: peel and wash ten large onions, cut each into two, and put them on to boil in water till they are tender. Then put in your tripe, and boil it ten minutes. Pour off almost all the liquor, shake a little flour into it, and put in some butter, with a little salt and mustard. Shake all over the fire till the butter is melted, then put it into your dish, and send it to table as hot as possible. Garnish with lemon or barberries. This dish is greatly admired in Ireland.

Harrico of Mutton.

CUT the best end of a neck of mutton into chops, in single ribs, flatten them, and fry them of a light brown

Then put them into a large saucepan, with two quarts of water, and a large carrot cut in slices; and when they have stewed a quarter of an hour, put in two turnips cut in square pieces, the white part of a head of celery, two cabbage lettuces fried, a few heads of asparagus, and season all with a little chyan pepper. Boil all together till tender, and put it into a tureen or soup-dish, without any thickening to the gravy.

Shoulder of Mutton surprised.

HALF boil a shoulder of mutton, and then put it into a stew-pan with two quarts of veal gravy, four ounces of rice, a little beaten mace, and a tea spoonful of mushroom powder. Stew it an hour, or till the rice is enough, and then take up your mutton and keep it hot. Put to the rice half a pint of cream, and a piece of butter rolled in flour; then shake it well, and boil it a few minutes. Lay your mutton on the dish, and pour your gravy over it. Garnish with pickles or barberries.

To dress the Umbles of Deer.

TAKE the kidney of a deer, with the fat of the heart: season them with a little pepper, salt, and nutmeg. First fry, and then stew them in some good gravy till they are tender. Squeeze in a little lemon; take the skirts, and stuff them with the forcemeat made with the fat of the venison, some fat of bacon, grated bread, pepper, mace, sage, and onion chopped very small. Mix it with the yolk of an egg. When the skirts are stuffed with this, tie them to the spit to roast; but first strew over them some thyme and lemon-peel. When they are done, lay the skirts in the middle of the dish, and then fricasee round it.

Mutton Kebobbed.

CUT a loin of mutton into four pieces, then take off the skin, rub them with the yolk of an egg, and strew over them a few crumbs of bread and a little parsley, shred fine. Spit and roast them, and keep basting them all the time with fresh butter in order to make the froth rise. When they are properly done, put a little brown gravy under them, and send them to table. Garnish with pickles.

Leg of Mutton a-la-haut Gout.

TAKE a fine leg of mutton that has hung a fortnight, (if the weather will permit,) and stuff every part of it with some cloves of garlic, rub it with pepper and salt, and then roast it. When it is properly done, send it up with some good gravy and red wine in the dish.

Leg of Mutton roasted with Oysters.

TAKE a fine leg of mutton that has hung two or three days, stuff every part of it with oysters, roast it, and when done, pour some good gravy into the dish, and garnish with horse-radish. If you prefer cockles you must proceed in the same manner.

Shoulder of Mutton en Epigram.

ROAST a shoulder of mutton till it is nearly enough, then carefully take off the skin about the thickness of a crown-piece, and also the shank-bone at the end. Season both the skin and shank-bone with pepper, salt, a little lemon-peel cut small, and a few sweet herbs and crumbs of bread: lay this on the gridiron till it is of a fine brown; and, in the meantime, take the rest of the meat, and cut it like a hash in pieces, about the bigness of a shilling. Save the gravy, and put to it, with a few spoonsful of strong gravy, a little nutmeg, half an onion cut fine, a small bundle of herbs, a little pepper and salt, some girkins cut very small, a few mushrooms, two or three truffles cut small, two spoonsful of wine, and a little flour dredged into it. Let all these stew together very slowly for five or six minutes, but be careful it does not boil. Take out the sweet herbs, lay the hash in the dish, and the broiled upon it. Garnish with pickles.

Sheep's Rumps and Kidneys.

BOIL six sheep's rumps in veal gravy: then lard your kidneys with bacon, and set them before the fire in a tin oven; as soon as the rumps become tender, rub them over with the yolk of an egg, a little grated nutmeg, and some chyan pepper. Skim the fat from the gravy, and put the gravy in a stew-pan, with three ounces of boiled rice, a spoonful of good cream, and a little catsup and mushroom powder. Thicken it with flour and butter, and give it a gentle boil. Fry your rumps till they are of a light brown; and when you dish them up, lay them round on the rice, so that the ends may meet in the middle; lay a kidney between every rump, and garnish with barberries and red cabbage. This makes a pretty side or corner dish.

Mutton Rumps a-la-Braise.

Boil six mutton rumps for fifteen minutes in water, then take them out, and cut them into two, and put them into a stew-pan, with half a pint of good gravy, a gill of white wine, an onion stuck with cloves, and a little salt and chyan pepper. Cover them close, and stew them till they are tender. Take them and the onion out, and thicken the gravy with a little butter rolled in flour, a spoonful of browning, and the juice of half a lemon. Boil it up till it is smooth, but not too thick. Then put in your rumps, give them a shake or two, and dish them up hot. Garnish with horse-radish and beet-root. For variety, you may leave the rumps whole, and lard six kidneys on one side, and do them the same as the rumps, only not boil them, and put the rumps in the middle of the dish, and kidneys round them, with the sauce over all.

Mutton Chops in Disguise.

Rub the chops over with pepper, salt, nutmeg, and a little parsley. Roll each in half a sheet of white paper, well buttered within-side, and close the two ends. Boil some hog's lard, or beef dripping, in a stew-pan, and put the steaks into it. Fry them of a fine brown, then take them out, and let the fat thoroughly drain from them. Lay them in your dish, and serve them up with good gravy in a sauce-boat. Garnish with horse-radish and fried parsley.

A Shoulder of Mutton called Hen and Chickens.

HALF roast a shoulder, then take it up, and cut off the blade at the first joint, and both the flaps, to make the blade round; score the blade round in diamonds, throw a little pepper and salt over it, and set it in a tin oven to broil. Cut the flaps and meat off the shank in thin slices, and put the gravy that came out of the mutton into a stew-pan, with a little good gravy, two spoonsful of walnut catsup, one of browning, a little chyan pepper, and one or two shalots. When your meat is tender, thicken it with flour and butter, put it into the dish with the gravy, and lay the blade on the top. Garnish with green pickles.

A Quarter of Lamb forced.

TAKE a large leg of lamb, cut a long slit on the back side, and take out the meat; but be careful you do not deface the other side. Then chop the meat small with marrow, half a pound of beef suet, some oysters, an anchovy washed, an onion, some sweet herbs, a little lemon-peel, and some beaten mace and nutmeg. Beat all these together in a mortar, stuff up the leg in the shape it was before, sew it up, and rub it all over with the yolks of eggs beaten; spit it flour it all over, lay it to the fire, and baste it with butter. An hour will roast it. In the meantime, cut the loin into steaks, season them with pepper, salt and nutmeg, lemon-peel cut fine, and a few herbs Fry them in fresh butter of a fine brown, then pour out all the butter, put in a quarter of a pint of white wine, shake it about, and then add half a pint of strong gravy, wherein good spice has been boiled, a quarter of a pint of oysters and the liquor, some mushrooms, and a spoonful of the pickle, a piece of butter rolled in flour, and the yolk of an egg beat fine; stir all these together till thick, then lay your leg of lamb in the dish, and the loin round it. Pour the sauce over them and garnish with lemon.

Lamb's Bits.

SKIN the stones, and split them; then lay them on

a dry cloth with the sweetbreads and the liver, and dredge them well with flour. Fry them in lard or butter till they are of a light brown, and then lay them in a sieve to drain. Fry a good quantity of parsley, lay your bits on the dish, the parsley in lumps over them, and pour round them melted butter.

Lamb a-la-Bechamel.

La Bechamel is nothing more than to reduce any thing to the consistence of cream, till it is thick enough to make a sauce. When it begins to thicken, put in the meat cut in slices, warm it without boiling, season it to your taste, and serve it up. All slices a-la-bechamel are done in the same manner.

Lamb Chops en Casarole.

Having cut a loin of lamb into chops, put yolks of eggs on both sides, and strew bread crumbs over them, with a few cloves and mace, pepper and salt mixed; fry them of a nice light brown, and put them round in a dish, as close as you can; leave a hole in the middle to put the following sauce in: all sorts of sweet herbs and parsley chopped fine, and stewed a little in some good thick gravy. Garnish with fried parsley.

Barbacued Pig.

Prepare a pig, about ten weeks old, as for roasting. Make a forcemeat of two anchovies, six sage leaves, and the liver of the pig, all chopped very small; then put them into a mortar with the crumb of half a penny loaf, four ounces of butter, half a tea-spoonful of chyan pepper, and half a pint of red wine. Beat them all together to a paste, put it into the pig's belly, and sew it up. Lay your pig down at a good distance before a large brisk fire, singe it well, put into your dripping-pan three bottles of red wine, and baste it well with this all the time it is roasting. When it is half done, put under the pig two penny loaves, and if you find your wine too much reduced, add more. When your pig is near enough, take the loaves and sauce out of your dripping-pan, and put to the sauce one anchovy chopped small, a bundle of sweet herbs, and half a lemon. Boil it a few minutes, then draw your pig, put a small lemon or apple in the pig's mouth, and a leaf on each side. Strain your sauce, and pour it on boiling hot. Send it up whole to table, and garnish with barberries and sliced lemon.

A Pig au Pere Duillet.

CUT off the head, and divide the body into quarters, lard them with bacon, and season them well with salt, pepper, nutmeg, cloves, and mace. Put a layer of fat bacon at the bottom of a kettle, lay the head in the middle, and the quarters round it. Then put in a bay-leaf, an onion shred, a lemon, with some carrots, parsley, and the liver, and cover it again with bacon. Put in a quart of broth, stew it for an hour, and then take it up. Put your pig into a stew-pan, pour in a bottle of white wine, cover it close, and let it stew very gently an hour. In the meantime, while it is stewing in the wine, take the first gravy it was stewed in, skim off the fat, and strain it. Then take a sweetbread cut into five or six slices, some truffles, morels, and mushrooms, and stew all together till they are enough. Thicken it with the yolks of two eggs, or a piece of butter rolled in flour; and when your pig is enough, take it out, and lay it in your dish. Put the wine it was stewed in to the sauce, then pour it all over the pig, and garnish with lemon. If it is to be served up cold, let it stand till it is so, then drain it well, and wipe it, that it may look white, and lay it in a dish, with the head in the middle, and the quarters round it. Throw some green parsley over all. Either of the quarters separately make a pretty dish.

A Pig Matelote.

HAVING taken out the entrails, and scalded your pig, cut off the head and pettitoes; then cut the body into four quarters, and put them, with the head and toes, into cold water. Cover the bottom of a stew-pan with slices of bacon, and place the quarters over them, with the pettitoes, and the head cut in two. Season the whole with pepper and salt, a bay-leaf, a little thyme, an onion, and add a bottle of white wine. Then lay on more slices of bacon, put over it a quart of water, and let it boil Skin and gut two large eels, and cut them in pieces about five or six inches long. When your pig is half done, put in your eels; then boil a dozen of large craw-fish, cut off the claws, and take off the shells of the tails. When your pig and eels are enough, lay your pig in the dish, and your pettitoes round it; but do not put in the head, as that will make a pretty cold dish. Then lay your eels and craw-fish over them, and take the liquor they were stewed in, skim off the fat, and add to it half a pint of strong gravy, thickened with a little piece of burnt butter. Pour this over it, and garnish with lemon and craw-fish. Fry the brains, and lay them round, and all over the dish. At grand entertainments this will do for a first course or remove.

Sheep's Trotters en Gratten

Boil them in water, and then put them into a stew-pan with a glass of white wine, half a pint of broth, as much cullis, a bunch of sweet herbs, with salt, whole pepper, and mace. Stew them by a slow fire till the sauce is reduced, then take out the herbs, and serve them upon a gratten. Sheep's trotters may be served with a ragoo of cucumbers.

SECT. II.

MADE DISHES of POULTRY. &c.

Turkey a-la-daub.

Bone your turkey, but let it be so carefully done, as not to spoil the look of it, and then stuff it with the following forcemeat: chop some oysters very fine, and mix them with some crumbs of bread, pepper, salt, shalots, and very little thyme, parsley, and butter. Having filled your turkey with this, sew it up, tie it in a cloth, and boil it white, but be careful not to boil it too much. Serve it up with good oyster sauce. Or you may make a rich gravy of the bones, with a piece of veal, mutton, and bacon: season with salt, pepper, shalots, and a little mace. Strain it off through a sieve; and having before half-boiled your turkey, stew it in this gravy just half an hour. Having well skimmed the gravy, dish up your turkey in it, after you have thickened it with a few mushrooms stewed white, or stewed palates, forcemeat balls, sweetbreads, or fried oysters, and pieces of lemon. Dish it with the breast upwards. You may add a few morels and truffles to your sauce.

Turkey in a hurry.

TRUSS a turkey with the legs inward, and flatten it as much as you can: then put it into a stew-pan, with melted lard, chopped parsley, shalots, mushrooms, and a little garlic; give it a few turns on the fire, and add the juice of half a lemon to keep it white. Then put it into another stew-pan, with slices of veal, one slice of ham, and melted lard, and every thing as used before; adding whole pepper and salt: cover it over with slices of lard, and set it about half an hour over a slow fire. then add a glass of white wine and a little broth, and finish the brazing: skim and sift the sauce, add a little cullis to make it rich, reduce it to a good consistence, put the turkey into your dish, and pour the sauce over it. Garnish with lemon.

Fowls a-la-Braise.

TRUSS your fowl as for boiling, with the legs in the body: then lay over it a layer of fat bacon cut in thin slices, wrap it round in beet-leaves, then in a caul of veal, and put it into a large saucepan with three pints of water, a glass of Madeira wine, a bunch of sweet herbs, two or three blades of mace, and half a lemon: stew it till it is quite tender, then take it up and skim off the fat; make your gravy pretty thick with flour and butter, strain it through a hair sieve, and put to it a pint of oysters and a tea-cupful of thick cream; keep shaking your pan over the fire, and when it has simmered a short ti ne, serve up your fowl with the bacon, beet-leaves, a..d caul on, and pour your sauce hot upon it. Garnish with barberries and red beet-root.

Fowls forced.

TAKE a l. rge fowl, pick it clean, draw it, cut it down the b ck, and take the skin off the whole; cut the flesh rom the bones, and chop it with half a pint of oyste s, one ounce of beef marrow, and a little pepper and salt. Mix it up with cream: then lay the meat on the bones, draw the skin over it, and sew up the back. Cut large thin slices of bacon, lay them on the breast of your fowl, and tie them on with pack-thread in diamonds. It will take an hour roasting by a moderate fire. Make a good brown gravy sauce, pour it into your dish, take the bacon off, lay n your fowl, and serve it up. Garnish with pickles, mushrooms, or oysters. It is proper for a side-dish at dinner, or top-dish for supper.

Fowls marinaded.

RAISE the skin from the breast-bone of a large fowl with your finger: then take a veal sweetbread and cut it small, a few oysters, a few mushrooms, an anchovy, some pepper, a little nutmeg, some lemon-peel, and a little thyme; chop all together small, and mix it with the yolk of an egg, stuff it in between the skin and the flesh, but take great care you do not break the skin: and then put what oysters you please in the body of the fowl. Paper the breast, and roast it. Make good gravy, and garnish with lemon. You may add a few mushrooms to the sauce.

Chickens chiringrate.

FLATTEN the breast-bones of your chickens with a rolling-pin, but be careful you do not break the skin. Strew some flour over them, then fry them in butter of a fine light brown, and drain all the fat out of the pan, but leave the chickens in. Lay a pound of gravy beef, with the same quantity of veal cut into thin slices, over your chickens, together with a little mace, two or three cloves, some whole pepper, an onion, a small bunch of sweet herbs, and a piece of carrot. Then pour in a quart of boiling water, cover it close, and let it stew a quarter of an hour. Then take out the chickens, and keep them hot: let the gravy boil till it is quite rich and good; then strain it off, and put it into your pan again, with two spoonsful of red wine and a few mushrooms. Put in your chickens to heat, then take them up, lay them in your dish, and pour your sauce over them. Garnish with lemon, and a few slices of cold ham broiled.

Chickens a-la-braise

TAKE a couple of fine chickens, lard them, and season them with pepper, salt, and mace; then put a layer of veal in the bottom of a deep stew-pan, with a slice or two of bacon, an onion cut in pieces, a piece of carrot, and a layer of beef: then put in the chickens with the breast downwards, and a bundle of sweet herbs; after that a layer of beef, and put in a quart of broth or water, cover it close, and let it stew very gently for an hour. In the meantime get ready a ragoo made thus: take two veal sweetbreads, cut them small, and put them into a saucepan, with a very little broth or water, a few cock's-combs, truffles, and morels cut small, with an ox-palate. Stew them all together, and when your chickens are done, take them up, and keep them hot; then strain the liquor they were stewed in, skim off the fat, and pour it into your ragoo; add a glass of red wine, a spoonful of catsup, and a few mushrooms: then boil all together with a few artichoke bottoms cut in four, and asparagus tops. If your sauce is not thick enough, put in a piece of butter rolled in flour: and when properly done, lay your chickens in the dish, and pour the ragoo over them. Garnish with lemon.

Chickens in savoury Jelly.

TAKE two chickens, and roast them. Boil some calf's feet to a strong jelly; then take out the feet, and skim off the fat; beat up the whites of three eggs, and mix them with half a pint of white vinegar, and the juice of three lemons, a blade or two of mace, a few peppercorns, and a little salt. Put them to your jelly; and when it has boiled five or six minutes, strain it several times through a jelly-bag till it is very clear. Then put a little in the bottom of a bowl large enough to hold your chickens, and when they are cold and the jelly set, lay them in with their breasts down. Then fill your bowl quite full with the rest of your jelly, which you must take care to keep from setting, so that when you pour it into your bowl it will not break. Let it stand all night; and the next day put your basin into warm water, pretty near the top. As soon as you find it loose in the basin, lay your dish over it, and turn it whole.

Chickens and Tongues.

BOIL six small chickens very white; then take six hogs' tongues boiled and peeled, a cauliflower boiled whole in milk and water, and a good deal of spinach boiled green. Then lay your cauliflower in the middle, the chickens close all round, and the tongues round them with the roots outwards, and the spinach in little heaps between the tongues. Garnish with small pieces of bacon toasted, and lay a piece on each of the tongues. This is a good dish for a large company.

Pullets a-la-Sainte Menehout.

HAVING trussed the legs in the body, slit them down the back, spread them open on a table, take out the thigh bones, and beat them with a rolling pin.—Season them with pepper, salt, mace, nutmeg, and sweet herbs. Then take a pound and a half of veal, cut it into thin slices, and lay it in a stew-pan. Cover it close, and set it over a slow fire, and when it begins to stick to the pan, stir in a little flour, shake it about till it is a little brown, and then pour in as much broth as will stew the fowls. Stir them together, and put in a little whole pepper, an onion, and a slice of bacon or ham. Then lay in your fowls, cover them close, and when they have stewed half an hour, take them out, lay them on the gridiron to brown on the inside, and then lay them before the fire to do on the outside. Strew over them the yolk of an egg, and some crumbs of bread, and baste them with a little butter. Let them be of a fine brown, and boil the gravy till there is about enough for sauce; then strain it, and put into it a few mushrooms, with a small piece of butter rolled in flour. Lay the pullets in the dish, pour the sauce over them, and garnish with lemon.

Ducks a-la-Braise.

Having dressed and singed your ducks, lard them quite through with bacon rolled in shred parsley, thyme, onions, beaten mace, cloves, pepper, and salt. Put in the bottom of a stew-pan a few slices of fat bacon, the same of ham or gammon of bacon, two or three slices of veal or beef: lay your ducks in with the breasts down, and cover them with slices, the same as put under them; cut a carrot or two, a turnip, one onion, a head of celery, a blade of mace, four or five cloves, and a little whole pepper. Cover them close down, and let them simmer a little over a gentle fire till the breasts are a light brown; then put in some broth or water, cover them as close down again as you can: stew them gently two or three hours till enough. Then take some parsley, an onion or shalot, two anchovies, and a few girkins or capers; chop them all very fine, put them into a stew-pan with part of the liquor from the ducks, a little browning, and the juice of half a lemon; boil it up, and cut the ends of the bacon even with the breasts of your ducks, lay them in your dish, pour the sauce hot upon them, and serve them up.

Ducks a-la-mode.

Take a coup e of fine ducks, cut them into quarters,

and fry them in butter till they are of a light brown. Then pour out all the fat, dust a little flour over them, and put in half a pint of good gravy, a quarter of a pint of red wine, an anchovy, two shalots, and a bundle of sweet herbs: cover them close, and let them stew a quarter of an hour. Take out the herbs, skim off the fat, and thicken your sauce with a bit of butter rolled in flour. Put your ducks into the dish, strain your sauce over them, and send them to table. Garnish with lemon or barberries.

Ducks a-la-Françoise.

Put two dozen of roasted chesnuts peeled into a pint of rich gravy, with a few leaves of thyme, two small onions, a little whole pepper, and a bit of ginger. Take a fine tame duck, lard it, and half roast it, then put it into the gravy, let it stew ten minutes, and add a quarter of a pint of red wine. When the duck is enough take it out, boil up the gravy to a proper thickness, skim it very clean from the fat, lay the duck in the dish, and pour the sauce over. Garnish with lemon.

A Goose a-la-mode.

Pick a large fine goose clean, skin and bone* it nicely, and take off the fat. Then take a dried tongue, and boil and peel it. Take a fowl, and treat it in the same manner as the goose; season it with pepper, salt, and beaten mace, and roll it round the tongue. Season the goose in the same manner, and put both tongue and fowl into the goose. Put it into a little pot that will just hold it, with two quarts of beef gravy, a bundle of sweet herbs, and an onion. Put some slices of ham, or good bacon, between the fowl and goose; then cover it close, and stew it over a fire for an hour very slowly. Then take up your goose,

---

* It may not be amiss to inform the cook, that the best method of boning a goose, or fowls of any sort, is to begin at the breast, and to take out the bones without cutting the back; for without this method, when it is sewed up, and you come to stew it, it generally bursts in the back, whereby the shape of it is spoiled.

and skim off all the fat, strain it, and put in a glass of red wine, two spoonsful of catsup, a veal sweetbread cut small, some truffles, mushrooms, and morels, a piece of butter rolled in flour, and, if wanted, some pep per and salt. Put the goose in again, cover it close, and let it stew half an hour longer. Then take it up, pour the ragoo over it, and garnish with lemon. You must remember to save the bones of the goose and fowl, and put them into the gravy when it is first set on. It will be an improvement if you roll some beef marrow between the tongue and the fowl, and between the fowl and the goose, as it will make them mellow, and eat the finer

A Goose marinaded.

Bone your goose, and stuff it with forcemeat made thus : take ten or twelve sage leaves, two large onions, and two or three large sharp apples ; chop them very fine, and mix them with the crumb of a penny loaf, four ounces of beef marrow, one glass of red wine, half a nutmeg grated, pepper, salt, and a little lemon-peel shred small, and the yolks of four eggs. When you have stuffed your goose with this, sew it up, fry it of a light brown, and then put it into a deep stew-pan, with two quarts of good gravy. Cover it close, and let it stew two hours ; then take it out, put it into a dish, and keep it warm. Skim the fat clean off from the gravy, and put into it a large spoonful of lemon-pickle, one of browning, and one of red wine, an anchovy shred fine, a little beaten mace, with pepper and salt to your palate. Thicken it with flour and butter, dish up your goose, strain the gravy over it, and send it to table.

Pigeons Compote.

Truss six young pigeons in the same manner as for boiling, and make a forcemeat for them thus :— Grate the crumb of a penny loaf, and scrape a quarter of a pound of fat bacon, which will answer the purpose better than suet. Chop a little parsley and thyme, two shalots, or an onion, some lemon-peel, and a little nutmeg grated; season them with pepper and salt, and mix them up with eggs. Put this forcemeat into the craws of the pigeons, lard them down the breast, and fry them brown. Then put them into a stew-pan, with some good brown gravy, and when they have stewed three quarters of an hour, thicken it with a piece of butter rolled in flour. When you serve them up, strain your gravy over them, and lay forcemeat balls round them.

French Pupton of Pigeons.

Put savory forcemeat, rolled out like paste, into a butter-dish. Then put a layer of very thin slices of bacon, squab pigeons, sliced sweetbread, asparagus tops, mushrooms, cock's-combs, a palate boiled tender, and cut into pieces, and the yolks of four eggs boiled hard. Make another forcemeat, and lay it over the whole like a pie-crust. Then bake it, and when it is enough, turn it into a dish, and pour in some good rich gravy.

Pigeons a-la-Braise.

Pick, draw, and truss some large pigeons, then take a stew-pan, and lay at the bottom some slices of bacon, veal, and onions; season the pigeons with pepper, salt, some spice beat fine, and sweet herbs. Put them into the stew-pan, and lay upon them some more slices of veal and bacon; let them stew very gently over a stove, and cover them down very close. When they are stewed, make a ragoo with veal sweetbreads, truffles, morels, champignons; the sweetbreads must be blanched and put into a stew-pan with a ladle full of gravy, a little cullis, the truffles, morels, &c. Let them all stew together with the pigeons. When they are enough, put them into a dish, and pour the ragoo over them.

Pigeons au Poise.

Cut off the feet of your pigeons, and stuff them with forcemeat in the shape of a pear; roll them in the yolk of an egg, and then in crumbs of bread. Put them into a dish well buttered, but do not let them touch each other, and send them to the oven. When they are enough, lay them in a dish, and pour in good gravy thickened with the yolk of an egg, or butter rolled in flour; but do not pour your gravy over the pigeons. Garnish with lemon.—This is a very genteel dish, and may be improved by the following variation; lay one pigeon in the middle, the rest round, and stewed spinach between, with poached eggs on the spinach. Garnish with notched lemon and orange cut in quarters, and have melted butter in boats.

Fricandeau of Pigeons.

After having larded all the upper part of your pigeons with bacon, stew them in the same manner as the fricandeau a-la-Bourgeoise, page 131.

Pigeons a-la-daub.

Put a layer of bacon into a large saucepan, then a layer of veal, a layer of coarse beef, and another little layer of veal, about a pound of beef, and a pound of veal, cut very thin, a piece of carrot, a bundle of sweet herbs, an onion, some black and white pepper, a blade or two of mace, and four or five cloves. Cover the saucepan close, set it over a slow fire, and draw it till it is brown, to make the gravy of a fine light brown. Then put a quart of boiling water, and let it stew till the gravy is quite rich and good. Strain it off, and skim off all the fat. In the meantime, stuff the bellies of the pigeons with forcemeat made thus: take a pound of veal, and a pound of beef suet, and beat both fine in a mortar; an equal quantity of crumbs of bread, some pepper, salt, nutmeg, beaten mace, a little lemon-peel cut small, some parsley cut small, and a very little thyme stripped. Mix all together with the yolks of two eggs, fill the pigeons with this, and flat the breasts down. Flour them, and fry them in fresh butter a little brown Then pour the fat clean out of the pan, and put the gravy to the pigeons. Cover them close, and let them stew a quarter of an hour, or till they are quite enough. Then take them up, lay them in a dish, and pour in your sauce. On each pigeon lay a bay-leaf, and on each leaf a slice of bacon. Garnish with a lemon notched.

Pigeons a-la-Soussel.

BONE four pigeons, and make a forcemeat as for pigeons compote. Stuff them, and put them into a stew-pan with a pint of veal gravy. Stew them half an hour very gently, and then take them out. In the meantime make a veal forcemeat, and wrap it all round them. Rub it over with the yolk of an egg, and fry them of a nice brown in good dripping. Take the gravy they were stewed in, skim off the fat, thicken with a little butter rolled in flour, the yolk of an egg, and a gill of cream beat up. Season it with pepper and salt, mix it altogether, and keep it stirring one way till it is smooth. Strain it into your dish, and put the pigeons on. Garnish with plenty of fried parsley.

Pigeons in a Hole.

PICK, draw, and wash four young pigeons, stick their legs in their bellies as you do boiled pigeons, and season them with pepper, salt, and beaten mace. Put into the belly of each pigeon a lump of butter the size of a walnut. Lay your pigeons in a pie-dish, pour over them a batter made of three eggs, two spoonsful of flour, and half a pint of good milk. Bake them in a moderate oven, and serve them to table in the same dish.

Jugged Pigeons.

PLUCK and draw six pigeons, wash them clean, and dry them with a cloth; season them with beaten mace, white pepper, and salt. Put them into a jug with half a pound of butter upon them. Stop up the jug close with a cloth, that no steam can get out, then set in a kettle of boiling water, and let it boil an hour and a half. Then take out your pigeons, put the gravy that is come from them into a pan, and add to it a spoonful of wine, one of catsup, a slice of lemon, half an anchovy chopped, and a bundle of sweet herbs. Boil it a little, and then thicken it with a piece of butter rolled in flour; lay your pigeons in the dish, and strain your gravy over them. Garnish with parsley and red cabbage.—This makes a very pretty side or corner dish.

Partridges a-la-Braise.

TAKE two brace of partridges, and truss the legs into the bodies; lard them, and season with beaten mace, pepper, and salt. Take a stew-pan, lay slices of bacon at the bottom, then slices of beef, and then slices of veal, all cut thin, a piece of carrot, an onion cut small, a bundle of sweet herbs, and some whole pepper. Put in the partridges with the breasts downwards, lay some thin slices of beef and veal over them, and some parsley shred fine. Cover them, and let them stew eight or ten minutes over a slow fire; then give your pan a shake, and pour in a pint of boiling water. Cover it close, and let it stew half an hour over a little quicker fire; then take out your birds, keep them hot, pour into the pan a pint of thin gravy, let them boil till there is about half a pint, then strain it off, and skim off all the fat. In the meantime have a veal sweetbread cut small, truffles and morels, cock's-combs, and fowls' livers stewed in a pint of good gravy half an hour, some artichoke-bottoms and asparagus tops, both blanched in warm water, and a few mushrooms. Then add the other gravy to this, and put in your partridges to heat. If it is not thick enough, put in a piece of butter rolled in flour. When thoroughly hot, put in your partridges into the dish, pour the sauce over them, and serve them to table.

Pheasants a-la-Braise.

COVER the bottom of your stew-pan with a layer of beef, a layer of veal, a little piece of bacon, a piece of carrot, an onion stuck with cloves, a blade or two of mace, a spoonful of pepper, black and white, and a bundle of sweet herbs. Having done this, put in your pheasant, and cover it with a layer of beef and a layer of veal Set it on the fire for five or six minutes, and then pour in two quarts of boiling gravy. Cover it close, and let it stew very gently an hour and a half. Then take up your pheasant, and keep it hot; let the gravy boil till it is reduced to about a pint, then strain it off, and put it in again. Put in a veal sweetbread that has been stewed with the pheasant, some truffles and morels, livers of fowls, artichoke-bottoms, and (if you have them) asparagus tops. Let these simmer in the gravy about five or six minutes, and then add two spoonsful of catsup, two of red wine, a spoonful of browning, and a little piece of butter rolled in flour. Shake all together, then put in your pheasant, with a few mushrooms, and let them stew about five or six minutes more. Then take up your pheasant, pour the ragoo over it, and lay forcemeat-balls round. Garnish with lemon.

Snipes, or Woodcocks, in surtout.

TAKE some forcemeat made of veal, as much beef-suet chopped and beat in a mortar, with an equal quantity of crumbs of bread; mix in a little beaten mace, pepper and salt, some parsley, a few sweet herbs, and the yolk of an egg. Lay some of this meat round the dish, and then put in the snipes, being first drawn and half roasted. Take care of the trail, chop it, and scatter it all over the dish. Take some good gravy, according to the bigness of your surtout, some truffles and morels, a few mushrooms, a sweetbread cut into pieces, and artichoke-bottoms cut small. Let all stew together, shake them, and take the yolks of two or three eggs, beat them up with a spoonful or two of white wine, and stir all together one way. When it is thick, take it off, let it cool, and pour it into the surtout. Put in the yolks of a few hard eggs here and there, season with beaten mace, pepper, and salt, to your taste; cover with the forcemeat all over, then rub on the yolks of eggs to colour it, and send it to the oven. Half an hour will do it sufficiently.

Snipes, with Purslain Leaves.

DRAW your snipes, and make a forcemeat for the

inside, but preserve your ropes for your sauce; spit them across upon a lark-spit, covered with bacon and paper, and roast them gently. For sauce you must take some prime thick leaves of purslain, blanch them well in water, put them into a ladle of cullis and gravy, a bit of shalot, pepper, salt, nutmeg, and parsley, and stew all together for half an hour gently. Have the ropes ready blanched and put in. Dish up your snipes upon thin slices of bread fried., squeeze the juice of an orange into your sauce, and serve them up.

Larks a-la-Françoise.

Truss your larks with the legs across, and put a sage-leaf over the breasts. Put them on a long thin skewer, and between every lark put a thin bit of bacon. Then tie the skewer to a spit, and roast them before a clear brisk fire; baste them with butter, and strew over them some crumbs of bread mixed with flour. Fry some crumbs of bread of a fine brown in butter. Lay the larks round the dish, and the bread-crumbs in the middle.

Florendine Hares.

Let your hare be a full-grown one, and let it hang up four or five days before you case it. Leave on the ears, but take out all the bones except those of the head, which must be left entire. Lay your hare on the table, and put into it the following forcemeat: take the crumb of a two-penny loaf, the liver shred fine, half a pound of fat bacon scraped, a glass of red wine, an anchovy, two eggs, a little winter savory, some sweet-marjorum, thyme, and a little pepper, salt, and nutmeg. Having put this into the belly, roll it up to the head, and fasten it with packthread, as you would a collar of veal. Wrap it in a cloth, and boil it an hour and a half in a saucepan, covered with two quarts of water. As soon as the liquor is reduced to about a quart, put in a pint of red wine, a spoonful of lemon-pickle, one of catsup, and the same of browning. Then stew it till it is reduced to a pint, and thicken it with butter rolled in flour. Lay round your hare a few morels, and four slices of forcemeat boiled in a caul of a leg of veal. When you dish it up, draw the jaw-bones, and stick them in the sockets of the eyes. Let the ears lie back on the roll, and stick a sprig of myrtle in the mouth. Strain your sauce over it, and garnish with barberries and parsley.

Florendine Rabbits.

SKIN three young rabbits, but leave on the ears, and wash and dry them with a cloth. Take out the bones as carefully as you can, but leave the head whole, and proceed in the same manner as before directed for the hare. Have ready a white sauce made of veal gravy, a little anchovy, and the juice of half a lemon, or a tea-spoonful of lemon-pickle. Strain it, and then put in a quarter of a pound of butter rolled in flour, so as to make the sauce pretty thick. Beat up the yolk of an egg, put to it some thick cream, nutmeg, and salt, and mix it with the gravy. Let it simmer a little over the fire, but not boil, then pour it over your rabbits, and serve them up. Garnish with lemon and barberries.

Jugged Hare.

CUT your hare into small pieces, and lard them here and there with little slips of bacon, season them with pepper and salt, and put them in an earthen jug, with a blade or two of mace, an onion stuck with cloves, and a bunch of sweet herbs. Cover the jug close, that nothing may get in; set it in a pot of boiling water, and three hours will do it. Then turn it into the dish, take out the onion and sweet herbs, and send it hot to table.

Rabbits surprised.

TAKE two young rabbits, skewer them, and put the same kind of pudding in them as for roasted rabbits. When they are roasted, take off the meat clean from the bones; but leave the bones whole. Chop the meat very fine, with a little shred parsley, some lemon-peel, an ounce of beef marrow, a spoonful of cream, and a little salt. Beat up the yolks of two eggs boiled hard, and a small piece of butter, in a marble mortar: then mix all together, and put it into a stew-pan. Having stewed it five minutes, lay it on the rabbits, where you took the meat off, and put it close down with your hand, to make them appear like whole rabbits. Then with a salamander brown them all over. Pour a good brown gravy, made as thick as cream, into the dish, and stick a bunch of myrtle in their mouths. Send them up to table, with their livers boiled and frothed.

Rabbits en Casserole.

CUT your rabbits into quarters, and then lard them or not, just as you please. Shake some flour over them, and fry them in lard or butter. Then put them into an earthen pipkin, with a quart of good broth, a glass of white wine, a little pepper and salt, a bunch of sweet herbs, and a small piece of butter rolled in flour. Cover them close, and let them stew half an hour; then dish them up, and pour the sauce over them. Garnish with Seville oranges cut into thin slices and notched.

Macaroni.

BROIL four ounces of macaroni till it is quite tender, then lay it on a sieve to drain, and put it into a stew-pan, with about a gill of cream, and a piece of butter rolled in flour. Boil it five minutes, pour it on a plate. Lay Parmasan cheese roasted all over it, and send it up in a water-plate.

Amulets.

TAKE six eggs, beat them up as fine as you can, strain them through a hair sieve, and put them into a frying-pan, in which must be a quarter of a pound of hot butter. Throw in a little ham scraped fine, with shred parsley, and season them with pepper, salt, and nutmeg. Fry it brown on the under side, and lay it on your dish, but do not turn it. Hold a hot salaman der over it for half a minute, te take off the raw look of the eggs. Stick curled parsley in it, and serve it up.

Amulets of Asparagus.

BEAT up six eggs with cream, boil some of the largest and finest asparagus, and, when boiled, cut off all the green in small pieces. Mix them with the eggs, and put in some pepper and salt. Make a slice of butter hot in the pan, put them in, and serve them up on buttered toast.

Oyster Loaves.

MAKE a hole in the top of some little round loaves, and take out all the crumb. Put some oysters into a stew-pan, with the oyster liquor, and the crumbs that were taken out of the loaves, and a large piece of butter: stew them together five or six minutes, then put in a spoonful of good cream, then fill your loaves. Lay a bit of crust carefully on the top of each, and put them in the oven to crisp.

Mushroom Loaves.

TAKE some small buttons, and wash them as for pickling. Boil them a few minutes in a little water, and put to them two large spoonsful of cream, with a bit of butter rolled in flour, and a little salt and pepper. Boil these up, then fill your loaves, and do them in the same manner as directed in the preceding article.

Eggs in Surtout.

BOIL half a pound of bacon cut into thin slices, and fry some bits of bread in butter: put three spoonsful of cullis into your dish, garnish the rim with fried bread, break some eggs in the middle, cover them with the rashers of bacon, and do them over a slow fire.

Eggs and Broccoli.

BOIL your broccoli tender, observing to save a large bunch for the middle, and six or eight little thick sprigs to stick round. Toast a bit of bread as large as you would have it for your dish or butter plate. Butter some eggs, thus: take six eggs or as many as you have occasion for, beat them well, put them into a saucepan, with a good piece of butter and a little salt; keep beating them with a spoon till they are thick enough, and then pour them on the toast. Set the largest bunch of broccoli in the middle, and the other little pieces round and about. Garnish the dish with little sprigs of broccoli. This is a pretty side dish or corner plate.

Spinach and Eggs.

PICK and wash your spinach very clean in several waters, then put it into a saucepan with a little salt; cover it close, and shake the pan often. When it is just tender, and whilst it is green, throw it into a sieve to drain, and then lay it in your dish. Have ready a stew-pan of water boiling, and break as many eggs into cups as you would poach. When the water boils put in the eggs, have an egg slice ready to take them out with, lay them on the spinach, and serve them up with melted butter in a cup. Garnish with orange cut into quarters.

To make Ramekins.

PUT a bit of Parmasan cheese into a stew-pan, bruising it with a quarter of a pound of fresh butter, a gill of water, very little salt, and an anchovy cut small; boil the whole well together, and put in as much flour as the sauce will suck up; keep it over the fire till it forms a thick paste, then put it into a stew-pan with the yolks of a dozen eggs, and beat up the whites quite stiff till they will bear an egg, then mix the whites with the rest. Drop them into square paper cases. If well made, the ramekins will be of a light and of a fine colour.

CHAPTER XIII.

VEGETABLES and ROOTS.

IN dressing these articles, the greatest attention must be paid to cleanliness. They are, particularly at some times of the year, subject to dust, dirt, and insects, so that if they are not properly cleansed, they will be unsatisfactory to those for whom they are provided, and disreputable to the cook. To avoid this, be careful first to pick off all the outside leaves, then wash them well in several waters, and let them lie some time in a pan of clean water before you dress them. Be sure your saucepan is thoroughly clean, and boil them by themselves in plenty of water. They should always be brought crisp to table, which will be effected by being careful not to boil them too much. Such are the general observations necessary to be attended to in dressing of Vegetables and Roots. We shall now proceed to particulars, beginning with

Asparagus.

Scrape all the stalks very carefully till they look white, then cut them all even alike, and throw them into a pan of clean water, and have ready a stew-pan with water boiling. Put some salt in, and when they are a little tender take them up. If you boil them too much, they will lose both their colour and taste. Cut the round off a small loaf, about half an inch thick, and toast it brown on both sides: then dip it into the liquor the asparagus was boiled in, and lay it in your dish. Pour a little melted butter over your toast, then lay your asparagus on the toast all round your dish, with the heads inwards, and send it to table, with melted butter in a basin. Some pour melted butter over them, but this is injudicious, as it makes the handling them very disagreeable.

Artichokes.

Twist off the stalks, then put them into cold water, and wash them well. When the water boils, put them in with the tops downwards, that all the dust and sand may boil out. About an hour and a half, or two hours, will do them. Serve them up with melted butter in cups.

Broccoli.

Carefully strip off all the little branches till you

come to the top one, and then with a knife peel off the hard outside skin that is on the stalks and little branches, and throw them into water. Have ready a stew-pan of water, throw in a little salt, and when it boils, put in your broccoli. When the stalks are tender, it is enough. Put in a piece of toasted bread, soaked in the water the broccoli was boiled in at the bottom of your dish, and put your broccoli on the top of it, as you do asparagus. Send them up to table laid in bunches, with butter in a boat.

Cauliflowers.

TAKE off the green part, then cut the flower into four parts, and lay them in water for an hour. Then have some milk and water boiling, put in the cauliflowers, and be sure to skim the saucepan well. When the stalks feel tender, take up the flowers carefully, and put them in a callender to drain. Then put a spoonful of water into a clean stew-pan, with a little dust of flour, about a quarter of a pound of butter, a little pepper and salt, and shake it round till the butter is melted, and the whole well mixed together. Then take half the cauliflower, and cut it as you would for pickling. Lay it into the stew-pan, turn it, and shake the pan round for about ten minutes, which will be sufficient time to do it properly. Lay the stewed in the middle of your plate, the boiled round it, and pour over it the butter in which the one-half was stewed. This is a delicate mode of dressing cauliflowers; but the usual way is as follows: cut the stalks off, leave a little green on, and boil them in spring water and salt for about fifteen minutes. Then take them out, drain them, and send them whole to table, with melted butter in a sauce-boat.

Green Peas.

LET your peas be shelled as short a time as you can before they are dressed, as otherwise they will lose a great part of their sweetness. Put them into boiling water, with a little salt and a lump of loaf sugar, and when they begin to dent in the middle, they are enough. Put them into a sieve, drain the water clear from them, and pour them into your dish. Put in them a good lump of butter, and stir them about with a spoon till it is thoroughly melted. Mix with them likewise a little pepper and salt. Boil a small bunch of mint by itself, chop it fine, and lay it in lumps round the edge of your dish. Melted butter is sometimes preferred to mixing it with the peas.

Windsor Beans.

THESE must be boiled in plenty of water, with a good quantity of salt in it, and when they feel tender, are enough. Boil and chop some parsley, put it into good melted butter, and serve them up with boiled bacon, and the butter and parsley, in a boat. Remember never to boil them with bacon, as that will greatly discolour them.

Kidney Beans.

FIRST carefully string them, then slit them down the middle, and cut them across. Put them into salt and water, and when the water boils in your saucepan, put them in with a little salt. They will be soon done, which may be known by their feeling tender. Drain the water clear from them, lay them in a plate, and send them up with butter in a sauce-boat.

Spinach.

BE careful to pick it exceeding clean, then wash it in five or six waters, put it into a saucepan that will just hold it, without water, throw a little salt over it, and cover it close. Put your saucepan on a clear quick fire, and when you find the spinach shrunk and fallen to the bottom, and the liquor that comes out boils up, it is done. Then put it into a clean sieve to drain, and just give it a gentle squeeze. Lay it on a plate, and send it to table, with melted butter in a boat.

Cabbages.

AFTER you have taken off the outer leaves, and well washed them, quarter them, and boil them in plenty of water, with a handful of salt. When they are tender, drain them on a sieve, but do not press them. Savoys and greens must be boiled in the same manner, but always by themselves, by which means they will eat crisp, and be of a good colour.

Turnips.

THESE may be boiled in the same pot with your meat, and, indeed, will eat best if so done. When they are enough, take them out, put them into a pan, mash them with butter, and a little salt, and in that state send them to table.

Another method of boiling turnips is thus: When you have pared them, cut them into little square pieces, then put them into a saucepan, and just cover them with water. As soon as they are enough, take them off the fire, and put them into a sieve to drain. Then put them into a saucepan, with a good piece of butter, stir them over the fire a few minutes, put them into your dish, and serve them up.

Carrots.

SCRAPE your carrots very clean, put them into the pot, and when they are enough, take them out and rub them in a clean cloth. Then slice them into a plate, and pour some melted butter over them. If they are young, half an hour will sufficiently boil them.

Parsnips.

THESE must be boiled in plenty of water, and when they are soft, which you may know by running a fork into them, take them up. Scrape them all fine with a knife, throw away all the sticky part, and send them to table, with melted butter in a sauce-boat.

Potatoes.

THESE must be boiled in so small a quantity of water as will be just sufficient to keep the saucepan from burning. Keep them close covered, and as soon as the skins begin to crack, they are enough. Having drained out all the water, let them remain in the saucepan covered for two or three minutes; then peel them, lay them in a plate, and pour some melted butter over them. Or when you have peeled them, you may do thus: lay them on the gridiron till they are of a fine brown, and then send them to table.

Potatoes scolloped.

HAVING boiled your potatoes, beat them fine in a bowl, with some cream, a large piece of butter, and a little salt. Put them into scollop-shells, make them smooth on the top, score them with a knife, and lay thin slices of butter on the tops of them. Then put them into a Dutch oven to brown before the fire.—This makes a pretty dish for a light supper.

Hops.

THEY are to be boiled in water, with a little salt, and eat as a salad, with salt, pepper, oil, and vinegar.

CHAPTER XIV.

PUDDINGS.

IN this degree of cookery some previous and general observations are necessary, the most material of which are, first, that your cloth be thoroughly clean, and before you put your pudding into it, dip it into boiling water, strew some flour over it, and then give it a shake. If it is a bread pudding, tie it loose; but if a batter pudding, close; and never put your pudding in till the water boils. All bread and custard puddings that are baked require time and a moderate oven; but batter and rice puddings a quick oven. Before you put your pudding into the dish for baking be careful always to moisten the bottom and sides with butter.

SECT. I.

BOILED PUDDINGS.

Bread Pudding.

TAKE the crumb of a penny loaf, cut it into very

thin slices, put it into a quart of milk, and set it over a a chafing-dish of coals till the bread has soaked up al the milk. Then put in a piece of butter, stir it round, and let it stand till it is cold; or you may boil your milk, and pour it over the bread, and cover it up close, which will equally answer the same purpose. Then take the yolks of six eggs, the whites of three, and beat them up with a little rose-water and nutmeg, and a little salt and sugar. Mix all well together, and put it into your cloth, tie it loose to give it room to swell, and boil it an hour. When done, put it into your dish, pour melted butter over, and serve it tc table.

Another, but more expensive, way of making a bread-pudding is this: cut thin all the crumb of a stale penny loaf, and put it into a quart of cream, set it over a slow fire, till it is scalding hot, and then let it stand till it is cold. Beat up the bread and the cream well together, and grate in some nutmeg. Take twelve bitter almonds, boil them in two spoonsful of water, pour the water to the cream, stir it in with a little salt, and sweeten it to your taste. Blanch the almonds in a mortar, with two spoonsful of rose or orange-flower water, till they are a fine paste; then mix them by degrees with the cream. Take the yolks of eight eggs, and the whites of four, beat them up well, put them into the cream likewise, and mix the whole well together. Dip your cloth into warm water, and flour it well, before you put in the pudding; tie it loose, and let it boil an hour. Take care the water boils when you put it in, and that it keeps so all the time. When it is enough, turn it into your dish. Melt some butter, and put in it two or three spoonsful of white wine or sack; give it a boil, and pour it over your pudding. Then strew a good deal of fine sugar over your pudding and dish, and send it hot to table. Instead of a cloth, you may boil it in a bowl or basin, which is indeed the better way of the two. In this case, when it is enough, take it up in the basin, and let it stand a minute or two to cool; then untie the string, wrap the cloth round the basin, lay your dish over it, and turn the pudding out; then take off the basin and cloth with great care, otherwise a light pudding will be subject to break in turning out.

Batter Pudding.

TAKE a quart of milk, beat up the yolks of six eggs, and the whites of three, and mix them with a quarter of a pint of milk. Then take six spoonsful of flour, a tea-spoonful of salt, and one of ginger. Put to these the remainder of the milk, mix all well together, put it into your cloth, and boil it an hour and a quarter. Pour melted butter over it when you serve it up.

A batter pudding may be made without eggs, in which case proceed thus: take a quart of milk, mix six spoonsful of flour with a little of the milk first, a tea-spoonful of salt, two of beaten ginger, and two of the tincture of saffron. Then mix all together, and boil it an hour.

Custard Pudding.

PUT a piece of cinnamon into a pint of thick cream, boil it, and add a quarter of a pound of sugar. When cold, put in the yolks of five eggs well beaten: stir this over the fire till it is pretty thick, but be careful it does not boil. When quite cold, butter a cloth well, dust it with flour, tie the custard in it very close, and boil it three quarters of an hour. When you take it up put it into a basin to cool a little; untie the cloth, lay the dish on the basin, and turn it carefully out. Grate over it a little sugar, and serve it up with melted butter and a little wine in a boat.

Quaking Pudding.

TAKE a quart of cream, boil it, and let it stand till almost cold; then beat up four eggs very fine, with a spoonful and a half of flour: mix them well with your cream: add sugar and nutmeg to your palate. Tie it close up in a cloth well buttered. Let it boil an hour, and then turn it carefully out Pour over it melted butter.

Sago Pudding.

BOIL two ounces of sago in a pint of milk till tender. When cold, add five eggs, two Naples biscuits, a little brandy, and sugar to the taste. Boil it in a basin, and serve it up with melted butter, and a little wine and sugar.

Marrow Pudding.

GRATE a small loaf into crumbs, and pour on them a pint of boiling hot cream. Cut a pound of beef marrow very thin, beat up four eggs well, and then add a glass of brandy, with sugar and nutmeg to your taste. Mix them all well together, and boil it three quarters of an hour. Cut two ounces of citron into very thin bits, and when you dish up your pudding, stick them all over it.

Biscuit Pudding.

POUR a pint of boiling milk or cream over six penny Naples biscuits grated, and cover it close. When cold, add the yolks of four eggs, the whites of two, some nutmeg, a little brandy, half a spoonful of flour, and some sugar. Boil it an hour in a china basin, and serve it up with melted butter, wine, and sugar.

Almond Pudding.

TAKE a pound of sweet almonds, and beat them as fine as possible, with three spoonsful of rose-water, and a gill of sack or white wine. Mix in half a pound of fresh butter melted, with five yolks of eggs, and two whites, a quart of cream, a quarter of a pound of sugar, half a nutmeg grated, one spoonful of flour, and three spoonsful of crumbs of bread. Mix all well together, and boil it. Half an hour will do it.

Tansey Pudding.

PUT as much boiling cream to four Naples biscuits grated as will wet them, beat them with the yolks of four eggs. Have ready a few chopped tansey-leaves, with as much spinach as will make it pretty green. Be careful not to put too much tansey in, because it will make it bitter. Mix all together when the cream is cold, with a little sugar, and set it over a slow fire till it grows thick, then take it off, and, when cold, put it in a cloth, well buttered and floured; tie it up close, and let it boil three quarters of an hour; then take it up in a basin, and let it stand one quarter, then turn it carefully out, and put white wine sauce round it.

Or you may do it thus:

TAKE a quarter of a pound of almonds, blanch them, and beat them very fine with rose-water; slice a French roll very thin, put in a pint of cream boiling hot; beat four eggs very well, and mix with the eggs, when beaten, a little sugar and grated nutmeg, a glass of brandy, a little juice of tansey, and the juice of spinach to make it green. Put all the ingredients into a stew-pan, with a quarter of a pound of butter, and give it a gentle boil. You may either put it into a cloth and boil it, or bake it in a dish.

Herb Pudding.

STEEP a quart of grits in warm water half an hour, and then cut a pound of hog's lard into little bits. Take of spinach, beets, parsley, and leeks, a handful of each: three large onions chopped small, and three sage leaves cut very fine. Put in a little salt, mix all well together, and tie it close. It will require to be taken up while boiling, in order to loosen the string.

Spinach Pudding.

PICK and wash clean a quarter of a peck of spinach, put it into a saucepan with a little salt, cover it close, and when it is boiled just tender, throw it into a sieve to drain. Then chop it with a knife, beat up six eggs, and mix with it half a pint of cream, and a stale roll grated fine, a little nutmeg, and a quarter of a pound of melted butter. Stir all well together, put it into the saucepan in which you boiled the spinach, and keep stirring it all the time till it begins to thicken. Then wet and flour your cloth well, tie it up, and boil it an hour. When done, turn it into your dish, pour melted butter over it, with the juice of Seville orange and strew on a little grated sugar.

Cream Pudding.

Boil a quart of cream with a blade of mace, and half a nutmeg grated, and then let it stand to cool. Beat up eight eggs, and three whites, and strain them well. Mix a spoonful of flour with them, a quarter of a pound of almonds blanched and beat very fine, with a spoonful of orange-flower or rose-water. Then by degrees mix in the cream, and stir a.: well together. Take a thick cloth, wet and flour it well, pour in your mixture, tie it close, and boil it half an hour. Let the water boil fast all the time, and, when done, turn it in your dish, pour melted butter over it, with a little wine or sack, and strew on the top fine sugar grated.

Hunting Pudding.

Mix eight eggs beat up fine with a pint of good cream, and a pound of flour. Beat them well together, and put to them a pound of beef suet finely chopped, a pound of currants well cleaned, half a pound of jar-raisins stoned and chopped small, two ounces of candied orange cut small, the same of candied citron, a quarter of a pound of powdered sugar, and a large nutmeg grated. Mix all together with half a gill of brandy, put it into a cloth, and boil it for four hours. Be sure to put it in when the water boils, and keep it boiling all the time. When done, turn it into a dish, and strew over it powdered sugar.

Steak Pudding.

Make a good crust, with flour and suet shred fine, and mix it up with cold water; season it with a little salt, and make it pretty stiff. Take either beef or mutton steaks, well season them with pepper and salt, and make it up as you would an apple pudding, tie it in a cloth, and put it in when the water boils. If a small pudding, it will take three hours: if a large one. five hours.

Calf's Foot Pudding.

MINCE very fine a pound of calf's feet, first taking out the fat and brown. Then take a pound and a half of suet, pick off all the skin, and shred it small. Take six eggs, all the yolks, and but half the whites, and beat them well. Then take the crumb of a half-penny roll grated, a pound of currants clean picked and washed, and rubbed in a cloth, as much milk as will moisten it with the eggs, a handful of flour, and a little salt, nutmeg, and sugar, to season it to your taste. Boil it four hours; then take it up, lay it in your dish, and pour melted butter over it. If you put white wine and sugar into the butter it will be a pleasing addition.

Prune Pudding.

TAKE a few spoonsful from a quart of milk, and beat in it six yolks of eggs and three whites, four spoonsful of flour, a little salt, and two spoonsful of beaten ginger. Then by degrees mix in the rest of the milk, and a pound of prunes. Tie it up in a cloth, boil it an hour, and pour over it melted butter. Damsons done in the same manner are equally good.

Plum Pudding.

CUT a pound of suet into small pieces, but not too fine, a pound of currants washed clean, a pound of raisins stoned, eight yolks of eggs, and four whites, half a nutmeg grated, a tea-spoonful of beaten ginger, a pound of flour, and a pint of milk. Beat the eggs first, then put to them half the milk, and beat them together; and, by degrees, stir in the flour, then the suet, spice and fruit, and as much milk as will mix it well together, very thick. It will take four hours boiling. When done, turn it into your dish, and strew over it grated sugar.

Hasty Pudding.

PUT four bay-leaves into a quart of milk, and set it on the fire to boil. Then beat up the yolks of two eggs with a little salt. Take two or three spoonsful of milk, and beat up with your eggs, take out the bay leaves, and stir up the remainder of the milk. Then with a wooden spoon in one hand, and flour in the other, stir it in till it is of a good thickness, but not too thick. Let it boil, and keep it stirring; then pour it into a dish, and stick pieces of butter in different places. Remember, before you stir in the flour to take out the bay-leaves.

Oatmeal Pudding.

TAKE a pint of whole oatmeal, and steep it in a quart of boiled milk over night. In the morning take half a pound of beef suet shred fine, and mix with the oatmeal and milk; then add to them some grated nutmeg and a little salt, with three eggs beat up, a quarter of a pound of currants, the same quantity of raisins, and as much sugar as will sweeten it. Stir the whole well together, tie it pretty close, and boil it two hours. When done, turn it into your dish, and pour over it melted butter.

Suet Pudding.

TAKE six spoonsful of flour, a pound of suet shred small, four eggs, a spoonful of beaten ginger, a teaspoonful of salt, and a quart of milk. Mix the eggs and flour with a pint of the milk very thick, and with the seasoning mix in the rest of the milk with the suet. Let your batter be pretty thick, and boil it two hours.

Veal Suet Pudding.

TAKE a three-penny loaf, and cut the crumb of it into slices. Boil and pour two quarts of milk on the bread, and then put to it one pound of veal suet melted down. Add to these one pound of currants, and sugar to the taste, half a nutmeg, and six eggs well mixed together. This pudding may be either boiled or baked; if the latter, be careful to well butter the inside of your dish.

Cabbage Pudding.

TAKE one pound of beef suet, and as much of the lean part of a leg of veal. Then take a little cabbage well washed, and scald it Bruise the suet, veal, and cabbage together in a marble mortar, and season it with mace, nutmeg, ginger, a little pepper and salt, and put in some green gooseberries, grapes, or barberries. Mix them all well with the yolks of four or five eggs well beaten. Wrap all up together in a green cabbage leaf, and tie it in a cloth. It will take about an hour boiling.

A Spoonful Pudding.

TAKE a spoonful of flour, a spoonful of cream or milk, an egg, a little nutmeg, ginger, and salt.. Mix all together, and boil it in a little wooden dish half an hour. If you think proper you may add a few currants.

White Puddings in Skins.

BOIL half a pound of rice in milk till it is soft, having first washed the rice well in warm water. Put it into a sieve to drain, and beat half a pound of Jordan almonds very fine with some rose-water. Wash and dry a pound of currants, cut in small bits a pound of hog's lard, beat up six eggs well, half a pound of sugar, a large nutmeg grated, a stick of cinnamon, a little mace, and a little salt. Mix them well together, fill your skins, and boil them.

Apple Pudding.

HAVING made a puff paste, roll it near half an inch thick, and fill the crust with apples pared and cored. Grate in a little lemon-peel, and, in the winter, a little lemon-juice, (as it quickens the apples,) put in some sugar, close the crust, and tie it in a cloth. A small pudding will take two hours boiling, and a large one three or four.

Apple Dumplings.

WHEN you have pared your apples, take out the core with the apple-corer, and fill up the hole with quince, orange-marmalade, or sugar, as may best suit you. Then take a piece of paste, make a hole in it, lay in your apples, put another piece of paste in the same form over it, and close it up round the side of the apples. Put them into boiling water, and about three quarters of an hour will do them. Serve them up with melted butter poured over them.

Suet Dumplings.

TAKE a pint of milk, four eggs, a pound of suet, a little salt and nutmeg, two tea-spoonsful of ginger, and such a quantity of flour as will make it into a light paste. When the water boils, make the paste into dumplings, and roll them in a little flour. Then put them into the water, and move them gently, to prevent their sticking. A little more than half an hour will boil them.

Raspberry Dumplings.

MAKE a good puff paste and roll it. Spread over it raspberry jam, roll it into dumplings, and boil them an hour. Pour melted butter into the dish, and strew over them grated sugar.

Yeast Dumplings.

MAKE a light dough with flour, water, yeast, and salt, as for bread, cover it with a cloth, and set it before the fire for half an hour. Then have a saucepan of water on the fire, and when it boils take the dough, and make it into round balls, as big as a large hen's egg. Then flatten them with your hand, put them into the boiling water, and a few minutes will do them. Take care that they do not fall to the bottom of the pot or saucepan, as in that case they will then be heavy, and be sure to keep the water boiling all the time. When they are enough, take them up, and lay them in your dish, with melted butter in a boat.

Norfolk Dumplings.

TAKE half a pint of milk, two eggs, a little salt, and make them into a good thick batter with flour. Have ready a clean saucepan of water boiling, and drop your batter into it, and two or three minutes will boil them; but be particularly careful that the water boils fast when you put the batter in. Then throw them into a sieve to drain, turn them into a dish, and stir a lump of fresh butter into them.

Hard Dumplings.

Make some flour and water, with a little salt, into a sort of paste. Roll them in balls in a little flour, throw them into boiling water, and half an hour will boil them. They are best boiled with a good piece of beef.

Potatoe Pudding.

Boil half a pound of potatoes till they are soft, then peel them, mash them with the back of a spoon, and rub them through a sieve to have them fine and smooth. Then take half a pound of fresh butter melted, half a pound of fine sugar, and beat them well together till they are quite smooth. Beat up six eggs, whites as well as yolks, and stir them in with a glass of sack or brandy. Pour it into your cloth, tie it up, and about half an hour will do it. When you take it out, melt some butter, put into it a glass of wine sweetened with sugar, and pour it over your pudding.

Black Puddings.

Before you kill a hog, get a peck of grits, boil them half an hour in water, then drain them, and put them in a clean tub, or large pan. Then kill your hog, save two quarts of the blood, and keep stirring it till it is quite cold; then mix it with your grits, and stir them well together. Season with a large spoonful of salt, a quarter of an ounce of cloves, mace, and nutmeg together, an equal quantity of each; dry it, beat it well, and mix in. Take a little winter savory, sweet-marjorum, and thyme, penny-royal stripped of the stalks, and chopped very fine, just enough to season them, and to give them a flavour, but no more. The next day take the leaf of the hog, and cut it into dice, scrape and wash the guts very clean, then tie one end, and begin to fill them; mix in the fat as you fill them; be sure to put in a good deal of fat, fill the skins three parts full, tie the other end, and make your pudding what length you please; prick them with a pin, and put them in a kettle of boiling water. Boil them very softly an hour, then take them out, and lav them on clean straw.

SECT. II

BAKED PUDDINGS.

Vermicelli Puddings.

TAKE four ounces of vermicelli, and boil it in a pint of new milk till it is soft, with a stick or two of cinnamon. Then put in half a pint of thick cream, a quarter of a pound of butter, the like quantity of sugar, and the yolks of four eggs beaten fine. Bake it without paste in an earthen dish.

Sweetmeat Pudding.

COVER your dish with a thin puff-paste, and then take candied orange or lemon-peel, and citron, of each an ounce. Slice them thin, and lay them all over the bottom of the dish. Then beat up eight yolks of eggs, and two whites, and put to them half a pound of sugar, and half a pound of melted butter. Mix the whole well together, put it on the sweetmeats, and send it to a moderate heated oven. About an hour will do it.

Orange Pudding

BOIL the rind of a Seville orange very soft, then beat it in a marble mortar with the juice, and put to it two Naples biscuits grated very fine, a quarter of a pound of sugar, half a pound of butter, and the yolks of six eggs. Mix them well together, lay a good puff-paste round the edge of your dish, and bake it an hour in a gentle oven. Or you may make it thus :

Take the yolks of sixteen eggs, beat them well with half a pint of melted butter, grate in the rinds of two fine Seville oranges, beat in half a pound of fine sugar, two spoonsful of orange-flower water, two of rose-water, a gill of sack, half a pint of cream, two Naples biscuits, or the crumb of a penny loaf soaked in cream, and mix all well together. Make a thin puff-paste, and lay it all round the rim, and over the dish. Then pour in the pudding, and send it to the oven.

Lemon Pudding.

TAKE three lemons, cut the rinds off very thin, and boil them in three quarts of water till they are tender. Then pound them very fine in a mortar, and have ready a quarter of a pound of Naples biscuits boiled up in a quart of milk or cream. Mix them and the lemon rind with it, and beat up twelve yolks and six whites of eggs very fine. Melt a quarter of a pound of fresh butter, and put in half a pound of sugar, and a little orange-flower water. Mix all well together, put it over the fire, keep it stirring till it is thick, and then squeeze in the juice of half a lemon. Put puff-paste round your dish, then pour in your pudding, cut some candied sweetmeats and strew over it, and bake it three quarters of an hour. Or you may make it in this manner:

Blanch and beat eight ounces of Jordan almonds with orange-flower water, and add to them half a pound of cold butter, the yolks of ten eggs, the juice of a large lemon, and half the rind grated fine. Work them in a marble mortar till they look white and light, then put the puff-paste on your dish, pour in your pudding, and bake it half an hour.

Almond Pudding

TAKE a little more than three ounces of the crumb of white bread sliced, or grated, and steep it in a pint and a half of cream. Then beat half a pint of blanched almonds very fine, till they are like a paste, with a little orange-flower water. Beat up the yolks of eight eggs, and the whites of four. Mix all well together, put in a quarter of a pound of white sugar, and stir in about a quarter of a pound of melted butter. Put it over the fire, and keep stirring it till it is thick. Lay a sheet of puff-paste at the bottom of your dish, and pour in the ingredients Half an hour will bake it

Rice Pudding.

Boil four ounces of ground rice till it is soft, then beat up the yolks of four eggs, and put to them a pint of cream, four ounces of sugar, and a quarter of a pound of butter. Mix them well together, and either boil or bake it. Or you may make it thus:

Take a quarter of a pound of rice, put it into a saucepan, with a quart of new milk, a stick of cinnamon, and stir it often to prevent its sticking to the saucepan. When boiled till thick, put it into a pan, stir in a quarter of a pound of fresh butter, and sweeten it to your palate. Grate in half a nutmeg, add three or four spoonsful of rose-water, and stir all well together. When it is cold, beat up eight eggs with half the whites, mix them well in, pour the whole in a buttered dish, and send it to the oven.

If you would make a cheap boiled rice pudding, proceed thus: Take a quarter of a pound of rice, and half a pound of raisins, and tie them in a cloth; but give the rice a good deal of room to swell. Boil it two hours, and when it is enough, turn it into your dish, and pour melted butter and sugar over it, with a little nutmeg. Or you may make it thus: Tie a quarter of a pound of rice in a cloth, but give it room for swelling. Boil it an hour, then take it up, untie it, and with a spoon stir in a quarter of a pound of butter. Grate some nutmeg, and sweeten it to your taste. Then tie it up close, and boil it another hour. Then take it up, turn it into your dish, and pour over it melted butter.

Millet Pudding.

Wash and pick clean half a pound of millet-seed, put it into half a pound of sugar, a whole nutmeg grated, and three quarts of milk, and break in half a pound of fresh butter. Butter your dish, pour it in, and send it to the oven.

Oat Pudding.

Take a pound of oats with the husks off, and lay them in new milk, eight ounces of raisins of the sun stoned, the same quantity of currants well picked and washed, a pound of suet shred fine, and six new laid eggs well beat up. Season with nutmeg, beaten ginger, and salt, and mix them all well together.

Transparent Pudding.

Beat up eight eggs well in a pan, and put to them half a pound of butter, and the same quantity of loaf sugar beat fine, with a little grated nutmeg. Set it on the fire, and keep stirring it till it is the thickness of buttered eggs. Then put it into a basin to cool, roll a rich puff-paste very thin, lay it round the edge of your dish, and pour in the ingredients. Put it into a moderate heated oven, and about half an hour will do it.

French Barley Pudding.

Beat up the yolks of six eggs, and the whites of three, and put them into a quart of cream. Sweeten it to your palate, and put in a little orange-flower water, or rose-water, and a pound of melted butter. Then put in six handsful of French barley, having first boiled it tender in milk. Then butter a dish, pour it in, and send it to the oven.

Potatoe Pudding.

Boil two pounds of white potatoes till they are soft, peel and beat them in a mortar, and rub them through a sieve till they are quite fine. Then mix in half a pound of fresh butter, melted, beat up the yolks of eight eggs, and the whites of three. Add half a pound of white sugar finely pounded, half a pint of sack, and stir them well together. Grate in half a large nutmeg, and stir in half a pint of cream. Make a puff-paste, lay it all over the dish, and round the edges; pour in your pudding, and bake it till it is of a fine light brown.

Lady Sunderland's Pudding.

Beat up the yolks of eight eggs with the whites of three, add to them five spoonsful of flour, with half a nutmeg, and put them into a pint of cream. Butter the insides of some small basins, fill them half full, and bake them an hour. When done, turn them out of the basins, and pour over them melted butter mixed with wine and sugar.

Citron Pudding.

TAKE a spoonful of fine flour, two ounces of sugar, a little nutmeg, and half a pint of cream. Mix them well together, with the yolks of three eggs. Put it into tea-cups, and divide among them two ounces of citron cut very thin. Bake them in a pretty quick oven, and turn them out upon a china dish.

Chesnut Pudding.

BOIL a dozen and a half of chesnuts in a saucepan of water for a quarter of an hour. Then blanch and peel them, and beat them in a marble mortar, with a little orange-flower or rose-water and sack, till they come to a fine thin paste. Then beat up twelve eggs with half the whites, and mix them well. Grate half a nutmeg, a little salt, and mix them with three pints of cream, and half a pound of melted butter. Sweeten it to your palate, and mix all together. Put it over the fire, and keep stirring it till it is thick. Lay a puff-paste all over the dish, pour in the mixture, and send it to the oven. When you cannot get cream, take three pints of milk, beat up the yolks of four eggs, and stir into the milk. Set it over the fire, stirring it all the time till it is scalding hot, and then mix it instead of cream.

Quince Pudding.

SCALD your quinces till they are very tender, then pare them thin, and scrape off all the soft part. Strew sugar on them till they are very sweet, and put to them a little ginger and a little cinnamon. To a pint of cream put three or four yolks of eggs, and stir your quinces in it till it is of a good thickness. Butter your dish, pour it in, and bake it. In the same manner you may treat apricots, or white-pear plums.

Cowslip Pudding.

CUT and pound small the flowers of a peck of cowslips, with half a pound of Naples biscuits grated, and three pints of cream. Boil them a little, then take them off the fire, and beat up sixteen eggs, with a little cream and rose-water. Sweeten to your palate. Mix it all well together, butter a dish, and pour it in. Bake it, and when it is enough, throw fine sugar over it, and serve it up.

Cheese-curd Puddings.

TURN a gallon of milk with rennet, and drain off all the curd from the whey. Put the curd into a mortar, and beat it with half a pound of fresh butter, till the butter and the curd are well mixed. Beat the yolks of six eggs, and the whites of three, and strain them to the curd. Then grate two Naples biscuits or a penny roll. Mix all these together, and sweeten to your palate. Butter your patty-pans, and fill them with the ingredients. Bake them in a moderately heated oven, and when they are done, turn them out into a dish. Cut citron and candied orange-peel into little narrow bits, about an inch long, and blanched almonds cut in long slips. Stick them here and there in the tops of the puddings, according to your fancy. Pour melted butter, with a little sack in it, into the dish, and throw fine sugar all over them.

Apple Pudding.

PARE twelve large apples, and take out the cores Put them into a saucepan, with four or five spoonsful of water, and boil them till they are soft and thick. Then beat them well, stir in a pound of loaf sugar, the juice of three lemons, and the peel of two cut thin and beat fine in a mortar, and the yolks of eight eggs Mix all well together, and bake it in a slack oven When done, strew over it a little fine sugar.

Newmarket Pudding.

SLICE and butter a French roll: put it into your

mould: between every layer put some dried cherries. Take half a pint of cream, and a pint of milk, eight eggs, six ounces of fine sugar, a glass of brandy, some nutmeg, and lemon-peel. Let your dish or mould be nicely buttered; and when done you may turn it out into the dish you serve it in.

A Muffin pudding may be made in the same way.

A Grateful Pudding.

To a pound of flour add a pound of white bread grated. Take eight eggs, but only half the whites; beat them up, and mix with them a pint of new milk. Then stir in the bread and flour, a pound of raisins stoned, a pound of currants, half a pound of sugar, and a little beaten ginger. Mix all well together, pour it into your dish, and send it to the oven. If you can get cream instead of milk it will be a material improvement.

Carrot Pudding

Scrape a raw carrot very clean, and grate it. Take half a pound of grated carrot and a pound of grated bread; beat up eight eggs, leave out half the whites, and mix the eggs with half a pint of cream. Then stir in the bread and carrot, half a pound of fresh butter melted, half a pint of sack, three spoonsful of orange-flower water, and a nutmeg grated. Sweeten to your palate. Mix all well together, and if it be not thin enough, stir in a little new milk or cream. Let it be of a moderate thickness, lay a puff-paste all over the dish, and pour in the ingredients. It will take an hour baking.

Yorkshire Pudding.

Take four large spoonsful of flour, and beat it up well with four eggs and a little salt. Then put to them three pints of milk, and mix them well together.—Butter a dripping-pan, and set it under beef, mutton, or a loin of veal. When the meat is about half roasted, put in your pudding, and let the fat drip on it.

When it is brown at top, cut it into square pieces and turn it over; and when the under side is browned also, send it to table on a dish.

CHAPTER XV.

PIES.

THERE are several things necessary to be particularly observed by the cook, in order that her labours and ingenuity under this head may be brought to their proper degree of perfection. One very material consideration must be, that the heat of the oven is duly proportioned to the nature of the article to be baked. Light paste requires a moderate oven; if it is too quick, the crust cannot rise, and will therefore be burned; and if too slow, it will be soddened, and want that delicate light brown it ought to have. Raised pies must have a quick oven, and be well closed up, or they will sink in their sides, and lose their proper shape. Tarts that are iced, should be baked in a slow oven, or the icing will become brown before the paste is properly baked.

Having made these general observations respecting the baking of pies, we shall now direct the cook how to make the different kinds of paste, as they must be proportioned in the qualities according to the respective articles for which they are to be used.

Puff Paste must be made thus: Take a quarter of a peck of flour, and rub it into a pound of butter very fine. Make it up into a light paste, with cold water, just stiff enough to work it up. Then roll it out about as thick as a crown piece; put a layer of butter all over, then sprinkle on a little flour, double it up, and roll it out again. Double and roll it, with layers of butter three times, and it will be properly fit for use.

Short Crust. Put six ounces of butter to eight of flour, and work them well together; then mix it up with as little water as possible, so as to have it a stiffish paste; then roll it out thin for use.

A good Paste for large Pies. Take a peck of flour, and put to it three eggs; then put in half a pound of suet, and a pound and a half of butter and suet, and as much of the liquor as will make it a good light crust. Work it up well, and roll it out.

A standing Crust for great Pies. Take a peck of flour and six pounds of butter boiled in a gallon of water: skim it off into the flour, and as little of the liquor as you can. Work it up well into a paste, and then pull it into pieces till it is cold. Then make it up into what form you please.

Paste for Tarts. Put an ounce of loaf sugar beat and sifted to one pound of fine flour. Make it into a stiff paste, with a gill of boiling cream, and three ounces of butter. Work it well, and roll it very thin.

Paste for Custards. To half a pound of flour put six ounces of butter, the yolks of two eggs, and three spoonsful of cream. Mix them together, and let them stand a quarter of an hour; then work it up and down, and roll it out very thin.

SECT. I.

MEAT PIES.

Beef Steak Bie.

TAKE some rump steaks, and beat them with a roll ing-pin, then season them with pepper and salt to your palate. Make a good crust, lay in your steaks, and then pour in as much water as will fill the dish. Put on the crust, send it to the oven and let it be well baked.

Mutton Pie.

TAKE off the skin and outside fat of a loin of mutton, cut it into steaks, and season them well with pepper and salt. Set them into your dish, and pour in as much water as will cover them. Then put on your crust, and let it be well baked.

A Mutton Pie a-la-Perigord.

TAKE a loin of mutton, cut it into chops, leaving the bone that marks the chop; cover your dish with paste, and put the chops on it: season them with salt and mixed spices: put truffles between them.—Cover them with slices of bacon, and spread over the whole butter the thickness of half a crown. Complete your pies with a short crust, and when baked add a good cullis mixed with a glass of white wine. It will take two hours to bake in a moderate oven.

A Veal Pie, made of the brisket part of the breast, may be done in the same manner, letting the veal first be stewed.

Veal Pie.

CUT a breast of veal into pieces, season them with pepper and salt, and lay them in your dish. Boil six or eight eggs hard, take the yolks only, and put them into different places in the pie, then pour in as much water as will nearly fill the dish, put on the lid and bake it well. A lamb pie must be done in the same manner.

A rich Veal Pie.

CUT a loin of veal into steaks, and season them with salt, pepper, nutmeg, and beaten mace. Lay the meat in your dish, with sweetbreads seasoned, and the yolks of six hard eggs, a pint of oysters, and half a pint of good gravy. Lay a good puff-paste round your dish, half an inch thick, and cover it with a lid of the same substance. Bake it an hour and a quarter in a quick oven. When it comes home, take off the lid, cut it into eight or ten pieces, and stick them round the inside of the rim of the dish. Cover the meat with slices of lemon, and send the pie hot tc table.

Lamb or Veal Pies in high Taste.

CUT your lamb or veal into small pieces, and season with pepper, salt, cloves, mace, and nutmegs beat fine. Make a good puff-paste crust, lay it in your dish, then put in your meat, and strew on it some stoned raisins and currants clean washed, and some sugar.—Then lay on some forcemeat-balls made sweet, and, if in the summer, some artichoke bottoms boiled; but if in winter, scalded grapes. Add to these some Spanish potatoes boiled, and cut into pieces, some candied citron, candied orange, lemon-peel, and three or four blades of mace. Put butter on the top, close up your pie, and bake it. Have ready against it is done the following composition: Mix the yolks of three eggs with a pint of wine, and stir them well together over the fire one way, till it is thick. Then take it off, put in sugar enough to sweeten it, and squeeze in the juice of a lemon. Raise the lid of your pie, put this hot into it, close it up again, and send it to table.

Venison Pasty.

TAKE a neck and breast of venison, bone them, and season them well with pepper and salt, put them into a deep pan, with the best part of a neck of mutton sliced and laid over them; pour in a glass of red wine, put a coarse paste over it, and bake it two hours in an oven; then lay the venison in a dish, pour the gravy over it, and put one pound of butter over it; make a good puff-paste, and lay it near half an inch thick round the edge of the dish; roll out the lid, which must be a little thicker than the paste on the edge of the dish, and lay it on; then roll out another lid pretty thin, and cut in flowers, leaves, or whatever form you please, and lay it on the lid. If you do not want it, it will keep in the pot that it was baked in eight or ten days; but let the crust be kept on, that the air may not get to it. A breast and shoulder of venison is the most proper for pasty.

Olive Pie.

CUT some thin slices from a fillet of veal, rub them over with the yolks of eggs, and strew on them a few crumbs of bread; shred a little lemon-peel very fine, and put it on them, with a little grated nutmeg, pepper, and salt; roll them up very tight, and lay them in a pewter dish; pour over them half a pint of good gravy, put half a pound of butter over it, make a light paste, and lay it round the dish. Roll the lid half ar inch thick, and lay it on.

Calf's Head Pie.

BOIL the head till it is tender, and then carefully take off the flesh as whole as you can. Then take out the eyes, and slice the tongue. Make a good puff-paste crust, cover the dish, and lay in your meat.—Throw the tongue over it, and lay the eyes, cut in two, at each corner. Season it with a little pepper and salt, pour in half a pint of the liquor it was boiled in, lay on it a thin top crust, and bake it an hour in a quick oven. In the meantime boil the bones of the head in two quarts of liquor; with two or three blades of mace, half a quarter of an ounce of whole pepper, a large onion, and a bundle of sweet herbs. Let it boil till it is reduced to about a pint, then strain it off, and add two spoonsful of catsup, three of red wine, a small piece of butter rolled in flour, and half an ounce of truffles and morels. Season it to your palate, and boil it. Roll half the brains with some sage, then beat them up, and add to them twelve leaves of sage chopped very fine. Then stir all together, and give it a boil. Take the other part of the brains, and beat them with some of the sage chopped fine, a little lemon-peel minced, and half a small nutmeg grated. Beat up with an egg, and fry it in little cakes of a fine light brown. Boil six eggs hard, of which take only the yolks, and when your pie comes home, take off the lid, lay the eggs and cakes over it, and pour in all the sauce. Send it hot to table with the lid.

Calf's Feet Pie.

BOIL your calf's feet in three quarts of water, with three or four blade of mace, anu let them boil gently till it is reduced to about a pint and a half. Then take out the feet, strain the liquor, and make a good crust. Cover your dish, then take the flesh from the bones, and put half into it. Strew over it half a pound of currants clean washed and picked, and half a pound of raisins stoned. Then lay on the rest of your meats, skim the liquor they were boiled in, sweeten it to your taste, and put in half a pint of white wine. Then pour all into the dish, put on your lid, and bake it an hour and a half.

Sweetbread Pie.

LAY a puff-paste half an inch thick at the bottom of a deep dish, and put a forcemeat round the sides. Cut some sweetbreads in pieces, three or four, according to the size the pie is intended to be made; lay them in first, then some artichoke bottoms, cut into four pieces each, then some cock's-combs, a few truffles and morels, some asparagus tops, and fresh mushrooms, yolks of eggs boiled hard, and forcemeat balls; season with pepper and salt. Almost fill the pie with water, cover it, and bake it two hours. When it comes from the oven, pour in some rich veal gravy, thickened with a very little cream and flour

Cheshire Pork Pie.

TAKE the shin and loin of pork, and cut it into steaks. Season them with pepper, salt, and nutmeg, and make a good crust. Put into your dish a layer of pork, then a layer of pippins pared and cored, and sugar sufficient to sweeten it. Then place another layer of pork, and put in half a pint of white wine. Lay some butter on the top, close your pie, and send it to the oven; if your pie is large, you must put in a pint of white wine.

Devonshire Squab Pie.

COVER your dish with a good crust, and put at the bottom of it a layer of sliced pippins, and then a layer of mutton steaks, cut from the loin, well seasoned with pepper and salt. Then put another layer of pippins, peel some onions, slice them thin, and put a layer of them over the pippins. Then put a layer of mutton and then pippins and onions. Pour in a pint of water, close up the pie, and send it to the oven.

SECT. II.

PIES *made of* POULTRY, *&c.*

A plain Goose Pie.

QUARTER your goose, season it well with pepper and salt, and lay it in a raised crust. Cut half a pound of butter into pieces, and put it in different places on the top; then lay on the lid, and send it to an oven moderately heated.

Another method of making a goose pie, with material improvements, is thus: Take a goose and a fowl, bone them, and season them well; put a forcemeat into the fowl, and then put the fowl into the goose. Lay these in a raised crust, and fill the corners with a little forcemeat. Put half a pound of butter on the top cut into pieces, cover it, send it to the oven, and let it be well baked. This pie may be eaten either hot or cold, and makes a pretty side-dish for supper.

Giblet Pie.

CLEAN two pair of giblets well, and put all but the livers into a saucepan, with two quarts of water, twenty corns of whole pepper, three blades of mace, a bundle of sweet herbs, and a large onion Cover them close, and let them stew very gently till they are tender. Have a good crust ready, cover your dish, lay at the bottom a fine rump steak seasoned with pepper and salt, put in your giblets, with the livers, and strain the liquor they were stewed in; then season it with salt, and pour it into your pie. Put on the lid, and bake it an hour and a half.

Duck Pie.

SCALD two ducks and make them very clean; then cut off the feet, the pinions, necks, and heads; take out the gizzards, livers, and hearts, pick all clean, and scald them. Pick out the fat of the inside, lay a good puff-paste crust all over the dish, season the ducks, both inside and out, with pepper and salt, and lay them in the dish with the giblets at each end properly seasoned. Put in as much water as will nearly fill the pie, lay on the crust, and let it be well baked.

Pigeon Pie.

Pick and clean your pigeons very nicely, and then season them with pepper and salt; or put some good forcemeat, or butter, pepper and salt, into each of their bellies. Then cover your dish with a puff-paste crust, lay in your pigeons, and put between them the necks, gizzards, livers, pinions, and hearts, with the yolk of a hard egg, and a beef steak in the middle. Put as much water as will nearly fill the dish, lay on the top crust, and bake it well.

Chicken Pie.

Season your chickens with pepper, salt, and mace. Put a piece of butter into each of them, and lay them in the dish with their breasts upwards. Lay a thin slice of bacon over them, which will give them an agreeable flavour. Then put in a pint of strong gravy, and make a good puff-paste. Put on the lid, and bake it in a moderately heated oven.

Another Method of making a Chicken Pie

Cover the bottom of the dish with a puff-paste, and upon that, round the side, lay a thin layer of forcemeat. Cut two small chickens into pieces, season them high with pepper and salt; put some of the pieces into the dish, then a sweetbread or two cut into pieces and well seasoned, a few truffles and morels, some artichoke bottoms cut each into four pieces, yolks of eggs boiled hard, chopped a little, and strewed over the top; put in a little water, and cover the pie. When it comes from the oven, pour in a rich gravy, thickened with a little flour and butter. To make the pie still richer, you may add fresh mushrooms, aspara gus tops, and cock's-combs.

Partridge Pie.

Take two brace of partridges, and truss them in the same manner as you do a fowl for boiling. Put some shalots into a marble mortar, with some parsley cut small, the livers of the partridges, and twice the quantity of bacon. Beat these well together, and season them with pepper, salt, and a blade or two of mace. When these are all pounded to a paste, add to them some fresh mushrooms. Raise the crust for the pie, and cover the bottom of it with the seasoning; then lay in the partridges, but no stuffing in them; put the remainder of the seasoning about the sides, and between the partridges. Mix together some pepper and salt, a little mace, some shalots shred fine, fresh mushrooms, and a little bacon beat fine in a mortar. Strew this over the partridges, and lay on some thin slices of bacon. Then put on the lid, and send it to the oven, and two hours will bake it. When it is done, remove the lid, take out the slices of bacon, and scum off the fat. Put in a pint of rich veal gravy, squeeze in the juice of an orange, and send it hot to table.

Hare Pie.

Cut your hare into pieces, and season it well with pepper, salt, nutmeg, and mace; then put it into a jug with half a pound of butter, close it up, set it in a copper of boiling water, and make a rich forcemeat with a quarter of a pound of scraped bacon, two onions, a glass of red wine, the crumb of a two-penny loaf, a little winter savory, the liver cut small, and a little nutmeg. Season it high with pepper and salt, mix it well up with the yolks of three eggs, raise the pie, and lay the forcemeat in the bottom of the dish. Then put in the hare, with the gravy that came out of it; lay on the lid, and send it to the oven. An hour and half will bake it.

Rabbit Pie.

Cut a couple of young rabbits into quarters; then take a quarter of a pound of bacon, and bruise it to pieces in a marble mortar, with the livers, some pepper, salt, a little mace, some parsley cut small, some chives, and a few leaves of sweet basil. When these are all beaten fine, make the paste, and cover the bottom of the pie with the seasoning. Then put in the rabbits, pound some more bacon in a mortar, and with it some fresh butter. Cover the rabbits with this, and lay over it some thin slices of bacon; put on the lid, and send it to the oven. It will take two hours baking. When it is done, remove the lid, take out the bacon, and skim off the fat. If there is not gravy enough in the pie, pour in some rich mutton or veal gravy boiling hot.

Another Method of making a Rabbit Pie, and which is particularly done in the County of Salop.

CUT two rabbits into pieces, with two pounds of fat pork cut small, and season both with pepper and salt to your taste. Then make a good puff-paste crust, cover your dish with it, and lay in your rabbits. Mix the pork with them; but take the livers of the rabbits, parboil them, and beat them in a mortar, with the same quantity of fat bacon, and a little sweet herbs, and some oysters. Season with pepper, salt, and nutmeg, mix it up with the yolk of an egg, and make it into little balls. Scatter them about your pie, with some artichoke bottoms cut in dices, and some cock's-combs, if you have them. Grate a small nutmeg over the meat, then pour in half a pint of red wine, and half a pint of water. Close your pie, and bake it an hour and a half in a quick but not too fierce an oven.

Fine Patties.

TAKE any quantity of either turkey, house-lamb, or chicken, and slice it with an equal quantity of the fat of lamb, loin of veal, or the inside of a sirloin of beef, and a little parsley, thyme, and lemon-peel shred. Put all into a marble mortar, pound it very fine, and season it with salt and white pepper. Make a fine puff-paste, roll it out into thin square sheets, and put the mea: in the middle. Cover the patties, close them all round, cut the paste even, wash them over with the yolk of an egg, and bake them twenty minutes in a quick oven. Have ready a little white gravy, seasoned with pepper, salt, and a little shalot, thickened up with cream, or butter. When the patties come out of the oven, make a hole in the top, and pour in some gravy; but take care not to put in too much, lest it should run out at the sides, and spoil the appearance.

To make any Sort of Timbale.

MAKE your paste thus: take a pound of flour, mix it well with a little water, a quarter of a pound of fresh butter or hog's lard, the yolks of two eggs, and a little salt; knead this paste well, that it may be firm; take a part and roll it to the sides of your stew-pan, put it in the bottom and round the sides, that it may take the form of the stew-pan; then put in any meat or fish you may think fit. You must butter your stew-pan well, to make it turn out. Cover it with what paste remains, and send it to the oven; or bury the stew-pan in hot embers, and cover it with a lid that will admit fire on the top. When turned out of the stew-pan, cut a hole in the top, and put in a rich gravy; replace the bit of crust, and serve it up.

SECT. III.

FRUIT PIES, &c.

Apple Pie.

MAKE a good puff-paste crust, and put it round the edge of your dish. Pare and quarter your apples, and take out the cores. Then lay a thick row of apples, and put in half the sugar you intend to use for your pie. Mince a little lemon-peel fine, spread it over the sugar and apples, squeeze in a little juice of a lemon; then scatter a few cloves over it, and lay on the rest of your apples and sugar, with another small squeeze of the juice of a lemon. Boil the parings of the apples and cores in some water, with a blade of mace, till the flavour is extracted; strain it, put in a little sugar, and boil it till it is reduced to a small quantity; then pour it into your pie, put on your crust, and send it to the oven. You may add to the apples a little quince or marmalade, which will greatly enrich the flavour. When the pie comes from the oven, beat up the yolks of two eggs, with half a pint of cream, and a little nutmeg and sugar. Put it over a slow fire, and keep stirring it till it is near boiling; then take off the lid of the pie, and pour it in. Cut the crust into small three-corner pieces, and stick them about the pie. A pear pie must be done in the same manner, only the quince or marmalade must be omitted

Apple Tart.

Scald eight or ten large codlins, let them stand till they are cold, and then take off the skins. Beat the pulp as fine as possible with a spoon: then mix the yolks of six eggs, and the whites of four. Beat all together very fine, put in some grated nutmeg, and sweeten it to your taste. Melt some good fresh butter, and beat it till it is of the consistence of fine thick cream. Then make a puff-paste, and cover a tin patty-pan with it; pour in the ingredients, but do not cover it with the paste. When you have baked it a quarter of an hour, slip it out of the patty-pan on a dish, and strew over it some sugar finely beaten and sifted.

Cherry Pie.

Having made a good crust, lay a little of it round the sides of your dish, and strew sugar at the bottom. Then lay in your fruit, and some sugar at the top. Put on your lid, and bake it in a slack oven. If you mix some currants with the cherries, it will be a considerable addition. A plum or gooseberry pie may be made in the same manner.

Mince Pies.

SHRED three pounds of meat very fine, and chop it as small as possible; take two pounds of raisins stoned and chopped very fine, the same quantity of currants, nicely picked, washed, rubbed, and dried at the fire. Pare half a hundred fine pippins, core them, and chop them small, take half a pound of fine sugar, and pound it fine, a quarter of an ounce of mace, a quarter of an ounce of cloves, and two large nutmegs, all beat fine, put them all into a large pan, and mix them well together with half a pint of brandy, and half a pint of sack, put it down close in a stone pot, and it will keep good three or four months. When you make your pies, take a little dish, somewhat larger than a soup plate, lay a very thin crust all over it; lay a thin layer of meat, and then a layer of citron, cut very thin, then a layer of mincemeat, and a layer of orange-peel, cut thin; over that a little meat; squeeze half the juice of a fine Seville orange or lemon, lay on your crust, and bake it nicely. These pies eat very fine cold. If you make them in little patties, mix your meats and sweetmeats accordingly. If you choose meat in your pies, parboil a neat's tongue, peel it, and chop the meat as fine as possible, and mix with the rest; or two pounds of the inside of a sirloin of beef boiled. But when you use meat, the quantity of fruit must be doubled.

Another Method of making Mince Pies.

TAKE a neat's tongue, and boil it two hours, then skin it, and chop it exceeding small. Chop very small three pounds of beef suet, three pounds of good baking apples, four pounds of currants clean washed, picked, and well dried before the fire, a pound of jar raisins stoned and chopped small, and a pound of powder sugar. Mix them all together, with half an ounce of mace, as much nutmeg, a quarter of an ounce of cloves, a quarter of an ounce of cinnamon, and a pint of French brandy. Make a rich puff-paste, and as you fill up the pie, put in a little candied citron and orange, cut in little pieces. What mincemeat you have to spare, put close down in a pot, and cover it up; but never put any citron or orange to it till you use it.

To make Mincemeat.

TAKE a pound of beef, a pound of apples, two pounds of suet, two pounds of sugar, two pounds of currants, one pound of candied lemon or orange-peel, a quarter of a pound of citron, an ounce of fine spices mixed together; half an ounce of salt, and six rinds of lemon shred fine. Let the whole of these ingredients be well mixed, adding brandy and wine sufficient to your palate.

Orange and Lemon Tarts.

TAKE six large oranges or lemons, rub them well with salt, and put them into water, with a handful of salt in it, for two days. Then change them every day with fresh water, without salt, for a fortnight. Boil them till they are tender, and then cut them into half quarters corner-ways as thin as possible. Take six pippins pared cored, and quartered, and put them into a pint of water. Let them boil till they break, then put the licuor to your oranges or lemons, half the pulp of the pippins well broken, and a pound of sugar.— Boil these together a quarter of an hour, then put it into a pot; and squeeze into it either the juice of an orange or lemon, according to which of the tarts you intend to make. Two spoonsful will be sufficient to give a proper flavour to your tart. Put fine puff-paste, and very thin, into your patty-pans, which must be small and shallow. Before you put your tarts into the oven, take a feather or brush, and rub them over with melted butter, and then sift some double refined sugar over them, which will form a pretty icing, and make them have a pleasing effect on the eye.

Tart de moi.

PUT round your dish a puff-paste, and then a layer of biscuit; then a layer of butter and marrow, another of all sorts of sweetmeats, or as many as you have, and thus proceed till your dish is full. Then boil a quart of cream, thicken it with eggs, and put in a spoonful of orange-flower water. Sweeten it with sugar to your taste, and pour it over the whole. Half an hour will bake it.

Artichoke Pie.

Boil twelve artichokes, break off the leaves and chokes, and take the bottoms clear from the stalks. Make a good puff-paste crust, and lay a quarter of a pound of fresh butter all over the bottom of your pie. Then lay a row of artichokes, strew a little pepper, salt, and beaten mace over them, then another row, strew the rest of your spice over them, and put in a quarter of a pound more of butter cut in little bits. Take half an ounce of truffles and morels, and boil them in a quarter of a pint of water. Pour the water into the pie, cut the truffles and morels very small, and throw them all over the pie. Pour in a gill of white wine, cover your pie, and bake it. When the crust is done, the pie will be enough.

Vermicelli Pie.

Season four pigeons with a little pepper and salt; stuff them with a piece of butter, a few crumbs of bread, and a little parsley cut small; butter a deep earthen dish well, and then cover the bottom of it with two ounces of vermicelli. Make a puff-paste, roll it pretty thick, and lay it on the dish, then lay in the pigeons, the breasts downwards, put a thick lid on the pie, and bake it in a moderate oven. When it is enough, take a dish proper for it to be sent to table in, and turn the pie on it. The vermicelli will be then on the top, and have a pleasing effect.

SECT. IV.

FISH PIES.

Eel Pie.

When you have skinned, gutted, and washed your eels very clean, cut them into pieces about an inch and a half long. Season them with pepper, salt, and a little dried sage rubbed small. Put them into your dish, with as much water as will just cover them. Make a good puff-paste, lay on the lid, and send your pie to the oven, which must be quick, but not so as to burn the crust.

Turbot Pie.

First parboil your turbot, and then season it with a little pepper, salt, cloves, nutmeg, and sweet herbs cut fine. When you have made your paste, lay the turbot in your dish, with some yolks of eggs, and a whole onion, which must be taken out when the pie is baked. Lay a good deal of fresh butter at the top, put on the lid, and send it to the oven.

Sole Pie.

Cover your dish with a good crust; then boil two pounds of eels till they are tender, pick the flesh from the bones, and put the bones into the liquor in which the eels were boiled, with a blade of mace and a little salt. Boil them till there is only a quarter of a pint of liquor left, and then strain it. Cut the flesh off the eels very fine, and mix with it a little lemon-peel chopped small, salt, pepper, and nutmeg, a few crumbs of bread grated, some parsley cut fine, an anchovy, and a quarter of a pound of butter. Lay this in the bottom of your dish. Cut the flesh from a pair of large soles, and take off the fins, lay it on the seasoning, then pour in the liquor the eels were boiled in, close up your pie, and send it to the table.

Flounder Pie.

Gut your flounders, wash them clean, and then dry them well in a cloth. Give them a gentle boil, and then cut the flesh clean from the bones, lay a good crust over the dish, put a little fresh butter at the bottom, and on that the fish. Season with pepper and salt to your taste. Boil the bones in the water the fish was boiled in, with a small piece of horse-radish, a little parsley, a bit of lemon peel, and a crust of bread. Boil it till there is just enough liquor for the pie, then strain it, and pour it over the fish. Put on the lid, and send it to a moderate heated oven.

Carp Pie.

SCRAPE off the scales, and then gut and wash a large carp clean. Take an eel, and boil it till it is almost tender; pick off all the meat, and mince it fine, with an equal quantity of crumbs of bread, a few sweet herbs, lemon-peel cut fine, a little pepper and salt, and grated nutmeg; an anchovy, half a pint of oysters parboiled and chopped fine, and the yolks of three hard eggs cut small. Roll it up with a quarter of a pound of butter, and fill the belly of the carp. Make a good crust, cover the dish, and lay in your fish. Save the liquor you boiled your eel in, put into it the eel bones, and boil them with a little mace, whole pepper, an onion, some sweet herbs, and an anchovy. Boil it till reduced to about half a pint, then strain it, and add to it about a quarter of a pint of white wine, and a piece of butter about the size of a hen's egg mixed in a very little flour. Boil it up, and pour it into your pie. Put on the lid, and bake it an hour in a quick oven.

Tench Pie.

PUT a layer of butter at the bottom of your dish, and grate in some nutmeg, with pepper, salt, and mace. Then lay in your tench, cover them with some butter, and pour in some red wine with a little water. Then put on the lid, and when it comes from the oven, pour in melted butter mixed with some good rich gravy.

Trout Pie.

TAKE a brace of trout, and lard them with eels; raise the crust, and put a layer of fresh butter at the bottom. Then make a forcemeat of trout, mushrooms, truffles, morels, chives, and fresh butter. Season them with salt, pepper, and spice; mix these up with the yolks of two eggs; stuff the trout with it, lay them in the dish, cover them with butter, put on the lid, and send it to the oven. Have some good fish gravy ready, and when the pie is done, raise the crust, and pour it in

Salmon Pie.

WHEN you have made a good crust, take a piece of fresh salmon, well cleansed, and season it with salt, mace, and nutmeg. Put a piece of butter at the bottom of your dish, and then lay in the salmon. Melt butter in proportion to the size of your pie, and then take a lobster, boil it, pick out all the flesh, chop it small, bruise the body, and mix it well with the butter. Pour it over your salmon, put on the lid, and let it be well baked.

Herring Pie.

HAVING scaled, gutted, and washed your herring clean, cut off their heads, fins, and tails. Make a good crust, cover your dish, and season your herrings with beaten mace, pepper, and salt. Put a little butter in the bottom of your dish, and then the herrings. Over these put some apples and onions sliced very thin. Put some butter on the top, then pour in a little water, lay on the lid, send it to the oven, and let it be well baked.

Lobster Pie.

BOIL two or three lobsters, take the meat out of the tails, and cut it into different pieces. Then take out all the spawn, and the meat of the claws; beat it well in a mortar, and season it with pepper, salt, two spoonsful of vinegar, and a little anchovy liquor. Melt half a pound of fresh butter, and stir all together, with the crumbs of a penny roll rubbed through a fine cullender, and the yolks of ten eggs. Put a fine puff-paste over your dish, lay in the tails first, and the rest of the meat on them. Put on the lid, and bake it in a slow oven.

CHAPTER XVI.

PANCAKES AND FRITTERS.

THE principal things to be observed, of a general nature, in dressing these articles is, that your pan be thoroughly clean, that you fry them in nice sweet lard, or fresh butter, of a light brown colour, and that the grease is thoroughly drained from them before you carry them to table.

Pancakes.

BEAT six or eight eggs well together, leaving out half the whites, and stir them into a quart of milk. Mix your flour first with a little of the milk, and then add the rest by degrees. Put in two spoonsful of beaten ginger, a glass of brandy, and a little salt, and stir all well together. Put a piece of butter into your stew-pan, and then pour in a ladleful of batter, which will make a pancake, moving the pan round, that the batter may spread all over it.—Shake the pan, and when you think one side is enough, turn it, and when both sides are done, lay it in a dish before the fire; and in like manner do the rest. Before you take them out of the pan, raise it a little, that they may drain, and be quite clear of grease. When you send them to table, strew a little sugar over them.

Cream Pancakes.

MIX the yolks of two eggs with half a pint of cream, two ounces of sugar, and a little beaten cinnamon, mace, and nutmeg. Rub your pan with lard, and fry them as thin as possible. Grate over them some fine sugar.

Rice Pancakes.

TAKE three spoonsful of flour and rice, and a quart of cream. Set it on a slow fire, and keep stirring it till it is as thick as pap. Pour into it half a pound of butter, and a nutmeg grated. Then pour it into an earthen pan, and when it is cold, stir in three or four spoonsful of flour, a little salt, and some sugar, and nine eggs well beaten. Mix all well together, and fry them nicely. When cream is not to be had, you must use new milk, but in that case you must add a spoonful more of the flour of rice.

Pink-coloured Pancakes.

Boil a large beet-root till it is tender, and then beat it fine in a marble mortar. Add the yolks of four eggs, two spoonsful of flour, and three spoonsful of cream. Sweeten it to your taste, grate in half a nutmeg, and add a glass of brandy. Mix all well together, and fry your pancakes in butter. Garnish them with green sweetmeats, preserved apricots, or green sprigs of myrtle. This makes a pretty corner-dish either for dinner or supper.

Clary Pancakes.

Take three eggs, three spoonsful of fine flour, and a litte salt. Beat them well together, and mix them with a pint of milk. Put lard into your pan, and when it is hot, pour in your batter as thin as possible, then lay in some clary leaves washed and dried, and pour a little more batter thin over them. Fry them of a nice brown, and serve them up hot.

Plain Fritters.

Grate the crumb of a penny loaf, and put it into a pint of milk; mix it very smooth, and when cold, add the yolks of five eggs, three ounces of sifted sugar, and some grated nutmeg. Fry them in hog's lard, and when done, pour melted butter, wine and sugar into the dish.

Custard Fritters.

Beat up the yolks of eight eggs with one spoonful of flour, half a nutmeg, a little salt, and a glass of brandy, add a pint of cream, sweeten it, and bake it in a small dish. When cold, cut it into quarters, and dip them in batter made of half a pint of cream, a quarter of a pint of milk, four eggs, a little flour, and a little ginger grated. Fry them in good lard or dripping, and when done strew over them some grated sugar.

Apple Fritters.

TAKE some of the largest apples you can get, pare and core them, and then cut them into round slices. Take half a pint of ale and two eggs, and beat in as much flour as will make it rather thicker than a common pudding, with nutmeg and sugar to your taste. Let it stand three or four minutes to rise. Dip your slices of apple into the batter, fry them crisp, and serve them up with sugar grated over them, and wine sauce in a boat.

Water Fritters.

TAKE five or six spoonsful of flour, a little salt, a quart of water, eight eggs well beat up, a glass of brandy, and mix them all well together. The longer they are made before dressed, the better. Just before you do them, melt half a pound of butter, and beat it well in. Fry them in hog's lard.

White Fritters.

TAKE two ounces of rice, wash it clean in water, and dry it before the fire. Then beat it very fine in a mortar, and sift it through a lawn sieve. Put it into a saucepan, just wet it with milk, and when it is thoroughly moistened, add to it another pint of milk. Set the whole over a stove, or very slow fire, and take care to keep it always moving. Put in a little ginger, and some candied lemon-peel grated. Keep it over the fire, till it is come almost to the thickness of a fine paste. When it is quite cold, spread it out with a rolling-pin, and cut it into little pieces, taking care they do not stick to each other. Flour your hands, roll up your fritters handsomely, and fry them. When done, strew on them some sugar, and pour over them a little orange-flower water.

Hasty Fritters.

PUT some butter into a stew-pan, and let it heat. Take half a pint of good ale, and stir into it by degrees a little flour. Put in a few currants, or chopped apples, beat them up quick, and drop a large spoonful at a time all over the pan. Take care they do not stick together; turn them with an egg-slice, and when they are of a fine brown, lay them on a dish, strew some sugar over them, and serve them hot to table.

Fritters Royal.

PUT a quart of new milk into a saucepan, and when it begins to boil, pour in a pint of sack, or wine. Then take it off, let it stand five or six minutes, skim off the curd, and put it into a basin. Beat it up well with six eggs, and season it with nutmeg. Then beat it with a whisk, and add flour sufficient to give it the usual thickness of batter; put in some sugar, and fry them quick.

Tansey Fritters.

POUR a pint of boiling milk on the crumb of a penny loaf, let it stand an hour, and then put in as much juice of tansey to it as will give it a flavour. Add to it a little of the juice of spinach, in order to make it green. Put to it a spoonful of ratafia water, or brandy, sweeten it to your taste, grate the rind of half a lemon, beat the yolks of four eggs, and mix them all together. Put them in a stew-pan, with a quarter of a pound of butter, stir it over a slow fire till it is quite thick; take it off, and let it stand two or three hours; then drop a spoonful at a time into a pan of boiling lard; and when done, grate sugar over them, and serve wine sauce in a boat. Garnish the dish with slices of orange.

Rice Fritters.

BOIL a quarter of a pound of rice in milk till it is pretty thick; then mix it with a pint of cream, four eggs, some sugar, cinnamon, and nutmeg, six ounces of currants washed and picked, a little salt, and as much flour as will make it a thick batter. Fry them in little cakes in boiling lard, and when done, send them up with white sugar and butter.

Chicken Fritters.

Put on a stew-pan with some new milk, and as much flour of rice as will be necessary to make it of a tolerable thickness. Beat three or four eggs, the yolks and whites together, and mix them well with the rice and milk. Add to them a pint of rich cream, set it over a stove, and stir it well. Put in some powdered ugar, some candied lemon-peel cut small, and some fresh-grated lemon-peel. Take all the white meat from a roasted chicken, pull it into small shreds, put it to the rest of the ingredients, and stir it all together. Then take it off, and it will be a very rich paste. Roll it out, cut it into small fritters, and fry them in boiling lard. Strew the bottom of the dish with sugar finely powdered. Put in the fritters, and shake some sugar over them.

Bilboquet Fritters.

Break five eggs into two handsful of fine flour, and put milk enough to make it work well together. Then put in some salt, and work it again. When it is well made, put in a tea-spoonful of powder of cinnamon, the same quantity of lemon-peel grated, and half an ounce of candied citron cut very small. Put on a stew-pan, rub it over with butter, and put in the paste. Set it over a very slow fire, and let it be done gently, without sticking to the bottom or sides of the pan. When it is in a manner baked, take it out, and lay it on a dish. Set on a stew-pan with a large quantity of lard; when it boils, cut the paste the size of a finger, and then cut it across at each end, which will rise and be hollow, and have a very good effect. Put them into the boiling lard; but great care must be taken in frying them, as they rise so much. When they are done, sift some sugar on a warm dish, lay on the fritters, and sift some more sugar over them.

Orange Fritters.

Take five or six sweet oranges, pare off the outside as thin as possible, and cut them in quarters; take out the seeds, and boil the oranges with a little sugar make a paste with some white wine, flour, a spoonful of fresh butter melted, and a little salt; mix it neither too thick nor too thin; it should rope in pouring from the spoon. Dip the quarters of your orange into this paste, and fry them in hog's lard till they are of a light brown. Serve them glazed with fine sugar and a salamander.

Strawberry Fritters.

MAKE a paste with some flour, a spoonful of brandy, a glass of white wine, and the whites of two eggs, beat it up stiff, with some lemon-peel shred fine; mix it well, not too thick or thin; dip some large strawberries into it, fry them, and glaze them with a salamander.

Any kind of fruit may be fried in the same manner; if not in season, preserved are better.

Strawberry Fritters.

MAKE a batter with flour, a spoonful of sweet oil, another of white wine, a little rasped lemon-peel, and the whites of two or three eggs; make it pretty soft, just fit to drop with a spoon. Mix some large strawberries with it, and drop them with a spoon into the hot fritters. When of a good colour take them out, and drain them on a sieve. When done, strew some sugar over them, or glaze them, and send them to table.

Raspberry Fritters.

GRATE the crumb of a French roll, or two Naples biscuits, and put to it a pint of boiling cream. When cold, add to it the yolks of four eggs well beat up.—Mix all well together with some raspberry juice; drop them into a pan of boiling lard in very small quantities. When done stick them with blanched almonds sliced.

Currant Fritters.

TAKE half a pint of ale that is not bitter, and stir into it as much flour as will make it pretty thick with a few currants. Beat it up quick, have the lard boiling, and put a large spoonful at a time into the pan.

German Fritters.

Take some well tasted crisp apples, pare, quarter, and core them; take the core quite out, and cut them into round pieces. Put into a stew-pan a quarter of a pint of French brandy, a table spoonful of fine sugar pounded, and a little cinnamon. Put the apples into this liquor, and set them over a gentle fire, stirring them often, but not to break them. Set on a stew-pan with some lard. When it boils drain the apples, dip them in some fine flour, and put them into the pan. Strew some sugar over the dish, and set it on the fire; lay in the fritters, strew a little sugar over them, and glaze them over with a red-hot salamander.

Almond Fraze.

Steep a pound of Jordan almonds blanched in a pint of cream, ten yolks of eggs, and four whites. Then take out the almonds, and pound them fine in a mortar; mix them again in the cream and eggs, and put in some sugar and grated white bread. Stir them all together, put some fresh butter into the pan, and as soon as it is hot, pour in the batter, stirring it in the pan till it is of a good thickness. When enough, turn it into a dish, and throw some sugar over it.

CHAPTER XVII

TARTS AND PUFFS.

WE have already given directions for making puff-paste for tarts, as also the making of Tarts as well as Pies, in the commencement of the fifteenth chapter. We have, therefore, here to treat only of those of a smaller and more delicate kind, concerning which the following general observations are necessary.

If you use tin patties to bake it, butter the bottoms, and then put on a very thin bit of crust, otherwise you will not be able to take them out; but if you bake them in glass or china, you need only use an upper crust. Put some fine sugar at the bottom, then lay in your fruit, strew more sugar at top, cover them, and bake them in a slack oven. Currants and rasp berries make an exceeding good tart, and require little baking.

Apples and pears intended for tarts must be managed thus: cut them into quarters, and take out the cores, then cut the quarters across, and put them into a saucepan, with as much water as will barely cover them, and let them simmer on a slow fire till the fruit is tender. Put a good piece of lemon-peel into the water with the fruit, and then have your patties ready. Lay fine sugar at bottom, then your fruit, and a little sugar at top. Pour over each tart one tea-spoonful of lemon-juice, and three of the liquor they were boiled in; then put on your lid, and bake them in a slack oven. Apricot tarts may be made in the same manner, only that you must not put in any lemon-juice.

Preserved fruit requires very little baking, and that which is very high preserved should not be baked at all. In this case, the crust should be first baked upon a tin the size of the intended tart; cut it with a marking iron, and when cold, take it off, and lay it on the fruit.

SECT. I.

DIFFERENT KINDS OF TARTS.

Raspberry Tart.

ROLL out some thin puff-paste, and lay it in a patty-pan; then put in some raspberries, and strew over them some very fine sugar. Put on the lid, and bake it. Then cut it open, and put in half a pint of cream, the yolks of two or three eggs well beaten, and a little sugar. Give it another heat in the oven, and it will be fit for use.

Green Almond Tarts.

GATHER some almonds off the tree before they

begin to shell, scrape off the down, and put them into a pan with some cold spring water. Then put them into a skillet with more spring water, set it on a slow fire, and let it remain till it just simmers. Change the water twice, and let them remain in the last till they begin to be tender. Then take them out, and dry them well in a cloth. Make a syrup with double refined sugar, put them into it, and let them simmer a short time. Do the same the next day, put them into a stone jar, and cover them very close, for if the least air comes to them, they will turn black. The yellower they are before they are taken out of the water, the greener they will be after they are done. Put them into your crust, cover them with syrup, lay on the lid, and bake them in a moderate oven.

Angelica Tarts.

PARE and core some golden pippins, or nonpareils; then the stalks of angelica, peel them, and cut them into small pieces; apples and angelica, of each an equal quantity. Boil the apples in just water enough to cover them, with lemon-peel, and fine sugar. Do them very gently till they become a thin syrup, and then strain it off. Put it on the fire with the angelica in it, and let it boil ten minutes. Make a puff-paste, lay it at the bottom of the tin, and then a layer of apples, and a layer of angelica, till it is full. Pour in some syrup, put on the lid, and send it to a very moderate oven.

Rhubarb Tarts.

TAKE the stalks of rhubarb that grow in a garden, peel them, and cut them into small pieces. Then do it in every respect the same as a gooseberry tart.

Spinach Tarts.

SCALD some spinach in boiling water, and then drain it quite dry. Chop it, and stew it in some butter and cream, with a very little salt, some sugar, some bits of citron, and very little orange-flower water

Put it into very fine puff-paste, and let it be baked in a moderate oven.

Petit Patties.

Make a short crust, and roll it thick; take a piece of veal, and an equal quantity of bacon and beef suet. Shred them all very fine, season them with pepper and salt, and a little sweet herbs. Put them into a stew-pan, and keep turning them about, with a few mushrooms chopped small, for eight or ten minutes. Then fill your patties, and cover them with crust. Colour them with the yolk of an egg, and bake them. These make a very pretty garnish, and give a handsome appearance to a large dish.

Orange Tarts.

Grate a little of the outside rind of a Seville orange; squeeze the juice of it into a dish, throw the peels into water, and change it often for four days.—Then set a saucepan of water on the fire, and when it boils put in the oranges; but mind to change the water twice to take out the bitterness. When they are tender, wipe them well, and beat them in a mortar till they are fine. Then take their weight in double-refined sugar, boil it into a syrup, and scum it very clean. Put in the pulp, and boil altogether till it is clear. Let it stand till cold, then put it into the tarts, and squeeze in the juice. Bake them in a quick oven.

Chocolate Tarts.

Rasp a quarter of a pound of chocolate, and a stick of cinnamon, and add to them some fresh lemon-peel grated, a little salt, and some sugar. Then take two spoonsful of fine flour, and the yolks of six eggs well beaten and mixed with some milk. Put all these into a stew-pan, and let them be a little time over the fire. Then take it off, put in a little lemon-peel cut small, and let it stand till it is cold. Beat up enough of the whites of eggs to cover it, and put it into puff-paste. When it is baked, sift some sugar over it, and glaze it with a salamander.

SECT. II.

PUFFS, &c.

Sugar Puffs.

BEAT up the whites of ten eggs till they rise to a high froth, and then put them into a marble mortar, with as much double-refined sugar as will make it thick. Then rub it well round the mortar, put in a few carraway seeds, and take a sheet of wafers, and lay it on as broad as a sixpence, and as high as you can. Put them into a moderately heated oven for about a quarter of an hour, and they will have a very white and delicate appearance.

Lemon Puffs.

TAKE a pound of double-refined sugar, bruise it, and sift it through a fine sieve. Put it into a bowl, with the juice of two lemons, and mix them together. Then beat the white of an egg to a very high froth, put it into your bowl, beat it half an hour, and then put in three eggs, with two rinds of lemons grated. Mix it well up, and throw sugar on your papers, drop on the puffs in small drops, and bake them in a moderately heated oven.

Almond Puffs.

TAKE two ounces of sweet almonds, blanch them, and beat them very fine with orange-flower water. Beat up the whites of three eggs to a very high froth, and then strew in a little sifted sugar. Mix your almonds with the sugar and eggs, and then add more sugar till it is as thick as paste. Lay it in cakes, and bake them in a slack oven on paper.

Chocolate Puffs.

BEAT and sift half a pound of double-refined sugar, scrape into it an ounce of chocolate very fine, and mix them together. Beat up the white of an egg to a very high froth, and strew into it your sugar and chocolate. Keep beating it till it is as thick as paste, then sugar your paper, drop them on about the size of a sixpence, and bake them in a very slow oven.

Curd Puffs.

PUT a little rennet into two quarts of milk, and when it is broken, put it into a coarse cloth to drain. Then rub the curd through a hair sieve, and put to it four ounces of butter, ten ounces of bread, half a nutmeg, a lemon-peel grated, and a spoonful of wine.—Sweeten with sugar to your taste, rub your cups with butter, and put them into the oven for about half an hour.

Wafers.

TAKE a spoonful of orange-flower water, two spoonsful of flour, two of sugar, and the same of milk. Beat them well together for half an hour; then make your wafer tongs hot, and pour a little of your batter in to cover your irons. Bake them on a stove fire, and as they are baking, roll them round a stick like a spigot. When they are cold, they will be very crisp, and are proper to be ate either with jellies or tea.

CHAPTER XVIII.

CHEESECAKES AND CUSTARDS.

SECT. I.

CHEESECAKES.

THE shorter time any cheesecakes are made, before put into the oven, the better; but more particularly almond or lemon cheesecakes, as standing long will make them grow oily, and give them a disagreeable appearance. Particular attention must likewise be paid to the heat of the oven, which must be moderate; for if it is too hot, they will be scorched, and consequently their beauty spoiled; and, if too slack, they will look black and heavy.

Common Cheesecakes.

Put a spoonful of rennet into a quart of new milk, and set it near the fire. When the milk is blood-warm, and broken, drain the curd through a coarse sieve. Now and then break the curd gently with your fingers, and rub into it a quarter of a pound of butter, the same quantity of sugar, a nutmeg, and two Naples biscuits grated; the yolks of four eggs, and the white of one, with an ounce of almonds well beaten with two spoonsful of rose-water, and the same of sack. Then clean and wash six ounces of currants, and put them into the curd. Mix all well together, fill your patty-pans, and send them to a moderate oven.

Fine Cheesecakes.

Put a pint of cream into a saucepan over the fire, and when it is warm, add to it five quarts of milk, immediately taken from the cow. Then put to it some rennet, give it a stir about, and when it is turned, put the curd into a linen cloth or bag. Let it drain well away from the whey, but do not squeeze it too much. Put it into a mortar, and pound it as fine as butter. Add to it half a pound of sweet-almonds blanched, and half a pound of macaroons, both beat exceeding fine, but if you have no macaroons, Naples biscuits will do. Then add the yolks of nine eggs well beaten up, a grated nutmeg, a little rose or orange-flower water, and half a pound of fine sugar. Mix all well together, and melt a pound and a quarter of butter, and stir it well in. Then make a puff-paste in this manner: take a pound of fine flour, wet it with cold water, roll it out, put into it by degrees a pound of fresh butter, and shake a little flour on each coat as you roll it. Then proceed to finish your business as before directed, and send them to the oven. For variety, when you make them of macaroons, put in as much tincture of saffron as will give them a high colour, but no currants. These may be called saffron cheesecakes.

Bread Cheesecakes.

SLICE a penny loaf as thin as possible, then pour on it a pint of boiling cream, and let it stand two hours. Then take eight eggs, half a pound of butter, and a nutmeg grated. Beat them well together, and mix them into the cream and bread, with half a pound of currants well washed and dried, and a spoonful of white wine or brandy. Bake them in patty-pans, or raised crust.

Rice Cheesecakes.

BOIL four ounces of rice till it is tender, and then put it into a sieve to drain. Mix with it four eggs well beaten up, half a pound of butter, half a pint of cream, six ounces of sugar, a nutmeg grated, and a glass of brandy or ratifia water. Beat them all well together, then put them into raised crusts, and bake them in a moderate oven.

Almond Cheesecakes.

TAKE four ounces of sweet almonds, blanch them, and put them into cold water; then beat them in a marble mortar, or wooden bowl, with some rose-water. Put to it four ounces of sugar, and the yolks of four eggs beat fine. Work it in the mortar, or bowl, till it becomes white and frothy, and then make a rich puff-paste as follows: take half a pound of flour, a quarter of a pound of butter, rub a little of the butter into the flour, mix it stiff with a little cold water, and then roll your paste straight out. Strew on a little flour, and lay over it, in thin bits, one third of your butter; throw a little more flour over the bottom, and do the like three different times. Then put the paste into your tins, fill them, grate sugar over them, and bake them in a gentle oven.

Or you may make Almond Cheesecakes thus:

TAKE four ounces of almonds, blanch them, and beat them with a little orange-flower water; add the yolks of eight eggs, the rind of a large lemon grated, half a pound of melted butter, and sugar to your taste; lay a thin puff-paste at the bottom of your tins, and little slips across. Add about half a dozen bitter almonds.

Lemon Cheesecakes.

Boil the peelings of two large lemons till they are tender; then pound them well in a mortar, with a quarter of a pound of loaf sugar, the yolks of six eggs, half a pound of fresh butter, and a little curd beat fine. Pound and mix all together, lay a puff-paste in your patty-pans, fill them half full, and bake them.

Orange cheesecakes must be done the same way; but you must boil the peel in two or three waters to deprive it of its bitter taste.

Citron Cheesecakes.

Beat the yolks of four eggs, and mix them with a quart of boiled cream. When it is cold, set it on the fire, and let it boil till it curds. Blanch some almonds, beat them with orange-flower water, and put them into cream with a few Naples biscuits, and green citron shred fine. Sweeten it to your taste, and bake them in cups.

SECT. II.

CUSTARDS.

In making of custards, the greatest care must be taken that your pan be well tinned; and always remember to put a spoonful of water into it, to prevent your ingredients sticking to the bottom.

Plain Custards.

Put a quart of good cream over a slow fire, with a little cinnamon, and four ounces of sugar. When it has boiled, take it off the fire, beat the yolks of eight eggs, and put to them a spoonful of orange-flower water, to prevent the cream from cracking. Stir them in by degrees as your cream cools, put the pan over a very slow fire, stir it carefully one way till it is almost boiling, and then pour it into cups.

Or you may make them in this manner:

TAKE a quart of new milk, sweeten to your taste, beat up well the yolks of eight eggs and the whites of four. Stir them into the milk, and bake it in china basins. Or put them into a china dish, and pour boiling water round them till the water is better than half way up their sides; but take care the water does not boil too fast, lest it should get into your cups, and spoil your custards.

Baked Custards.

BOIL a pint of cream with some mace and cinnamon, and when it is cold, take four yolks and two whites of eggs, a little rose and orange-flower water and sack, and nutmeg and sugar to your palate. Mix them well together, and bake it in cups.

Rice Custards.

PUT a blade of mace and a quartered nutmeg into a quart of cream; boil it, then strain it, and add to it some whole rice boiled, and a little brandy. Sweeten it to your palate, stir it over the fire till it thickens, and serve it up in cups, or a dish. It may be used either hot or cold.

Almond Custards.

TAKE a quarter of a pound of almonds, blanch and beat them very fine, and then put them into a pint of cream, with two spoonsful of rose-water. Sweeten it to your palate, beat up the yolks of four eggs very fine, and put it in. Stir all together one way over the fire till it is thick, and then pour it into cups.

Lemon Custards.

TAKE half a pound of double-refined sugar, the juice of two lemons, the rind of one pared very thin, the inner rind of one boiled tender, and rubbed through a sieve, and a pint of white wine. Let them boil for some time, then take out the peel, and a little of th liquor, and set it to cool. Pour the rest into the dish you intend for it, beat four yolks and two whites of eggs, and mix them with your cool liquor. Strain them into your dish, stir them well together, and set them on a slow fire in boiling water. When it is enough, grate the rind of a lemon on the top, and brown it over with a hot salamander. This may be eaten either hot or cold.

Orange Custards.

Boil very tender the rind of half a Seville orange, and then beat it in a mortar till it is very fine. Put to it a spoonful of the best brandy, the juice of a Seville orange, four ounces of loaf sugar, and the yolks of four eggs. Beat them all well together for ten minutes, and then pour in by degrees a pint of boiling cream. Keep beating them till they are cold, then put them in custard cups and set them in a dish of hot water. Let them stand till they are set, then take them out, and stick preserved orange on the top. These, like the former, may be served up either hot or cold.

CHAPTER XIX.

CAKES, BISCUITS, &c.

ONE very material matter to be attended to in making these articles is, that all your ingredients are ready at the time you are going to make them, and that you do not leave them till your business is done, but be particularly observant with respect to the eggs when beaten up, which, if left at any time, must be again beaten, and by that means your cake will not be so light as it otherwise would and ought to be. If you use butter to your cakes, be careful in beating it to a fine cream before you mix the sugar with it. Cakes made with rice. seeds, or plums, are best baked with wooden girths, as thereby the heat will penetrate into the middle, which will not be the case if baked in pots or tins. The heat of the oven must be proportioned to the size of the cake.

A Good Common Cake.

Take six ounces of ground rice, and the same quantity of flour, the yolks and whites of nine eggs, half a pound of lump sugar, pounded and sifted, and half an ounce of carraway seeds. Mix these well together, and bake it an hour in a quick oven.

A Rich Seed Cake.

Take a pound and a quarter of flour well dried, a pound of butter, a pound of loaf sugar, beat and sifted, eight eggs, two ounces of carraway seeds, one nutmeg grated, and its weight in cinnamon. First beat your butter to a cream, then put in your sugar; beat the whites of your eggs by themselves, and mix them with your butter and sugar, and then beat up the yolks and mix with the whites. Beat in your flour, spices, and seed, a little before you send it away. Bake it two hours in a quick oven.

A Pound Cake Plain.

Beat a pound of butter in an earthen pan, till it is like a fine thick cream, then beat in nine whole eggs till quite light. Put in a glass of brandy, a little lemon-peel shred fine; then work in a pound and a quarter of flour. Put it into your hoop or pan, and bake it for one hour.

A pound plum cake is made the same, with putting one pound and a half of clean washed currants, and half a pound of candied lemon or orange-peel.

Cream Cakes.

Beat the whites of nine eggs to a stiff froth, stir it gently with a spoon, lest the froth should fall, and to every white of an egg grate the rinds of two lemons. Shake in gently a spoonful of double-refined sugar sifted fine, lay a wet sheet of paper on a tin, and with a spoon drop the froth in little lumps on it, at a small distance from each other. Sift a good quantity of sugar over them, set them in the oven after the bread is out, and close up the mouth of it, which will occasion the froth to rise. As soon as they are coloured they will be sufficiently baked; then take them out, and put two bottoms together; lay them on a sieve, and set them to dry in a cool oven.

Wedding or Christening Cake.

TAKE three pounds and three quarters of butter, four pounds and a half of flour, three pounds of sugar, six pounds of currants, one pound and a half of candied lemon-peel, half a pound of almonds, half a pound of citron, thirty eggs, and a pint of brandy and milk. Beat your butter in a pan till it is like thick cream, but be sure not to make it too hot; then add your eggs by degrees, till they are quite light; then beat in half your flour, then put your milk and brandy in; grate the rinds of six lemons, and put in the rest of your flour, currants, candied lemon-peel, almonds, and half an ounce of spices, beat and sifted through a fine sieve, such as cloves, mace, nutmegs, cinnamon, and allspice; only put half an ounce of the whole in. If you bake the whole in one cake it will take three hours, but must not be baked too quick.

Rice Cakes.

BEAT the yolks of fifteen eggs for near half an hour with a whisk; then put to them ten ounces of loaf-sugar sifted fine, and mix them well together. Then put in half a pound of ground rice, a little orange-water or brandy, and the rinds of two lemons grated. Then put in the whites of seven eggs well beaten, and stir the whole together for a quarter of an hour. Put them in a hoop, and set them in a quick oven for half an hour, and they will be properly done.

Gingerbread Cakes.

Take three pounds of flour, a pound of sugar, the same quantity of butter rolled in very fine, two ounces of beaten ginger, and a large nutmeg grated. Then take a pound of treacle, a quarter of a pint of cream, and make them warm together. Work up the bread stiff, roll it out, and make it up into thin cakes. Cut them out with a tea-cup or small glass, or roll them round like nuts, and bake it in a slack oven on tin plates.

Bath Cakes or Buns.

TAKE half a pound of butter, and one pound of flour; rub the butter well into the flour; add five eggs, and a tea-cup full of yeast. Set the whole well mixed up before the fire to rise; when sufficiently rose, add a quarter of a pound of fine powder sugar, an ounce of carraways well mixed in, then roll them out in little cakes, and bake them on tins. They may either be eat for breakfast or tea.

Shrewsbury Cakes.

BEAT half a pound of butter to a fine cream, and put in the same weight of flour, one egg, six ounces of beaten and sifted loaf-sugar, and half an ounce of carraway seeds. Mix them with a paste, roll them thin, and cut them round with a small glass, or little tins; prick them, lay them on sheets of tin; and bake them in a slow oven.

Portugal Cakes.

MIX into a pound of fine flour a pound of loaf-sugar beat and sifted, and rub it into a pound of pure sweet butter till it is thick like grated white bread; then put to it two spoonsful of rose-water, two of sack, and ten eggs, and then work them well with a whisk, and put in eight ounces of currants. Butter the tin pans, fill them but half full, and bake them. If made without currants, they will keep half a year.

Saffron Cakes.

TAKE a quartern of fine flour, a pound and a half of butter, three ounces of carraway seeds, six eggs well beaten, a quarter of an ounce of cloves and mace fine beaten together, a little cinnamon pounded, a pound of sugar, a little rose-water and saffron, a pint and a half of yeast, and a quart of milk. Mix all together lightly in the following manner: first boil your milk and butter, then skim off the butter, and mix it with your flour, and a little of the milk. Stir the yeast into the rest, and strain it. Mix it with the flour, put in your seeds and spice, rose-water, tincture of saffron, sugar, and eggs Beat it all well up, and bake it in a hoop or pan well buttered. Send it to a quick oven, and an hour and a half will do it.

Prussian Cakes.

Take half a pound of dried flour, a pound of beaten and sifted sugar, the yolks and whites of seven eggs beaten separately, the juice of a lemon, the peels of two finely grated, and half a pound of almonds beat fine with rose-water. When you have beat the whites of the eggs to a froth, put in the yolks, and every thing else except the flour, and beat them well together. Shake in the flour just before you set it in the oven, and be particularly careful to beat the whites and yolks separately, otherwise your cake will be heavy, and very unpleasant.

Queen Cakes.

Take a pound of sugar, and beat and sift it; a pound of well dried flour, a pound of butter, eight eggs, and half a pound of currants washed and picked; grate a nutmeg, and the same quantity of mace and cinnamon. Work your butter to a cream, and put in your sugar; beat the whites of your eggs near half an hour, and mix them with your sugar and butter. Then beat your yolks near half an hour, and put them to your butter. Beat the whole well together, and when it is ready for the oven put in your flour, spices, and currants. Sift a little sugar over them, and bake them in tins.

Almond Cakes.

Take two ounces of butter, and one pound of sweet

almonds, blanched and beat, with a little rose or orange flower water, and the white of one egg; half a pound of sifted loaf sugar, eight yolks and three whites of eggs, the juice of half a lemon and the rind grated. Mix the whole well together, and either bake it in one large pan or several small ones.

Little Plum Cakes.

Take half a pound of sugar finely powdered, two pounds of flour well dried, four yolks and two whites of eggs, half a pound of butter washed with rose-water, six spoonsful of cream warmed, and a pound and a half of currants unwashed, but picked and rubbed very clean in a cloth. Mix all well together, then make them up into cakes, bake them in a hot oven, and let them stand half an hour till they are coloured on both sides. Then take down the oven lid, and let them stand to soak. You must rub the butter well into the flour, then the eggs and cream, and then the currants.

Ratifia Cakes.

First blanch, and then beat half a pound of sweet almonds, and the same quantity of bitter almonds in fine orange, rose, or ratifia water, to keep the almonds from oiling. Take a pound of fine sugar pounded and sifted, and mix it with your almonds. Have ready the whites of four eggs well beaten, and mix them lightly with the almonds and sugar. Put it into a preserving-pan, and set it over a moderate fire. Keep stirring it one way until it is pretty hot, and, when a little cool, form it in small rolls, and cut it into thin cakes. Dip your hands in flour, and shake them on them; give each a light tap with your finger, and put them on sugar papers. Sift a little sugar on them before you put them into the oven, which must be quite slack.

Apricot Cakes.

Take a pound of ripe apricots, scald and peel them, and, as soon as you find the skin will come off, take out the stones. Beat the fruit in a mortar to a pulp:

then boil half a pound of double-refined sugar, with a spoonful of water, skim it well, and put to it the pulp of your apricots. Let it simmer a quarter of an hour over a slow fire, and keep stirring it all the time. Then pour it into shallow flat glasses, turn them out upon glass plates, put them into a stove, and turn them once a day till they are dry.

Orange Cakes.

QUARTER what quantity you please of Seville oranges that have very good rinds, and boil them in two or three waters till they are tender, and the bitterness gone off. Skim them, and then lay them on a clean napkin to dry. Take all the skins and seeds out of the pulp with a knife, shred the peels fine, put them to the pulp, weigh them, and put rather more than their weight of fine sugar into a pan, with just as much water as will dissolve it. Boil it till it becomes a perfect sugar, and then by degrees, put in your orange-peels and pulp. Stir them well before you set them on the fire; boil it very gently till it looks clear and thick, and then put them into flat-bottomed glasses. Set them in a stove, and keep them in a constant and moderate heat; and when they are candied on the top, turn them out upon glasses.

Lemon Cakes.

TAKE the whites of ten eggs, put to them three spoonsful of rose or orange-flower water, and beat them an hour with a whisk. Then put in a pound of beaten and sifted sugar, and grate into it the rind of a lemon. When it is well mixed put in the juice of half a lemon, and the yolks of ten eggs beat smooth.—Just before you put it into the oven, stir in three quarters of a pound of flour, butter your pan, put it into a moderate oven, and an hour will bake it.

Currant Cakes.

DRY well before a fire a pound and a half of fine flour, take a pound of butter, half a pound of fine loaf sugar well beaten and sifted, four yolks of eggs, four spoonsful of rose-water, the same of sack, a little mace, and a nutmeg grated. Beat the eggs well, and put them to the rose-water and sack. Then put to it the sugar and butter. Work them all together, and then strew in the currants and flour, having taken care to have them ready warmed for mixing. You may make six or eight cakes of them; but mind to bake them of a fine brown, and pretty crisp

Whigs.

PUT half a pint of warm milk to three quarters of a pound of fine flour, and mix in it two or three spoonsful of light barm. Cover it up, and set it before the fire an hour, in order to make it rise. Work into the paste four ounces of sugar, and the same quantity of butter. Make it into cakes or whigs, with as little flour as possible, and a few seeds, and bake them in a quick oven.

Common Biscuits.

BEAT eight eggs well up together, and mix with them a pound of sifted sugar with the rind of a lemon grated. Whisk it about till it looks light, and then put in a pound of flour, with a little rose-water. Sugar them over, and bake them on tins, or on papers.

Sponge Biscuits.

Beat the yolks of twelve eggs for half an hour; then put in a pound and a half of sugar beat and sifted, and whisk it till you see it rise in bubbles. Then beat the whites to a strong froth, and whisk them well with your sugar and yolks. Work in fourteen ounces of flour, with the rinds of two lemons grated. Bake them in tin moulds buttered, and in a quick oven.—They will take about half an hour baking; but before you put them into the oven, remember to sift pounded sugar over them.

Spanish Biscuits.

TAKE the yolks of eight eggs, beat them half an hour, and then put to them eight spoonsful of sifted sugar. Then beat the whites to a strong froth, and work them well with the yolks and sugar. Put in four spoonsful of flour, and a little lemon-peel cut fine Mix all well together, and bake them on paper.

Drop Biscuits.

BEAT up the whites of six eggs, and the yolks of ten, with a spoonful of rose-water, and then put in ten ounces of beaten and sifted loaf sugar. Whisk them well for half an hour, and then add an ounce of carraway-seeds crushed a little, and six ounces of fine flour. Mix the whole well together, drop them on papers, and bake them in a moderately heated oven.

Lemon Biscuits.

TAKE the yolks of ten eggs, and the whites of five, and beat them well together, with four spoonsful of orange-flower water, till they froth up. Then put in a pound of loaf sugar sifted, beat it one way for half an hour or more, put in half a pound of flour, with the raspings of two lemons, and the pulp of a small one. Butter your tin, and bake it in a quick oven; but do not stop up the mouth at first, for fear it should scorch. Dust it with sugar before you put it into the oven.

Macaroons.

BLANCH and beat fine a pound of sweet almonds, and put to them a pound of sugar and a little rose-water, to keep them from oiling. Then beat the whites of seven eggs to a froth, put them in, and work the whole well together. Drop them on wafer-paper, grate sugar over them, and put them into the oven.

Green Caps.

HAVING gathered as many codlins as you want just before they are ripe, green them in the same man ner as for preserving. Then rub them over with a little oiled butter, grate double-refined sugar over them, and set them in the oven till they look bright, and sparkle like frost. Then take them out, and put them into a china dish. Make a very fine custard, and pour it round them. Stick single flowers in every apple, and serve them up.

Black Caps.

TAKE out the cores, and cut into halves twelve large apples. Place them on a tin patty-pan as close as they can lie, with the flat side downwards. Squeeze a lemon into two spoonsful of orange-flower water, and pour it over them. Shred some lemon-peel fine, and throw over them, and grate fine sugar over all. Set them in a quick oven, and half an hour will do them. When you send them to table, strew fine sugar all over the dish.

Snow Balls.

PARE and take out the cores of five large baking apples, and fill the holes with orange or quince marmalade. Then make some good hot paste, roll your apples in it, and make your crust of an equal thickness. Put them in a tin dripping-pan, bake them in a moderate oven, and when you take them out, make icing for them, directions for which you will find at the close of the second section in the next chapter. Let your icing be about a quarter of an inch thick, and set them at a good distance from the fire till they are hardened; but take care you do not let them brown. Put one in the middle of a dish, and the others round it.

CHAPTER XX.

THE ART OF CONFECTIONARY.

SECT. I.

THE METHOD OF PREPARING SUGARS AND COLOURS.

THE first process in the art of confectionary is that of *clarifying sugars*, which requires great care and attention, and must be done according to the following direction:

Break the white of an egg into your preserving-pan, put to it four quarts of water, and beat it up to a froth with a whisk. Then put in twelve pounds of sugar, mix all together, and set it over the fire. When it boils put in a little cold water, and in this manner proceed as many times as may be necessary, till the scum appears thick on the top. Then remove it from the fire, and when it is settled take off the scum, and pass it through a straining-bag. If the sugar should not appear very fine, give it another boil before you strain it.—This is the first operation, having done which you may proceed to clarify your sugar to either of the following degrees:

1. *Smooth or Candy Sugar.*—After having gone through the first process, as before directed, put what quantity you may have occasion for over the fire, and let it boil till it is smooth. This you may know by dipping your skimmer into the sugar, and then touching it between your fore-finger and thumb, and immediately on opening them, you will observe a small thread drawn between, which will immediately break, and remain on a drop on your thumb, which will be a sign of its being in some degree of smoothness. Then give it another boiling, and it will draw into a larger string, when it will have acq ired the first degree, from whence we proceed to,

2. *Bloom Sugar.*—In this degree of refining sugar, you must boil it longer than in the former process, and then dip your skimmer in, shaking off what sugar you can into the pan then blow with your mouth strongly through the holes, and if certain bladders, or bubbles, go through, it will be a proof that it has acquired the second degree

3. *Feathered Sugar.*—To prove this degree, dip the skimmer into the sugar when it has boiled longer than in the former degrees. When you have so done, first shake it over the pan, then give it a sudden flirt behind you, and if it is enough, the sugar will fly off like feathers.

4. *Crackled Sugar.*—Boil your sugar longer than in the preceding degree; then dip a stick into it, and immediately put it into a pan of cold water, which you must have by you for that purpose. Draw off the sugar that hangs to the stick into the water, and if it becomes hard, and snaps, it has acquired the proper degree; but if otherwise, you must boil it again till it answers that trial. Be particularly careful that the water you use for this purpose is perfectly cold, otherwise you will be greatly deceived.

5. *Carmel Sugars.*—To obtain the last degree, your sugar must boil longer than in either of the former operations. You must prove it by dipping a stick, first into the sugar, and then into cold water; but this you must observe, that when it comes to the carmel height, it will, the moment it touches the water, snap like glass, which is the highest and last degree of refining sugar. When you boil this, take care that your fire is not too fierce, lest it should, by flaming up the sides of the pan, cause the sugar to burn, discolour it, and thereby destroy all your labour.

Having thus described the various degrees of refining sugar, we shall now point out the method of preparing those colours with which they may be tinged, according to the fancy, and the different purposes for which they are to be used.

Red Colour.

To make this colour, boil an ounce of cochineal in half a pint of water, for above five minutes; then add half an ounce of cream of tartar, and half an ounce of pounded alum, and boil the whole on a slow fire about as long again. In order to know if it is done, dip a pen into it, write on white paper, and if it shows the colour clear, it is sufficient. Then take it off the fire, add two ounces of sugar, and let it settle. Pour it clear off, and keep it in a bottle well stopped for use.

Blue Colour.

This colour is only for present use, and must be made thus: put a little warm water into a plate, and rub an indigo stone in it till the colour is come to the tint you would have it. The more you rub it, the higher the colour will be.

Yellow Colour.

This is done by pouring a little water into a plate, and rubbing it with a bit of gamboge. It may also be done with yellow lily thus: take the heart of the flower, infuse the colour with milk-warm water, and preserve it in a bottle well stopped.

Green Colour.

Trim the leaves of some spinach, boil them about half a minute in a little water, then strain it clear off, and it will be fit for use.

Any alteration may be made in these colours, by mixing to what shade you think proper; but on these occasions taste and fancy must be your guide.

Devices in Sugar.

Steep gum-tragacanth in rose-water, and with some double-refined sugar make it into a paste. Colour it to your fancy, and make up your device in such forms as you may think proper. You may have moulds made in various shapes for this purpose, and your devices will be pretty ornaments placed on the top of iced cakes.

Sugar of Roses in various figures.

Chip off the white part of some rose-buds, and dry them in the sun. Pound an ounce of them very fine; then take a pound of loaf-sugar, wet it in some rose-water, and boil it to a candy height; then put in your powder of roses, and the juice of a lemon. Mix all well together, then put it on a pie-plate, and cut it into lozenges, or make it into any kind of shapes or figures your fancy may draw. If you want to use them as ornaments for a desert, you may gild or colour them to your taste.

SECT. II.

CREAMS *and* JAMS.

Orange Cream.

Pare off the rind of a Seville orange very fine, and then squeeze out the juice of four oranges. Put them into a stew-pan, with a pint of water, and eight ounces of sugar; mix with them the whites of five eggs well beat, and set the whole over the fire. Stir it one way till it becomes thick and white, then strain it through a gauze, and keep stirring it till it is cold. Then beat the yolks of five eggs very fine, and put it into your pan with some cream and the other articles. Stir it over a slow fire till it is ready to boil, and pour it into a basin, and having stirred it till it is quite cold, put it into your glasses.

Lemon Cream.

Cut off the rinds of two lemons as thin as you can, then squeeze out the juice of three, and add to them a pint of spring water. Mix with them the whites of six eggs beat very fine, sweeten it to your taste, and keep stirring it till it thickens, but be careful it does not boil. Strain it through a cloth, then mix with it the yolks of six eggs well beat up, and put it over the fire to thicken. Then pour it into a bowl, and when it is thoroughly cold, put it into your glasses.

Hartshorn Cream.

TAKE four ounces of the shavings of hartshorn, boil them in three pints of water till it is reduced to half a pint, and then run it through a jelly-bag. Put to it a pint of cream, and four ounces of fine sugar, and let it just boil up. Put it into jelly-glasses, let it stand till it is cold, and then, by dipping your glasses into scalding water, it will slip out whole. Then stick them all over with slices of almonds cut lengthways. It is generally eaten with white wine and sugar.

Burnt Cream.

TAKE a little clarified sugar, put it into your sugar-pan, and let it boil till it colours in the pan; then pour in your cream, stirring it all the time till the sugar is dissolved. The cream may be made in the following manner: to a pint of cream take five eggs, a quarter of a pound of fine sugar, and a spoonful of orange-flower water; set it over the fire, stirring it till it is thick; but be sure it does not boil, or else it will curdle.

Burnt Cream another Way.

BOIL a pint of cream with sugar and a little lemon-peel shred fine; and then beat up the yolks of six, and the whites of four eggs separately. When your cream has got cool, put in your eggs, with a spoonful of orange-flower water, and one of fine flour. Set it over the fire, keep stirring it till it is thick, and then pour it into a dish. When it is cold, sift a quarter of a pound of fine sugar all over it, and hold a hot salamander over it till it is of a nice light brown colour.

Blanched Cream.

TAKE a quart of very thick cream, and mix with it some fine sugar and orange-flower water. Boil it, and beat up the whites of twenty eggs, with a little cold cream; strain it, and when the cream is upon the boil, pour in the eggs, and keep stirring it till it comes to a thick curd. Then take it up, and strain it through a hair sieve; beat it well with a spoon till it is cold, and then put it into a dish.

Cream a-la Franchipane.

Put two spoonsful of flour into a stew-pan, with some grated lemon-peel, some dried orange-flowers shred fine, and a little salt; beat up the yolks and whites of six eggs, with a pint of milk, and a bit of sugar; make it boil, and stir it over the fire half an hour: when cold, use it to make a franchipane pie or tartlets, for which nothing more is necessary than to put it upon a puff-paste, and when it is cold glaze it with sugar. You may put in a few ratifia biscuits to give it a flavour.

Whipt Cream.

Take the whites of eight eggs, a quart of thick cream, and half a pint of sack. Mix them together, and sweeten it to your taste with double-refined sugar. You may perfume it, if you please, with a little musk or ambergris tied in a rag, and steeped a little in the cream. Whip it up with a whisk, and some lemon-peel tied in the middle of the whisk. Take the froth with a spoon, and lay it in your glasses or basins. This put over fine tarts has a pretty appearance.

Spanish Cream.

Take three spoonsful of flour of rice sifted very fine, the yolks of three eggs, three spoonsful of water, and two of orange-flower water. Then put to them one pint of cream, and set it upon a good fire; keep stirring it till it is of a proper thickness, and then pour it into cups.

Steeple Cream.

Take five ounces of hartshorn and two ounces of isinglass, and put them into a stone bottle; fill it up with fair water to the neck; put in a small quantity of gum-arabic and gum-dragon; then tie up the bottle very close, and set it into a pot of water, with hay at the bottom. When it has stood six hours, take it out, and let it stand an hour before you open it; then strain it, and it will be a strong jelly. Take a pound of blanched almonds, beat them very fine, mix it with a pint of thick cream, and let it stand a little; then strain it out, and mix it with a pound of je. y; set it over the fire till it is scalding hot, and sweeten it to your taste with double-refined sugar. Then take it off, put in a little amber, and pour it into small high gallipots. When it is cold, turn them, and lay cold cream about them in heaps. Be careful it does not boil when you put in the crean .

Barley Cream.

Take a small quantity of pearl barley, boil it in milk and water till it is tender, and then strain off the liquor. Put your barley into a quart of cream, and let it boil a little. Take the whites of five eggs, and the yolk of one, and beat them up with a spoonful of fine flour, and two spoonsful of orange-flower water. Then take the cream off the fire, mix in the eggs by degrees, and set it over the fire again to thicken. Sweeten it to your taste, and pour it into basins for use.

Pistachio Cream.

Take out the kernels of half a pound of pistachio nuts, and beat them in a mortar with a spoonful of brandy. Put them into a pan with a pint of good cream, and the yolks of two eggs beat fine. Stir it gently over the fire till it grows thick, and then put it into a china soup-plate. When it is cold, stick it over with small pieces of the nuts, and send it to table.

Tea Cream.

Boil a quarter of an ounce of fine hyson tea with half a pint of milk; then strain it, and put in half a pint of cream, and two spoonsful of rennet. Set it over some hot embers in the dish you intend to send to table, and cover it with a tin plate. When it is thick it will be done, and fit to serve up.

Coffee Cream.

Boil three ounces of coffee with a pint and a half of water, and when it has boiled up four or five times, let it settle, and pour it off clear. Put it into a stew-pan, with a pint of milk sweetened to your taste, and let it boil till there remains no more than sufficient for the size of your dish: beat up the yolks of six eggs with a little flour, and then add some cream; strain it through a sieve into your stew-pan, and thicken it over the fire. Serve it up, after passing a hot salamander, not too hot, over it.

Chocolate Cream.

TAKE a quarter of a pound of the best chocolate, and having scraped it fine, put to it as much water as will dissolve it. Then beat it half an hour in a mortar, and put in as much fine sugar as will sweeten it, and a pint and a half of cream. Mill it, and as the froth rises, lay it on a sieve. Put the remainder of your cream in posset-glasses, and lay the frothed cream upon them.

Chocolate Cream another Way.

SCRAPE two squares of chocolate, and put them into a stew-pan, with four ounces of sugar, a pint of milk, and half a pint of cream; let it boil till a third is consumed, and when nearly cold, beat up the yolks of seven eggs with it, and strain the whole through a sieve. Set your cream over the fire to thicken, but it must not boil.

Pompadour Cream.

BEAT the whites of five eggs to a strong froth, then put them into a pan, with two spoonsful of orange-flower water, and two ounces of sugar. Stir it gently for three or four minutes, then put it into your dish, and pour melted butter over it. This must be served up hot, and makes a pretty corner dish for a second course at dinner.

Ratifia Cream.

TAKE six large laurel leaves, and boil them in a quart of thick milk with a little ratifia, and when it has boiled throw away the leaves Beat the yolks of four eggs with a little cold cream, and sweeten it with sugar to your taste. Then thicken the cream with your eggs, and set it over the fire again, but do not let it boil. Keep stirring it all the time one way, and then pour it into china dishes. This must be served up cold.

Raspberry Cream.

Rub a quart of raspberries, or raspberry-jam, through a hair sieve, to take out the seeds, and then mix it well with cream. Sweeten it with sugar to your taste; then put it into a stone jug, and raise a froth with a chocolate mill. As your froth rises, take it off with a spoon, and lay it upon a hair sieve. When you have got as much froth as you want, put what cream remains into a deep china dish, or punch-bowl, pour your frothed cream upon it as high as it will lie on.

Ice Cream.

To a pound of preserved fruit, which may be of what kind you choose, add a quart of good cream, the juice of two lemons squeezed into it, and some sugar to your palate. Let the whole be rubbed through a fine hair sieve, and if raspberry, strawberry, or any red fruit, you must add a little cochineal to heighten the colour: have your freezing pot nice and clean, and put your cream into it, cover it, and put it into your tub with ice beat small, and some salt; turn the freezing pot quick, and as the cream sticks to the sides scrape it down with your ice spoon, and so on till it is froze. The more the cream is worked with the spoon the smoother and better flavoured it will be. After it is well froze, take it out, and put it into ice shapes with fresh salt and ice; when you serve it, carefully wash the shapes, for fear any salt should adhere to them; dip them in water luke-warm, and send them up to table.

Fruit Ices may be made either with water or cream If water, two pounds of fruit, a pint of spring water, a pint of clarified sugar, and the juice of two lemons.

Chocolate, coffee, ginger, vanilla, biscuit, and *noyeau*, are all custard ices, and must be set over the fire like set creams, and froze like the others when the custard is cold. Observe, no flour must be used in set creams for ices.

Raspberry Jam.

LET your raspberries be thoroughly ripe, and quite dry. Mash them fine, and strew them in their own weight of loaf-sugar, and half their weight of the juice of white currants. Boil them half an hour over a clear slow fire, skim them well, and put them into pots, or glasses. Tie them down with brandy papers, and keep them dry. Strew on the sugar as soon as you can after the berries are gathered, and in order to preserve their fine flavour, do not let them stand long before you boil them.

Strawberry Jam.

BRUISE very fine some scarlet strawberries gathered when quite ripe, and put to them a little juice of red currants. Beat and sift their weight in sugar, strew it over them, and put them into a preserving-pan. Set them over a clear slow fire, skim them, boil them twenty minutes, and then put them into glasses.

Apricot Jam.

GET some of the ripest apricots you can. Pare and cut them thin, and then infuse them in an earthen pan till tender and dry. To every pound and a half of apricots, put a pound of double-refined sugar, and three spoonsful of water. Boil your sugar to a candy height, and then put it upon your apricots. Stir them over a slow fire till they look clear and thick, but be careful they do not boil; then pour them into your glasses.

Gooseberry Jam.

CUT and pick out the seeds of fine large green gooseberries, gathered when they are full grown but not ripe. Put them into a pan of water, green them, and put them into a sieve to drain. Then beat them in a marble mortar, with their weight in sugar. Take a quart of gooseberries, boil them to a mash in a quart of water, squeeze them, and to every pint of liquor put a pound of fine loaf-sugar. Then boil and skim it, put in your green gooseberries, and having boiled them till they are very thick, clear, and of a pretty green, put them into glasses.

Black Currant Jam.

GATHER your currants when they are thoroughly ripe and dry, and pick them clean from the stalks. Then bruise them well in a bowl, and to every two pounds of currants, put a pound and a half of loaf-sugar finely beaten. Put them into a preserving-pan, boil them half an hour, skim and stir them all the time, and then put them into pots.

Icings for Cakes, or various Articles in Confectionary.

TAKE a pound of double-refined sugar pounded and sifted fine, and mix it with the whites of twenty-four eggs in an earthen pan. Whisk them well for two or three hours till it looks white and thick, and then, with a broad thin board, or bunch of feathers, spread it all over the tops and sides of the cake. Set it at a proper distance before a clear fire, and keep turning it continually, that it may not lose its colour; but a cool oven is best, where an hour will harden it.

Or you may make it thus:

BEAT the whites of three eggs to a strong froth: bruise a pound of Jordan almonds very fine with rose-water, and mix your almonds with the eggs lightly together. Then beat a pound of loaf-sugar very fine, and put it in by degrees. When your cake (or what ever article it may be) is enough, lay on your icing.

SECT. III.

JELLIES, SYLLABUBS, &c.

Calf's Feet Jelly.

BOIL two calf's feet well cleaned in a gallon of water till it is reduced to a quart, and then pour it into a pan. When it is cold, skim off all the fat, and take the jelly up clean. Leave what settling may remain at the bottom, and put the jelly into a saucepan, with a pint of mountain wine, half a pound of loaf-sugar and the juice of four lemons. Add to these the whites of six or eight eggs well beat up; stir all well together, put it on the fire, and let it boil a few minutes. Pour it into a large flannel bag, and repeat it till it runs clear; then have ready a large china basin, and put into it some lemon-peel cut as thin as possible. Let the jelly run into the basin, and the lemon-peel will not only give it a pleasing colour, but a grateful flavour. Fill your glasses, and it will be fit for use.

Hartshorn Jelly.

Boil half a pound of hartshorn in three quarts of water over a gentle fire, till it becomes a jelly. If you take out a little to cool, and it hangs on a spoon, it is enough. Strain it while it is hot, put it into a well-tinned saucepan, and add to it a pint of Rhenish wine, and a quarter of a pound of loaf-sugar. Beat the whites of four eggs or more to a froth, stir it altogether that the whites may mix well with the jelly, and pour it in as if you were cooling it. Let it boil two or three minutes, then put in the juice of three or four lemons, and let it boil a minute or two longer. When it is finely curdled, and of a pure white colour, have ready a swan-skin jelly-bag over a china basin, pour in your jelly, and pour it back again till it is as clear as rock-water; then set a very clean china basin under, have your glasses as clean as possible, and with a clean spoon fill them. Have ready some thin rind of lemons, and when you have filled half your glasses, throw your peel into the basin. When the jelly is all run out of the bag, with a clean spoon fill the rest of the glasses, and they will look of a fine amber colour. Put in lemon and sugar to your palate, but remember to make it pretty sweet, otherwise it will not be palatable. No fixed rule can be given for putting in the ingredients, which can only be regulated according to taste and fancy.

Orange Jelly.

TAKE three ounces of isinglass, and a quart of water, let it boil till the isinglass is all dissolved, then put in three quarters of a pound of fine sugar, the juice of four lemons, and twelve oranges if small, if large eight; let the rinds of six of the oranges be rubbed on some sugar, and scraped into your isinglass while boiling; when done, strain it through a fine lawn sieve; if you have any dried crocus flowers to boil in your jelly it will give it a fine yellow tinge, and leave no taste.

Fruit in Jelly.

PUT into a basin half a pint of clear calf's feet jelly, and when it is set and stiff, lay in three fine peaches, and a bunch of grapes with the stalk upwards. Put over them a few vine leaves, and then fill up your bowl with jelly. Let it stand till the next day, and then set your basin to the brim in hot water. When you perceive it gives way from the basin, lay your dish over it, turn your jelly carefully out, and serve it to table.

Blanc Mange.

THERE are various methods of making this jelly, but the best, and those most usually practised are three; the first of which is termed *green*, and is prepared from isinglass in the following manner:

Having dissolved your isinglass, put to it two ounces of sweet, and the same quantity of bitter almonds, with some of the juice of spinach to make it green, and a spoonful of French brandy. Set it over a stove fire in a saucepan, and let it remain till it is almost ready to boil; then strain it through a gauze sieve, and when it grows thick, put it into a melon mould, let lie till the next day, and then turn it out. You may garnish it with red and white flowers.

The second method of preparing this jelly is also from isinglass, and must be done thus: put into a quart of water an ounce of isinglass, and let it boil till it is reduced to a pint; then put in the whites of four eggs, with two spoonsful of rice water, and sweeten it to your taste. Run it through a jelly-bag, and then put to it two ounces of sweet and one-ounce of bitter almonds. Give them a scald in your jelly, and then run them through a hair sieve. Then put it into a china bowl, and the next day turn it out. Garnish with flowers or green leaves, and stick all over the top blanched almonds cut lengthways.

The third sort of blanc mange is called *clear*, and is prepared thus: skim off the fat, and strain a quart of strong calf's feet jelly. Then beat the whites of four eggs, and put them to your jelly. Set it over the fire, and keep stirring it till it boils. Then pour it into a jelly-bag, and run it through several times till it is clear. Beat an ounce of sweet and the same quantity of bitter almonds to a paste, with a spoonful of rose-water squeezed through a cloth. Then mix it with the jelly, and add to it three spoonsful of very good cream. Set it again over the fire, and keep stirring it till it almost boils. Pour it into a bowl, stir it very often till it is almost cold, then wet your moulds, and fill them.

Jaunmange.

TAKE three quarters of an ounce of isinglass and half a pint of water boiled together till the isinglass is just dissolved, then put in the rind and juice of a lemon, half a pint of mountain wine, and sugar to your palate; after it is all boiled together, let it stand till almost cold, then add four yolks of eggs. Put it again on the fire, till it almost boils, then strain it through a fine lawn sieve, and keep stirring it till cold.

Black Currant Jelly.

LET your currants be thoroughly ripe, and quite dry; strip them clear from the stalks, and put them into a large stew-pot. To every ten quarts of currants put one quart of water. Tie paper close over them, and set them for two hours in a cool oven. Then squeeze them through a very fine cloth, and to every quart of juice add a pound and a half of loaf-sugar broken into small pieces. Stir it gently till the sugar is melted, and when it boils, take off the scum quite clean. Let it boil pretty quick over a clear fire, till it jellies, which is known by dipping the skimmer into your jelly and holding it in the air; when it hangs to the spoon in a drop, it is done. You may also put some into a plate to try, and if there comes a thick skin, it is done. If the jelly is boiled too long it will lose its flavour, and shrink very much. Pour it into pots, cover them with brandy papers, and keep them in a dry place. Red and white jelly is made in the same manner.

Riband Jelly.

TAKE out the great bones of four calf's feet, and put the meat into a pot with ten quarts of water, three ounces of hartshorn, the same quantity of isinglass, a nutmeg quartered, and four blades of mace. Boil it till it comes to two quarts, then strain it through a flannel bag, and let it stand twenty-four hours. Then scrape off all the fat from the top very clean, slice the jelly, and put to it the whites of six eggs beaten to a froth. Boil it a little, and strain it through a flannel bag. Then run the jelly into little high glasses, and run every colour as thick as your finger; but observe, that one colour must be thoroughly cold before you put on another; and that which you put on must be blood-warm, otherwise they will mix together. You must colour red with cochineal, green with spinach, yellow with saffron, blue with syrup of violets, and white with thick cream.

Savoury Jelly.

TAKE some thin slices of lean veal and ham, and put them into a stew-pan, with a carrot or turnip, and two or three onions. Cover it, and let it sweat on a slow fire till it is of a deep brown colour. Then put to it a quart of very clear broth, some whole pepper, mace, a little isinglass, and salt to your palate. Boil it ten minutes, then strain it, skim off all the fat, and put to it the whites of three eggs. Then run it several times through a jelly-bag till it is perfectly clear and pour it into your glasses.

Common Syllabubs.

PUT a pint of cider and a bottle of strong beer into a large bowl, grate in a small nutmeg, and sweeten it to your taste. Then milk from the cow as much milk as will make a strong froth. Let it stand an hour, and then strew over it a few currants well washed, picked, and plumed before the fire; and it will be fit for use.

Whipt Syllabub.

RUB a lump of loaf sugar on the outside of a lemon, and put it into a pint of thick cream, and sweeten it to your taste. Then squeeze in the juice of a lemon, and add a glass of Madeira wine, or French brandy. Mill it to a froth with a chocolate-mill, take off the froth as it rises, and lay it in a hair sieve. Then fill one half of your glasses a little more than half full with white wine, and the other half of your glasses a little more than half full with red wine. Then lay your froth as high as you can, but take care that it is well drained on your sieve, otherwise it will mix with the wine, and your syllabub be spoiled.

Solid Syllabub.

To a quart of rich cream put a pint of white wine, the juice of two lemons, with the rind of one grated, and sweeten it to your taste. Whip it up well, and take off the froth as it rises. Put it upon a hair sieve, and let it stand in a cool place till the next day. Then half fill your glasses with the skim, and heap up the froth as high as you can. The bottom will look clear, and it will keep several days.

Lemon Syllabubs.

TAKE a quarter of a pound of loaf sugar, and rub upon the outer rinds of two lemons, till you have got all the essence out of them. Then put the sugar into a pint of cream, and the same quantity of white wine. Squeeze in the juice of both lemons, and let it stand for two hours. Then mill it with a chocolate-mill to raise the froth, and take it off with a spoon as it rises, or it will make it heavy, Lay it upon a hair sieve to drain, then fill your glasses with the remainder, and lay on the froth as high as you can. Let them stand all night, and they will be fit for use.

Everlasting Syllabubs.

TAKE half a pint of Rhenish wine, half a pint of sack, with the juice of two large Seville oranges, and put them into two pints and a half of thick cream. Grate in just the yellow rind of three lemons, and put in a pound of double-refined sugar well beaten and sifted. Mix all together with a spoonful of orange-flower water, and with a whisk beat it well together for half an hour. Then, with a spoon, take off the froth, lay it on a sieve to drain, and fill your glasses. These will keep better than a week, and should always be made a day before they are wanted. The best way to whip a syllabub is this: have a fine large chocolate-mill, which you must keep on purpose, and a large deep bowl to mill them in, as this way they will be done quicker, and the froth be the stronger. For the thin that is left at the bottom, have ready some calf's feet jelly boiled and clarified, in which must be nothing but the calf's feet boiled to a hard jelly. When it is cold, take off the fat, clear it with the whites of eggs, run it through a flannel bag, and mix it with the clear left of the syllabub. Sweeten it to your palate, give it a boil, and then pour it into basins, or such other vessels as you may think proper. When cold, turn it out, and it will be exceeding fine.

A Hedgehog.

TAKE two pounds of blanched almonds, and beat them well in a mortar, with a little canary and orange-flower water to keep them from oiling. Work them into a stiff paste, and then beat in the yolks of twelve, and the whites of seven eggs. Put to it a pint of cream, sweeten it to your taste, and set it on a clear fire. Keep it constantly stirring till it is thick enough to make into the form of an hedgehog. Then stick it full of blanched almonds, slit and stuck up like the bristles of a hedgehog, and then put it into a dish. Take a pint of cream, and the yolks of four eggs beat up, and sweeten it to your palate. Stir the whole together over a slow fire till it is quite hot, and then pour it into the dish round the hedgehog, and let it stand till it is cold, when its form will have a pleasing effect.

Flummery.

TAKE an ounce of bitter and the same quantity of sweet almonds, put them in a basin, and pour over them some boiling water to make the skins come off. Then strip off the skins, and throw the kernels into cold water; take them out, and beat them in a marble mortar, with a little rose-water to keep them from oiling; and when they are beat, put them into a pint of calf's feet stock: set it over the fire, and sweeten it to your taste with loaf sugar. As soon as it boils, strain it through a piece of muslin or gauze; and when it is a little cold, put it into a pint of cream, and keep stirring it often till it grows thick and cold. Wet your moulds in cold water, and pour in the flummery. Let them stand about six hours before you turn them out; and if you make your flummery stiff, and wet your moulds, it will turn out without putting them into warm water, which will be a great advantage to the look of the figures, as warm water gives a dulness to the flummery.

French Flummery.

PUT an ounce of isinglass beat very fine into a quart of cream, and mix them well together. Let it boil gently over a slow fire for a quarter of an hour, and keep it stirring all the time. Then take it off, sweeten it to your taste, and put in a spoonful of rose-water, and another of orange-flower water. Strain it, and pour it into a glass or basin, and when it is cold turn it out.

Green Melon in Flummery.

TAKE a little stiff flummery, and put into it some bitter almonds, with as much juice of spinach as will make it of a fine pale green. When it becomes as thick as good cream, wet your melon-mould, and put it in. Then put a pint of clear calf's feet jelly into a large basin, and let them stand all night. The next day turn out your melon, and lay it in the middle of your basin and jelly. Then fill up your basin with jelly that is beginning to set, and let it stand all night. The next morning turn it out in the same manner as directed for the *Fruit in Jelly*. See p. 245. For ornament, put on the top a garland of flowers.

Solomon,s Temple in Flummery.

TAKE a quart of stiff flummery, and divide it into three parts. Make one part a pretty thick colour with a little cochineal bruised fine, and steeped in French brandy. Scrape an ounce of chocolate very fine, dissolve it in a little strong coffee, and mix it with another part of your flummery, to make it a light stone colour. The last part must be white. Then wet your temple-mould, and fit it in a pot to stand even. Fill the top of the temple with red flummery for the steps, and the four points with white. Then fill it up with chocolate flummery, and let it stand till the next day. Then loosen it round with a pin, and shake it loose very gently; but do not dip your mould in warm water, as that will take off the gloss, and spoil the colour. When you turn it out, stick a small sprig of flowers down from the top of every point, which will not only strengthen it, but give it a pretty appearance. Lay round it rock candy sweetmeats.

SECT. IV.

PRESERVING FRUIT, &c.

SOME general rules are necessary to be observed in

this part of the Art of Confectionary, and which we shall previously notice as well for the instruction as reputation of those whose province it may be occasionally to use such articles. In the first place remember, that in making your syrups, the sugar is well pounded and dissolved before you set it on the fire, which will not only make the scum rise well, but cause the syrup to have its proper colour. When you preserve cherries, damsons, or any other kind of stone fruit, cover them with mutton-suet rendered, in order to keep out the air, which, if it penetrate, will totally destroy them. All wet sweetmeats must be kept in a dry and cool place, as they will be subject to grow mouldy and damp, and too much heat will destroy their virtue. Dip writing paper into brandy, lay it close to the sweetmeats, cover them quite tight with paper, and they will keep for any length of time without receiving the least injury. Without these precautions, all art and endeavours will prove ineffectual.

Apricots.

Gather your apricots before your stones become hard, put them into a pan of cold spring water with plenty of vine leaves; set them over a slow fire till they are quite yellow, then take them out, and rub them with a flannel and salt to take off the lint. Put them into the pan to the same water and leaves, cover them close, set them at a good distance from the fire till they are a fine light green, then take them carefully up, and pick out all the bad-coloured and broken ones. Boil the best gently two or three times in a thin syrup, and let them be quite cold each time before you boil them. When they look plump and clear, make a syrup of double-refined sugar, but not too thick; give your apricots a gentle boil in it, and then put them into your pots or glasses. Dip paper in brandy, lay it over them, tie it close, and keep them in a dry place for use.

Peaches.

Get the largest peaches you can, but do not let

them be too ripe. Rub off the lint with a cloth, and then run them down the seam with a pin skin deep, and cover them with French brandy. Tie a bladder over them, and let them stand a week. Then take them out, and make a strong syrup for them. Boil and skim it well, then put in your peaches, and boil them till they look clear; then take them out, and put them into pots or glasses. Mix the syrup with the brandy, and when it is cold, pour it on your peaches. Tie them so close down with a bladder, that no air can come to them, otherwise they will turn black, and be totally spoiled.

Quinces.

These may be preserved either whole or in quarters, and must be done thus: pare them very thin and round, put them into a saucepan, fill it with hard water, and lay the parings over the quinces to keep them down. Cover your saucepan close, that none of the steam may get out, set them over a slow fire till they are soft, and of a fine pink colour, and then let them stand till they are cold. Make a good syrup of double refined sugar, and boil, and skim it well; then put in your quinces, let them boil ten minutes, take them off, and let them stand two or three hours. Then boil them till the syrup looks thick, and the quinces clear. Put them into deep jars, with the syrup, and cover them close with brandy-paper and leather.

Barberries.

To preserve barberries for tarts, you must proceed thus: pick the female branches clean from the stalk; take their weight of loaf sugar, and put them into a jar. Set them in a kettle of boiling water till the sugar is melted, and the barberries quite soft, and then let them stand all night. The next day put them into a preserving pan, and boil them fifteen minutes, then put them into jars, tie them close, and set them by for use

If you intend to preserve your barberries in bunches you must proceed as follows: having procured the finest female barberries, select all the largest branches, and then pick the rest from the stalks. Put them in as much water as will make a syrup for your bunches. Boil them till they are soft, then strain them through a sieve, and to every pint of juice put a pound and a half of loaf sugar. Boil and skim it well, and to every pint of syrup put half a pound of barberries in bunches. Boil them till they look very fine and clear, then put them carefully into pots or glasses, and tie them close down with paper dipped in brandy.

Pine-Apples.

THESE must be taken before they are ripe, and laid in strong salt and water for five days. Then put into the bottom of a large saucepan a handful of vine-leaves, and put in your pine-apples. Fill your pan with vine-leaves, and then pour in the salt and water they were laid in. Cover it up very close, set them over a slow fire, and let them stand till they are of a fine light green. Have ready a thin syrup, made of a quart of water, and a pound of double-refined sugar. When it is almost cold, put it into a deep jar, and put in the pine-apples with their tops on. Let them stand a week, and take care they are well covered with the syrup. When they have stood a week, boil your syrup again, and pour it carefully into your jar, lest you break the tops of your pine-apples. Let it stand eight or ten weeks, and during that time give the syrup two or three boilings to keep it from moulding. Let your syrup stand till it is near cold before you put it on; and when your pine-apples look quite full and green, take them out of the syrup, and make a thick syrup of three pounds of double-refined sugar, with as much water as will dissolve it. Boil and skim it well, put a few slices of white ginger into it, and when it is nearly cold, pour it upon your pineapples. Tie them down close with a bladder, and they will keep many years without shrinking.

Grapes.

TAKE some close bunches (whether white or red is

immaterial) not too ripe, and lay them in a jar. Put to them a quarter of a pound of sugar-candy, and fill the jar with common brandy. Tie them up close with a bladder, and set them in a dry place.

Morello Cherries.

GATHER your cherries when they are full ripe, take off the stalks, and prick them with a pin. To every pound of cherries put a pound and a half of loaf-sugar. Beat part of your sugar, strew it over them, and let them stand all night. Dissolve the rest of your sugar in half a pint of the juice of currants, set it over a slow fire, and put in the cherries with the sugar, and give them a gentle scald. Then take them carefully out, boil your syrup till it is thick, pour it upon the cherries, and tie them down close.

Green Codlins, or other Fine Sauce Apples.

GATHER them when they are about the size of a large walnut, with the stalks and a leaf or two on them. Put a handful of vine leaves into a pan of spring water; then put a layer of codlins, then one of vine leaves, and so on till the pan is full. Cover it close to prevent the steam getting out, and set it on a slow fire. When you find them soft, take off the skins with a penknife, and then put them in the same water with the vine leaves, which must be quite cold, otherwise they will be apt to crack. Put in a little roach alum, and set them over a very slow fire till they are green, which will be in three or four hours. Then take them out, and lay them on a sieve to drain. Make a good syrup, and give them a gentle boil once a day for three days. Then put them into small jars, cover them close with brandy-paper, tie them down tight, and set them in a dry place. They will keep all the year.

Golden Pippins.

BOIL the rind of an orange very tender, and let it lay in water two or three days. Take a quart of golden pippins, pare, core, quarter, and boil them to a strong jelly, and run it through a jelly-bag. Then take twelve of the largest pippins, pare them, and scrape out the cores. Put a pint of water into a stew-pan, with two pounds of loaf sugar. When it boils, skim it, and put in your pippins, with the orange rind in thin slices. Let them boil fast till the sugar is very thick, and will almost candy. Then put a pint of the pippin-jelly, and boil them fast till the jelly is quite clear. Then squeeze in the juice of a lemon, give it a boil, and with the orange-peel, put them into pots or glasses, and cover them close.

Green Gage Plums.

Get the finest plums you can, gathered just before they are ripe. Put a layer of vine-leaves at the bottom of your pan, then a layer of plums, and then vine leaves and plums alternately, till the pan is nearly filled. Then put in as much water as it will hold, set it over a slow fire, and when the plums are hot, and begin to crack, take them off, and pare off the skins very carefully, putting them into a sieve, as you do them. Then lay them in the same water, with a layer of leaves between as you did at first, and cover them so close that no steam can get out. Hang them at a great distance from the fire till they are green, which will take at least five or six hours. Then take them carefully up, lay them on a hair sieve to drain, make a good syrup, and give them a gentle boil in it twice a day for two days. Then take them out, put them into a fine clear syrup, and cover them close down with brandy-paper.

Oranges.

Take what number of Seville oranges you think proper, cut a hole at the stalk end of each, about the size of a sixpence, and scoop out the pulp quite clean; tie them separately in pieces of muslin, and lay them in spring water for two days. Change the water twice every day, and then boil them in the muslin on a slow fire till they are quite tender. As the water wastes, put more hot water into the pan, and keep them covered. Weigh the oranges before you scoop them, and to every pound put two pounds of double-refined sugar, and a pint of water. Boil the sugar and water with the juice of the oranges to a syrup, skim it well, let it stand till it is cold, then take the oranges out of the muslin, put them into the pan, and let them boil half an hour. If they are not quite clear, boil them once a day for two or three days. Then pare and core some green pippins, and boil them till the water is strong of the apple; but do not stir them, and only put them down with the back of a spoon. Strain the water through a jelly-bag till it is quite clear, and then to every pint of water put a pound of double-refined sugar, and the juice of a lemon strained fine. Boil it up to a strong jelly, drain the oranges out of the syrup, and put them into glass jars, or pots the size of an orange, with the holes upwards. Pour the jelly over them, cover them with papers dipped in brandy, and tie them close down with a bladder. You may preserve lemons in the same manner.

Raspberries.

GATHER your raspberries on a dry day, when they are just turning red, with the stalks on about an inch long. Lay them singly on a dish, then beat and sift their weight of double-refined sugar, and strew it over them. To every quart of raspberries take a quart of red-currant juice, and put to it its weight of double-refined sugar. Boil and skim it well, then put in your raspberries, and give them a scald. Take them off, and let them stand for two hours. Then set them on again, and make them a little hotter. Proceed in this manner two or three times till they look clear; but do not let them boil, as that will make the stalks come off. When they are tolerably cool, put them in jelly-glasses with the stalks downwards. White raspberries must be preserved in the same manner, only observing, that instead of red you use white-currant juice.

Strawberries.

GATHER the finest scarlet strawberries you can, with the stalks on, before they are too ripe. Lay them separately on a china dish, then beat and sift twice their weight of double-refined sugar, and strew it over them. Take a few ripe scarlet strawberries, crush them, and put them into a jar, with their weight of double-refined sugar beat small. Cover them close, and let them stand in a kettle of boiling water till they are soft, and the syrup is extracted from them. Then strain them through a muslin rag into a preserving pan, boil and skim it well, and when it is cold, put in your whole strawberries, and set them over the fire till they are milk warm. Then take them off, and let them stand till they are quite cold. Set them on again, and make them a little hotter, and do so several times till they look clear; but do not let them boil, as that will bring off their stalks. When the strawberries are cold, put them into jelly-glasses, with the stalks downwards, and fill up your glasses with the syrup. Put over them papers dipped in brandy, and tie them down close.

Currants in Bunches.

STONE them, and tie six or seven bunches together with a thread to a piece of split deal about four inches long. Put them into the preserving-pan with their weight of double-refined sugar beaten and finely sifted, and let them stand all night. Then take some pippins, pare, core, and boil them, and press them down with the back of a spoon, but do not stir them. When the water is strong of the apple, add to it the juice of a lemon, and strain it through a jelly-bag till it runs quite clear. To every pint of your liquor put a pound of double-refined sugar, and boil it up to a strong jelly. Then put it to your currants, and boil them till they look clear. Cover them in the preserving-pan with paper till they are almost cold, and then put the bunches of currants into your glasses, and fill them up with jelly. When they are cold, wet papers in brandy and lay over them; then put over them another paper, and tie them up close. This method must be pursued with either white or red currants.

To preserve currants for tarts, you must proceed thus: to every pound of currants take a pound of sugar.

Put your sugar into a preserving-pan, with as much juice of currants as will dissolve it. When it boils, skim it, put in your currants, and boil them till they are clear. Put them into a jar, lay brandy-paper over them, and tie them down close.

Gooseberries.

Get the largest green gooseberries you can, and pick off the black eye, but not the stalk. Set them over the fire in a pot of water to scald, but do not let them boil, as that will spoil them. When they are tender, take them up, and put them into cold water. Then take a pound and a half of double-refined sugar to a pound of gooseberries, and clarify the sugar with water, a pint to a pound of sugar. When your syrup is cold, put the gooseberries singly into your preserving-pan, put the syrup to them, and set them on a gentle fire. Let them boil, but not so fast as to break them; and when they have boiled, and you perceive the sugar has entered them, take them off, cover them with white paper, and set them by all night. The next day take them out of the syrup, and boil the syrup till it begins to be ropy. Skim it, and put it to them again, set them on a slow fire, and let them simmer gently till you perceive the syrup will rope. Then take them off, set them by till they are cold, and cover them with brandy-paper.

If you preserve red gooseberries, you must proceed thus: put a pound of loaf-sugar into a preserving-pan, with as much water as will dissolve it, and boil and skim it well. Then put in a quart of rough red gooseberries, and let them boil a little. Set them by till the next day, and then boil them till they look clear, and the syrup is thick. Then put them into pots, or glasses, and cover them with brandy-paper.

Gooseberries in imitation of Hops.

Take the largest green walnut gooseberries you can get, and cut them at the stalk end into four quarters. Leave them whole at the blossom end, take out all the seeds, and put five or six one in another. Take a needleful of strong thread, with a large knot at the end; run the needle through the bunch of gooseberries, tie a knot to fasten them together, and they will resemble hops, put cold spring water into your pan, with a large handful of vine leaves at the bottom; then three or four layers of gooseberries, with plenty of vine leaves between every layer, and over the top of your pan. Cover it so that no steam can get out, and set them on a slow fire. Take them off as soon as they are scalding hot, and let them stand till they are cold. Put them into a sieve to drain, and make a thin syrup thus: to every pint of water put a pound of common loaf sugar, and boil it and skim it well. When it is about half cold, put in your gooseberries, let them stand till the next day, give them one boil a day for three days. Then make a syrup thus: to every pint of water put in a pound of fine sugar, a slice of ginger, and a lemon-peel cut lengthways very fine. Boil and skim it well, give your gooseberries a boil in it, and when they are cold, put them into glasses or pots, lay brandy-paper over them, and tie them up close

Damsons.

Put your damsons into a skillet over the fire, with as much water as will cover them. When they have boiled, and the liquor is pretty strong, strain it out, and add to every pound of damsons wiped clean, a pound of single-refined sugar. Put one third of your sugar into the liquor, set it over the fire, and when it simmers put in the damsons. Let them have one good boil, then take them off, and cover them up close for half an hour. Then set them on again, and let them simmer over the fire after turning them. Then take them out, put them into a basin, strew all the sugar that was left on them, and pour the hot liquor over them. Cover them up, let them stand till the next day, and then boil them up again till they are enough. Then take them up, and put them into pots; boil the liquor till it jellies, and when it is almost cold, pour it on them. Cover them with paper, tie them close, and set them in a dry place.

Walnuts

THERE are three different ways of preserving walnuts, namely, white, black, and green. To preserve them white, you must pare them till the white appears, and nothing else. As you do them, throw them into salt and water, and let them lie there till your sugar is ready. Take three pounds of good loaf sugar, put it into your preserving-pan, set it over a charcoal fire, and put as much water to it as will just wet the sugar Let it boil, and have ready ten or twelve whites of eggs strained, and beat up to a froth. Cover your sugar with the froth as it boils, and skim it. Then boil and skim it till it is as clear as crystal, and throw in your walnuts. Just give them a boil till they are tender, then take them out, and lay them in a dish to cool. When they are cold, put them into your preserving-pot, and pour the sugar as warm as milk over them. When they are quite cold tie them up.

In preserving walnuts black, you must proceed thus: take those of the smaller kind, put them into salt and water, and change the water every day for nine days. Then put them into a sieve, and let them stand in the air till they begin to turn black. Then put them into a jug, pour boiling water over them, and let them stand till the next day. Put them into a sieve to drain, stick a clove in each end of the walnuts, put them into a pan of boiling water, and let them boil five minutes. Then take them up, make a thin syrup, and scald them in it three or four times a day, till your walnuts are black and bright. Then make a thin syrup with a few cloves, and a little ginger cut in slices. Skim it well, pour in your walnuts, boil them five or six minutes, and then put them into jars. Lay brandy-paper over them, and tie them down close with a bladder. The longer they are kept, the better they will eat, as time takes off their bitterness

Green walnuts must be prepared by the following mode: wipe them very dry, and lay them in salt and water for twenty-four hours. Then take them out, and wipe them very clean. Have ready a skillet of boiling water, throw them in, let them boil a minute, and then take them out. Lay them on a coarse cloth, and boil your sugar as directed for the white walnuts. Then just give them a scald in the sugar, take them up, and lay them to cool. Put them into your preserving-pot, and proceed as directed for the preserving of white walnuts.

Cucumbers.

TAKE the greenest cucumbers, and the most free from seeds you can get; some small to preserve whole, and others large to cut into pieces. Put them into strong salt and water in a straight mouthed jar, with a cabbage-leaf to keep them down. Set them in a warm place till they are yellow, then wash them out, and set them over the fire in fresh water, with a little salt, and a fresh cabbage-leaf over them. Cover the pan very close, but take care they do not boil. If they are not of a fine green, change your water, and that will help them. Then cover them as before, and make them hot. When they become of a good green take them off the fire, and let them stand till they are cold. Then cut the large ones into quarters, take out the seed and soft part, then put them into cold water, and let them stand two days; but change the water twice every day to take out the salt. Take a pound of single-refined sugar, and half a pint of water; set it over the fire, and, when you have skimmed it clean, put in the rind of a lemon, and an ounce of ginger with the outside scraped off. When your syrup is pretty thick, take it off; and when cold wipe the cucumbers dry, and put them in. Boil the syrup once in two or three days for three weeks, and strengthen it if necessary. When you put the syrup to your cucumbers, be sure that it is quite cold. Cover them close, and set them in a dry place.

SECT. V.

DRYING *and* CANDYING.

BEFORE you proceed to dry and candy any kind of fruit, let it be first preserved, and so dried in a stove or before the fire, that all the syrup may be totally extracted. When you have boiled your sugar to the candy height, dip in the fruit, and lay them in dishes in your stove to dry; then put them into boxes, and keep them in a place where they cannot receive injury either from heat or damp

Dried Apricots

TAKE as many apricots as will amount to about a pound weight, pare and stone them, and then put them into a preserving-pan. Pound and sift half a pound of double-refined sugar, strew a little among them, and lay the rest over them. When they have been twenty-four hours in this state, turn them three or four times in the syrup, and then boil them pretty quick till they look clear. When they are cold, take them out, and lay them on glasses. Then put them into a stove, and turn them the first day every half hour, the second day every hour, and so on till they are perfectly dry. Put them into boxes covered, and set them by for use.

Dried Peaches.

PARE and stone some of the finest peaches you can get; then put them into a saucepan of boiling water, let them boil till they are tender, and then lay them on a sieve to drain. Put them again into the same saucepan, and cover them with their own weight in sugar. Let them lie two or three hours, and then boil them till they are clear, and the syrup pretty thick. Cover them close, and let them stand all night; scald them well, and then take them off to cool. When they are quite cold, set them on again till they are thoroughly hot, and continue this for three or four days. Then lay them on plates, and turn them every day til1 they are quite dry.

Candied Angelica.

CUT your angelica in lengths when young, cover it close, and boil it till it is tender. Then peel it, put it in again, and let it simmer and boil till it is green. Then take it up, dry it with a cloth, and to every pound of stalks put a pound of sugar. Put your stalks into an earthen pan, beat your sugar, strew it over them, and let them stand two days. Then boil it till it is clear and green, and put in a cullender to drain. Beat another pound of sugar to powder, and strew it over the angelica; then lay it on plates, and let it stand in a slack oven till it is thoroughly dry.

Green Gage Plums dried.

MAKE a thin syrup of half a pound of single-refined sugar, skim it well, slit a pound of plums down the seam, and put them into the syrup. Keep them scalding hot till they are tender, and take care they are well covered with syrup, or they will lose their colour. Let them stand all night, and then make a rich syrup thus: to a pound of double-refined sugar put two spoonsful of water, skim it well, and boil it almost to a candy. When it is cold, drain your plums out of the first syrup, and put them into the thick syrup; but be careful to let the syrup cover them. Set them on the fire to scald till they look clear, and then put them into a china bowl. When they have stood a week, then take them out, and lay them on china dishes. Then put them into a stove, and turn them once a day till they are dry.

Dried Cherries.

TAKE what quantity of morello cherries you think proper, stone them, and to every pound of cherries put a pound and a quarter of fine sugar; beat and sift it over your cherries, and let them stand all night. Then take them out of their sugar, and to every pound of sugar put two spoonsful of water. Boil and skim it well, and then put in your cherries. Let your sugar boil over them, the next morning strain them, and to every pound of syrup put half a pound more sugar.

Boil it till it is a little thicker, then put in your cherries, and let them boil gently. The next day strain them, put them into a stove, and turn them every day till they are dry.

Dried Damsons.

GATHER your damsons when they are full ripe, spread them on a coarse cloth, and set them in a very cool oven. Let them stand a day or two, and if they are not then properly dried, put them in for a day or two longer. Then take them out, lay them in a dry place, and they will eat like fresh plums, though even in the midst of winter.

Candied Cassia.

TAKE as much of the powder of brown cassia as will lie upon a half-crown, with as much musk and ambergris as you think proper. Pound them both well together. Then take a quarter of a pound of sugar, boil it to a candy height, put in your powder, and mix it well together. Pour it into saucers, which must be buttered very thin, and when cold, it will slip out.

Lemon and Orange Peels Candied.

CUT your lemons or oranges long-ways, take out all the pulp, and put the rinds into a pretty strong salt and hard water for six days. Then boil them in a large quantity of spring water till they are tender. Take them out, and lay them on a hair sieve to drain. Then make a thin syrup of fine loaf sugar, a pound to a quart of water. Put in your peels, and boil them half an hour, or till they look clear, and have ready a thick syrup, made of fine loaf sugar, with as much water as will dissolve it. Put in your peels, and boil them over a slow fire till you see the syrup candy about the pan and peels. Then take them out, and grate fine sugar all over them. Lay them on a hair sieve to drain, and set them in a stove, or before the fire to dry.

Candied Ginger.

TAKE an ounce of race ginger grated fine, a pound of loaf sugar beat fine, and put them into a preserving pan, with as much water as will dissolve the sugar. Stir them well together over a very slow fire till the sugar begins to boil. Then stir in another pound of sugar beat fine, and keep stirring it till it grows thick. Then take it off the fire, and drop it in cakes upon earthen dishes. Set them in a warm place to dry, and they will be hard and brittle, and look white.

Candied Horehound.

LET your horehound be boiled in water till the juice is quite extracted. Take your sugar, and boil it up to a feather, then add your juice to the sugar, and let it boil till it is again the same height. Stir it with a spoon against the sides of your sugar-pan, till it begins to grow thick, then pour it out into a paper case that is dusted with fine sugar, and cut it into squares. You may dry the horehound, and put it into the sugar finely powdered and sifted.

Candied Almond Cake, or Gateau Noga.

TAKE some fine powder sugar, put it into your stew-pan, and stir it over the fire till the sugar is nearly dissolved; have ready half a pound of almonds sliced and parched. Put them into the sugar you have over the fire, and keep stirring them well about till your almonds are a nice brown; take a jelly-mould or stew-pan, oil it well, and put your almonds into it; keep them well up to the sides, and when cold, you may turn it out to cover a burnt cream or boiled custard; or it may be served up just as it is. Sometimes they are ornamented like Savoy cakes, and look very handsome

Candied Rhubarb Cakes.

TAKE an ounce of rhubarb in powder, an ounce of fine powder-ginger, eighteen ounces of sugar, three drops of oil of peppermint; boil your sugar up to a feather, then mix all the ingredients, stirring them till it begins to grain. Have ready a square paper case, sugared with fine powder sugar: when cold, cut them in square pieces.

Compote of Crude Orange.

CUT the upper part of six sweet oranges in such a manner as to put them together as if they were whole. Pierce the pulps in several places with a little knife, and put in some fine powder sugar; then replace the pieces you have cut off, and serve them up in your desert.

Compote of Apples

TAKE a dozen of golden pippins, pare them nicely, and take the core out with a small penknife; put them into some water, and let them be well scalded; then take a little of the water with some sugar, and a few apples which may be sliced into it, and let the whole boil till it comes to a syrup: then pour it over your pippins, and garnish them with dried cherries and lemon-peel cut fine. You must take care that your pippins are not split.

Compote of Pears.

LET what quantity of pears you wish to be nicely scalded till soft, then take them out, pare them, and throw them into cold water to harden; take some sugar, cinnamon, red wine, and cloves, and put your pears into it; let them gently boil till a syrup: you may add some cochineal to give them a fine colour.

Compote of Quinces.

THESE may be cut in quarters and done in the same way as the apples, taking care that the quinces are done quite tender before you put them into the sugar. Let the syrup of all your compotes be thick before you dish them up.

Orange Chips.

GET some of the best Seville oranges you can, pare them at least about a quarter of an inch broad, and if you can keep the parings whole, they will have a pretty effect. When you have pared as many as you intend, put them into salt and spring water for a day or two; then boil them in a large quantity of spring water till they are tender, and drain them on a sieve. Have ready a thin syrup made of a quart of water, and a pound of sugar. Boil them a few at a time, to keep them from breaking till they look clear. Then put them into a syrup made of fine loaf sugar, with as much water as will dissolve it, and boil them to a candy height. When you take them up, lay them on a sieve, and grate double-refined sugar over them. Then put them in a stove, or before the fire to dry.

Orange Marmalade.

Get the clearest Seville oranges you can, cut them in two, take out all the pulp and juice into a basin, and pick all the skins and seeds out of it. Boil the rinds in hard water till they are tender, and change the water two or three times while they are boiling. Then pound them in a marble mortar, and add to it the juice and pulp. Then put them in the preserving-pan with double its weight of loaf sugar, and set it over a slow fire. Boil it rather more than half an hour, put it into pots, cover it with brandy-paper, and tie it close down.

Apricot Marmalade.

Apricots that are too ripe for keeping best answer this purpose. Boil them in syrup till they will mash, and then beat them in a marble mortar to a paste. Take half their weight of loaf sugar, and add just water enough to dissolve it. Boil and skim it till it looks clear, and the syrup like a fine jelly. Then put it into your sweetmeat glasses, and tie it up close.

Quince Marmalade

These must likewise be full ripe for the purpose of making marmalade. Pare them, and cut them into quarters; then take out the cores, and put the fruit into a saucepan. Cover them with the parings; nearly fill the saucepan with spring-water, cover it close, and let them stew over a slow fire till they are soft and of a pink colour. Then pick out the quinces from the parings, and beat them to a pulp in a marble mortar. Take their weight of fine loaf sugar, put as much water to it as will dissolve it, and boil and skim it well. Then put in your quinces, boil them gently three quarters of an hour, and keep stirring them all the time. When it is cold, put it into flat pots, tie it down close, and set it by for use.

Transparent Marmalade.

CUT very pale Seville oranges into quarters, take out the pulp, put it into a basin, and pick out the skins and seeds. Put the peels into a little salt and water, and let them stand all night. Then boil them in a good quantity of spring water till they are tender, cut them in very thin slices, and put them into the pulp. To every pound of marmalade put a pound and a half of double-refined sugar, finely beaten, and boil them together gently for twenty minutes; but if not clear and transparent in that time boil it five or six minutes longer. Keep stirring it gently all the time, and take care you do not break the slices. When it is cold, put it into jelly or sweetmeat glasses, and tie them down tight with brandy-paper and a bladder over them.

Burnt Almonds.

TAKE two pounds of almonds, and put them into a stew-pan, with the same quantity of sugar, and a pint of water. Set them over a clear coal fire, and let them boil till you find the almonds crack. Then take them off, and stir them about till they are quite dry. Put them in a wire sieve, and sift all the sugar from them. Put the sugar into the pan again with a little water, and give it a boil. Then pour four spoonsful of cochineal to the sugar to colour it, put the almonds into the pan, and keep stirring them over the fire till they are quite dry. Then put them into a large glass, and they will keep all the year.

Raspberry Paste.

MASH a quart of raspberries, strain one half, and put the juice to the other half. Boil them a quarter of an hour, put to them a pint of red currant juice, and let them boil all together till your raspberries are enough. Then put a pound and a half of double-refined sugar into a pan, with as much water as will dissolve it, and boil it to a sugar again. Put in your raspberries and juice, give them a scald, and pour it into glasses or plates. Then put them into a stove, and turn them at times till they are thoroughly dry.

Currant Paste.

CURRANT paste may be either red or white, according to the colour of the currants you use. Strip your currants, put a little juice to them to keep them from burning, boil them well, and rub them through a hair sieve. Then boil it a quarter of an hour, and to a pint of juice put a pound and a half of double-refined sugar pounded and sifted. Shake in your sugar, and when it is melted, pour it on plates. Dry it in the same manner as the raspberry paste, and turn it into any form you like best.

Gooseberry Paste.

TAKE some full grown red gooseberries, just on the turn for ripening, cut them in halves, and pick out all the seeds. Have ready a pint of currant juice, and boil your gooseberries in it till they are tender. Put a pound and a half of double-refined sugar into your pan, with as much water as will dissolve it, and boil it to sugar again. Then put all together, and make it scalding hot, but do not let it boil. Pour it into your plates or glasses, and dry it as before directed.

SECT. VI.

ORNAMENTS *in* CONFECTIONARY.

Artificial Fruit.

AT a proper time of the year, take care to save the stalks of the fruit, with the stones to them. Get some tins neatly made in the shape of the fruit you intend to imitate, leaving a hole at the top, to put in the stone and stalk. They must be so contrived as to open in the middle, to take out the fruit, and there must also be made a frame of wood to fix them in. Great care must be taken to make the tins very smooth in the inside, otherwise their roughness will mark the fruit; and that they be made exactly of the shape of the fruit that they are intended to represent. Being prepared with your tins, proceed thus: take two cow-heels, and a calf's foot, boil them in a gallon of soft water till they are all boiled to rags, and when you have a full quart of jelly, strain it through a sieve. Then put it into a saucepan, sweeten it, put in a lemon-peel perfumed, and colour it like the fruit you intend to imitate. Stir all together, give it a boil, and fill your tins: then put in the stones and the stalks just as the fruit grows, and when the jelly is quite cold, open your tins, and put on the bloom, which may be done by carefully dusting on powder-blue. Keep them covered to prevent the dust getting to them; and to the eye, art will be an excellent substitute for nature

A Dish of Snow

TAKE twelve large apples, and put them into a saucepan with cold water. Set them over a slow fire, and when they are soft, pour them into a hair sieve; take off the skins, and put the pulp into a basin. Then beat the whites of twelve eggs to a very strong froth; beat and sift half a pound of double-refined sugar, and strew it into the eggs. Work up the pulp of your apples to a strong froth, then beat them altogether till they are like a stiff snow. Lay it upon a china dish, and heap it up as high as you can. Set round it green knots of paste, in imitation of Chinese rails, and stick a sprig of myrtle in the middle of the dish.

Moonshine.

GET a piece of tin the shape of a half moon, as deep as a half pint basin, and one in the shape of a large star, and two or three lesser ones. Boil two calf's feet in a gallon of water till it comes to a quart, then strain it off, and when cold, skim off the fat. Take half the jelly, and sweeten it with sugar to your palate. Beat up the whites of four eggs, stir all together over a slow fire till it boils, and then run it through a flannel bag till clear. Put it in a clean saucepan, and take an ounce of sweet almonds, blanched, and beat very fine in a marble mortar, with two spoonsful of rose-water, and two of orange-flower water. Then strain it through a coarse cloth, mix it with the jelly, put in four spoonsful of thick cream, and stir it altogether till it boils. Then have ready the dish you intend it for, lay the tin in the shape of a half moon in the middle, and the stars round it. Lay little weights on the tins, to keep them in the place where you put them. Then pour the moonshine into the dish; and when it is quite cold, take out the tins. Then fill up the vacancies with clear calf's feet jelly. You may colour your moonshine with cochineal and chocolate, to make it look like the sky, and your moon and stars will then shine the brighter. Garnish it with rock candy sweetmeats.

Floating Island.

Take a soup-dish of a size proportioned to what you intend to make: but a deep glass set on a china dish will answer the purpose better. Take a quart of the thickest cream you can get, and make it pretty sweet with fine sugar. Pour in a gill of sack, grate in the yellow rind of a lemon, and mill the cream till it is of a thick froth: then carefully pour the thin from the froth into a dish. Cut a French roll, or as many as you want, as thin as you can, and put a layer of it as light as possible on the cream, then a layer of currant jelly, then a very thin layer of roll, then hartshorn jelly, then French roll, and over that whip your froth which you saved off the cream, well milled up, and lay it on the top as high as you can heap it. Ornament the rim of your dish with figures, fruits, or sweetmeats, as you please. This looks very pretty on the middle of a table, with candles round it; and you may make it of as many different colours as you fancy, according to what jellies, jams, or sweetmeats you have.

Desert Island.

TAKE a lump of paste and form it into a rock three inches broad at the top; then colour it, and set it in the middle of a deep china dish. Set a cast figure on it with a crown on its head, and a knot of rock candy at its feet: then make a roll of paste an inch thick, and stick it on the inner edge of the dish, two parts round. Cut eight pieces of eringo-roots, about three inches long, and fix them upright to the roll of paste on the edge. Make gravel walks of shot comfits round the dish, and set small figures in them. Roll out some paste, and cut it open like Chinese rails. Bake it, and fix it on either side of the gravel walks with gum, and form an entrance where the Chinese rails are, with two pieces of eringo-root for pillars.

Chinese Temple, or Obelisk.

TAKE an ounce of fine sugar, half an ounce of butter, and four ounces of fine flour. Boil the sugar and butter in a little water, and when it is cold, beat up an egg, and put it to the water, sugar, and butter. Mix it with the flour, and make it into a very stiff paste: then roll it as thin as possible, have a set of tins in the form of a temple, and put the paste upon them. Cut it in what form you please upon the separate parts of your tins, keeping them separate till baked; but take care to have the paste exactly the size of the tins. When you have cut all these parts, bake them in a slow oven, and when cold, take them out of the tins, and join the parts with strong isinglass and water with a camel's hair brush. Set them one upon the other, as the forms of the tin moulds will direct you. If you cut it neatly, and the paste is rolled very thin, it will be a beautiful corner for a large table. If you have obelisk moulds, you may make them the same way for an opposite corner. Be careful to make the pillars stronger than the top, that they may not be crushed by their weight

These ornamental decorations in confectionary are calculated to embellish grand entertainments, and it is certain they have all a very pleasing effect on the sight; out their beauties depend entirely on the abilities and ingenuity of the artist.

CHAPTER XXI.

PICKLING.

PICKLES are essentially necessary to be kept in all houses, but particularly such as contain large families; nor will the prudent and judicious housekeeper be without them; and this for two reasons; first, to avoid the inconvenience of sending for them when wanted; and secondly, from being assured that they are done as they ought to be, that is, that they shall have their proper colour without that artifice which is likely to be prejudicial to those who use them. It is too common a practice to make use of brass utensils in order to give the pickles a fine green; but this pernicious custom is easily avoided by heating the liquor, and keeping it in a proper degree of warmth before you pour it on the articles to be pickled. It is usual to put pickles into earthen jars, but stone jars are by far the best, for though they are more expensive in the first purchase, they will be found much cheaper in the end; the earthen vessels are porous, and will consequently admit the air, and spoil the pickles, especially if they stand any length of time; but this will not be the case with stone jars. Remember, that when you take any pickle out of your jars, be sure never to do it with your fingers, as that will spoil the pickle; but always make use of a spoon, which you should keep entirely for that purpose.

Having mentioned these necessary and general observations relative to pickling, we shall now proceed to particulars, beginning with

Mangoes.

THE proper cucumbers to be used for this purpose

are those of the largest sort, which must be taken from the vines before they are too ripe, or yellow at the ends. Cut a piece out of the side, and take out the seeds with an apple-scraper or a tea-spoon. Then put them into very strong salt and water for eight or nine days, or till they are yellow. Stir them well two or three times every day, and put them into a pan with a large quantity of vine leaves both over and under them. Beat a little roach alum very fine, and put it into the salt and water they came out of. Pour it on your cucumbers, and set them on a very slow fire for four or five hours till they are pretty green. Then take them out, and drain them in a hair sieve, and when they are cold, put to them a little horse-radish, then mustard-seed, two or three heads of garlic, a few pepper-corns, a few green cucumbers sliced in small pieces, then horse-radish, and the same as before-mentioned, till you have filled them. Then take the piece you cut out, and sew it on with a large needle and thread, and do all the rest in the same manner. Have ready the following pickle: to every gallon of vinegar put an ounce of mace, the same of cloves, two ounces of sliced ginger, the same of long pepper, Jamaica pepper, three ounces of mustard-seed tied up in a bag, four ounces of garlic, and a stick of horse-radish cut in slices. Boil them five minutes in the vinegar, then pour it upon your pickles, tie them down close, and keep them for use.

Girkins.

Put a quantity of spring water into a large earthen pan, and to every gallon put two pounds of salt. Mix them well together, and throw in five hundred girkins. When they have been two hours in the salt and water, take them out, and put them to drain; and when they are thoroughly dry, put them into your jar. Take a gallon of the best white wine vinegar, and put it in a saucepan, with half an ounce of cloves and mace, an ounce of allspice, the same quantity of mustard-seed, a stick of horse-radish cut in slices, six bay-leaves, two or three races of ginger, a nutmeg cut in pieces, and a handful of salt. Boil up all together, and pour it over the girkins. Cover them close down, and let them stand twenty-four hours. Then put them into your saucepan, and let them simmer over the fire till they are green; but be careful not to let them boil, as that will spoil them. Then put them into your jar, and cover them down close till they are cold. Then tie them over with a bladder and a piece of leather, and put them in a dry cold place.

Cucumbers.

For the purpose of pickling, choose the smallest cucumbers you can get, and be careful they are as free from spots as possible. Put them into strong salt and water for nine or ten days, or till they are quite yellow, and stir them twice a day, at least, or they will grow soft. When they are perfectly yellow, pour the water from them, and cover them with plenty of vine leaves. Set your water over the fire, and when it boils, pour it upon them, and set them upon the hearth to keep warm. When the water is nearly cold, make it boiling hot again, and pour it upon them. Proceed in this manner till you perceive they are of a fine green, which they will be in four or five times. Be careful to keep them well covered with vine leaves, with a cloth and dish over the top to keep in the steam, which will help to green them the sooner. When they are greened, put them into a hair sieve to drain, and then make the following pickle for them: to every two quarts of white wine vinegar, put half an ounce of mace, or ten or twelve cloves, an ounce of ginger cut into slices, the same of black pepper, and a handful of salt. Boil them all together for five minutes, pour it hot upon your pickles, and tie them down with a bladder for use.

Cucumbers in slices.

Take some large cucumbers before they are too ripe, slice them of the thickness of a crown-piece, and put them into a pewter dish. To every dozen of cu cumbers slice two large onions thin, and so on till you have filled your dish, or have got the quantity you intend to pickle; but remember to put a handful of salt between every row. Then cover them with another pewter dish, and let them stand twenty-four hours. Then put them into a cullender, and when they are thoroughly dry, put them into a jar, cover them over with white wine vinegar, and let them stand four hours. Pour the vinegar from them into a saucepan, and boil it with a little salt. Put to the cucumbers a little mace, a little whole pepper, a large race of ginger sliced, and then pour on them the boiling vinegar. Cover them close, and when they are cold, tie them down, and they will be ready for use in a few days.

To Keep Cucumbers.

CHOOSE those that are small, and not too old; put them in jars, and pour over a brine like the French beans; (see p. 281;) when you use them take the rind out, and dress them in the same manner as others.

Walnuts.

THERE are various methods of pickling walnuts, in order to have them of different colours, the number of which are four, namely, black, white, olive colour, and green; each of which we shall describe in their proper order.

To pickle walnuts *black*, you must gather them before the shells get too hard, which may be known by running a pin into them, and always gather them when the sun is hot upon them. Put them into strong salt and water for nine days, and stir them twice a day, observing to change the salt and water every three days. Then put them into a hair sieve, and let them stand in the air till they turn black. Put them into strong stone jars, and pour boiling vinegar over them; cover them up, and let them stand till they are cold. Then give the vinegar three more boilings, pour it each time on the walnuts, and let it stand till it is cold between every boiling. Then tie them down with paper and a bladder over them, and let them stand two months. When that time has elapsed, take them out of the vinegar, and make a pickle for them thus: to every two quarts of vinegar put half an ounce of mace. and the same of cloves; of black pepper, Jamaica pepper, long pepper, and ginger, an ounce each, and two ounces of common salt. Boil it ten minutes, then pour it hot on your walnuts, tie them close down, and cover them with paper and a bladder.

To pickle walnuts *white*, you must proceed thus. having procured a sufficient quantity of walnuts, of the largest size, and taken the before-mentioned precaution that the shells are not too hard, pare them very thin till the white appears, and throw them into spring water and a handful of salt as you do them. Let them lie in the water six hours, and put a thin board upon them to keep them under the water. Then set a stew-pan with some clean spring water on a charcoal fire. Take your nuts out of the water, put them into the stew-pan, and let them simmer four or five minutes, but be careful they do not boil. Then have ready a pan of spring water with a handful of salt in it, and stir it till the salt is melted; then take your nuts out of the stew-pan with a wooden ladle, or spoon, and put them into the cold water and salt. Let them stand a quarter of an hour, with the board lying on them to keep them down as before; for if they are not kept under the liquor they will turn black. Then lay them on a cloth, and put them into your jar, with some blades of mace and nutmeg sliced thin. Mix your spice between your nuts, and pour distilled vinegar over them. When your jar is properly filled with nuts, pour mutton fat over them, tie them down close with a bladder and leather, and set them in a dry place.

Walnuts to be pickled of an *olive colour*, must be managed thus: having gathered your walnuts, with the same precautions as before directed, put them into strong ale allegar, and tie them down under a bladder and paper to keep out the air. Let them stand twelve months, then take them out of the allegar, and make for them a pickle of strong allegar. To every quart, put half an ounce of Jamaica pepper, the same of long pepper, a quarter of an ounce of mace, the same of cloves, a head of garlic, and a little salt. Boil them altogether five or six minutes, and then pour it upon your walnuts. As it gets cold, boil it again three times, and pour it on them. Then tie them down with a bladder, and paper over it; and if your allegar is good, they will keep several years, without either turning colour or growing soft. You may make very good catsup of the allegar that comes from the walnuts, by adding a pound of anchovies, an ounce of cloves, the same of long and black pepper, a head of garlic, and half a pound of common salt, to every gallon of allegar. Boil it till it is half reduced, and skim it well. Then bottle it for use, and it will keep a great while.

To pickle walnuts *green*, proceed as follows: make use of the large double or French walnuts, gathered before the shells are hard. Wrap them singly in vine leaves, put a few vine leaves in the bottom of your jar, and nearly fill it with your walnuts. Take care they do not touch one another, and put a good many leaves over them. Then fill your jar with good allegar, cover them close that the air cannot get in, and let them stand for three weeks. Then pour the allegar from them, put fresh leaves at the bottom of another jar, take out your walnuts, and wrap them separately in fresh leaves as quick as possibly you can. Put them into your jar with a good many leaves over them, and fill it with white wine vinegar. Let them stand three weeks, pour off your vinegar, and wrap them up as before, with fresh leaves at the bottom and top of your jar. Take fresh white wine vinegar, put salt in it till it will bear an egg, and add to it mace, cloves, nutmeg, and garlic. Boil it about eight minutes, and then pour it on your walnuts. Tie them close with a paper and a bladder, and set them by for use. Be careful to keep them covered, and when you take any out for use, if the whole should not be wanted, do not put those left again into the jar, for by that means the whole may be spoiled.

Red Cabbage.

SLICE your cabbage crossways, then put it on an earthen dish, and sprinkle a handful of salt over it. Cover it with another dish, and let it stand twenty-four hours. Then put it into a cullender to drain, and lay it into your jar. Take a sufficient quantity of white wine vinegar to cover it, a few cloves, a little mace, and allspice. Put them in whole, with a little cochineal bruised fine. Then boil it up, and pour it either hot or cold upon your cabbage. If the former, let it stand till cold, and then tie it down for use.

Onions.

TAKE a sufficient number of the smallest onions you can get, and put them into salt and water for nine days, observing to change the water every day. Then put them into jars, and pour fresh boiling salt and water over them. Let them stand close covered till they are cold, then make some more salt and water, and pour it boiling hot upon them. When it is cold, put your onions into a hair sieve to drain, then put them into wide-mouthed bottles, and fill them up with distilled vinegar. Put into every bottle a slice or two of ginger, a blade of mace, a tea-spoonful of sweet oil, (which will keep the onions white,) a bay-leaf, and as much salt as will lay on a sixpence. Cork them well up, so that no air can get to them, and set them in a dry place.

Samphire.

TAKE what quantity of green samphire you think proper, put it into a clean pan, throw over it two or three handsful of salt, and cover it with spring water. When it has lain twenty-four hours, put it into a clean saucepan, throw in a handful of salt, and cover it with good vinegar. Cover the pan close, set it over a slow fire, let it stand till it is just green and crisp, and then take it off at that moment; for should it remain till it is soft, it will be totally spoiled. Put it into your pickling-pot, and cover it close. When it is quite cold tie it down with a bladder and leather, and set it by for use. Samphire may be preserved all the year by keeping it in very strong brine of salt and water, and just before you want to use it, put it for a few minutes into some of the best vinegar.

Kidney Beans.

TAKE some young small beans, and put them into strong salt and water for three days, stirring them two or three times each day. Then put them into a pan with vine leaves both under and over them, and pour on them the same water they came out of. Cover them close, and set them over a very slow fire till they are of a fine green. Then put them into a hair sieve to drain, and make a pickle for them of white wine vinegar, or fine ale allegar. Boil it five or six minutes with a little mace, Jamaica pepper, and a race or two of ginger sliced. Then pour it hot upon the beans, and tie them down with a bladder and paper.

To preserve French Beans.

TAKE any quantity of French beans you think fit, choosing those that are tender and least stringy; having cut off the ends, boil them a quarter of an hour, and shift them into cold water; then dry them, and put them into the jars in which you mean to keep them. Pour over your brine till it rises to the rim of the jar, then put over some butter that has been heated and is half cold, which will congeal upon the French beans, and keep them from the air. If you do not like to put butter you must put mutton suet in the same way. To make the brine, you must take two thirds water and one of vinegar; add several pounds according to the quantity of brine you would make, a pound to three pints. Set it over the fire till the salt is melted; let it settle, and before you use it pour it off clear.

Barberries.

TAKE a quantity of barberries not over ripe, pick off the leaves and dead stalks, and put them into jars, with a large quantity of strong salt and water, and tie them down with a bladder. When you see a scum rise on the barberries, put them into fresh salt and water; but they need no vinegar, their own natural sharpness being fully sufficient to preserve them. Cover them close, and set them by for use.

Beet Roots.

Boil the roots till they are tender, and take off the skins, cut them in slices, gimp them in the shape of wheels, or what other form you please, and put them into a jar. Take as much vinegar as you think will cover them, and boil it with a little mace, a race of ginger sliced, and a few small pieces of horse-radish. Pour it hot upon the roots, and tie them down close.

Radish Pods.

Gather your radish pods when they are quite young, and put them into salt and water all night; the next day boil the salt and water they were laid in, pour it upon the pods, and cover your jar close to keep in the steam. When it is nearly cold, make it boiling hot, and pour it on again, and continue doing so till the pods are quite green. Then put them into a sieve to drain, and make a pickle for them of white wine vinegar, with a little mace, ginger, long pepper, and horse-radish. Pour it boiling hot upon your pods, and when it is almost cold, make your vinegar twice as hot as before, and pour it upon them. Tie them down with a bladder, and set them in a dry place.

Cauliflowers.

Take the whitest and closest cauliflowers you can get, break the flowers into bunches, and spread them on an earthen dish. Lay salt all over them, and let them stand for three days to draw out all the water. Then put them into jars, and pour boiling salt and water upon them. Let them stand all night, then drain them in a hair sieve, and put them into glass jars. Fill up your jars with distilled vinegar, and tie them close down.

Artichoke Bottoms.

Boil your artichokes till you can pull off all the leaves, and thoroughly clear the bottoms. Put them into salt and water for an hour, then take them out, and lay them on a cloth to drain. When they are dry, put them into large wide-mouthed glasses, with a little mace and sliced nutmeg between, and fill them with distilled vinegar. Cover them with mutton fat melted, and tie them down with leather and a bladder.

To preserve Artichokes.

They may be quartered, the chokes taken out, and done exactly the same as the French beans.

Nasturtiums.

The most proper time for gathering the berries is soon after the blossoms are gone off. Put them into cold salt and water, and change the water for three days successively. Make your pickle of white wine vinegar, mace, nutmeg sliced, shalots, pepper-corns, salt, and horse-radish. Make your pickle pretty strong, but do not boil it. When you have drained your berries, put them into a jar, pour the pickle to them, and tie them down close.

Mushrooms.

Take the smallest mushrooms you can get, put them into spring water, and rub them with a piece of new flannel dipped in salt. Throw them into cold water as you do them, which will make them keep their colour; then put them into a saucepan, and throw a handful of salt over them. Cover them close, and set them over the fire four or five minutes, or till you find they are thoroughly hot, and the liquor is drawn out from them. Then lay them between two clean cloths till they are cold, put them into glass bottles, and fill them up with distilled vinegar. Put a blade or two of mace and a tea-spoonful of sweet oil into every bottle. Cork them up close, and set them in a cool place. If you have not any distilled vinegar, you may use white wine vinegar, or ale allegar will do; bu must be boiled with a little mace, salt, and a few slices of ginger; and it must stand till it is cold before you pour it on your mushrooms.

Mushroom Catsup.

TAKE a quantity of the full grown flaps of mushrooms, crush them well with your hands, and then strew a quantity of salt all over them. Let them stand all night, and the next day put them into stew-pans. Set them in a quick oven for twelve hours, and then strain them through a hair sieve. To every gallon of liquor put of cloves, Jamaica and black pepper, and ginger, one ounce each, and half a pound of common salt. Set it on a slow fire, and let it boil till half the liquor is wasted away. Then put it into a clean pot, and when it is quite cold, bottle it for use.

Mushroom Powder.

GET the largest and the thickest buttons you can peel them, and cut off the root end, but do not wash them. Spread them separately on pewter dishes, and set them in a slow oven to dry. Let the liquor dry up into the mushrooms, as that will make the powder much stronger, and let them continue in the oven till you find they will powder. Then beat them in a marble mortar, and sift them through a fine sieve, with a little chyan pepper and pounded mace. Bottle it quite clear, and keep it in a dry place.

Walnut Catsup.

Put what quantity of walnuts you think proper into jars, cover them with strong cold ale allegar, and tie them close for twelve months. Then take out the walnuts from the allegar, and to every gallon of the liquor put two heads of garlic, half a pound of anchovies, a quart of red wine, and of mace, cloves, long, black, and Jamaica pepper, and ginger, an ounce each. Boil them all together till the liquor is reduced to half the quantity, and the next day bottle it for use.

Another Method of making Walnut Catsup.

TAKE green walnuts before the shell is formed, and grind them in a crab-mill, or pound them in a marble mortar. Squeeze out the juice through a coarse cloth, and put to every gallon of juice a pound of anchovies, the same quantity of bay-salt, four ounces of Jamaica pepper, two of long and two of black pepper; of mace, cloves, and ginger, each an ounce, and a stick of horse-radish. Boil all together till reduced to half the quantity, and then put it into a pot. When it is cold, bottle it close, and in three months it will be fit for use.

Indian Pickle, or Picalillo.

TAKE a cauliflower, a white cabbage, a few small cucumbers, radish-pods, kidney-beans, and a little beet-root, or any other thing commonly pickled. Put them into a hair sieve; and throw a large handful of salt over them. Set them in the sun or before the fire, for three days to dry. When all the water is run out of them, put them into a large earthen pot in layers, and between every layer put a handful of brown mustard-seed. Then take as much ale allegar as you think will cover it, and to every four quarts of allegar put an ounce of turmeric. Boil them together, and put it hot upon your pickle. Let it stand twelve days upon the hearth, or till the pickles are of a bright yellow colour, and most of the allegar sucked up. Then take two quarts of strong ale allegar, an ounce of mace, the same of white pepper, a quarter of an ounce of cloves, and the same of long pepper and nutmeg. Beat them all together, and boil them ten minutes in the allegar. Then pour it upon your pickles, with four ounces of peeled garlic. Tie it close down, and set it by for use.

Asparagus.

GET the largest asparagus you can, cut off the white ends, and wash the green ends in spring water. Then put them into a pan of clean water, and let them lie in it two or three hours. Put as much spring water into a stew-pan as will nearly fill it, and throw in a large handful of salt. Set it on the fire, and when it boils put in your grass, not tied up, but loose, and not too many at a time, lest you break the heads. Just scald them, and no more; then take them out with a broad skimmer, and lay them on a cloth to cool. Make your pickle with a gallon or more (according to the quantity of your asparagus) of white wine vinegar, and an ounce of bay salt. Boil it, and put your asparagus into your jar. To a gallon of pickle put two nutmegs, a quarter of an ounce of mace, and the same quantity of whole white pepper. Pour the pickle hot over the asparagus, and cover them with a linen cloth three or four times double; and when they have stood a week, boil the pickle again. Let them stand a week longer, then boil the pickle again, and put it on hot as before. When they are cold, cover them close, tie them tight down, and keep them in a dry place.

Parsley pickled Green.

MAKE a strong salt and water that will bear an egg, and throw into it a large quantity of curled parsley. Let it stand a week, then take it out to drain, make a fresh salt and water as before, and let it stand another week. Then drain it well, put it into spring water, and change it three days successively. Then scald it in hard water till it becomes green, take it out, and drain it quite dry. Boil a quart of distilled vinegar a few minutes, with two or three blades of mace, a nutmeg sliced, and a shalot or two. When it is quite cold, pour it on your parsley, with two or three slices of horse-radish, and keep it for use.

Peaches.

GATHER your peaches when they are at the full growth, and just before the time of their turning ripe; and be sure they are not bruised. Take as much spring water as you think will cover them, and make it salt enough to bear an egg, for which purpose you must use an equal quantity of bay and common salt. Then lay in your peaches, and put a thin board over them to keep them under the water. When they have been three days in this state, take them out, wipe them very carefully with a fine soft cloth, and lay them in your jar. Then take as much white wine vinegar as will fill your jar, and to every gallon put one pint of the best well made mustard, two or three heads of garlic, a good deal of ginger sliced, and half an ounce of cloves, mace, and nutmegs. Mix your pickle well together, and pour it over your peaches. Tie them up close, and in two months they wi.. be fit for use.

Nectarines and apricots must be pickled in the same manner.

Golden Pippins.

Take a number of the finest pippins you can procure, free from spots and bruises, put them into a preserving-pan with cold spring water, and set them on a charcoal fire. Keep stirring them with a wooden spoon till they will peel, but do not let them boil. When you have peeled them, put them into the water again, with a quarter of a pint of the best vinegar, and a quarter of an ounce of alum. Cover them close with a pewter dish, and set them on a charcoal fire again, but do not let them boil. Keep turning them now and then till they look green, then take them out, and lay them on a cloth to cool. When they are quite cold, put to them the following pickle: to every gallon of vinegar put two ounces of mustard-seed, two or three heads of garlic, a good deal of ginger sliced, half an ounce of cloves, mace, and nutmeg. Mix your pickle well together, pour it over your pippins, and cover them close.

Grapes.

Let your grapes be of their full growth, but not ripe. Cut them into small bunches fit for garnishing, and put them into a stone jar, with vine-leaves between every layer of grapes. Then take spring water, as much as will cover them, and put into it a pound of bay salt, and as much white salt as will make it bear an egg. Dry your bay salt, and pound it before you put it in, and that will make it melt the sooner. Put it into a pot, and boil and skim it well; but take off only the black scum. When it has boiled a quarter of an hour, let it stand to cool and settle; and when it is almost cold pour the clear liquor on the grapes, lay vine-leaves on the top, tie them down close with a linen cloth, and cover them with a dish. Let them stand twenty-four hours, then take them out, lay them on a cloth, cover them over with another, and let them dry between the cloths. Then take two quarts of vinegar, a quart of spring water, and a pound of coarse sugar. Let it boil a little, skim it very clean as it boils, and let it stand till it is quite cold. Dry your jar with a cloth, put fresh vine-leaves at the bottom and between every bunch of grapes, and on the top. Then pour the clear of the pickle on the grapes, fill your jar that the pickle may be above the grapes, and having tied a thin piece of board in a flannel, lay it on the top of the jar, to keep the grapes under the liquor. Tie them down with a bladder and leather, and when you want them for use, take them out with a wooden spoon. Be careful you tie them up again quite close, for, should the air get in, they will be inevitably spoiled.

Red Currants.

TAKE a quantity of white wine vinegar, and to every quart put in half a pound of Lisbon sugar. Then pick the worst of your currants and put them into this liquor; but put the best of your currants into glasses. Then boil your pickle with the worst of your currants, and skim it very clean. Boil it till it looks of a fine colour, and let it stand till it is cold. Then strain it through a cloth, wringing it to get all the colour you can from the currants. Let it stand to cool and settle, then pour it clear into the glasses in a little of the pickle, and when it is cold, cover it close with a bladder and leather. To every half pound of sugar put a quarter of a pound of white salt.

Caveach, or pickled Mackarel.

TAKE half a dozen of large mackarel, and cut them

into round pieces. Then take an ounce of beaten pepper, three large nutmegs, a little mace, and a handful of salt. Mix your salt and beaten spice together, then make two or three holes in each piece, and with your finger thrust the seasoning into the holes. Rub the pieces all over with the seasoning, fry them brown in oil, and let them stand till they are cold. Then put them into vinegar, and cover them with oil. If well covered, they will keep a considerable time, and are most delicious eating.

Smelts.

At that time of the year when smelts are seasonably abundant, take a quarter of a peck of them, and wash, clean, and gut them. Take half an ounce of pepper, the same quantity of nutmegs, a quarter of an ounce of mace, half an ounce of saltpetre, and a quarter of a pound of common salt. Beat all very fine, and lay your smelts in rows in a jar. Between every layer of smelts strew the seasoning, with four or five-bay leaves. Then boil some red wine, and pour over them a sufficient quantity to cover them. Cover them with a plate, and when cold stop them down close, and put them by for use. A few make a very pretty supper.

Oysters.

Take two hundred of the newest and best oysters you can get, and be careful to save the liquor in a pan as you open them. Cut off the black verge, saving the rest, and put them into their own liquor. Then put all the liquor and oysters into a kettle, boil them half an hour on a gentle fire, and do them very slowly, skimming them as the scum rises. Then take them off the fire, take out the oysters, and strain the liquor through a fine cloth. Then put in the oysters again, take out a pint of the liquor when hot, and put thereto three quarters of an ounce of mace, and half an ounce of cloves. Just give it one boil, then put it to the oysters, and stir up the spices well among them. Then put in about a spoonful of salt, three quarters of a pint of the best white wine vinegar, and a quarter of an ounce of whole pepper: let them stand till they are cold, and put the oysters, as many as you well can, into the barrel. Put in as much liquor as the barrel will hold, letting them settle awhile, and they will soon be fit to eat. Or you may put them in stone jars, cover them close with a bladder and leather, and be sure they are quite cold before you cover them up.

In like manner you may do cockles and muscles, with this difference only, that there is not any thing to be picked off the cockles, and as they are small, the before-mentioned ingredients will be sufficient for two quarts of muscles; but take great care to pick out the crabs under the tongues, and the little pus which grows at the roots. Both cockles and muscles must be washed in several waters to cleanse them from grit. Put them into a stew-pan by themselves, cover them close, and when they open, pick them out of the shell, from the liquor, and proceed as directed for oysters.

Artificial Anchovies.

THESE must be made in the following manner to a peck of sprats put two pounds of common salt, a quarter of a pound of bay salt, four of saltpetre, two ounces of prunella salt, and a small quantity of cochineal Pound all in a mortar, put them into a stone-pan, a row of sprats, then a layer of your compound, and so on alternately to the top. Press them hard down, cover them close, let them stand six months, and they will be fit for use. Remember that your sprats are as fresh as you can possibly get them, and that you neither wash or wipe them, but do them as they come out of the water.

Ox Palates.

WASH the palates well with salt and water, and put them into a pipkin with some clean salt and water. When they are ready to boil, skim them well, and put to them as much pepper, cloves, and mace, as will give them a quick taste. When they are boiled tender, which will require four or five hours, peel them, and cut them into small pieces, and let them cool. Then make the pickle of an equal quantity of white wine and vinegar. Boil the pickle, and put in the spices that were boiled in the palates. When both the pickle and palates are cold, lay your palates in a jar, and put to them a few bay-leaves, and a little fresh spice. Pour the pickle over them, cover them close, and keep them for use.

CHAPTER XXII.

COLLARING.

ONE very material thing to be generally and indispensably observed in the business of collaring any kind of meat is, that you roll it up well, and bind it as tight as possible, otherwise when it is cut it will break in pieces, and its beauty be entirely lost. Be careful that you boil it enough, but not too much, and let it be quite cold before you put it into the pickle. After it has lain all night in the pickle, take off the binding, put it into a dish, and when it is cut, the skin will look clear, and the meat have its proper solidity.

Venison.

BONE a side of venison, take away all the sinews, and cut it into square collars of what size you please. It will make two or three collars. Lard it with fat clear bacon, and cut your lard as big as the top of your finger, and three or four inches long. Season your venison with pepper, salt, cloves, and nutmeg. Roll up your collars, and tie them close with coarse tape; then put them into deep pots with seasonings at the bottoms, some fresh butter, and three or four bay-leaves. Put the rest of the seasoning and butter on the top, and over that some beef-suet, finely shred and beaten. Then cover up your pots with coarse paste, and bake them four or five hours. After that take them out of the oven, and let them stand a little, take out your venison, and let it drain well from the gravy.

add more butter to the fat, and set it over a gentle fire to clarify. Then take it off, let it stand a little, and skim it well. Make your pots clean, or have pots ready fit for each collar. Put a little seasoning and some of your clarified butter at the bottom; then put in your venison, and fill up your pot with clarified butter, and be sure that your butter be an inch above the meat. When it is thoroughly cold, tie it down with double paper, and lay a tile on the top. They will keep six or eight months; and you may, when you use a pot, put it for a minute into boiling water, and it will come out whole. Let it stand till it is cold, stick it round with bay-leaves, and a sprig at the top, and serve it up.

Breast of Veal.

Bone your veal, and beat it a little. Rub it over with the yolk of an egg, and strew on it a little beaten mace, nutmeg, pepper and salt: a large handful of parsley chopped small, with a few sprigs of sweet marjorum, a little lemon-peel shred fine, an anchovy chopped small, and mixed with a few crumbs of bread. Roll it up very tight, bind it hard with a fillet, and wrap it in a clean cloth. Boil it two hours and a half in soft water, and when it is enough, hang it up by one end, and make a pickle for it, consisting of a pint of salt and water, with half a pint of vinegar. Before you send it to table, cut off a slice at each of the ends. Garnish with pickles and parsley.

Breast of Mutton.

Pare off the skin of a breast of mutton, and with a sharp knife nicely take out all the bones, but be careful you do not cut through the meat. Pick all the fat and meat off the bones, then grate some nutmeg all over the inside of the mutton, a very little beaten mace, a little pepper and salt, a few sweet herbs shred small, a few crumbs of bread, and the bits of fat picked off the bones. Roll it up tight, stick a skewer in to hold it together, but do it in such a manner that the collar may stand upright in the dish. Tie a packthread across it to hold it together, spit it, then roll the caul of a breast of veal all round it, and roast it. When it has been about an hour at the fire, take off the caul, dredge it with flour, baste it well with fresh butter, and let it be of a fine brown. It will require on the whole, an hour and a quarter roasting. For sauce take some gravy beef, cut and hack it well, then flour it, and fry it a little brown. Pour into your stew-pan some boiling water, stir it well together, and then fill your pan half full of water. Put in an onion, a bunch of sweet herbs, a little crust of bread toasted, two or three blades of mace, four cloves, some whole pepper, and the bones of the mutton. Cover it close, and let it stew till it is quite rich and thick. Then strain it, boil it up with some truffles and morels, a few mushrooms, a spoonful of catsup, and (if you have them) two or three bottoms of artichokes. Put just enough salt to season the gravy, take the packthread off the mutton, and set it upright in the dish. Cut the sweetbread into four pieces, and boil it of a fine brown, and have ready a few forcemeat balls fried. Lay these round your dish, and pour in the sauce. Garnish with sliced lemon.

Beef.

TAKE a piece of thin flank of beef, and bone it; cut off the skin, and salt it with two ounces of saltpetre, two ounces of sal prunella, the same quantity of bay-salt, half a pound of coarse sugar, and two pounds of common salt. Beat the hard salts very fine, and mix all together. Turn it every day, and rub it well with the brine for eight days; then take it out, wash it, and wipe it dry. Take a quarter of an ounce of cloves, a quarter of an ounce of mace, twelve corns of allspice, and a nutmeg beat very fine, with a spoonful of beaten pepper, a large quantity of chopped parsley, and some sweet herbs shred fine. Sprinkle this mixture on the beef, and roll it up very tight; put a coarse cloth round it, and tie it very tight with beggar's tape. Boil it in a copper of water, and if it is a large collar, it will take six hours boiling, but a small one will be done in five. When it is done, take it out, and put it into a press; but if you have not that convenience, put it between two boards, with a weight on the uppermost, and let it remain in that state till it is thoroughly cold. Then take it out of the cloth, cut it into thin slices, lay them on a dish, and serve them to table. Garnish your dish with raw parsley.

Calf's Head.

TAKE a calf's head with the skin on, scald off the hair, take out all the bones carefully from the neck, and lay it some time in warm milk to make it look white. Boil the tongue, peel it, cut that and the palate into thin slices, and put them and the eyes into the middle of the head. Take some pepper, salt, cloves, and mace, and beat them fine; and add to them some grated nutmeg, scalded parsley, thyme, savory, and sweet marjorum, cut very small. Beat up the yolks of three or four eggs, spread them over the head, and then strew on the seasoning. Roll it up very tight, tie it round with tape, and boil it gently for three hours in as much water as will cover it. When you take it out, season the pickle with salt, pepper, and spice, and add to it a pint of white wine vinegar. When it is cold put in the collar, and cut it in handsome slices when you send it to table.

Pig.

BONE your pig, and then rub it all over with pepper and sait beaten fine, a few sage leaves, and sweet herbs chopped small. Roll it up tight, and bind it with a fillet. Fill your boiler with soft water, put in a bunch of sweet herbs, a few pepper-corns, a blade or two of mace, eight or ten cloves, a handful of salt, and a pint of vinegar. When it boils, put in your pig, and let it boil till it is tender. Then take it up, and when it is almost cold, bind it over again, put it into an earthen pot, and pour the liquor your pig was boiled in upon it. Be careful to cover it close down after you cut any for use.

Eels.

WHEN you have thoroughly cleansed your eel, cut off the head, tail, and fins, and take out the bones. Lay it flat on the back, and then grate over it a small nutmeg, with two or three blades of mace beat fine, and a little pepper and salt, and strew on these a handful of parsley shred fine, with a few sage leaves chopped small. Roll it up tight in a cloth, and bind it tight. If it is of a middle size, boil it in salt and water three quarters of an hour, and hang it up all night to drain. Add to the pickle a pint of vinegar, a few pepper-corns, and a sprig of sweet marjorum; boil it ten minutes, and let it stand till the next day. Then take off the cloth, and put your eels into the pickles. When you send them to table, lay them either whole in the plate, or cut them in slices. Garnish with green parsley. Lampreys may be done in the same manner.

Mackarel.

GUT your mackarel, and slit them down the belly; cut off their heads, take out the bones, and be careful not to cut them in holes. Then lay them flat upon their backs, season them with mace, nutmeg, pepper, and salt, and a handful of parsley shred fine; strew it over them, roll them tight, and tie them well separately in cloths. Boil them gently twenty minutes in vinegar, salt, and water, then take them out, put them into a pot, and pour the liquor on them, or the cloth will stick to the fish. Take the cloth off the fish the next day, put a little more vinegar to the pickle, and keep them for use. When you send them to table garnish with fennel and parsley, and put some of the liquor under them.

Salmon.

TAKE a side of salmon, cut off the tail, then wash the fleshy part well, and dry it with a cloth. Rub it over with the yolks of eggs, and make some forcemeat with what you cut off at the tail end. Take off the skin, and put to it some parboiled oysters, a tail or two of lobsters, the yolks of three or four eggs boiled hard, six anchovies, a handful of sweet herbs chopped small, a little salt, cloves, mace, nutmeg, pepper, and grated bread. Work all these well together, with yolks of eggs, lay it over the fleshy part, and strew on it a little pepper and salt. Then roll it up into a collar, and bind it with broad tape. Boil it in water, salt, and vinegar, but let the liquor boil before you put it in, and throw in a bunch of sweet herbs, with some sliced ginger and nutmeg. Let it boil gently near two hours, and then take it up. Put it into a pan, and when the pickle is cold, put it to your salmon, and let it lay in it till wanted. If you cover it with clarified butter, it will keep a considerable time.

CHAPTER XXIII.

POTTING.

IN this mode of cookery, be sure to make it a rule, that whatever you do it is well covered with clarified butter before you send it to the oven, tie it close with strong paper, and let it be well baked. When it comes from the oven, pick out every bit of skin you can, and drain away the gravy, otherwise the article potted will be apt to turn sour. Beat your seasoning very fine, and strew it on gradually. Before you put it into your pot, press it well, and before you put on your clarified butter, let it be perfectly cold.

SECT. I.

MEAT *and* POULTRY.

Venison.

RUB your venison all over with red wine; season it with beaten mace, pepper and salt; put it into an earthen dish, and pour over it half a pint of red wine, and a pound of butter, and then send it to the oven. If it be a shoulder, put a coarse paste over it, and let it lay in the oven all night. When it comes out, pick the meat clean from the bones, and beat it in a marble mortar, with the fat from your gravy. If you find it not sufficiently seasoned, add more, with clarified butter, and keep beating it till it becomes like a fine paste. Then press it hard down into your pots, pour clarified butter over it, and keep it in a dry place.

Hares.

Case your hare, wash it thoroughly clean, then cut it up as you would do for eating; put it into a pot, and season it with pepper, salt, and mace. Put on it a pound of butter, tie it down close, and bake it in a bread oven. When it comes out, pick the meat clean from the bones, and pound it very fine in a mortar, with the fat from your gravy. Then put it close down in your pots, and pour over it clarified butter.

Marble Veal.

Boil, skin, and cut a dried tongue as thin as possible, and beat it well with near a pound of butter, and a little beaten mace, till it is like a paste. Have ready some veal stewed, and beat in the same manner. Then put some veal into potting-pots, thin some tongue in lumps over the veal. Do not lay on your tongue in any form, but let it be in lumps, and it will then cut like marble. Fill your pot close up with veal, press it very hard down, and pour clarified butter over it. Remember to keep it in a dry place, and when you send it to table, cut it into slices. Garnish it with parsley.

Tongues

Take a fine neat's tongue, and rub it well over with an ounce of saltpetre and four ounces of brown sugar, and let it lie two days. Then boil it till it is quite tender, and take off the skin and side bits. Cut the tongue in very thin slices, and beat it in a marble mortar with a pound of clarified butter, and season it to your taste with pepper, salt, and mace. Beat all as fine as possible, then press it close down in small potting-pots, and pour over them clarified butter.

Geese and Fowls.

Boil a dried tongue till it is tender; then take a goose and a large fowl, and bone them. Take a quarter of an ounce of mace, the same quantity of olives, a large nutmeg, a quarter of an ounce of black pepper, and beat all well together, add to these a spoonful of salt, and rub the tongue and inside of the fowl well with them. Put the tongue into the fowl, then season the goose, and fill it with the fowl and tongue, and the goose will look as i. it was whole. Lay it in a pan that will just hold it, melt fresh butter enough to cover it, send it to the oven, and bake it an hour and a half. Then take out the meat, drain the butter carefully from it, and lay it on a coarse cloth till it is cold. Then take off the hard fat from the gravy, and lay it before the fire to melt. Put your meat again into the pot, and pour your butter over it. If there is not enough, clarify more, and let the butter be an inch above the meat. It will keep a great while, cut fine, and look beautiful, and when you cut it let it be cross-ways. It makes a very pretty corner-dish for dinner, or side-dish for supper.

Beef.

Take half a pound of brown sugar, and an ounce of saltpetre, and rub it into twelve pounds of beef. Let it lie twenty-four hours; then wash it clean, and dry it well with a cloth. Season it to your taste with pepper, salt, and mace, and cut it into five or six pieces. Put it into an earthen pot, with a pound of butter in lumps upon it, set it in a hot oven, and let it stand three hours, then take it out, cut off the hard outsides, and beat it in a mortar. Add to it a little more pepper, salt, and mace. Then oil a pound of butter in the gravy and fat that came from your beef, and put in as you find necessary; but beat the meat very fine. Then put it into your pot, press it close down, pour clarified butter over it, and keep it in a dry place.

Another method of potting beef, and which will greatly imitate venison, is this: Take a buttock of beef and cut the lean of it into pieces of about a pound weight each. To eight pounds of beef take four ounces of saltpetre, the same quantity of bay-salt, half a pound of white salt, and an ounce of sal prunella. Beat all the salt very fine, mix them well together, and rub them into the beef. Then let it lie four days, turning it twice a day. After that put it into a pan, and cover it with pump water, and a little of its own brine. Send it to the oven, and bake it till it is tender; then drain it from the gravy, and take out all the skin and sinews. Pound the meat well in a mortar, lay it in a broad dish, and mix on it an ounce of cloves and mace, three quarters of an ounce of pepper, and a nutmeg, all beat very fine. Mix the whole well with the meat, and add a little clarified fresh butter to moisten it. Then press it down into pots very hard, set them at the mouth of the oven just to settle, and then cover them two inches thick with clarified butter. When quite cold, cover the pots over with white paper tied close, and set them in a dry place. It will keep good a considerable time.

Pigeons.

Pick and draw your pigeons, cut off the pinions, wash them clean, and put them in a sieve to drain. Then dry them with a cloth, and season them with pepper and salt. Roll a lump of butter in chopped parsley, and put it into the pigeons. Sew up the vents, then put them into a pot with butter over them, tie them down, and set them in a moderately heated oven. When they come out, put them into your pots, and pour clarified butter over them.

Woodcocks.

Take six woodcocks, pluck them, and draw out the train. Skewer their bills through their thighs, put their legs through each other, and their feet upon their breasts. Season them with three or four blades of mace, and a little pepper and salt. Then put them into a deep pot, with a pound of butter over them, and tie a strong paper over them. Bake them in a moderate oven, and when they are enough, lay them on a dish to drain the gravy from them, then put them into potting-pots; take all the clear butter from your gravy, and put it upon them. Fill up your pots with clarified butter. Keep them in a dry place for use Snipes must be done in the same manner.

SECT. II.

FISH.

TAKE a large eel, and when you have skinned, washed clean, and thoroughly dried it with a cloth, cut it into pieces about four inches long. Season them with a little beaten mace and nutmeg, pepper, salt, and a little sal prunella beat fine. Lay them in a pan, and pour as much clarified butter over them as will cover them. Bake them half an hour in a quick oven; but the size of your eels must be the general rule to determine what time they will take baking. Take them out with a fork, and lay them on a coarse cloth to drain. When they are quite cold, season them again with the like seasoning, and lay them close in the pot. Then take off the butter they were baked in clear from the gravy of the fish, and set it in a dish before the fire. When it is melted, pour the butter over them, and put them by for use. You may bone your eels, if you choose; but in that case you must put in no sal prunella.

Salmon.

TAKE a large piece of fresh salmon, scale it, and wipe it clean. Then season it with Jamaica pepper, black pepper, mace, and cloves, beat fine, and mixed with salt, and a little sal prunella: then pour clarified butter over it, and bake it well. When it is done, take it out carefully, and lay it on a cloth to drain. As soon as it is quite cold, season it again, lay it close in your pot, and cover it with clarified butter. Or you may pot it in this manner:

Scale and clean a whole salmon, slit it down the back, dry it well, and cut it as near the shape of your pot as you can. Then take two nutmegs, an ounce of mace and cloves beaten, half an ounce of white pepper, and an ounce of salt. Then take out all the bones, cut off the tail and the head below the fins Season the scaly side first, and lay that at the bottom of the pot; then rub the seasoning on the other side, cover it with a dish, and let it stand all night. It must be put double, and the scaly sides top and bottom. Put some butter at the bottom and top, and cover the pot with some stiff coarse paste. If it is a large fish, it will require three hours baking; but if a small one, two hours will be sufficient. When it comes out of the oven, let it stand half an hour, then uncover it, raise it up at one end that the gravy may run out, and put a trencher and weight on it effectually to answer this purpose. When the butter is cold take it out clear from the gravy, add more butter to it, and put it in a pan before the fire. When it is melted pour it over the salmon, and as soon as it is cold, paper it up, put it in a dry place, and it will keep a considerable time. Carp, tench, trout, and several other sorts of fish, may be potted in the same manner.

Lobster.

Boil a live lobster in salt and water, and stick a skewer in the vent to prevent the water getting in. As soon as it is cold, take out all the flesh, beat it fine in a mortar, and season it with beaten mace, grated nutmeg, pepper, and salt. Mix all together, melt a piece of butter the size of a walnut, and mix it with the lobster as you beat it. When it is beat to a paste, put it into your pot, and press it down as close and hard as you can. Then set some butter in a deep broad pan before the fire, and when it is all melted, take off the scum at the top, if any, and pour the clear butter over the fish as thick as a crown-piece. The whey and churn-milk will settle at the bottom of the pan; but take care that none of that goes in, and always let your butter be very good, or you will spoil all. If you choose it, you may put in the meat whole, with the body mixed among it, laying them as close together as you can, and pouring the butter over them.

CHAPTER XXIV.

CURING VARIOUS KINDS OF MEATS, SOUSINGS, &c.

Hams

CUT off a fine ham from a fat hind quarter of pork Take two ounces of saltpetre, a pound of coarse sugar, a pound of common salt, and two ounces of sal prunella; mix all together, and rub it well. Let it lie a month in this pickle, turning and basting it every day; then hang it in a wood smoke in a dry place, so that no heat comes to it; and, if you intend to keep them long, hang them a month or two in a damp place, and it will make them cut fine and short. Never lay these hams in water till you boil them, and then boil them in a copper, if you have one, or the largest pot you have. Put them into the water cold, and let them be four or five hours before they boil. Skim the pot well, and often, till it boils. If it is a very large one, three hours will boil it; if a small one, two hours will do, provided it is a great while before the water boils. Take it up half an hour before dinner, pull off the skin, and throw raspings, finely sifted, all over. Hold a red-hot salamander over it, and when dinner is ready, take a few raspings in a sieve, and sift all over the dish, then lay in your ham, and with your finger make figures round the edge of your dish. Be sure to boil your ham in as much water as you can, and keep skimming it all the time it boils. The pickle you take your ham out of will do finely for tongues. Let them lay in it a fortnight, and then lay them in a place where there is wood smoke, to dry. When you broil any slices of ham or bacon, have some boiling water ready, let them lay a minute or two in it, and then put them on a gridiron. This is a very good method, as it takes out the violence of the salt, and makes them have a fine flavour.

Hams the Yorkshire Way.

MIX well together half a peck of salt, three ounces of saltpetre, half an ounce of sal prunella, and five pounds of very coarse salt. Rub the hams well with this: put them into a large pan or pickling-tub, and lay the remainder on the top. Let them lie three days, and then hang them up. Put as much water to the pickle as will cover the hams, adding salt till it will bear an egg, and then boil and strain it. The next morning put in the hams, and press them down so that they may be covered. Let them lay a fortnight, then rub them well with bran, and dry them. The quantity of ingredients here directed, is for doing three middle-sized hams at once, so that if you do only one, you must proportion the quantity of each article.

New England Hams.

GET two fine hams, and in the mode of cure for this purpose, proceed as follows: take two ounces of sal prunella, beat it fine, rub it well in, and let them lie twenty-four hours. Then take half a pound of bay-salt, a quarter of a pound of common salt, and one ounce of saltpetre, all beat fine, and half a pound of the coarsest sugar. Rub all these well in, and let them lie two or three days. Then take some white common salt, and make a pretty strong brine, with about two gallons of water and half a pound of brown sugar. Boil it well, and scum it when cold; put in the hams, and turn them every two or three days in the pickle for three weeks. Then hang them up in a chimney, and smoke them well a day or two with horse litter. Afterwards let them hang about a week on the side of the kitchen chimney, and then take them down. Keep them dry in a large box, and cover them well with bran. They will keep good in this state for a year, though if wanted, may be used in a month.

Bacon.

TAKE off all the inside fat of a side of pork, and lay it on a long board or dresser, that the blood may run from it. Rub it well on both sides with good salt, and let it lie a day. Then take a pint of bay-salt, a quarter of a pound of saltpetre, and beat them both fine; two pounds of coarse sugar, and a quarter of a peck of common salt. Lay your pork in something that will hold the pickle, and rub it well with the above ingredients. Lay the skinny side downwards, and baste it every day with a pickle for a fortnight. Then hang it in a wood-smoke, and afterwards in a dry but not hot place. Remember that all hams and bacons should hang clear from every thing, and not touch the wall. Take care to wipe off the old salt before you put it into the pickle, and never keep bacon or hams in a hot kitchen, or in a room exposed to the rays of the sun, as all these matters will greatly contribute to make them rusty.

Mutton Hams.

TAKE a hind quarter of mutton, cut it like a ham, and rub it well with an ounce of saltpetre, a pound of coarse sugar, and a pound of common salt, mixed well together. Lay it in a deepish tray with the skin downward, and baste it with the pickle every day for a fortnight. Then roll it in sawdust, and hang it in a wood-smoke for a fortnight. Then boil it, and hang it up in a dry place. You may dress it whole, or cut slices off, and broil them, which will eat well, and have an excellent flavour.

Beef Hams.

CUT the leg of a fat Scotch or Welch ox as nearly in the shape of a ham as you can. Take an ounce of bay-salt, an ounce of saltpetre, a pound of common salt, and a pound of coarse sugar, which will be a sufficient quantity for about fourteen or fifteen pounds of beef; and if a greater or less quantity of meat, mix your ingredients in proportion. Pound these ingredients, mix them well together, rub your meat with it, turn it every day, and at the same time baste it well with the pickle. Let it lie in this state for a month, then take it out, roll it in bran or sawdust, and hang it in a wood-smoke for a month. Then take it down, hang it in a dry place, and keep it for use. You may dress it in whatever manner you please, and as occasion may require. If you boil a piece of it, and let it be till it is cold, it will eat very good, and shives like Dutch beef; or it is exceeding fine cut into rashers and broiled, with poached eggs laid on the tops.

Neat's Tongue.

SCRAPE your tongue clean, dry it well with a cloth, and then salt it with common salt, and half an ounce of saltpetre well mixed together. Lay it in a deep pan, and turn it every day for a week or ten days. Then turn it again, and let it lay a week longer. Take it out of the pan, dry it with a cloth, strew flour on it, and hang it up in a moderate warm place to dry.

Hung Beef.

MAKE a strong brine with bay-salt, saltpetre, and pump-water; put a rib of beef into it, and let it lay for nine days. Then hang it up a chimney where wood or sawdust is burnt. When it is a little dry, wash the outside with bullock's blood two or three times, to make it look black; and when it is dry enough boil it, and serve it up with such kind of vegetables as you think proper.

Another method of preparing hung beef is this: take the navel-piece, and hang it up in your cellar as long as it will keep good, and till it begins to be a little sappy; then take it down, cut it into three pieces, and wash it in sugar and water, one piece after another. Then take a pound of saltpetre, and two pounds of bay-salt, dried and pounded small. Mix with them two or three spoonsful of brown sugar, and rub your beef well with it in every place. Then strew a sufficient quantity of common salt all over it, and let the beef lie close till the salt is dissolved, which will be in six or seven days. Then turn it every other day for a fortnight, and after that hang it up in a warm but not hot place. It may hang a fortnight in the kitchen, and when you want it, boil it in bay-salt and pump-water till it is tender. It will keep when boiled, two or three months, rubbing it with a greasy cloth, or putting it two or three minutes into boiling water to take off the mouldiness.

Dutch Beef.

TAKE a buttock of beef, cut off all the fat, and rub the lean all over with brown sugar. Let it lie two or three hours in a pan or tray, and turn it two or three times. Then salt it with saltpetre and common salt, and let it lay a fortnight, turning it every day. After the expiration of this time, roll it very straight in a coarse cloth, put it into a cheese-press for a day and a night, and then hang it to dry in a chimney. When you boil it put it into a cloth, and when cold, it will cut like Dutch beef.

Hunting Beef.

TAKE a pound of salt, two ounces of saltpetre, a quarter of a pound of brown sugar, one ounce of corianders, one ounce of cloves, half an ounce of mace, half an ounce of nutmeg, two ounces of allspice, a quarter of a pound of pepper, half an ounce of chyan pepper, and two ounces of ginger; let the whole be ground and well mixed. Take your buttock of beef and rub it well with the spices, and keep turning and rubbing it every day, one month: when your beef is to be done, take a deep pan, put in your beef with plenty of fat over and under, taking care that your beef does not touch the bottom of the pan. Cover your pan down close so that the steam does not come out, which may be prevented by putting a paste to the cover made of flour and water. Send it to the oven, and if moderate it will be done enough in five hours. It should not be taken out of your pan till quite cold; be sure to have plenty of fat, as there must not be any water put in.

Pickled Pork.

BONE your pork, and then cut it into pieces of a size suitable to lay in the pan in which you intend to put it. Rub your pieces first with saltpetre, and then with two pounds of common salt, and two of bay-salt, mixed together. Put a layer of common salt at the bottom of your pan or tub, cover every piece over with common salt, and lay them one upon another as even as you can, filling the hollow places on the sides with salt. As your salt melts on the top, strew on more, lay a coarse cloth over the vessel, a board over that, and a weight on the board to keep it down. Cover it close, strew on more salt as may be occasionally necessary, and it will keep good till the very last bit.

Mock Brawn.

TAKE the head, and a piece of the belly-part of a young porker, and rub them well with saltpetre. Let them lay three days, and then wash them clean. Split the head and boil it, take out the bones, and cut it into pieces. Then take four cow-heels boiled tender, cut them in thin pieces, and lay them in the belly-piece of pork, with the head cut small. Then roll it up tight with sheet-tin, and boil it four or five hours. When it comes out, set it up on one end, put a trencher on it within the tin, press it down with a large weight, and let it stand all night. Next morning take it out of the tin, and bind it with a fillet. Put it into cold salt and water, and it will be fit for use. If you change the salt and water every four days, it will keep for a long time.

Turkey soused in Imitation of Sturgeon.

DRESS a fine large turkey, dry and bone it, then tie it up as you do a sturgeon, and put it into the pot, with a quart of white wine, a quart of water, the same quantity of good vinegar, and a large handful of salt; but remember that the wine, water, and vinegar, must boil before you put in the turkey, and that the pot must be well skimmed before it boils. When it is enough, take it out, and tie it tighter; but let the liquor boil a little longer. If you think the pickle wants more vinegar or salt, add them when it is cold, and pour it upon the turkey. If you keep it covered close from the air, and in a cool dry place, it will be equally good for some months. Some admire it more than sturgeon, and it is generally eaten with oil, vinegar, and sugar, for sauce.

To make fine Sausages.

TAKE six pounds of young pork, free from skin, gristles, and fat. Cut it very small, and beat it in a mortar till it is very fine. Then shred six pounds of beef-suet very fine, and free from all skin. Take a good deal of sage, wash it very clean, pick off the leaves, and shred it fine. Spread your meat on a clean dresser or table, and then shake the sage all over it, to the quantity of about three large spoonsful. Shred the thin rind of a middling lemon very fine, and throw them over the meat, and also as many sweet herbs as, when shred fine, will fill a large spoon. Grate over it two nutmegs, and put to it two tea-spoonsful of pepper, and a large spoonful of salt. Then throw over it the suet, and mix all well together. Put it down close in a pot, and when you use it, roll it up with as much egg as will make it roll smooth. Make them of the size of a sausage, and fry them in butter, or good dripping. Be careful the butter is hot before you put them in, and keep rolling them about while they are doing. When they are thoroughly hot, and of a fine light brown, take them out, put them into a dish, and serve them up. Veal mixed with pork, and done in this manner, eats exceeding fine.

Oxford Sausages.

TAKE a pound of young pork, fat and lean, without skin or gristle, a pound of lean veal, and a pound of beef-suet, chopped all fine together; put in half a pound of grated bread, half the peel of a lemon shred fine, a nutmeg grated, six sage-leaves washed and chopped very fine, a tea-spoonful of pepper and two of salt, some thyme, savory, and marjorum, shred fine. Mix all well together, and put it close down in a pan till you use it. Roll it out the size of a common sausage, and fry them in fresh butter of a fine brown, or broil them over a clear fire, and send them to table as hot as possible.

CHAPTER XXV

METHODS OF KEEPING VEGETABLES, FRUITS, &c

To keep Green Peas till Christmas.

PEAS for this purpose must be chosen very fine, young and fresh gathered. Shell them, and put them into boiling water with some salt in it. When they have boiled five or six minutes, throw them into a cullender to drain. Then lay a cloth four or five times double on a table, and spread them on it. Dry them well, and having your bottles ready, fill them and cover them with mutton-fat fried. Cork them as close as possible, tie a bladder over them, and set them in a cool place. When you use them, boil the water, put in a little salt, some sugar, and a piece of butter. As soon as they are enough, throw them into a sieve to drain; then put them into a saucepan with a good piece of butter, keep shaking it round till the butter is all melted, then turn them into a dish, and send them to table.

To keep Gooseberries.

PUT an ounce of roche-alum, beat very fine, into a large pan of boiling hard water. When you have picked your gooseberries, put a few of them into the bottom of a hair sieve, and hold them in the boiling water till they turn white. Then take out the sieve, and spread the gooseberries between two clean cloths. Put more gooseberries in your sieve, and then repeat it till they are done. Put the water into a glazed pot till next day; then put your gooseberries into wide-mouthed bottles, pick out all the cracked and broken ones, pour the water clear out of the pot, and fill your bottles with it. Then cork them loosely, and let them stand a fortnight. If they rise to the corks, draw them out, and let them stand two or three days uncorked. Then cork them quite close, and they will keep good several months.

Another method of keeping gooseberries is this: Pick them as large and dry as you can, and having taken care that your bottles are clean and dry, fill and cork them. Set them in a kettle of water up to the neck, and let the water boil very slowly till you find the gooseberries are coddled; then take them out, and put in the rest of the bottles till all are done. Have ready some rosin melted in a pipkin, and dip the necks of the bottles into it, which will prevent all air from getting in at the cork. Keep them in a cool dry place, and when you use them they will bake as red as a cherry, and have their natural flavour.

To keep Mushrooms.

TAKE large buttons, wash them in the same manner as for stewing, and lay them on sieves with the stalks upwards. Throw over them some salt, to draw out the water. When they are properly drained, put them into a pot, and set them in a cool oven for an hour. Then take them out carefully, and lay them to cool and drain. Boil the liquor that comes out of them with a blade or two of mace, and boil it half away. Put your mushrooms into a clean jar well dried, and when the liquor is cold, pour it into the jar, and cover your mushrooms with it. Then pour over them rendered suet; tie a bladder over the jar, and set them in a dry closet, where they will keep very well the greater part of the winter. When you use them, take them out of the liquor, pour over them boiling milk, and let them stand an hour. Then stew them in the milk a quarter of an hour, thicken them with flour, and a large quantity of butter; but be careful you do not oil it. Then beat the yolks of two eggs in a little cream, and put it into the stew; but do not let it boil after you have put in the eggs. Lay unroasted sippets round the inside of the dish, then serve them up, and they will eat nearly as good as when fresh gathered. If they do not taste strong enough, put in a little of the liquor. This is a very useful liquor, as it will give a strong flavour of fresh mushrooms to all made dishes.

To Bottle Damsons.

TAKE your damsons before they are too ripe, put

them into wide-mouthed bottles, and cork them down tight; then put them into a moderate oven, and about three hours will do them. You must be careful your oven is not too hot, or it will make your fruit fly. All kinds of fruits that are bottled may be done in the same way, and if well done will keep two years. After they are done they must be put away, with the mouth downward, in a cool place, to keep them from fermenting.

*** Remember, that every species of the vegetable tribe designed for future use, at times out of the natural season, must be kept in dry places, as damps will not only cover them with mould, but will also deprive them of their fine flavour. It must likewise be observed, that while you endeavour to avoid putting them into damp places, you do not place them where they may get warm, which will be equally detrimental; so that a proper attention must be paid to the observance of a judicious medium. When you boil any dried vegetables, always allow them plenty of water.

CHAPTER XXVI.

POSSETS, GRUELS, &c.

Sack Possets.

BEAT up the yolks and whites of fifteen eggs, and then strain them; then put three quarters of a pound of white sugar into a pint of canary, and mix it with your eggs in a basin; set it over a chafing-dish of coals, and keep continually stirring it till it is scalding hot. In the mean time grate some nutmeg in a quart of milk, and boil it, and then pour it into your eggs, and wine while they are scalding hot. As you pour it hold your hand very high, and let another person keep stirring it all the time. Then take it off, set it before the fire half an hour, and serve it up.

Another method of making sack-posset is this: take four Naples biscuits, and crumble them into a quart of new milk when it boils. Just give it a boil, take it off, grate in some nutmegs, and sweeten it to your palate. Then pour in half a pint of sack, keep stirring it all the time, put it into your basin, and send it to table.

Wine Posset.

BOIL the crumb of a penny loaf in a quart of milk till it is soft, then take it off the fire, and grate in half a nutmeg. Put in sugar to your taste, then pour it into a china bowl, and put in by degrees a pint of Lisbon wine. Serve it up with toasted bread upon a plate.

Ale Posset.

TAKE a small piece of white bread, put it into a pint of milk, and set it over the fire. Then put some nutmeg and sugar into a pint of ale, warm it, and when your milk boils, pour it upon the ale. Let it stand a few minutes to clear, and it will be fit for use

Orange Posset.

TAKE the crumb of a penny loaf grated fine, and put it into a pint of water, with half the peel of a Seville orange grated, or sugar rubbed upon it to take out the essence. Boil all together till it looks thick and clear. Then take a pint of mountain wine, the juice of half a Seville orange, three ounces of sweet almonds, and one of bitter, beat fine, with a little French brandy, and sugar to your taste. Mix all well together, put it into your posset, and serve it up. Lemon posset must be made in the same manner.

White Caudle.

TAKE two quarts of water, and mix it with four spoonsful of oatmeal, a blade or two of mace, and a piece of lemon-peel. Let it boil, and keep stirring it often. Let it boil a quarter of an hour, and be careful not to let it boil over, then strain it through a coarse sieve. When you use it sweeten it to your taste, grate in a little nutmeg, and what wine you think proper; and if it is not for a sick person, squeeze in the juice of a lemon.

Brown Caudle.

MIX your gruel as for the white caudle, and wher

you have strained it, add a quart of ale that is not bitter. Boil it, then sweeten it to your palate, and add half a pint of white wine or brandy. When you do not put in white wine or brandy, let it be half ale.

White Wine Whey.

PUT in a large basin half a pint of skimmed milk and half a pint of wine. When it has stood a few minutes, pour in a pint of boiling water. Let it stand a little, and the curd will gather in a lump, and settle at the bottom. Then pour your whey into a china bowl, and put in a lump of sugar, a sprig of balm, or a slice of lemon.

Water Gruel.

PUT a large spoonful of oatmeal into a pint of water, and stir it well together, and let it boil three or four times, stirring it often; but be careful it does not boil over. Then strain it through a sieve, salt it to your palate, and put in a good piece of butter. Stir it about with a spoon till the butter is all melted, and it will be fine and smooth.

Barley Gruel.

PUT a quarter of a pound of pearl-barley, and a stick of cinnamon, into two quarts of water, and let it boil till it is reduced to one quart. Then strain it through a sieve, add a pint of red wine, and sweeten it to your taste.

Orgeat Paste.

TAKE three quarters of a pound of sweet almonds, and a quarter of a pound of bitter almonds, blanch and pound them in your mortar, wetting them from time to time with orange-flower water that they may not oil. When they are pounded very fine, add three quarters of a pound of fine pounded sugar to it, and mix the whole into a stiff paste, and then put it into your pots for use. This paste will keep six months. When you wish to use it, you may take a piece about the size of an egg and mix it with half a pint of water, and squeeze it through a fine napkin.

CHAPTER XXVII

MADE WINES, &c.

A STRICT and attentive management in the making of these articles is the grand means by which they are to be brought to a proper state of perfection; and without which, labour, expense, and disrepute, will be the final, and disagreeable consequences. To prevent the last, and promote the first, let a due observance be paid to the following general rules: do not let such wines as require to be made with boiling water stand too long after drawn, before you get them cold, and be careful to put in your barm in due time, otherwise it will fret after being put into the cask, and can never be brought to that state of fineness it ought to be. Neither must you let it work too long in the butt, as it will be apt to take off the sweetness and flavour of the fruit or flowers from which it is made. Let your vessels be thoroughly clean and dry, and before you put in the wine, give them a rince with a little brandy. When the wine has done fermenting, bung it up close, and after being properly settled, it will draw to your wishes.

Raisin Wine.

PUT two hundred weight of raisins, with all their stalks into a large hogshead, and fill it up with water. Let them steep a fortnight, stirring them every day. Then pour off the liquor, and press the raisins. Put both liquors together into a nice clean vessel that will just hold it, for remember, it must be quite full. Let it stand till it is done hissing, or making the least noise, then stop it close, and let it stand six months. Then peg it, and if quite clear, rack it off into another vessel. Stop it again close, and let it stand three months longer. Then bottle it, and when wanted, rack it off into a decanter.

An excellent Wine from Smyrna Currants.

To every gallon of water put two pounds and three quarters of brown sugar, and one pound and a half of

Smyrna currants. Boil the sugar and water for half an hour, and fine it with whites of eggs; when near cold, put some fresh barm to it, and let it stand in the tub seven or eight days, stirring it once a day. Cut your currants a little with a chopping knife, then put them into a barrel, and pour the wine on them. Have ready some isinglass dissolved in a little of the wine, and put it into the barrels, stirring it every day for six or eight weeks, then close it up, and in about nine months it will be ready to bottle.

Currant Wine.

Gather your fruit on a fine dry day, and when they are quite ripe. Strip them from the stalks, put them into a large pan, and bruise them with a wooden pestle. Let them lay twenty-four hours to ferment, then run the liquor through a hair sieve, but do not let your hands touch it. To every gallon of liquor put two pounds and a half of white sugar, stir it well together, and put it into your vessel. To every six gallons put in a quart of brandy, and let it stand six weeks. If it is then fine, bottle it; but if not, draw it off as clear as you can into another vessel, or large bottles, and in a fortnight put it into smaller bottles, cork them close, and set it by for use.

Gooseberry Wine.

Gather your gooseberries in dry weather, and at the time when they are about half ripe. Gather about a peck in quantity, and bruise them well in a clean tub. Then take a horse-hair cloth, and press them as much as possible without breaking the seeds. When you have squeezed out all the juice, put to every gallon three pounds of fine dry pounded sugar. Stir it all together till the sugar is dissolved, and then put it into a vessel or cask, which must be quite filled. If the quantity is ten or twelve gallons, let it stand a fortnight, but, if it is a twenty gallon cask, it must stand three weeks. Set it in a cool place; then draw it off from the lees, and pour in the clear liquor again. If it is a ten gallon cask, let it stand three months; if a twenty gallon cask, four months; then bottle it off, and it will draw clear and fine.

Mulberry Wine.

GATHER your mulberries when they are in the state of changing from red to black, and at that time of the day when they are dry from the dew having been taken off by the heat of the sun. Spread them loose on a cloth, or a clean floor, and let them lay twenty-four hours. Then put them into a convenient vessel for the purpose, squeeze out all the juice, and drain it from the seeds. Boil up a gallon of water to each gallon of juice you get out of them; then skim the water well, and add a little cinnamon slightly bruised. Put to each gallon six ounces of white sugar-candy finely beaten. Skim and strain the water, when it has been taked off, and is settled; and put to it some more juice of the mulberries. To every gallon of the liquor, add a pint of white or rhenish wine. Let it stand in a cask to purge or settle for five or six days, and then draw off the wine, and keep it in a cool place.

Raspberry Wine.

PICK some of the finest raspberries you can get, bruise them, and strain them through a flannel bag into a stone jar. To each quart of juice put a pound of double-refined sugar, then stir it well together, and cover it close. Let it stand three days, and then pour it off clear. To a quart of juice put two pints of white wine, and then bottle it off. In the course of a week it will be fit for use.

Damsom Wine.

AFTER you have gathered your damsons, which must be on a dry day, weigh them and then bruise them. Put them into a stein that has a tap in it, and to every eight pounds of fruit put a gallon of water. Boil the water, skim it, and pour it scalding hot on your fruit. When it has stood two days draw it off, and put it into a vessel, and to every gallon of liquor put two pounds and a half of fine sugar. Fill up the vessel and stop it close, and the longer it stands the better. When you draw it off, put a lump of sugar into every bottle.

Orange Wine.

Boil six gallons of spring water three quarters of an hour, with twelve pounds of the best powder sugar, and the whites of eight or ten eggs well beaten. When it is cold, put it in six spoonsful of yeast. Take the juice of twelve lemons, which, being pared, must stand with about two pounds of white sugar in a tankard, and in the morning skim off the top, and put it in the water. Then add the juice and rinds of fifty oranges, but not the white parts of the rinds, and then let them work all together for forty-eight hours. Then add two quarts of Rhenish or white wine, and put it into your vessel.

Orange wine may be made with raisins, in which case proceed thus: take thirty pounds of new Malaga raisins picked clean, chop them small, and take twenty large Seville oranges, ten of which you must prepare as thin as for preserving. Boil about eight gallons of soft water till one third of it is wasted, and let it cool a little. Then put five gallons of it hot upon your raisins and orange-peel, stir it well together, cover it up, and when it is cold, let it stand five days, stirring it once or twice a day. Then pass it through a hair sieve, and with a spoon press it as dry as you can Put it in a rundlet fit for use, and put to it the rinds of the other ten oranges, cut as thin as the first. Then make a syrup of the juice of twenty oranges, with a pound of white sugar, which must be done the day before you tun the wine. Stir it well together, and stop it close. Let it stand two months to clear, and then bottle it off. This wine greatly improves by time, and will drink much better at the end of the third year than the first.

Lemon Wine.

Pare off the rinds of six large lemons, cut them,

and squeeze out the juice. Steep the rinds in the juice, and put to it a quart of brandy. Let it stand three days in an earthen pot close stopped; then squeeze six more, and mix it with two quarts of spring water, and as much sugar as will sweeten the whole. Boil the water, lemons, and sugar together, and let it stand till it is cool. Then add a quart of white wine, mix them together, and run it through a flannel bag into some vessel. Let it stand three months, and then bottle it off. Cork your bottles well, keep it cool, and it will be fit to drink in a month or six weeks.

Lemon wine may be made to drink like citron water, the method of which is as follows: pare fine a dozen of lemons very thin, put the peels into five quarts of French brandy, and let them stand fourteen days. Then make the juice into a syrup with three pounds of single-refined sugar, and when the peels are ready, boil fifteen gallons of water with forty pounds of single-refined sugar for half an hour. Then put it into a tub, and when cool, add to it one spoonful of barm, and let it work two days. Then turn it, and put in the brandy, peels, and syrup. Stir them altogether, and close up your cask. Let it stand three months, then bottle it, and it will be as pale and fine as any citron water.

Grape Wine.

Put a gallon of water to a gallon of grapes. Bruise the grapes well, let them stand a week without stirring, and then draw off the liquor. Put to a gallon of the wine three pounds of sugar, and then put it into a vessel, but do not fasten it up with your bung till it has done hissing. Let it stand two months, and it will draw clear and fine. If you think proper you may then bottle it, but remember your cork is quite close, and keep it in a good dry cellar.

Cherry Wine.

Gather your cherries when they are quite ripe, pull them from the stalks, and press them through a hair-sieve. To every gallon of liquor put two pounds of lump sugar finely beaten, then stir it together, and put it into a vessel that will just contain it. When it has done working, and ceases to make any noise, stop it very close for three months, and then bottle it off for use.

Elder Wine.

Pick your elder-berries when they are full ripe, put them into a stone jar, and set them in the oven, or in a kettle of boiling water till the jar is hot through; then take them out, and strain them through a coarse sieve, wringing the berries, and put the juice into a clean kettle. To every quart of juice, put a pound of fine Lisbon sugar, let it boil, and skim it well. When it is clear and fine, pour it into a cask. To every ten gallons of wine, add an ounce of isinglass dissolved in cider, and six whole eggs. Close it up, let it stand six months, and then bottle it.

Apricot Wine.

Put three pounds of sugar into three quarts of water, let them boil together, and skim it well. Then put in six pounds of apricots pared and stoned, and let them boil till they are tender. Take out the apricots, and when the liquor is cold, bottle it up For present use the apricots will make good marmalade.

Quince Wine.

Gather twenty large quinces, when they are dry and full ripe. Wipe them clean with a coarse cloth, and grate them with a large grate or rasp as near the cores as you can; but do not touch the cores. Boil a gallon of spring-water, throw in your quinces, and let them boil softly about a quarter of an hour. Then strain them well into an earthen pan on two pounds of double-refined sugar. Pare the peel of two large lemons, throw them in, and squeeze the juice through a sieve. Stir it about till it is very cold, and then toast a thin slice of bread very brown, rub a little yeast on it, and let the whole stand close covered twenty-four hours. Then take out the toast and lemon, put the wine in a cask, keep it three months, and then bottle it. If you make a twenty gallon cask, let it stand six months before you bottle it; and remember, when you strain your quinces, to wring them hard in a coarse cloth.

Blackberry Wine.

Let your berries be full ripe when you gather them for this purpose. Put them into a large vessel either of wood or stone, with a tap in it, and pour upon them as much boiling water as will cover them. As soon as the heat will permit you to put your hand into the vessel, bruise them well till all the berries are broken. Then let them stand covered till the berries begin to rise towards the top, which they will do in three or four days. Then draw off the clear into another vessel, and add to every ten quarts of this liquor one pound of sugar. Stir it well in, and let it stand to work a week or ten days in another vessel like the first. Then draw it off at the cork through a jelly-bag into a large vessel. Take four ounces of isinglass, and lay it to steep twelve hours in a pint of white wine. The next morning boil it upon a slow fire till it is all dissolved. Then take a gallon of your blackberry juice, put in the dissolved isinglass, give them a boil together, and pour all into the vessel. Let it stand a few days to purge and settle, then draw it off, and keep it in a cool place.

Turnip Wine.

Take what quantity of turnips you think proper, pare and slice them, put them into a cider-press, and squeeze out all the juice. To every gallon of juice put three pounds of lump sugar, put both into a vessel just large enough to hold them, and add to every gallon of juice half a pint of brandy. Lay something over the bung for a week; and when you are sure it has done working, bung it down close. Let it stand three months, then draw it off into another vessel, and when it is fine, put it into bottles.

Birch Wine.

This wine must be made at that time of the year when the liquor from the birch-trees can be best procured. This is in the beginning of March, when the sap is rising, and before the leaves shoot out; for when the sap is coming forward, and the leaves appear, the juice, by being long digested in the bark, grows thick and coloured, which before was thin and clear. The method of procuring the juice is, by boring holes in the body of the tree and putting fossets, which are usually made of the branches of elder, the pith being taken out. You may, without hurting the tree, if it is large, tap it in several places, four or five at a time, and by that means save, from a good many trees, several gallons every day. If you do not get enough in one day, the bottles in which it drops must be corked close, and rosined or waxed; however, make use of it as soon as you can. Take the sap, and boil it as long as any scum will rise, skimming it all the time. To every gallon of liquor put four pounds of good sugar and the thin peel of a lemon. Then boil it half an hour, and keep skimming it well. Pour it into a clean tub, and when it is almost cold, set it to work with yeast spread upon a toast. Let it stand five or six days, stirring it often. Then take a cask just large enough to hold all the liquor, fire a large match dipped in brimstone, and throw it into the cask, stop it close till the match is extinguished, then turn your wine, and lay the bung on lightly till you find it has done working. Stop it close, and, after three months, bottle it off.

Rose Wine.

Put into a well-glazed earthen vessel three gallons of rose-water drawn with a cold still. Put into it a sufficient quantity of rose-leaves, cover it close, and set it for an hour in a kettle or copper of hot water, to to take out the whole strength and flavour of the roses. When it is cold, press the rose-leaves hard into the liquor, and steep fresh ones on it, repeating it till the liquor has got the full strength of the roses. To every gallon of liquor put three pounds of loaf sugar, and stir it well that it may melt and disperse in every part. Then put it into a cask, or other convenient vessel, to ferment, and throw into it a piece of bread toasted hard and covered with yeast. Let it stand a month, when it will be ripe, and have all the fine flavour and scent of the roses. If you add some wine and spices, it will be a considerable improvement. By the same mode of infusion, wines may be made from any other flowers that have an odoriferous scent, and grateful flavour.

Ginger Wine.

Put seven pounds of Lisbon sugar into four gallons of spring water, boil them a quarter of an hour, and keep skimming it all the time. When the liquor is cold, squeeze in the juice of two lemons, and then boil the peels with two ounces of ginger, in three pints of water, for an hour. When it is cold, put it all together into a barrel, with two spoonsful of yeast, a quarter of an ounce of isinglass beat very thin, and two pounds of jar raisins. Then close it up, let it stand seven weeks, and then bottle it off.

Balm Wine.

Boil forty pounds of sugar in nine gallons of water for two hours, skim it well, and put it into a tub to cool. Take two pounds and a half of the tops of balm, bruise them, and put them into a barrel with a little new yeast, and when the liquor is cold, pour it on the balm. Mix it well together, and let it stand twenty-four hours, stirring it frequently during the time. Then close it up, and let it stand six weeks, at the expiration of which rack it off, and put a lump of sugar into every bottle. Cork it well, and it will be better the second year than the first.

Mead Wine.

There are different kinds of this wine; but those generally made are two, namely, sack-mead and cowslip-mead. Sack mead is made thus: to every gallon of water put four pounds of honey, and boil it three quarters of an hour, taking care properly to skim it To each gallon add half an ounce of hops, then boi. it half an hour, and let it stand till the next day. Then put it into your cask; and to thirteen gallons of the liquor add a quart of brandy or sack. Let it be tightly closed till the fermentation is over, and then stop it up very close. If you make as much as fills a large cask, you must not bottle it off till it has stood a year.

To make cowslip-mead you must proceed thus: put thirty pounds of honey into fifteen gallons of water, and boil it till one gallon is wasted; skim it, take it off the fire, and have ready sixteen lemons cut in half. Take a gallon of the liquor, and put it to the lemons. Pour the rest of the liquor into a tub, with seven pecks of cowslips, and let them stand all night: then put in the liquor with the lemons, eight spoonsful of new yeast, and a handful of sweet-brier; stir all well together, and let it work three or four days. Then strain it, pour it into your cask, let it stand six months, and then bottle it off for use.

Raspberry Brandy.

Mix a pint of water with two quarts of brandy, and put them into a pitcher large enough to hold them, with four pints of raspberries. Put in half a pound of loaf-sugar, and let it remain for a week close covered. Then take a piece of flannel, with a piece of Holland over it, and let it run through by degrees. In about a week it will be perfectly fine, when you may rack it off; but be careful the bottles are well corked.

Orange Brandy.

Put into three quarts of brandy the chips of eighteen Seville oranges, and let them steep a fortnight in a stone bottle close stopped. Boil two quarts of spring water, with a pound and a half of the finest sugar, near an hour very gently. Clarify the water and sugar with the white of an egg, then strain it through a jelly-bag, and boil it near half away. When it is cold strain the brandy into the syrup.

Lemon Brandy.

MIX five quarts of water with one gallon of brandy; then take two dozen of lemons, two pounds of the best sugar, and three pints of milk. Pare the lemons very thin, and lay the peel to steep in the brandy twelve hours. Squeeze the lemons upon the sugar, then put the water to it, and mix all the ingredients together. Let it stand twenty-four hours, and then strain it.

Black Cherry Brandy.

STONE eight pounds of black cherries, and put on them a gallon of the best brandy. Bruise the stones in a mortar, and then put them into your brandy. Cover them up close, and let them stand a month or six weeks. Then pour it clear from the sediments, and bottle it. Morello cherries managed in this manner, make a fine rich cordial.

CHAPTER XXVIII.

CORDIAL WATERS.

IN the process of making these articles, several things are necessary to be observed, in order to bring them to their proper state of perfection. If your still is an alembic, you must fill the top with cold water when you set it on, and close the bottom with a little stiff paste made of flour and water. If you use a hot still, when you put on the top, dip a cloth in white lead and oil, and lay it close over the ends, and a coarse cloth well soaked in water on the top; and when it becomes dry from the heat of the fire, wet it and lay it on again. It will require but little fire, but what there is must be as clear as possible. All simple waters must stand two or three days before they are bottled off, that the fiery taste which they will naturally receive from the still may be fully extracted.

Rose Water.

GATHER your roses when they are dry and full blown, pick off the leaves, and to every peck put a quart of water. Then put them into a cold still, and make a slow fire under it; for the more gradually it is distilled, the better it will be. Then bottle it, and in two or three days you may cork it up for use.

Lavender Water.

To every pound of lavender-neps put a quart of water. Put them into a cold still, and make a slow fire under it. Distil it off very slowly, and put it into a pot till you have distilled all your water. Then clean your still well out, put your lavender-water into it, and distil it off as slowly as before. Then put it into bottles, cork them quite close, and set them by for use.

Peppermint Water.

GATHER your peppermint when it is full grown, and before it seeds. Cut it into short lengths, put it into your still, and cover it with water. Make a good fire under it, and when it is near boiling, and the still begins to drop, if you find your fire too hot, draw a little away, that the liquor may not boil over. The slower your still drops, the clearer and stronger will be the water; but at the same time you must not let it get too weak. The next morning bottle it off, and after it has stood two or three days, to take off the fiery taste of the still, cork it well, and it will preserve its strength a considerable time.

Surfeit Water.

TAKE scurvy-grass, brook-lime, water-cresses, Roman wormwood, rue, mint, balm, sage, and chives, of each one handful; poppies, if fresh, half a peck; but if they are dry, only half that quantity; cochineal and saffron, six-penny worth of each: aniseeds, carraway-seeds, coriander-seeds, and cardamum seeds, of each · ounce; two ounces of scraped liquorice, a pound o split figs, the same quantity of raisins of the sun st ed, an ounce of juniper-berries bruised, an ounce of aten nutmeg, an ounce of mace bruised, and the sau of sweet fennel seeds also bruised; a few flowers of rosemary, marigold, and sage. Put all these into a large stone jar, and pour on them three gallons of French brandy. Cover it close, and let it stand near the fire for three weeks. Stir it three times a week, and at the expiration of that time strain it off. Bottle your liquor, and pour on the ingredients a quart more of French brandy. Let it stand a week, stirring it once a day; then distil it in a cold still, and you will have a fine white surfeit water. Bottle it close, and it will retain its virtues a considerable time.

CHAPTER XXIX.

THE ART OF BREWING.

TO complete the Housekeeper's knowledge in all domestic concerns, it is essentially necessary she should be properly acquainted with the method of brewing malt-liquors, more especially should she be the principal provider for a numerous family. This business will therefore form the subject of the present chapter. and the mode to be pursued throughout the whole process we shall endeavour to lay down in so clear, concise, and intelligent a manner, as may easily guide the unacquainted, and perhaps, in some degree, be materially beneficial to those already informed.

SECT. I.

The Principles on which a Copper should be built for Brewing.

THERE are several things that demand peculiar notice previous to the actual process of brewing malt liquors; and those are with respect to the various implements necessary to effect and facilitate a proper execution of so important a business.

The first thing that presents itself among these is the copper, the proper position of which, and manner of its being set are matters that require very attentive consideration. The most beneficial mode to be adopted is this: divide the heat of the fire by a stop; and if the door and draught be in a direct line, the stop must be erected from the middle of each outline of the grating, and parallel with the centre sides of the copper; by which method the middle of the fire will be directly under the bottom of the copper. The stop is composed of a thin wall in the centre of the right and left sides of the copper, which is to ascend half the height of it. On the top must be left a cavity, from four to six inches, for a draught for that half part of the fire which is next the door of the copper; and then the building must close all round to the finishing at the top. By this method the heat will communicate from the outward part of the fire round the outward half of your copper, through the cavity, as well the farthest part of the flue, which also contracts a conjunction of the whole, and causes the flame to glide gently and equally round the bottom of the copper.

The advantages derived from your copper being set in this manner are very great, nor is the saving of fuel the least object of consideration among them. It has a material pre-eminence over wheel-draughts; for with them, if there is not particular attendance given to the hops, by stirring them down, they are apt to stick to the sides, and scorch, which will deprive the liquor of having its sweet and proper flavour. By the before mentioned method the copper will last many years more than it will by the wheel-draught; for that draws with so much violence, that should your liquor be beneath the communication of the fire, your copper will thereby be liable to injury; whereas by the other method, you may boil half a copper full without fear of any bad consequence.

SECT. II.

On the proper Management of Vessels for Brewing, and the necessity of keeping them in due Order.

On the preceding day that you intend to brew

make a strict examination into all your vessels, that they are thoroughly clean, and in a proper state for use. They should never be converted to any other purpose, except for the use of making wines; and, even in that case, after done with, should be properly cleansed, and kept in a place free from dirt. Let your cask be well cleaned with boiling water; and if the bung-hole is large enough, scrub them well with a small birch-broom, or brush. If you find them bad, and a very musty scent comes from them, take out the heads, and let them be scrubbed clean with a hand brush, sand, and fullers'-earth. When you have done this, put on the head again, and scald it well, then throw in a piece of unslacked lime, and stop the bung close. When they have stood some time, rince them well with cold water, and they will be properly prepared for use.

The greatest attention must likewise be paid to the care of your coolers, which are implements of very material consequence; for, if they are not properly kept in order, your liquor, from a secret and unaccountable cause, abstracts a nauseousness that will entirely destroy it. This often proceeds from wet having been infused in the wood, as it is sometimes apt to lodge in the crevices of old coolers, and even infect them to such a degree, that it will not depart, though many washings and scaldings are applied. One cause incidental to this evil is, suffering women to wash in a brewhouse, which ought by no means to be permitted, where any other convenience can be had; for nothing can be more hurtful than the remnants of dirty soap suds left in vessels calculated only for the purpose of brewing.

When you prepare the coolers, be careful never to let the water stand too long in them, as it will soak in, and soon turn putrid, when the stench will enter the wood, and render them almost incurable. To prevent such consequences, as well as to answer good purposes, it has been recommended, where fixed brewhouses are intended, that all coolers should be leaded. It must be admitted, in the first place, that such are exceeding cleanly; and, secondly, that it expedites the cooling part of your liquor worts, which is very neces sary to forward it for working, as well as afterwards for cooling the whole; for evaporation causes considerably more waste than proper boiling. It is also indispensably necessary that your coolers be well scoured with cold water two or three times, cold water being more proper than hot to effect a perfect cleansing, especially if they are in a bad condition, from undiscovered filth that may be in the crevices. The application of warm water will drive the infection farther; so that if your liquor be let into the coolers, and any remain in the crevices, the heat will collect the foulness, and render the whole both disagreeable and unwholesome.

The mash-tub in particular must be kept perfectly clean; nor must the grains be left in the tub any longer than the day after brewing, lest it should sour the tub; for if there is a sour scent in the brewhouse before your beer is tunned, it will be apt to infect your liquor and worts. From such inconveniences, the necessity of cleanliness in utensils for brewing is sufficiently obvious.

SECT. III.

Directions for the Management of the Mash-tub, Penstaff, &c.

To render your mash-tub more perfect and lasting, you should have a circular piece of brass or copper, to inlay and line the whole where the penstaff enters, to let the wort run off into the underback. The penstaff should be also strongly ferrelled with the same metal, and both well and taperly finished, so that you can place it properly. By this method you have it run from the fineness of a thread to the fulness of an inch tube, &c. first dressing your mask-basket with straw, fern, or small bushy furze without stems, six or eight inches in from the bottom of your basket, and set quite perpendicularly over the whole, with the penstaff through the centre of the basket, and the middle of the furze or fern, and fastened to the hole of the tub. To steady it properly, you must have a piece of iron let into a staple fastened to the tub, at the nearest part opposite the basket, and to reach nearly to it; and from that piece another added on a jointed swivel, or any other contrivance, so as to be at liberty to let round the basket like a dog's collar, and to enter into the staple formed in the same to pin it fast, and by adding a half circular turn into the collar, in which you have room to drive in a wedge, which will keep it safe down to the bottom, where there can be no danger of its being disturbed by stirring the mash, which will otherwise sometimes be the case. When you let go, you will raise the penstaff to your own degree of running, and then fasten the staff, by the help of two wedges tightened between the staff and the basket.

In process of time the copper work, like every thing else, will become defective, and when this is the case, you may repair the imperfection by the following simple method. Work the penstaff in the brass socket with emery and water, or oil, which will make it perhaps more perfect than when new. The like method is sometimes taken even with taps just purchased, in order to prevent their decaying so soon as they otherwise would.

A very material addition may be made to the convenience of the underbacks, by having a piece of copper to line the hole in the bottom, which may be stopped with a cloth put singly round a large tap; and when it is fastened down for the wort to run, it will be necessary to put a large weight on the tap, which will prevent its flying up by the heat. When the liquor is pumped clean out of the back, the cloth round the tap will enable you to take out the tap with ease; and there should be a drain below the underback to carry off the water, which will enable you to wash it perfectly clean with very little trouble. This drain should be made with a clear descent, so as no damp may remain under the back. With the conveyance of water running into your copper, you may be enabled to work that water in a double quantity, your underback being filled, by the means of letting it in at your leisure, out of your copper, through a shoot to the mash-tub, and so to the underback. Thus you will have a reserve against the time you wish to fill your copper, which may be completed in a few minutes, by pumping while the under tap is running. Thus much for the principal utensils in brewing, which we again recommend to be always kept in a perfect state of cleanliness.

SECT. IV

Of the proper Time of Brewing.

The month of March is generally considered as one of the principal seasons for brewing malt liquor for long keeping; and the reason is, because the air at that time of the year is, in general, temperate, and contributes to the good working or fermentation of the liquor, which principally promotes its preservation and good keeping. Very cold, as well as very hot weather, prevents the free fermentation or working of liquors; so that, if you brew in very cold weather, unless you use some means to warm the cellar while new drink is working, it will never clear itself in the manner you would wish, and the same misfortune will arise if, in very hot weather, the cellar is not put into a temperate state; the consequence of all which will be, that such drink will be muddy and sour, and, perhaps, in such a degree, as to be past recovery. Such accidents often happen, even in the proper season for brewing, and that owing to the badness of the cellar; for when they are dug in springy grounds, or are subject to damps in the winter, the liquor will chill, and become vapid or flat. When cellars are of this nature, it is advisable to make your brewings in March, rather than in October; for you may keep your cellars temperate in summer, but cannot warm them in winter. Thus your beer brewed in March will have due time to settle and adjust itself before the cold can do it any material injury.

All cellars for keeping liquor should be formed in such a manner, that no external air can get into them; for the variation of the air abroad, were there free admission of it into the cellars, would cause as many alterations in the liquors, and would thereby keep them in so unsettled a state, as to render them unfit for drinking. A constant temperate air digests and softens malt liquors; so that they taste quite soft and smooth to the palate; but in cellars which are unequal, by letting in heats and colds, the liquor will be apt to sustain very material injury.

SECT. V.

On the Quality of Water proper for Brewing.

It has evidently appeared from repeated experience, that the water best in quality for brewing is river-water, such as is soft, and has received those benefits which naturally arise from the air and sun; for this easily penetrates into the grain, and extracts its virtues. On the contrary, hard waters astringe and bind the power of the malt, so that its virtue is not freely communicated to the liquor. There are some who hold it as a maxim, that all water that will mix with soap is fit for brewing, which is the case with most river-water; and it has been frequently experienced, that when the same quantity of malt has been used to a barrel of river-water, as to a barrel of spring-water, the brewing from the former has excelled the other in strength above five degrees in twelve months keep. It is likewise to be observed, that the malt was not only the same in quantity for one barrel as for the other, but was the same in quality, having been all measured from the same heap. The hops were also the same, both in quality and quantity, and the time of boiling equal in each. They were worked in the same manner, and tunned and kept in the same cellar

This is the most demonstrable and undeniable proof that the difference took place from the difference of the quality of the water.

Various experiments have been tried by gentlemen in different counties to ascertain the truth of this very essential difference in malt liquors, arising from the quality of the water; but after all, they have been left in a state of perplexity.

One circumstance has greatly puzzled the ablest brewers, and that is, when several gentlemen in the same town have employed the same brewer, have had the same malt, the same hops, and the same water, and brewed in the same month, and broached their drink at the same time, yet one has had beer exceeding fine, strong, and well-tasted, while the others have had hardly any worth drinking. In order to account for this very singular difference, three reasons may be advanced. First, it might arise from the difference of the weather, which might happen at the several brewings in this month, and make an alteration in the working of the liquors. Secondly, the yeast, or barm, might be of different sorts, or in different states, wherewith these liquors were worked; and, thirdly, the cellars might not be equally adapted for the purpose. The goodness of such drink as is brewed for keeping, in a great measure depends on the proper form and temperature of the cellars in which it is placed.

Beer made at Dorchester, which in general is greatly admired, is, for the most part, brewed with chalky-water, which is to be had in most parts of that county; and as the soil is generally chalk, the cellars being dug in that dry soil, contribute to the good keeping of their drink, it being of a close texture, and of a drying quality, so as to dissipate damps; for it has been found by experience that damp cellars are injurious to the keeping of liquor, as well as injurious to the casks.

Water that is naturally of a hard quality may be, in some degree, softened by exposing it to the air and sun, and putting into it some pieces of soft chalk to infuse; or, when the water is set on to boil, in order to be poured on the malt, put into it a quantity of bran, which will take off some part of its sharpness, and make it better extract the virtues of the malt.

SECT. VI.

Of the Quality of the Malt and Hops most proper to be chosen for Brewing, with some necessary Observations on the Management of each.

THERE are two sorts of malt, the general distinction between which is, that the one is high, and the other low dried. The former of these, when brewed, produces a liquor of a deep brown colour; and the other, which is the low dried, will produce a liquor of a pale colour. The first is dried in such a manner as rather to be scorched than dried, and is much less wholesome than the pale mait. It has likewise been found by experience, that brown malt, although it may be well brewed, will sooner turn sharp than the pale; from whence, among other reasons, the latter is entitled to pre-eminence.

We have farther proofs of this distinction from various people, but particularly one:—A gentleman, who has made the Art of Brewing his study for many years, *and who* gives his opinion and knowledge in words to this purpose, says, brown malt makes the best drink when it is brewed with a course river water, such as that of the Thames about London; and that likewise being brewed with such water makes very good ale; but that it will not keep above six months without turning stale, even though he allows fourteen bushels to the hogshead. He adds, that he has tried the high-dried malt to brew beer with for keeping and hopped it accordingly; and yet he could never brew it so as to drink soft and mellow like that brewed with pale malt. There is, he says, an acid quality in the high-dried malt, which occasions those who drink it to be greatly troubled with that disorder called the heart burn.

What we have here said with respect to malt, refers only to that made of barley; for wheat-malt, pea-malt, or high coloured liquor, will keep some years, and drink soft and smooth, but they are very subject to have the flavour of mann.

Malt high dried should not be used in brewing till it has been ground ten days or a fortnight, as it will then yield much stronger drink than from the same quantity ground but a short time before it is used. On the contrary, pale malt, which has not received much of the fire, must not remain ground above a week before it is used.

With respect to hops, the newest are by far the best. They will, indeed, remain very good for two years, but after that they begin to decay, and lose their flavour, unless great quantities are kept together, in which case they will keep good much longer than in small quantities. In order the better to preserve them, they should be kept in a very dry place, contrary to the practice of those who deal in them, who making self-interest their first consideration, keep them as damp as they can to increase their weight.

It will happen, in the course of time, that hops will grow stale, decayed, and lose their natural bitterness; but this defect may be removed, by unbagging them, and sprinkling them with aloes and water.

From what has been said, it is evident that every one of the particulars mentioned should be judiciously chosen before you commence brewing, otherwise you will sustain a loss, which will be aggravated by your labours being in vain. It is likewise to be observed, that the yeast or barm with which you work your liquor, must be well considered, for otherwise, even by that alone, a good brewing may be totally destroyed. Be always particularly careful that you are provided with every necessary article previous to your commencing the business of brewing; for if the wort waits for any thing that should be immediately at hand, it will be attended with very bad consequences.

SECT. VII.

The Process, or Practical Part of Brewing.

HAVING, in the preceding sections, fully explained the necessary precautions to be taken previous to the commencement of this very important business, we shall now proceed to give a concise detail of every thing that is necessary to be observed and attended to in the regular process of it, from the malt being first malted, to the liquor being turned off for the cellar.

Your utensils being all properly cleansed and scalded, your malt ground, your water in the copper boiling, and your penstaff well set, you must then proceed to mash, by putting a sufficient quantity of boiling water into your tub, in which it must stand until the greater part of the steam is gone off, or till you can see your own shadow in it. It will be then necessary that one person should pour the malt gently in, while another is carefully stirring it; for it is equally essential that the same care should be observed when the mash is thin as when thick. This being effectually done, and having a sufficient reserve of malt to cover the mash, to prevent evaporation, you may cover your tub with sacks, &c. and leave your malt three hours to steep, which will be a proper time for the extraction of its virtues.

Before you let the mash run, be careful to be prepared with a pail to catch the first flush, as that is generally thickish, and another pail to be applied while you return the first on the mash, and so on for two or three times, or, at least, till it runs fine.

By this time, your copper should be boiling, and a convenient tub placed close to your mash-tub. Let into it through your spout half the quantity of boiling water you mean to use for drawing off your best wort; after which you must instantly turn the tap to fill up again, which, with a proper attention to the fire, will boil in due time. During such time, you must slop the mash with this hot water out of the convenient tub, in moderate quantities, every eight or ten minutes till the whole is consumed; and then let off the remaining quantity, which will be boiling hot, to the finishing process for strong beer.

Having proceeded thus far, fill your copper, and let it boil as quick as possible for the second mash, whether you intend it either for ale or small beer. Being thus far prepared, let off the remaining quantity of water into your tub, as you did for the strong beer; but if you would have small beer besides, you must act accordingly, by boiling a proper quantity off in due time, and letting it into the tub as before.

With respect to the quantity of malt, twenty-four bushels will make two hogsheads of as good strong beer as any person would wish to drink, as also two hogsheads of very decent ale. The strong beer made from this quantity of malt should be kept two or three years before it is tapped, and the ale never less than one. If your mash is only for one hogshead, it should be two hours in running off; if for two hogsheads, two hours and a half; and for any greater quantity, three hours.

Particular attention must be paid to the time of steeping your mashes. Strong beer must be allowed three hours; ale, one hour; and, if you draw small beer after, half an hour. By this mode of proceeding, your boilings will regularly take place of each other, which will greatly expedite the business. Be careful, in the course of mashing, that it is thoroughly stirred from the bottom, and especially round the muck-basket, for, being well shaken, it will prevent a stagnation of the whole body of the mash. This last process demands peculiar attention, for without it your beer will certainly be foxed, and, at best, will have a very disagreeable flavour.

In the preparation for boiling, the greatest care must be taken to put the hops in with the first wort, or it will char in a few minutes. As soon as the copper is full enough, make a good fire under it; but be careful in filling it to leave room enough for boiling. Quick boiling is part of the business that requires very par ticular attention. Great caution should likewise be observed when the liquor begins to swell in waves in the copper. If you have no attendant, be particular attentive to its motions; and being provided with an iron rod of a proper length, crooked at one end, and jagged at the other, then with the crook you are enabled to open the furnace, or copper-door, and with the other end push in the damper without stirring from your station; but on the approach of the first swell you will have sufficient time to proportion your fire, as care should be taken that it is not too fierce. When the boil is properly got under, you may increase the fire so that it may boil briskly.

In order to ascertain the proper time the liquor should boil, you may make use of the following expedient: take a clean copper bowl dish, dip out some of the liquor, and when you discover a working, and the hops sinking, then conclude it to be sufficiently boiled. Long and slow boiling is not only pernicious, but it likewise wastes the liquor; for the slower it boils the lower it drops and singes to your copper; whereas, quick boiling has a contrary effect. Essence of malt is extracted by length of boiling, by which you can make it to the thickness of honey or treacle. In some parts of Yorkshire they value their liquor for its great strength, by its affecting the brain for two or three days after intoxication. This is the effect of long boiling; for in that county they boil liquor for three hours; and what is still worse, when it sinks in the copper, from the waste in boiling, they every now and then add a little fresh wort, which, without doubt, must produce stagnation, and, consequently, impurities.

When your liquor is properly boiled, be sure to traverse a small quantity of it over all the coolers so as to get a proper quantity cold immediately to set to work; but if the airiness of your brewhouse is not sufficient to expedit a quantity soon, you must traverse a second quantity over the coolers, and then let it into shallow tubs. Put these into any passage where there is a thorough draft of air, but where no rain or other wet can get to it. Then let off the quantity of two baring-tubsfull from the first one, the second and third coolers, which may be soon got cold, to be ready for a speedy working, and then the remaining part that is in your copper may be quite let out into the first cooler. In the mean time mend the fire, and also attend to the hops, to make a clear passage through the strainer.

Having proceeded thus far, as soon as the liquor is done running, return to your business of pumping; but be careful to remember, that, when you have got four or five pails full, you then return all the hops into the copper for the ale.

By this time the small quantity of liquor traversed over your coolers being sufficiently cooled, you must proceed to set your liquor to work, the manner of doing which is as follows:

Take four quarts of barm, and divide half of it into small vessels, such as clean bowls, basins, or mugs, adding thereto an equal quantity of wort, which should be almost cold. As soon as it ferments to the top of the vessel, put it into two pails, and when that works to the top, put one into a baring-tub, and the other into another. When you have half a baring-tub full together, you may put the like quantity to each of them, and then cover them over, until it comes to a fine white head. This may be perfectly completed in three hours, and then put those two quantities into the working guile. You may now add as much wort as you have got ready; for, if the weather is open, you cannot work it too cold. If you brew in cold frosty weather, keep the brewhouse warm: but never add hot wort to keep the liquor to a blood heat, that being a bad maxim; for hot wort put to cold, as well as cold to hot, is so intemperate in its nature, that it stagnates the proper operation of the barm.

Be particularly careful that your barm be not from foxed beer, that is, beer heated by ill management in its working; for in that case it is likely to carry with it the contagion. If your barm be flat, and you cannot procure that which is new, the method of recovering 'ts working is, by putting to it a pint of warm sweet wort, of your first letting off, the heat to be about half the degree of milk-warm. then give the vessel that contains it a shake, and it will soon gather strength, and be fit for use.

With respect to the quantity of hops necessary to be used, remember that half a pound of good hops is sufficient for a bushel of malt.

The last, and most simple operation in the business of brewing is, that of tunning, the general methods of doing which are, either by having it carried into the cellar on men's shoulders, or conveying it thither by means of leathern pipes commonly used for that purpose.

Your casks being perfectly clean, sweet and dry, and placed on the stand ready to receive the liquor, first skim off the top barm, then proceed to fill your casks quite full, and immediately bung and peg them close. Bore a hole with a tap-borer near the summit of the stave at the same distance from the top, as the lower tap-hole is from the bottom, for working through that upper hole, which is a clean and more effectual method than working it over the cask; for, by the above method, being so closely confined, it soon sets itself into a convulsive motion of working, and forces itself fine, provided you attend to the filling of your casks five or six times a day. This ought to be carefully attended to, for, by too long an omission, it begins to settle, and being afterwards disturbed, it raises a sharp fermentation, which produces an incessant working of a spurious froth that may continue for some weeks, and, after all, give your beer a disagreeable taste.

One material caution necessary to be kept in remembrance is this: that however careful you may be in attending to all the preceding particulars, yet if your casks are not kept in good order, still the brewing may be spoiled. New casks are apt to give liquor a bad taste, if they are not well scalded and seasoned several days successively before they are used; and old casks, if they stand any time out of use, are apt to grow musty

Having thus gone through the practical part of brewing, and brought the liquor from the mash-tub to the cask, we shall now proceed to

SECT. VIII.

Containing the proper Management of Malt Liquors, with some necessary Observations on the Whole.

In order to keep strong beer in a proper state of preservation, remember, that when once the vessel is broached, regard must be paid to the time in which it may be expended; for, if there happens to be a quick draught for it, then it will last good to the very bottom; but if there is likely to be but a slow draught, then do not draw off quite half before you bottle it, otherwise it will grow flat, dead, or sour.

In proportion to the quantity of liquor which is enclosed in one cask, so will it be a shorter or longer time in ripening. A vessel, which contains two hogsheads of beer, will require twice as much time to perfect itself as one of a hogshead; and it is found, by experience, that no vessel should be used for strong beer (which is intended to be kept) less than a hogshead, as one of that quantity, if it is fit to draw in a year, will have body enough to support it for two, three, or four years, provided it has a sufficient strength of malt and hops, which is the case with Dorchester beer.

With respect to the management of small beer, the first consideration should be to make it tolerably good in quality, which, in various instances, will be found truly economical; for if it is not good, servants, for whom it is principally calculated, will be feeble in summer time, incapable of strong work, and subject to various disorders. Besides, when the beer is bad, a great deal will be thrown away; whereas, on the contrary, good wholesome drink will be valued, and consequently taken care of. It is advisable therefore, where there is a good cellaring, to brew a stock of small beer in March or October, or in both months, to be kept, if possible, in hogsheads.

The beer brewed in March should not be tapped till October, nor that brewed in October till the March following; having thus regard to the quantity, that a family, of the same number of working people, will drink at least one third more in summer than in winter.

In order to fine beer, some people, who brew with high dried barley malt, put a bag, containing about three pints of wheat into every hogshead of liquor, which has had the desired effect, and made the beer drink soft and mellow. Others again, have put about three pints of wheat-malt into a hogshead, which has produced the like effect.

But all malt liquors, however well they may be brewed, may be spoiled by bad cellaring; be subject to ferment in the cask, and consequently turn thick and sour. When this happens to be the case, the best way of bringing the liquor to itself is, to open the bung-hole of the cask for two or three days; and if that does not stop the fermentation, then put in about two or three pounds of oyster shells, washed, dried well in an oven, and then beaten to a fine powder. After you have put it in stir it a little, and it will soon settle the liquor, make it fine, and take off the sharp taste. When you find this effected, draw it off into another vessel, and put a small bag of wheat, or wheat-malt into it, in proportion to the size of the vessel. It sometimes occurs, that such fermentations will happen in liquor from a change of weather, if it is in a bad cellar, and will, in a few months, fall fine of itself, and grow mellow.

In some country places remote from principal towns, it is a practice to dip whisks into yeast, then beat it well, and hang up the whisks, with the yeast in them, to dry; and if there be no brewing till two months afterwards, the beating and stirring one of the whisks in new wort will soon raise a working or fermentation. It is a rule, that all liquor should be worked well in the tun, before it is put into the vessel, otherwise it will not easily grow fine. Some follow the rule of beating down the yeast pretty often while it is in the tun, and keep it there working for two or three days, observing to put it into the vessel just when the yeast begins to fall. This liquor is in general very fine, whereas, on the contrary, that which is put into the vessel soon after it is brewed will be several months before it comes to a proper state of perfection.

We have before taken notice of the season for brewing malt liquors to keep. But it may not be improper further to observe, that if the cellars are subject to the heat of the sun, or warm summer air, it will be best to brew in October, that the liquor may have time to digest before the warm season comes on; and if cellars are subject to damp, and to receive water, the best time will be to brew in March. Some experienced brewers always choose to brew with the pale malt in March, and the brown in October; supposing, that the pale malt, being made with a less degree of fire than the other, wants the summer sun to ripen it; and so, on the contrary, the brown, having had a larger share of the fire to dry it, is more capable of defending itself against the cold of the winter season.

All that remains further to be said relative to the management of malt liquors, we shall preserve in

SECT. IX.

Containing the proper Method of bottling Malt Liquors.

As a necessary preparation for executing this business properly, great attention must be paid to your bottles, which must first be well cleaned and dried; for wet bottles will make the liquor turn mouldy or mothery, as it is called; and by wet bottles a great deal of good beer is frequently spoiled. Though the bottles may be clean and dry, yet, if the corks are not new and sound, the liquor will be still liable to be damaged; for, if the air can get into the bottles, the liquor will grow flat, and never rise. Many who have flattered themselves they knew how to be saving, by using old corks on this occasion, have spoiled as much liquor as stood them in four or five pounds, only for want of laying out three or four shillings. If bottles are corked as they should be, it will be difficult to draw the cork without a screw; and to secure the drawing of the cork without breaking, the screw ought to go through the cork, and then the air must necessarily find a passage where the screw has passed. If a cork had once been in a bottle, though it has not been drawn with a screw, yet that cork will turn musty as soon as exposed to the air, and will communicate its ill flavour to the bottle in which it is next put, and spoil the liquor that way. In the choice of corks, take those that are soft and clear from specks. You may also observe, in the bottling of liquor, that the top and middle of the hogshead are the strongest, and will sooner rise in the bottles than the bottom. When you begin to bottle a vessel of any liquor, be sure not to leave it till all is completed, otherwise it will have different tastes.

If you find a vessel of liquor begins to grow flat whilst it is in common draught, bottle it, and into every bottle put a piece of loaf sugar of about the size of a walnut, which will make it rise and come to itself: and, to forward its ripening, you may set some bottles in hay in a warm place; but straw will not assist its ripening.

If you should have the opportunity of brewing a good stock of small beer in March and October, some of it may be bottled at the end of six months, putting into every bottle a lump of loaf sugar; which, in the summer, will make it a very pleasant and refreshing drink. Or if you happen to brew in summer, and are desirous of brisk small beer, as soon as it is done working, bottle it as before directed.

Where your cellars happen not to be properly calculated for the preservation of your beer, you may use the following expedient · Sink holes in the ground, put into them large oil-jars, and fill up the earth close about the sides. One of the jars will hold about two dozen bottles, and will keep the liquor in proper order; but care must be taken that the tops of the jars are kept close covered. In winter time, when the weather is frosty, shut up all the lights or windows of your cellars, and cover them close with horse-dung, which will keep your beer in a very proper and temperate state.

We shall close this section and chapter with that information, which, if properly attended to, may be found, at times, of the highest convenience and utility.

To Preserve Yeast.

If you wish to preserve a large stock of yeast, which will keep and be of use for several months, either for brewing, or to make bread or cakes, you must follow these directions. When you have plenty of yeast, and are apprehensive of a future scarcity, take a quantity of it, stir and work it well with a whisk, until it becomes liquid and thin. Then get a large wooden platter, cooler or tub, clean and dry, and with a soft brush lay a thin layer of yeast on the tub, and turn the mouth downwards, that no dust may fall upon it, but so that the air may get under to dry it. When that coat is very dry, then lay on another, and so on till you have a sufficient quantity, even two or three inches thick, always taking care that the yeast is very dry in the tub before you lay any more on, and this will keep good for several months. When you have occasion to use this yeast, cut a piece off, and lay it into warm water; then stir it together, and it will be fit for use. If it is for brewing, take a large handful of birch tied together, dip it into the yeast, and hang it up to dry. In this manner you may do as many as you please; but take care no dust comes to it. When your beer is fit to set to work, throw in one of these, and it will make it work as wel. as if you had made fresh yeast.

CHAPTER XXX.

DIRECTIONS FOR TRUSSING POULTRY, &c.

THERE are various reasons why the experienced and prudent housekeeper should be properly acquainted with this necessary preparation to the Art of Cookery. In London every article is generally trussed by the poulterer of whom it is bought; but it frequently happens that, either from inexperience or negligence of the servants, and want of knowledge in the cook, the article appears on the table with disgrace. Another very substantial reason for the cook having this knowledge is, that the families in which they serve are frequently in counties where there are no poulterers, and consequently they are under the necessity of killing and trussing their own poultry. To be prepared, therefore, for the execution of this business, we recommend a proper attention to the following general rules be careful that all the stubs are perfectly taken out; and when you draw any kind of poultry, you must be very particular to avoid breaking the gall, for should that happen, no means can be used to take away that bitterness, which will totally destroy the natural and proper taste of the article dressed. Great care should likewise be taken that you do not break the gut joining to the gizzard; for, should this happen, the inside will be gritty, and the whole spoiled. These are to be attended to as general matters. We shall proceed to particulars, beginning with

Turkeys.

HAVING properly picked your turkey, break the leg bone close to the foot, and draw out the strings from the thigh, for which purpose you must hang it on a hook fastened against the wall. Cut off the neck close to the back; but be careful to leave the crop skin sufficiently long to turn over the back. Then proceed to take out the crop, and loosen the liver and gut at the throat end with your middle finger. Then cut off the vent, and take out the gut. Pull out the gizzard with a crooked, sharp pointed iron, and the liver will soon follow; but be careful not to break the gall. Wipe the inside perfectly clean with a wet cloth; having done which, cut the breast-bone through on each side close to the back, and draw the legs close to the crops. Then put a cloth on the breast, and beat the high bone down with a rolling-pin till it lies flat. If the turkey is to be trussed for boiling, cut the legs off; then put your middle finger into the inside, raise the skin of the legs, and put them under the apron of the turkey. Put a skewer into the joint of the wing and the middle joint of the leg, and run it through the body and the other leg and wing. The liver and gizzard must be put in the pinions; but be careful first to open the gizzard and take out the filth, and the gall of the liver Then turn the small end of the pinion on the back, and tie a packthread over the ends of the legs to keep them in their places. If the turkey is to be roasted, leave the legs on, put a skewer in the joint of the wing, tuck the legs close up, and put the skewer through the middle of the legs and body. On the other side, put another skewer in at the small part of the leg. Put it close on the outside of the sidesman, and put the skewer through, and the same on the other side. Put the liver and gizzard between the pinions, and turn the point of the pinion on the back. Then put, close above the pinions, another skewer through the body of the turkey.

If turkey-poults, they must be trussed as follow: take the neck from the head and body, but do not remove the neck skin. They are drawn in the same manner as a turkey. Put a skewer through the joint of the pinion, tuck the legs close up, run the skewer through the middle of the leg, through the body, and so on the other side. Cut off the under part of the bill, twist the skin of the neck round, and put the head on the point of the skewer, with the bill-end forwards. Another skewer must be put in the sidesman, and the legs placed between the sidesman and apron on each side. Pass the skewer through all, and cut off the toe-nails. It is very common to lard them on the breast. The liver and gizzard may or may not be used, as you like.

Fowls.

When you have properly picked your fowls, cut off the neck close to the back. Then take out the crop, and with your middle finger loosen the liver and other matters. Cut off the vent, draw it clean, and beat the breast-bone flat with a rolling-pin. If your fowl is to be boiled, cut off the nails of the feet, and tuck them down close to the legs. Put your finger into the inside, and raise the skin of the legs; then cut a hole in the top of the skin, and put the legs under. Put a skewer in the first joint of the pinion, bring the middle of the leg close to it, put the skewer through the middle of the leg, and through the body; and then do the same on the other side. Having opened the gizzard, take out the filth, and the gall out of the liver. Put the gizzard and the liver in the pinion, turn the points on the back, and tie a string over the tops of the legs to keep them in their proper place. If your fowl is to be roasted, put a skewer in the first joint of the pinion, and bring the middle of the leg close to it. Put the skewer through the middle of the leg, and through the body, and do the same on the other side. Put another skewer in the small of the leg, and through the sidesman; do the same on the other side, and then put another through the skin of the feet. You must not forget to cut off the nails of the feet.

Chickens.

With respect to picking and drawing, they must be done in the same manner as fowls. If they are to be boiled, cut off the nails, give the sinews a nich on each side of the joint, put the feet in at the vent, and then peel the rump. Draw the skin tight over the legs, put a skewer in the first joint of the pinion, and bring the middle of the leg close. Put the skewer through the middle of the legs and through the body, and d·

the same on the other side. Clean the gizzard, and take out the gall in the liver; put them into the pinions, and turn the points on the back. If your chickens are to be roasted, cut off the feet, put a skewer in the first joint of the pinions, and bring the middle of the leg close. Run the skewer through the middle of the leg, and through the body, and do the same on the other side. Put another skewer into the sidesman, put the legs between the apron and the sidesman, and run the skewe through. Having cleaned the liver and gizzard, put them in the pinions, turn the points on the back, and pull the breast skin over the neck.

Geese.

HAVING picked and stubbed your goose clean, cut the feet off at the joint, and the pinion off the first joint. Then cut off the neck almost close to the back; but leave the skin of the neck long enough to turn over the back. Pull out the throat, and tie a knot at the end. With your middle finger loosen the liver and other matters at the breast end, and cut it open between the vent and the rump. Having done this, draw out all the entrails, excepting the soul. Wipe it out clean with a wet cloth, and beat the breast bone flat with a rolling-pin. Put a skewer into the wing, and draw the legs close up. Put the skewer through the middle of the leg, and through the body, and the same on the other side. Put another skewer in the small of the leg, tuck it close down to the sidesman, run it through, and do the same on the other side. Cut off the end of the vent, and make a hole large enough for the passage of the rump, as by that means it will much better keep in the seasoning.

Ducks are trussed in the same manner, except that the feet must be left on, and turned close to the legs.

Pigeons.

WHEN you have picked them, and cut off the neck close to the back, then take out the crop, cut off the vent, and draw out the guts and gizzard, but leave the liver for a pigeon has no gall. If they are to be roasted, cut off the toes, cut a slit in one of the legs, and put the other through it. Draw the leg tight to the pinion, put a skewer through the pinions, legs, and body, and with the handle of the knife break the breast flat. Clean the gizzard, put it in one of the pinions, and turn the points on the back. If you intend to make a pie of them, you must cut the feet off at the joint, turn the legs, and stick them in the sides close to the pinions. If they are to be stewed or boiled, they must be done in the same manner.

Wild Fowl.

HAVING picked them clean, cut off the neck close to the back, and with your middle finger loosen the liver and guts next the breast. Cut off the pinions at the first joint, then cut a slit between the vent and the rump, and draw them clean. Clean them properly with the long feathers on the wing, cut off the nails, and turn the feet close to the legs. Put a skewer in the pinion, pull the legs close to the breast, and run the skewer through the legs, body, and the other pinion. First cut off the vent, and then put the rump through it. The directions here given are to be followed in trussing every kind of wild fowl.

Pheasants and Partridges.

HAVING picked them very clean, cut a slit at the back of the neck, take out the crop, and loosen the liver and gut next the breast with your fore-finger, then cut off the vent and draw them. Cut off the pinion at the first joint, and wipe out the inside with the pinion you have cut off. Beat the breast bone flat with a rolling-pin, put a skewer in the pinion, and bring the middle of the legs close. Then run the skewer through the legs, body, and the other pinion, twist the head, and put it on the end of the skewer, with the bill fronting the breast. Put another skewer into the sidesman, and put the legs close on each side the apron, and then run the skewer through all. If you would wish to make the pheasant (if it is a cock) have a pleasing appearance on the table, leave the beautiful feathers on the head, and cover them gently with paper to prevent their being injured by the heat of the fire You may likewise save the long feathers in the tail to stick in the rump when roasted. If they are for boiling, put the legs in the same manner as in trussing a fowl.

All kinds of moor game must be trussed in the same manner.

Woodcocks and Snipes.

As these birds are remarkably tender to pick, especially if they should not happen to be quite fresh, the greatest care must be taken how you handle them; for even the heat of the hand will sometimes take off the skin, which will totally destroy the beautiful appearance of the bird. Having picked them clean, cut the pinions of the first joint, and with the handle of a knife beat the breast-bone flat. Turn the legs close to the thighs, and tie them together at the joints. Put the thigh close to the pinions, put a skewer into the pinions, and run it through the thighs, body, and the other pinion. Skin the head, turn it, take out the eyes, and put the head on the point of the skewer, with the bill close to the breast. Remember, that these birds must never be drawn.

Larks.

When you have picked them properly, cut off their heads, and the pinions of the first joint. Beat the breast-bone flat, and turn the feet close to the legs, and put one into the other. Draw out the gizzard. and run a skewer through the middle of the bodies. Tie the skewer fast to the spit when you put them down to roast. Wheat ears, and other small birds. must be done in the same manner.

Hares.

Having cut off the four legs at the first joint, raise the skin of the back, and draw it over the hind legs. Leave the tail whole draw the skin over the back, and slip out the fore-legs. Cut the skin off the neck and head; but take care to leave the ears on, and mind to skin them. Take out the liver, lights, &c. and be sure to draw the gut out of the vent. Cut the sinews that lie under the hind-legs, bring them up to the fore-legs, put a skewer through the hind-leg, then through the fore-leg under the joint, run it through the body, and do the same on the other side. Put another skewer through the thick part of the hind-legs and body, put the head between the shoulders, and run a skewer through to keep it in its place. Put a skewer in each ear to make them stand erect, and tie a string round the middle of the body over the legs to keep them in their place. A young fawn must be trussed just in the same manner, except that the ears must be cut off.

Rabbits must be cased much in the same manner as hares, only observing to cut off the ears close to the head. Cut open the vent, and slit the legs about an inch up on each side of the rump. Make the hind-legs lie flat, and bring the ends to the fore-legs. Put a skewer into the hind-leg, then into the fore-leg, and through the body. Bring the head round, and put it on the skewer. If you want to roast two together, truss them at full length with six skewers run through them both, so that they may be properly fastened on the spit.

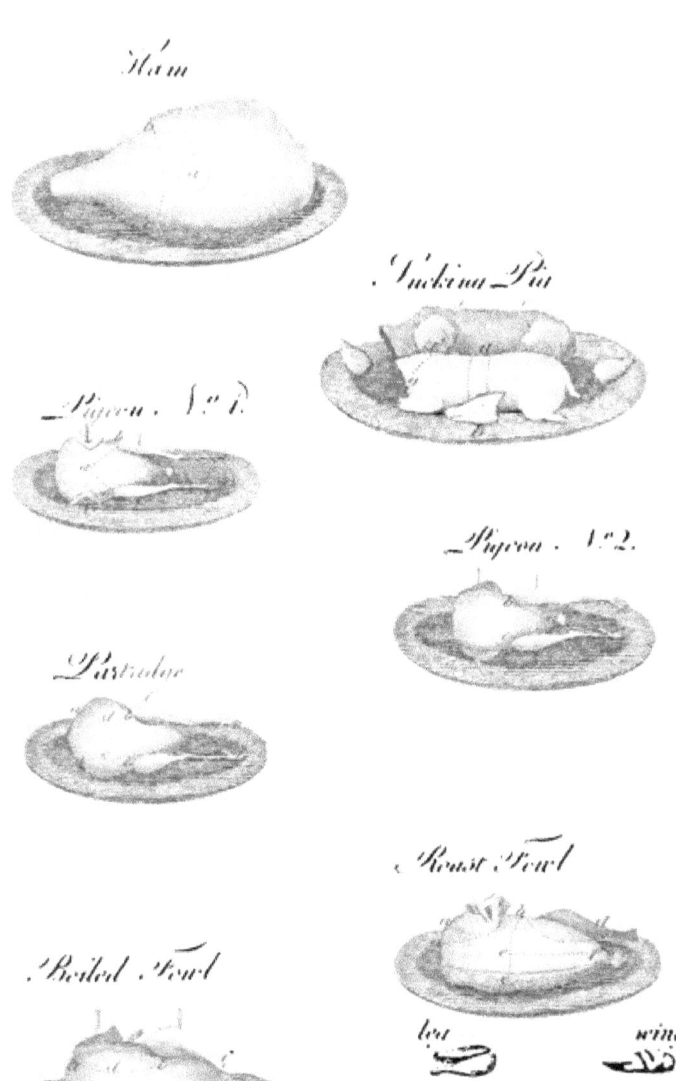
Ham
Sucking Pig
Pigeon. No. 1.
Pigeon. No. 2.
Partridge
Roast Fowl
Boiled Fowl
leg
wing
neck
bone

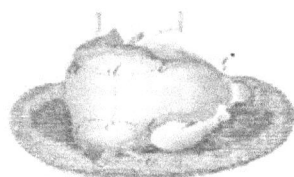

THE

ART OF CARVING.

NOTHING can be more disagreeable to a person who is placed at the head of a table, and whose business it is to pay the necessary honours to guests invited, than to be defective in not being properly able to carve the different articles provided. From the want of knowledge in this particular, it must naturally become no less painful to the person who undertakes the task, than uncomfortable to those who are waiting for the compliment of being served. Abilities and dexterity in this art are striking qualifications in the eyes of every company, and are material instruments of forming the necessary and polite graces of the table.

The instructions here laid down by words, are materially enlivened by the representations of the respective articles described, so that the young and inexperienced may, by proper attention to the description, and reference to the plates, soon make themselves proficients in this useful and polite art.

We shall commence the subject with describing the method of carving

A Roast Fowl.

IN the plate the fowl is placed in the centre, and is represented as lying on its side, with one of the legs, wings, and neck-bone, taken off. Whether the fowl is roasted or boiled, it must be cut up in the same manner. A roasted fowl is sent to table nearly in the same manner as a pheasant, excepting that the pheasant has the head tucked under one of the wings, whereas the fowl has the head cut off before it is dressed. In a boiled fowl (which is represented in the same plate) the legs are bent inwards, and tucked into the belly; but, previous to its being sent to table, the skewers are withdrawn. The most convenient method of cutting up a fowl is to lay it on your plate, and, as you separate the joints, in the line *a*, *b*, *d*, put them into the dish.

The legs, wings, and merry-thought being removed, the next thing is to cut off the neck-bones. This is done by putting in the knife at *g*, and passing it under the long broad part of the bone in the line *g*, *h*, then lifting it up, and breaking off the end of the shorter part of the bone, which cleaves to the breast-bone. All the parts being thus separated from the carcase, divide the breast from the back, by cutting through the tender ribs on each side, from the neck quite down to the vent or tail. Then lay the back upwards on your plate, fix your fork under the rump, and laying the edge of your knife in the line *b*, *e*, *c*, and pressing it down, lift up the tail, or lower part of the back, and it will readily divide with the help of your knife in the line *b, e, e*. In the next place, lay the lower part of the back upwards in your plate, with the rump from you, and cut off the side-bones, (or sidesmen, as they are generally called,) by forcing the knife through the rump-bone in the line *e, f*, when your fowl will be completely cut up.

Boiled Fowl.

We have before observed, that a boiled fowl is cut up in the same manner as one roasted. In the representation of this the fowl is complete, whereas in that part of the other it is in part dissected. Those parts, which are generally considered as the most prime, are the wings, breast, and merry-thought, and next to these the neck-bones, and sidesmen. The legs of boiled fowls are more tender than those that are roasted; but every part of a chicken is good and juicy. As he thigh bones of a chicken are very tender, and easily broken with the teeth, the gristles and marrow render them very delicate. In the boiled fowl the leg should be separated from the drum-stick, at the joint, which is easily done, if the knife is introduced into the hollow, and the thigh-bone turned back from the leg-bone.

Partridge.

The Partridge is here represented as just taken from the spit; but before it is served up, the skewers must be withdrawn. It is cut up in the same manner as a fowl. The wings must be taken off in the lines *a, b*, and the merry-thought in the line *c, d*. The prime parts of a partridge are, the wings, breast, and merry-thought. The wing is considered as the best, and the tip of it reckoned the most delicate morsel of the whole.

Pigeons.

Here are the representations of two, the one with the back uppermost, and the other with the breast.—That with the back uppermost is marked No. 1. and that with the breast No. 2. Pigeons are sometimes cut up in the same manner as chickens. But as the lower part, with the thigh, is in general most preferred, and as, from its small size, half a one is not too much for most appetites, they are seldom carved now, otherwise than by fixing the fork at the point *a*, entering the knife just before it, and dividing the pigeon into two, cutting away in the lines *a, b*, and *a, c*, No. 1, at the same time bringing the knife out at the back, in the direction *a, b*, and *a, c*, No. 2.

A Pheasant.

In the representation here given, the bird appears in a propet state for the spit, with the head tucked under one of the wings. When laid in the dish, the skewers drawn, and the bird carried to table, it must be carved as follows: fix your fork on that part of the breast where the two dots are marked, by which means you will have a full command of the bird, and can turn it as you think proper. Slice down the breast in the lines *a, b*, and then proceed to take off the leg on one side, in the direction *d, e*, or in the circular dotted line *b*, *d*. This done, cut off the wing on the same side, in the line *c*, *d*. When you have separated the leg and wing on one side, do the same on the other, and then cut off, or separate from the breast-bone, on each side of the breast, the parts you before sliced or cut down. Be very attentive in taking off the wing. Cut it in the notch *a*, for if you cut too near the neck, as at *g*, you will find yourself interrupted by the neck-bone, from whence the wing must be separated. Having done this, cut off the merry-thought in the line *f*, *g*, by passing the knife under it towards the neck. With respect to the remaining parts, they are to be cut up in the same manner as directed for a roast fowl. The parts most admired in a pheasant are, first, the breast, then the wings, and next the merry-thought.

A Goose.

LET the neck-end lie before you, and begin by cutting two or three long slices on each side the breast, in the lines *a*, *b*, quite to the bone. Cut these slices from the bone, then take off the leg, turning the goose up on one side, putting the fork through the small end of the leg bone, and pressing it close to the body, which, when the knife has entered at *d*, will easily raise the joint. Then pass the knife under the leg in the direction *d*, *e*. If the leg hangs to the carcase, at the point *e*, turn it back with the fork, and, if the goose is young, it will easily separate. Having removed the leg, proceed to take off the wing, by passing the fork through the small end of the pinion, pressing it close to the body, and entering the knife at the notch *c*, and passing it under the wing in the direction *c*, *d*. This is a very nice thing to hit, and can only be acquired by practice. When you have taken off the leg and wing on one side, do the same on the other. Then cut off the apron in the line *f*, *e*, *g*, having done which, take off the merry-thought in the line *i*, *h*. All the other parts are to be taken off in the same manner as directed for the fowl. A goose is seldom quite dissected, unless the company is very large, in which case the above method must be pursued.

The parts of a goose most esteemed are, the slices from the breast; the fleshy part of the wing, which may be divided from the pinion; the thigh-bone, (or drum-stick as it is called,) the pinion, and the side-bones. If sage and onions are put into the body of the goose, (which is by most approved of,) when you have cut off the limbs, draw it out with a spoon at the place from whence the apron is taken, and mix it with the gravy, which should first be poured boiling hot into the body of the goose. Some people are particularly fond of the rump, which, after being nicked with a knife, is peppered and salted, and then broiled till it is of a nice light brown; and this is distinguished by the epithet of *a devil*. The same is likewise done by the rump of a turkey.

Haunch of Venison.

FIRST cut it across down the bone, in the line *b*, *c*, *a*, then turn the dish with the end *d*, towards you, put in the point of the knife at *c*, and cut it down as deep as you can in the direction *c*, *d*, so that the two strokes will then form the resemblance of the letter T. Having cut it thus, you may cut as many slices as are necessary, according to the number of the company, cutting them either on the right or left. As the fat lies deeper on the left between *d* and *a*, those who are fond of fat, (as is the case with most admirers of venison,) the best flavoured and fattest slices will be found on the left of the line *c*, *d*, supposing the end *d* turned towards you. In cutting the slices, remember that they must not be either too thick or too thin. With each slice of lean add a proper proportion of fat, and put a sufficient quantity of gravy into each plate. Currant-jelly should always be on the table for those who choose it. Indeed this is generally used by most.

A Fore-Quarter of Lamb.

This joint is always roasted, and when it comes to table, before you can help any one, you must separate the shoulder from the breast and ribs, (or what is by some called the coast,) by passing the knife under, in the direction *c*, *g*, *d*, *e*. The shoulder, being then taken off, the juice of a lemon, or Seville orange, should be squeezed upon the part it was taken from, a little salt added, and the shoulder replaced. The gristly part must then be separated from the ribs in the line *f*, *g*, and then all the preparatory business to serving will be done. The ribs are generally most esteemed, and one, two, or more may be easily separated from the rest, in the line *a*, *b* : but to those who prefer the gristly part, a piece or two may be cut off in the lines *h*, *i*, &c. If you should have a fore-quarter of grass lamb that runs large, the shoulder, when cut off, must be put into another dish, and carved in the same manner as a shoulder of mutton.

A Pig.

A pig is seldom sent whole to table, but is usually cut up by the cook, who takes off the head, splits the body down the back, and garnishes the dish with the chops and ears.

Before you help any one at table, first separate the shoulders from the carcase, and then the legs, according to the direction given by the dotted line *c*, *d*, *e*. The most delicate part of a pig is that about the neck, which may be cut off in the line *f*, *g*. The next best parts are the ribs, which may be divided in the line *a*, *b*, &c. and the others are pieces cut from the legs and shoulders. Indeed the bones of a pig are little else than gristle, so that it may be cut in any part without the least difficulty. It produces such a variety of delicate bits, that the fancies of most may be readily gratified.

Shoulder of Mutton.

This is a very fine joint, and by many preferred to the leg, it being very full of gravy, if properly roasted, and producing many nice bits. The figure No. 1, represents it as laid in the dish with the back uppermost. When it is first cut, it should be in the hollow part of it in the direction *a*, *b*, and the knife should be passed deep to the bone. The gravy will then run fast into the dish, the part will immediately open, and many fine slices will be readily cut from it. The prime part of the fat lies on the outer edge, and is to be cut out in thin slices in the direction *e f*. If many are at table, and the hollow part cut in the line *a, b*, is eaten, some very good and delicate slices may be cut out on each side the ridge of the blade-bone, in the direction *c, d*. The line between these two dotted lines, is that in the direction of which the edge, or ridge of the blade-bone lies, and cannot be cut across.

No. 2 represents the under-side, where there are two parts very full of gravy, and such as many prefer to the upper-side. One is a deep cut in the direction *g, h*, accompanied with fat, and the other all lean, in a line from *i* to *k*. The parts above the shank are coarse and dry; but yet some prefer this to the rich and more juicy parts.

A Saddle of Mutton.

This is by some called a chine of mutton, and consists of the two loins together, the back-bone running down the middle of the tail. When you carve it you must cut a long slice in either of the fleshy parts, on the side of the back-bone, in the direction *a, b*. There is seldom any great length of tail left on, but if it is sent up with the tail, many will be fond of it, and it may be easily divided into several pieces, by cutting between the joints of the tail, which are about an inch apart.

A Cod's Head.

Fish in general requires very little carving, the fleshy parts being those principally esteemed. A cod's head and shoulders, when in season, and properly boiled, is a very genteel and handsome dish. When cut, it should be done with a spoon fish-trowel, and the parts about the back-bone on the shoulders are the most firm and best. Take off a piece quite down to the bone, in the direction *a, b, c, d*, putting in the spoon at *a, c*, and with each slice of fish give a piece of the sound, which lies underneath the back-bone and lines it, the meat of which is thin, and a little darker coloured than the body of the fish itself, this may be got by passing a knife or spoon underneath, in the direction *d, f*. About the head are many delicate parts, some fine kernels, and a great deal of the jelly kind. The jelly parts lie about the jaw bones, and the firm parts within the head. Some are fond of the palate, and others the tongue, which likewise may be got, by putting a spoon into the mouth, in the direction of the line *e*.

A Piece of Boiled Salmon.

The fattest and richest part of salmon is the belly; it is therefore customary to give to those who like both, a thin slice of each; the one cut out of the belly in the direction *c, d*, the other out of the back in the line *a. b*. Most people who are fond of salmon generally like the skin, so that the slices must be cut thin with the skin on.

A Mackarel.

Slit the fish all along the back in the line *a, c, b*, and take off the whole side, as far as the line *b c*, not too near the head, as the meat above the gills is generally black, and ill flavoured. The roe of a male fish is soft, but that of the female is hard, and full of small eggs.

A Calf's Head.

In carving this, begin by cutting the flesh quite along the cheek bone, in the direction *c*, *b*, from whence several handsome slices may be taken. In the fleshy part, at the end of the jaw-bone, lies part of the throat-sweet-bread, which may be cut into, in the line *c*, *d*, and which is esteemed the best part in the head. Many like the eye, which is to be cut from its socket *a*, by forcing the point of the knife down to the bottom of one edge of the socket, and cutting quite round, keeping the point of the knife slanting towards the middle, so as to separate the meat from the bone. The palate is also reckoned by some very delicate: it lies on the under side of the roof of the mouth; is a wrinkled, white, thick skin, and may be easily separated from the bone by a knife, by raising the head with your left hand. There is also some nice tender bits on the under side, covering the under jaw, and some delicately gristly fat to be pared off about the ear, *g*. In the upper-jaw is the large tooth behind, which, having several cells, and being full of jelly, is called the sweet-tooth; but its delicacy is more in the name than any thing else. When you serve any person with a slice of the head, you must inquire whether they choose to have any of the tongue and brains, which are generally served up in a separate dish. A slice from the thick part of the tongue, near the root, is the best.

Leg of Mutton.

A leg of wether Mutton, which is by far the best flavoured, may be readily known by the kernel, or little round lump of fat, just above the letters *a*, *e*. This joint, whether boiled or roasted, is carved in the same manner. The person who does this business should turn the joint towards him as it here lies, the shank to the left hand; then holding it steady with his fork, he should cut it deep on the fleshy part, in the hollow of the thigh, quite to the bone, in the direction *a*, *b*. Then will he cut it right through the kernel of fat called the *pope's eye*, of which many are particularly fond. The most juicy parts of the leg are in the thick part of it, from the line *a*, *b*, upward, towards *e*; but many prefer the drier part, about the shank or knuckle, which some call the venison part, from its eating so short; but this is certainly the coarsest part of the joint. The fat lies chiefly on the ridges *e*, *e*, and is to be cut in the direction *e*, *f*. In order to cut out what is by some called the cramp-bone, and by others the gentleman's bone, you must take hold of the shank-bone with your left hand, and cutting down to the thigh-bone at the point *d*, then passing the knife under the cramp-bone, in the direction *d*, *c*, it may easily be cut out.

A Ham.

A ham is cut two ways, either across in the line *b*, *c*, or in the circular line in the middle, taking out a small piece as at *a*, and cutting thin slices in a circular direction, thus enlarging it by degrees. This

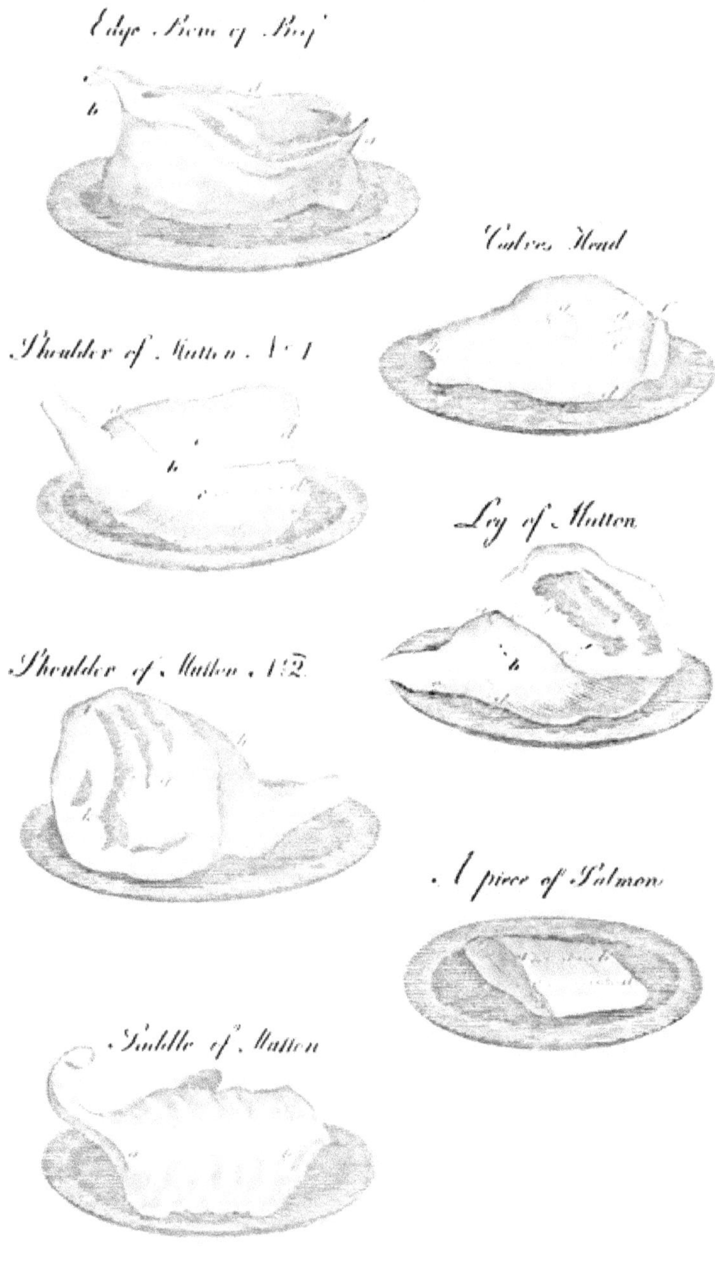
Edge Bone of Beef
Calves Head
Shoulder of Mutton No. 1
Leg of Mutton
Shoulder of Mutton No. 2
A piece of Salmon
Saddle of Mutton

last method is, to preserve the gravy and keep it moist, which is thus prevented from running out.

Piece of Sirloin of Beef.

As a whole sirloin is too large for families in general, so we have here only represented a part, either of which must be carved in the same manner. It is drawn as standing up in the dish, in order to show the inside, or upper part; but when sent to table, it is always laid down, so that the part described by the letter *c*, lies close on the dish. The part *c*, *d*, then lies uppermost, and the line *a*, *b*, underneath. The meat on the upper side of the ribs is firmer, and of a closer texture, than the fleshy part underneath, which is by far the most tender, and of course preferred by many. To those who like the upper side, the outside slice should be first cut off, quite down to the bone, in the direction *c*, *d*. Some people, however, instead of beginning to carve at either end, cut it in the middle of the most leshy part. For those who prefer the inside, several slices may be cut in the direction of the line *a*, *b*, pressing the knife down to the bone. But wherever the slices are cut they must be of a moderate substance, neither too thick nor too thin.

Edge-bone of Beef.

The outside of this joint is generally injured in its flavour from the water in which it is boiled; a thick slice must therefore be cut off, the whole length of the joint, beginning at *a*, and cutting it all the way even and through the whole surface, from *a* to *b*. The soft fat, which resembles marrow, lies on the back below the letter *d*, and the firm fat must be cut in thin horizontal slices at the points *c*; but as some people like the soft, and some the firm fat, it is necessary to ask the company which they prefer. The upper part, as it is generally placed in the dish, is the handsomest, fullest of gravy, most tender, and enriched with fat; but there are some who prefer a slice from the under-side, though it is lean and dry. The skewer that keeps the meat properly together when boiling is here shown at *a*. This should be drawn out before it is served up; or, if it is necessary to leave the skewer in, it should be a silver one.

Brisket of Beef.

This is a part always boiled, and must be cut in the direction *a*, *b*, quite down to the bone, after having cut off the outside, or first slice, which must be cut pretty thick. The fat cut with this slice is a firm, gristly fat, but a softer fat is found underneath for those who prefer it.

Breast of Veal.

A breast of veal must be cut across quite through, dividing the gristles from the rib-bones: this is called cutting the brisket from the ribs. The brisket may be cut into pieces as wanted; for some prefer this part to the ribs. There requires no great direction how to separate the ribs, since nothing more is required than to put the knife in at the top between any two, and continue downwards till they are separated. Remember to give a piece of the sweetbread to every one you help, as that is reckoned particularly delicate.

Fillet of Veal.

This part of the calf is the same as that called the buttock in the ox. Many people think the outside slice of a fillet of veal a delicacy, because it is most savoury; but as some think otherwise, the question should be asked before any one is helped. If no one chooses the first slice, lay it in the dish, and the second cut will be exceeding white and delicate; but take care to cut it even and close to the bone. A fillet of veal is always stuffed under the skirt or flap, with a pudding, or forcemeat. This you must cut deep into, in a line with the surface of the fillet, and take out a thin slice. This, and a thin slice of fat cut from the skirt, must be given to each person at table.

Sparerib of Pork.

This is carved by cutting out slices in the thick part at the bottom of the bones. When the fleshy part is all cut away, the bones, which are esteemed very sweet picking, may be easily separated. Few people admire the gravy of pork, it being too strong for most stomachs.

Rabbits.

To *unlace* a rabbit, the back must be turned downward, and the apron divided from the belly. This done, slip your knife between the kidneys, loosening the flesh on each side. Then turn the belly, cut the back crossways between the wings, and draw your knife down both sides of the back-bone, dividing the sides and legs from the back. Observe not to pull the leg too violently from the bone, when you open the side; but with great exactness lay open the sides from scut to shoulder, and then put the legs together.

Woodcocks.

To *thigh* a woodcock, you must raise the legs and wings in the same manner as you do a fowl, only open the head for the brains. In like manner you *thigh* curlews, plovers, or snipes, using no other sauce than salt.

Mallards or Ducks.

To *unbrace* a mallard or duck, first raise the pinions and legs, but do not cut them off. Then raise the merry-thought from the breast, and lace it down both sides with your knife.

Buttock of Beef.

This part is always boiled, and requires little directions as to the carving of it. A thick slice should be first taken off all round it. When you come to the juicy and prime part of it, you must be careful to cut it even, that it may have a graceful figure, should it be brought to table cold the next day.

THE NEW

FAMILY RECEIPT-BOOK

German method of Clarifying and Preserving Fresh Butter.

A VALUABLE article, the original communication of an ingenious traveller, who resided many years in Germany. "The peculiar advantage of clarified butter," says this gentleman, "though but little known in England, is unequalled for most culinary purposes, for frying, and for general use in long sea-voyages, where no fresh butter is to be had. Indeed this purified butter is equal to the best virgin oils of Florence, Aix, or Lucca, for frying in perfection. At Vienna, and in many other parts of Germany, it is sold in all the shops. The best is purified at the dairies, during the cheapest season, and sent to market in barrels and tubs; it is then clarified. Set a large clean tinned copper vessel on a trivet, over a charcoal fire; and put in the new butter, before it has taken any ill taste, but not in large portions at a time. With the quantity of about fifty pounds, add a large onion peeled and cut crossway. The whole must be closely watched, and kept skimming the moment it begins to boil; and the fire then slackened, that it may only simmer for five minutes; after which, if it cannot be suddenly removed, the fire to be immediately extinguished. The onion then taken out, the butter to be left standing till every impurity sinks to the bottom; as all that has not risen to the skimmer never fails doing. Large tin canisters, stone jars, or wooden vessels made air-tight, holding about fifty pounds each, should receive the liquid butter, and be kept closely covered up for use. This butter should be constantly taken out as it is wanted, with a wooden spoon; neither the hand, nor any metal, ever suffered to touch it."

Queen Elizabeth's Cordial Electuary.

BOIL a pint of the best honey; and, having carefully taken off all the scum, put into the clarified liquid a bundle of hyssop which has been well bruised, previously to tying it up, and let them boil together till the honey tastes strongly of the hyssop. Then strain out the honey very hard; and, putting into it a quarter of an ounce each of powdered liquorice root and aniseed, half that quantity of pulverized elecampane and angelica roots, and one pennyweight each of finely beaten pepper and ginger, let the whole boil together a short time, being well stirred all the while. After which, pour it into a gallipot, or a small jar, and continue stirring till it is quite cold. Keep it covered up for use; and, whenever troubled with straitness at the stomach, or shortness of breath, take some of the electuary on a bruised stick of liquorice, which will speedily afford relief. This is said to have been Queen Elizabeth's favourite remedy for all oppression at the stomach and shortness of breath, with which complaints her majesty had been much afflicted; she lived till seventy-three years of age.

Genuine Friar's Balsam

Put four ounces of sarsaparilla cut in short pieces, two ounces of China root sliced thin, and an ounce of Virginian snake-weed cut small, with one quart of spirits of wine, in a two quart bottle. Set it in the sun, or any equal degree of heat, shaking it two or three times a day, till the spirit be tinctured of a fine golden yellow. Then clear off the infusion into another bottle; and, putting in eight ounces of gum guaicum, set it in the sun, or other similar heat; shaking it very often, till all the gum be dissolved, except the dregs, which will generally be about ten or twelve days. It must now be a second time cleared from the dregs; and, having received an ounce of Peruvian balsam, be well shaken, and again placed in the sun for two days; after which, an ounce of balm of Gilead being added, it is to be once more shaken together, and finally set in the sun for fourteen days, when it will become quite fit for use, and keep many years. There were, formerly, scarcely any complaints, either external or internal, for which this admirable balsam was not considered as an effectual remedy. It has, in truth, many virtues, when properly made; but, as a mere vulnerary, for common flesh wounds, the simpler and cheaper balsams, sold under the names of Friar's Balsam, Turlington's balsam, and the Traumatic Balsam of the London Dispensatory, are usually efficacious. Neither of these, however, nor any of the other compound balsams, or restorative drops, formed on the basis of this true Friar's balsam, are so well adapted for internal use; and some of them, as commonly manufactured for sale, are quite unfit for any such purpose. The dose of genuine Friar's balsam, for consumptions, or any inward ulcer, &c. is about half a table spoonful, on a lump of sugar, or in any liquid vehicle, once or twice a day, according to the urgency of the case, using moderate exercise while in the habit of taking it. In any soreness of the stomach, and for some coughs, twenty or thirty drops occasionally taken, often give complete relief; and, in almost every weakness or debility, they may be advantageously resorted to, as well as by persons afflicted with scorbutic complaints, and other taints or impurities of the blood.

Excellent Lozenges for the Heart-burn.

Take calcined oyster shells, as found on the sea-coast, where they are so blanched by time as to appear, both within and without, of the whiteness of mother of pearl; dry them well by he fire, and then beat and sift them as fine as possible. In half a pound of this powder mix half a pound of loaf sugar well beaten and sifted; and wet it with a spoonful or two of milk and water, so as to form a very stiff paste. Then mould the whole into neat lozenges, of any form or size, and bake them very dry in so slack an oven as not to discolour them; this will be effected after every thing else is drawn. These lozenges so effectually destroy that acidity in the stomach which causes the heart-burn, as not only to prevent the disagreeable sensation it occasions, but greatly to promote digestion. Their power in neutralizing acids may be easily tried, by dissolving one of them in a glass of the sharpest vinegar.

Decoction of the Beards of Leeks, for the Stone and Gravel.

CUT off a large handful of the beards of leeks; and put them in a pot or pipkin with two quarts of water, covered closely up, and to be kept simmering till the liquor is reduced to a quart; then to be poured off, and drank every morning, noon, and evening, about the third part of a pint each time. Half the quantity, or less, may be sufficient for children, according to their respective ages, and the violence of the disease. The most desperate condition of this painful disorder has frequently been cured by this seemingly-simple remedy in little more than a month. It is best to keep making it fresh every two or three days, which indeed is the case with most vegetable decoctions.

Instant Relief for a Pain and Lax State of the Bowels.

TAKE twelve drops of laudanum in half a gill of spirituous cinnamon-water; or, if that cannot be immediately had, in the best brandy. This will seldom fail to give instant relief; but, should it so fail in the first instance, it may be repeated in about an hour.

The true Daffy's Elixir.

THE popular medicine sold under this name is differently made by different venders. The following, however, is considered as the genuine receipt for making it.—Take five ounces of aniseeds, three ounces of fennel-seeds, four ounces of parsley-seeds, six ounces of Spanish liquorice, five ounces of senna, one ounce of rhubarb, three ounces of elecampane-root, seven ounces of jalap, twenty-one drachms of saffron, six ounces of manna, two pounds of raisins, a quarter of an ounce of cochineal, and two gallons of brandy. Stone the raisins, slice the roots, and bruise the jalap. Then mix the whole together; and, after letting them stand close covered for fifteen days, strain out the elixir. So favourite a remedy has Daffy's elixir been for all colicky pains, during the last hundred years, that many families have been enriched by its preparation and sale; a few of whom there is reason to believe, have used not half the ingredients above enumerated. The cheap stuff, commonly sold as Daffy's elixir, is little more than an infusion of aniseeds, liquorice, and jalap, in the coarsest and most fiery malt spirit, lowered with common water.

Infallible Remedy for the Ague.

MIX a quarter of an ounce each of finely powdered Peruvian bark, grains of paradise, and long pepper, in a quarter of a pound of treacle; of which mixture, take a third part immediately as the cold fit commences, washing it down with half a quartern of the best French brandy. As the cold fit goes off, and the fever approaches, take a third part, with the like quantity of brandy; and, on the following morning, fasting, swallow the remainder, and the same quantity of brandy as before. This excellent electuary, which is said never to fail, perfectly cured an afflicted person, after being most grievously tormented for the greater part of four years, having almost every fit accompanied by delirium, during which period innumerable other remedies had been tried in vain. The person from whom it was obtained, declared that he had cured many hundred persons, and never met with but a single instance where the three doses did not immediately effect a cure, and even then a second three completely prevailed. To children under nine years of age, only half the above quantities must be given.

Bayley's Patent Cakes for Liquid Blacking.

THIS blacking has been the scource of an ample fortune to the patentee, the celebrated Mr. Bayley, of Cockspur-street, Charing-cross, whose exclusive right has lately expired. It is made, according to the specification in the patent office, with one part of the gummous juice which issues from the shrub called goat's thorn, during the months of June, July, and August; four parts of river-water; two parts of neat's-foot, or some other softening and lubricating oil; two parts of a deep blue colour, prepared from iron and copper; and four parts of brown sugar candy. The water is then evaporated till the composition becomes of a proper consistence, when it is formed into cakes of such a size as to produce, when dissolved in hot water, a pint of liquid blacking.

An Incomparable Fumigation, or Vapour, for a Sore Throat.

TAKE a pint of vinegar, and an ounce of myrrh; boil them well together about half an hour, and then pour the liquid into a basin. Place over the basin the large part of a funnel which fits it; and, the small end being taken into the mouth of the patient, the fume will be inhaled, and descend to the throat. It must be used as hot as it can possibly be borne; and should be renewed every quarter of an hour, till a cure is effected This excellent remedy will seldom or never fail, if resolutely persisted in, only for a day or two, and sometimes a very few hours, in the most dangerous state of either an inflammatory or putrid sore throat, or even a quinsy.

Dr. Fullar's Vapour for a Quinsy.

TAKE powdered pepper, one ounce; milk, a quart; and boil them to a pint and a half. Put the whole into a glass bottle with a small neck, and let the vapour be received as hot as can be endured with open mouth. "This euporiston," says that learned physican, "more powerfully than any gargle whatsoever, attenuates, melts down, and draws forth, tough phlegm; which, by obstructing the glands and spongy flesh, and hindering the free passage of blood and humours through them, occasions the inflammation and tumour; and, therefore, it more effectually takes off this perilous distemper than any of them." This, it is to be remarked, is only recommended for a quinsy. It affords good professional authority, however, for the preferable use of such vaporous inhalements over common gargles and other medicines, in dangerous complaints of the throat, lungs, &c.

Fine Red Ink.

Boil four ounces of best raspings of Brazil-wood, and one ounce each of crystals of tartar and powdered alum in a quart of the clearest river-water, till half the fluid be evaporated. While it is yet sufficiently warm, dissolve in it an ounce each of double-refined sugar, and the whitest gum arabic. This fine ink is said to preserve its lively red hue much longer than any other known preparation for the same purpose. The common red ink, which is certainly far cheaper, and will do very well for most occasions, is made by infusing four ounces of Brazil-wood raspings with two drachms of powdered alum, in a pint each of vinegar and rain-water, for two or three days, and afterward boiling them over a moderate fire till a third part of the fluid has evaporated. It is then to stand two or three days; and, being filtered through blotting-paper, to be preserved in closely-corked bottles for use.

Method of Cleansing and Polishing Rusty Steel.

After well oiling the rusty parts of the steel, let it remain two or three days in that state, then wipe it dry with clean rags, and polish with emery or pumice-stone, on hard wood. Frequently, however, a little unslacked lime, finely powdered, will be sufficient, after the oil is cleaned off. Where a very high degree of polish is requisite, it will be most effectually obtained by using a paste composed of finely levigated blood-stone and spirits of wine. Bright bars, however, are admirably cleaned in a few minutes, by using a small portion of fine corn emery, and afterward finishing with flour of emery or rotten-stone; all of which may be had at any ironmonger's. This last very simple method will, perhaps, render any other superfluous.

A fine Balsamic Elixir for confirmed Coughs and Consumptions.

Take a pint of the finest old rum, two ounces of balsam of Tolu, an ounce and a half of Strasburg turpentine, an ounce of powdered extract of Catechu, formerly called Japan earth, and half an ounce each of gum guaiacum and balsam of copavia. Mix them well together in the bottle; and keep it near the fire, closely corked, for ten days, frequently well shaking it during that time. Afterwards let it stand two days to settle, and pour off the clear for use. Half a pint of rum may then be poured over the dregs; and, being treated for twelve days in the same manner as the first, will produce more elixir, and equally good. The dose may be from fifty to a hundred, or even two hundred drops, according to the urgency of the case, taken twice or thrice a day in a wine glass of water.

Admiral Gascoigne's Tincture of Rhubarb.

Take half an ounce each of powdered rhubarb, myrrh, cochineal, and hierapicra, and put them in a bottle with one quart of the best double-distilled aniseed water. When it has stood four days, it is fit for immediate use and may be taken, a small wine-glass at time, for any pains in the stomach or bowels. In the valuable co..ection whence this is extracted, is the following memorandum--"There is not a better receipt in the world!"

German Cure for a Consumption.

Take a pound of pure honey, and let it boil gently in a stewpan; then, having washed, scraped clean, and finely grated with a sharp grater, two large sticks of fresh horse-radish, stir into the honey as much as you possibly can. It must remain in a boiling state about five minutes, but stirred so as not to burn; after which, put it into small earthen pots, or a jar, and keep it covered up for use. Two or three table spoonsful a day, or more, according to the strength of the patient, and some time persisted in, is said to perform wonders, even where there is a confirmed phthisis pulmonalis, or consumption of the lungs. It is also serviceable in all coughs where the lungs are greatly affected.

Easy and effectual Cure for Wens.

Put a quantity of salt and water into a saucepan, and boil it four or five minutes; with which, while tolerably hot, bathe the entire surface of the wen, however large; and continue so to do, even after it is cold. Every time, before applying it, stir up the salt deposited at the bottom of the basin, and incorporate it again with the water. In this manner the wen must be rubbed well over, at least ten or twelve times every twenty-four hours; and, frequently in less than a fortnight, a small discharge takes place, without any pain, which a gentle pressure soon assists to empty the whole contents. In particular instances, it is necessary to continue the application several weeks, or even months: but it is said always finally to prevail, where resolutely persisted in, and that without occasioning pain or inconvenience of any kind, there being not the smallest previous notice of the discharge. A person who had, for many years, been an object of attraction in the streets of London, from having a most enormous wen hanging on his neck and breast, being suddenly seen, with astonishment, completely divested of it, was asked how he had lost it, without the appearance of any scar or other disfigurement; when he declared, that he had been happily relieved of his incumbrance, in a very few months, by simply rubbing it with the old rusty fat and brine of bacon. This undoubted fact may serve as a hint, should the still simpler preparation of salt and water ever seem likely to prove insufficiently powerful.

Genuine Lozenges for the Piles, as used in the West Indies, and other warm climates.

Take four ounces of fine powdered loaf sugar, two ounces of flour of sulphur, and a sufficient quantity of mucilage of gum tacamahaca dissolved in red rose water to form the whole into a paste for lozenges. Having made it up in lozenges of the desired form, dry them before the fire, or in an oven after every thing has been drawn. Take, of these lozenges, about the weight of a drachm daily. This is a mos valuable medicine for that disagreeable and dreadful complaint;

which prevails much, and is a peculiarly grievous and even dangerous disease in the West India Islands, as well as in most other hot climates. It is, however, generally found completely efficacious, even in those regions.

Easy Method of cleaning Paper Hangings.

CUT into eight half-quarters a quartern loaf two days old; it must neither be newer nor staler. With one of these pieces, after having blown off all the dust from the paper to be cleaned by means of a good pair of bellows, begin at the top of the room, holding the crust in the hand, and wiping lightly downward with the crumb, about half a yard at each stroke, till the upper part of the hangings is completely cleaned all round. Then go again round, with the like sweeping stroke downward, always commencing each successive course a little higher than the upper stroke had extended, till the bottom be finished. This operation, if carefully performed, will frequently make very old paper look almost equal to new. Great caution must be used not by any means to rub the paper hard, nor to attempt cleaning it the cross or horizontal way. The dirty part of the bread, too, must be each time cut away, and the pieces renewed as soon as at all necessary.

Sir John Hill's Specific for the Scurvy.

SIR John's own description of this excellent remedy will convey its virtues. "There is in the hands of one person only a medicine of very great efficacy in the cure of the scurvy, leprosy, and other desperate cutaneous disorders. Its effect is certain; but it is kept at so exorbitant a price, that only persons of fortune can have the advantage of it.

"A gentleman of great worth and goodness applied some months since to the person who possesses it, in favour of two daughters of a country clergyman. He did not desire it should be given, but requested it at any moderate price. He was refused. A bottle of the medicine was afterward procured, and put into my hands to examine. It appeared to me, on many trials, to be an infusion of the root of the common great water-dock, and nothing else. I have made an infusion of that root, which perfectly agrees with it in taste, smell, and colour, and, what is more important, in virtues.

"This is no modern invention; the plant was long since known and celebrated: it is the famous *Britannica antiquorum vera* of authors, concerning which such wonders are recorded in the cure of scurvies; but, like many other English plants, it has long been neglected.

"I beg you to make this public for the service of those whom the common remedies have failed to cure, and whose fortunes do not afford their going to the person hitherto possessed of the secret for redress. The method of infusion and decoction both will answer better than that by infusion alone, and what I have directed to several who have found great benefit from it, is made thus:

"Weigh half a pound of the fresh root of great water-dock, cut it into thin slices, put it in a stone jar, and pour upon it a gallon of boiling water, cover it up, and let it stand twenty-four hours: then put the whole into a saucepan, and boil it about eight minutes. After this let it stand to be quite cold, then strain it off without squeezing. Drink a half pint basin of this twice a-day, avoid high seasoned food, and use moderate exercise.

"The great good I have seen from this makes me desirous that all may know of it who want it.

"I am, Sir, your humble servant,

"JOHN HILL."

Russian Method of preserving Green Peas for Winter.

PUT into a kettle of boiling hot water any quantity of fresh-shelled green peas: and, after letting them just boil up, pour them into a colander. When the liquor has drained away, empty them into a large thick cloth, cover them over with another, make them quite dry, set them once or twice in a cool oven, to harden a little; after which put the peas into paper bags, and hang them up in the kitchen for use. To prepare them, when wanted, they are first well soaked for an hour or more; and then boiled in cold water, with a few sprigs of mint, and a little butter. Green peas are sometimes kept in England, by scalding and drying alone, without putting them in an oven; they are afterward bottled like gooseberries or damsons covered by clarified suet, closed up with cork and resin, and either buried in the earth or kept in a cool cellar; being boiled, when wanted, till quite tender, with mint, butter, and sugar. This last article, at least, is certainly an improvement on the Russian method. A dish of green peas, thus prepared, has sometimes agreeably surprised friends at a Christmas dinner.

Admirable Wash for the Hair, said to Thicken its Growth better than Bear's Grease.

TAKE two ounces each of rosemary, maidenhair, southernwood, myrtle berries, and hazel bark; and burn them to ashes on a clean hearth, or in an oven: with these ashes make a strong ley, with which wash the hair at the roots every day, and keep it cut short. This lixivium, or wash, it is said, will destroy the worm at the root; and prove far more effectual than bear's grease or pomatum, which rather feed than destroy that unsuspected enemy to the hair.

Excellent Remedy for Swelled Legs and a Relaxed Stomach.

TAKE six ounces of the common bitter infusion, consisting of gentian root and outer rind of Seville orange, with or without coriander seeds; one ounce of tincture of senna; and a drachm of compound spirits of lavender. Mix them together, and take four spoonsful every other night on going to bed. To prevent swelled legs from breaking, make a decoction of marshmallow leaves, rue, camomile, and southernwood, boiled in a quart of ale or stale beer; and foment them with flannels wrung out of the liquor, as hot as can be borne without scalding, three or four times a day. After bathing, anoint them with a little ointment of marshmallows; and should they even be broke, only cover the holes with dry lint, while bathing or fomenting the legs, and afterwards dress them with the ointment, and take a little cooling physic.

Fine Raspberry Vinegar.

THIS excellent article in domestic management is both grateful to the palate, and a very effectual remedy for complaints in the chest. It is made, at very little expense, in the following manner: Pour three pints of the best white-wine vinegar over a pound and a half of fine red raspberries, in a stone jar or china bowl, for neither glazed earthenware nor any metal must be used: the next day, strain the liquor over a like quantity of fresh raspberries; and the day following do the same. Then drain the liquid as much as possible without pressing the fruit; and pass it through a cotton bag previously wetted with plain vinegar, merely for preventing waste, into a stone jar, with a pound of loaf sugar in large lumps to every pint of the vinegar. As soon as the sugar is melted, stir the liquor, and put the jar into a saucepan of water, to simmer for some time; skim it carefully; and, when cold, bottle it for use. A large spoonful, in a small tumbler of water, with a very little sugar, makes a most pleasant and refreshing beverage, either for invalids or persons in health.

Genuine Turlington's Balsam.

THIS is a very good vulnerary balsam for common uses; and may be safely taken internally, where the genuine friar's balsam is not at hand. The receipt for making the true Turlington's balsam, or drops, is as follows: Take an ounce of the Peruvian balsam; two ounces of the best liquid storax; three ounces of gum Benjamin, impregnated with almonds; and half an ounce each of the best aloes, myrrh, frankincense, angelica roots, and the flowers of St. John's wort. Beat all these ingredients in a mortar, and put them into a large glass bottle; adding a pint and a quarter of the best spirits of wine. Let the bottle stand by the kitchen fire, or in the chimney corner, two days and nights; then decant it off, in small bottles well corked and sealed, to be kept ready for use. The same quantity of spirits of wine poured on the ingredients, well shaken up, and placed near the fire, or in some other warm situation, about six or eight days and nights, will serve for slight occasions, on being bottled in a similar manner.

Cephalic Snuff.

TAKE half an ounce each of sage, rosemary, lilies of the valley, and the tops of sweet marjoram, with a drachm each of asarabacca root, lavender flowers, and nutmeg. Reduce the whole composition to a fine powder; and take it like common snuff, as often as may be necessary for the relief of the head, &c. There are many more powerful cephalic snuffs, for particular medicinal purposes, but few so generally useful, agreeable, and innocent, to be used at pleasure.

Cheap and excellent Composition for preserving Weather-Boarding, Paling, and all other Works liable to be injured by the Weather.

LIME, it is well known, however well burnt, will soon become slacked by exposure in the open air, or even if confined in a situation not remarkably dry, so as to crumble of itself into powder. This is called air-slacked lime, in contradistinction to that which is slacked in the usual way by being mixed with water. For the purpose of making the present useful composition to preserve all sorts of wood work exposed to the vicissitudes of the weather, take three parts of this air-slacked lime, two of wood ashes, and one of fine sand; pass them through a fine sieve, and add as much linseed oil to the composition as will bring it to a proper consistence for working with a painter's brush. As particular care must be taken to mix it perfectly, it should be ground on a stone slab with a proper muller, in the same manner as painters grind their white lead, &c. but, where these conveniences are not at hand, the ingredients may be mixed in a large pan, and well beaten up with a wooden spatula. Two coats of this composition being necessary, the first may be rather thin; but the second should be as thick as it can conveniently be worked. This most excellent composition for preserving wood when exposed to the injuries of the weather, is highly preferable to the customary method of laying on tar and ochre. It is, indeed, every way better calculated for the purpose, being totally impenetrable by water; and, so far from being liable to injury by the action of the weather or heat of the sun, that the latter, though such a powerful enemy to tar and ochred palings, &c. even hardens, and consequently increases the durability of, the present proposed composition, which forms an article of public utility not only much cheaper than paint, but prodigiously more lasting.

Art of making Brillau's incomparable Liquid for changing the Colour of the Hair, &c.

This is said to be the best liquid in the world for making the hair curl, as well as for changing that which is disagreeably sandy to a very pleasing colour. The method of preparing it is as follows: Take two ounces of scrapings of lead, an ounce of hartshorn shavings, a quarter of an ounce of litharge of gold, and a drachm of camphor; put them into a pint of soft water, and let them boil for half an hour. When cold and fine, pour the liquid off, and add to it a drachm each of the sugar of lead and rosemary flowers. Boil these up together; pour off the liquid; and, when fine, it is fit for immediate use.

Dutch Method of extracting beautiful Colours from Flowers, Leaves, Roots, &c.

Take the flowers, leaves, or roots, whatever quantity wished, and bruise them nearly to a pulp; then, putting it into a glazed earthen vessel, pour filtered water sufficient to cover it, adding a table spoonful of a strong solution of pure pot-ash to every pint of water. After boiling, in a proper vessel, the whole over a moderate fire till the liquor has obviously imbibed as much of the colour as can possibly be obtained from the pulp, decant the fluid part through a cloth or blotting paper, and gradually drop into it a solution of alum, which precipitates the colouring matter to the bottom. Having secured the powder, continue to wash it in several fresh waters, and, at length, filtering it again through blotting-paper, dry the remaining powder; from which prepare the finest pigments, for water colours, by trituration on marble, with clarified gum-water, and then form them into cakes, cones, &c. for sale. A fine violet colour is in this manner prepared by the Dutch from that flower; the most delicately rosaceous red, from the small French rose and other beautiful red roses; and a most brilliant azure, from the blossoms of the corn blue-bottle.

Excellent Remedy for the Dropsy.

TAKE sixteen large nutmegs, eleven spoonsful of broom ashes dried and burnt in an oven, an ounce and a half of bruised mustard-seed, and a handful of scraped horse-radish; put the whole into a gallon of strong mountain wine, and let it stand three or four days. A gill, or half a pint, according to the urgency of the disease and strength of the patient, is to be drank every morning fasting, taking nothing else for an hour or two after.

Another powerful Remedy for the Dropsy.

TAKE a sufficient quantity of pelitory of the wall, put it in pump water, and let it simmer over the fire till reduced to half its quantity, then add honey to make it into a good syrup, of which take two-thirds to one-third of a glass of Geneva, two or three times in a day till relieved. This actually cured the Editor's mother, after her legs had burst and discharged water several times; and the cure was so effectual, that she never had that sad disorder afterwards.

Of the fining of Malt Liquors.

IT is most desirable to have beer fine of itself, which it seldom fails to do in due time, if rightly brewed and worked; but as disappointments sometimes happen, it will be necessary to know what to do in such cases.

Ivory shavings boiled in the wort, or hartshorn shavings put into the cask just before it is bunged down, will do much towards fining and keeping the liquor from growing stale.

Isinglass is the most common thing made use of in fining all sorts of liquors; first beat it well with a hammer or mallet, and lay it in a pail, and then draw off about two gallons of the liquor, to be fined upon it, and let it soak two or three days; and when it is soft enough to mix with the liquor, take a whisk, and stir it about till it is all of a ferment, and white froth; and frequently add the whites and shells of about a dozen eggs, which beat in with it, and put all together into the cask: then with a clean mopstick, or some such thing, stir the whole together; and then lay a cloth or piece of paper over the bung hole, till the ferment is over, and then bung it up close: in a few days it will fall fine.

But if it is wanted to fine only a small quantity, take half an ounce of unslacked lime, and put it into a pint of water, and stir it well together, and let it stand for two or three hours, or till the lime settle to the bottom; then pour the water off clear, and throw away the sediment; then take half an ounce of insinglass cut small, and boil it in the lime water till it dissolves; then let it cool, and pour it into the vessel, &c.

To make Elderberry Beer, or Ebulum.

TAKE a hogshead of the first and strong wort, and boil in the same one bushel of picked elderberries, full ripe; strain off, and when cold, work the liquor in the hogshead, and not in any open tun or tub; and, after it has lain in the cask about a year, bottle it; and it will be a most rich drink, which they call Ebulum; and has often been preferred to port wine, for its pleasant taste and healthful quality.

N. B. There is no occasion for the use of sugar in this operation; because the wort has strength and sweetness enough in itself to answer that end; but there should be an infusion of hops added to the liquor, by way of preservation and relish.

Some likewise hang a small bag of bruised spices in the vessel White ebulum may be made with pale malt and white elderberries.

Easy method of Drying and Preserving Currants in Bunches

BEAT well up the whites of eggs, or a little gum arabic dissolved in water; and, after dipping in the bunches, and letting them get a little dry, roll them in finely powdered loaf sugar. Lay them on a sieve in a stove to dry; and keep turning them, and adding sugar till they become perfectly dried. Not only red, white, and black currants, but even grapes in bunches, may be thus dried and preserved. They should be carefully kept dry, in boxes neatly lined with paper.

Dr. Stoughton's celebrated Stomachic Elixir.

PARE off the thin yellow rinds of six large Seville oranges, and put them in a quart bottle, with an ounce of gentian root scraped and sliced, and half a drachm of cochineal. Pour over these ingredients a pint of the best brandy; shake the bottle well, several times, during that and the following day; let it stand two days more to settle, and clear it off into bottles for use. Take one or two tea-spoonsful morning and afternoon in a glass of wine, or even in a cup of tea. This is an elegant but simple preparation, little differing from the compound tincture of gentian either of the London or Edinburgh Dispensatories; the former adding half an ounce of canella alba, (white cinnamon,) and the latter only substituting for the cochineal of Stoughton, half an ounce of husked and bruised seeds of the lesser cardamom. In deciding on their respective merits, it should seem, that Stoughton's elixir has the advantage in simplicity, and, perhaps, altogether as a general and elegant stomachic. Indeed, for some particular intentions, both the London and Edinburgh compositions may have their respective claims to preference: in a cold stomach, the cardamom might be useful; and, in a laxative habit, the canella alba. As a family medicine, however, to be at all times safely resorted to, there is no need to hesitate recommending Dr. Stoughton's elixir.

Cure for a Pimpled Face.

TAKE an ounce each of liver of sulphur, roche-alum, and common salt; and two drachms each of sugar-candy and spermaceti. Pound and sift these articles; then put the whole into a quart bottle, and add half a pint of brandy, three ounces of white lily water, and the same quantity of pure spring water. Shake it well together, and keep it for use. With this liquid, the face is to be freely and frequently bathed; remembering always first to shake the bottle, and, on going to bed, lay all over the face linen which has been dipped in it. In ten or twelve days at farthest, it is said a perfect cure will be effected of this very unpleasant complaint, as nothing in this composition can possibly prove prejudicial.

Curious method of separating Gold or Silver from Lace, without burning it.

CUT in pieces the gold or silver lace intended to be divested of any thing but the pure metal; tie it up tightly in linen, and boil it in soap ley, till the size appear considerably diminished: then take the cloth out of the liquid; and, after repeatedly rinsing it in cold water, beat it well with a mallet, to extract all the alkaline particles. On opening the linen, to the great astonishment of those who have never before witnessed the process, the metallic part will be found pure and undiminished, in all its natural brightness, without a single thread.

Permanent Red Ink for marking Linen.

THIS useful preparation, which was contrived by the late learned and ingenious Dr. Smellie of Edinburgh, who was originally a printer in that city, may be used either with types, a hair pencil, or even with a pen: take half an ounce of vermilion, and a drachm of salt of steel; let them be finely levigated with linseed oil, to the thickness or limpidity required for the occasion. This has not only a very good appearance; but will, it is said, be found perfectly to resist the effects of acids, as well as of all alkaline leys. It may be made of other colours, by substituting the proper articles instead of vermilion.

Portable Balls for taking out Spots from Clothes.

SPOTS of grease, &c. are in general easily removed from woollen cloth of all descriptions by means of portable balls prepared in the following manner: Take fuller's earth, dried so as to crumble into powder, and moisten it well with lemon juice; then add a small quantity of pure pulverised pearl-ashes, and work up the whole into a thick paste. Roll this paste into small balls, let them completely dry in the heat of the sun, and they are then fit for immediate use. The manner of using them is, by moistening with water the spots on the cloth, rubbing the ball over them, and leaving it to dry in the sun, when, on washing the spots with common water, and often with brushing alone, the spots instantly disappear.

Art of preparing a newly-discovered Permanent Green Pigment, both for Oil and Water Colours.

A GREEN colour, at once beautiful and durable, discovered by the ingenious M. Kinnman, member of the Swedish Academy. The process by which it is produced is thus described: Dissolve, in aqua fortis, a small quantity of zinc; and, in aqua regia, some strongly calcined cobalt: each solution to be made in a different vessel, and to remain till the respective liquids be completely saturated. When they are both ready, mix one part of the former with two parts of the latter; and, having prepared a hot and clarified solution of potash, pour in a quantity exactly equal to the whole of both the other solutions, for the purpose of precipitating the mixture. After it has subsided, the fluid part should be decanted, and the sediment evaporated to dryness over the fire, till it assumes a green colour. It is necessary, however, that it should be repeatedly washed with filtered water, before it can be used; but, this being effected, it becomes fit for both oil and water colours, as it is sufficiently fixed to withstand all the effects of the air and the sun; which the inventor fully ascertained, by an experience of more than ten years. By means of this preparation, also the ingenious inventor adds, that painters may readily combine their yellow and ultramarine, so as to form a most beautiful and permanent green.

Stewed Oysters in French Rolls.

TAKE any quantity of oysters, and wash them in their own liquor. Then, straining it, put it in again with them, and add a little salt, ground pepper, beaten mace, and grated nutmeg. Let them stew a little together, and thicken them up with a great deal of butter. In the mean time, cut the tops off a few French rolls, and take out sufficient crumb to admit some of the oysters, which must be filled in boiling hot, and set over a stove, or chafing-dish of coals, till they are quite hot through; filling them up with more liquor, or some hot gravy, as the former soaks in. When they are sufficiently moistened, serve them up in the manner of puddings.

Dr. Anderson's admirable Improvement on the common Mode of salting Butter.

THIS ingenious gentleman, in his celebrated Recreations, first published the following directions for an improved mode of preserving salt butter; which he had experienced as not only more effectually to preserve it from any taint of rancidity than the general old method of using common salt only, but also to make it look better, and taste sweeter, richer, and more marrowy, than if it had been cured with common salt alone. Take of the best common salt, two parts; of saltpetre, one part; and of sugar, one part; beating them up together, so that they may be completely blended. To every pound of the butter add an ounce of this composition, mix it well in the mass, and close it up for use. Butter thus prepared will keep good for three years, and cannot be distinguished from what has been recently salted. It may be necessary to remark, indeed, that butter cured in the above excellent manner, does not taste well till it has stood at least two or three weeks. Dr. Anderson is of opinion that such butter would keep during the longest voyages, if it could be so stowed as not to melt by heat of climate, and thus occasion the salts to separate.

Method of expeditiously Fattening Chickens.

Among the many silly prejudices which exist in England against the more general use of rice, is that of remarking its total unfitness for feeding fowls. This may be true enough, if it be given them in so hard a state as to pass without dissolution; but, perhaps, there is scarcely any thing which will sooner fatten the most delicate chickens than this very article, when it is properly prepared: Take, for that purpose, a quantity of rice, and grind or pound it into a fine flour; mix sufficient for present use with milk and a little coarse sugar; stir the whole well over the fire, till it makes a thick paste; and feed the chickens, in the day-time only, by putting as much of it as they can eat, but no more, into the troughs, belonging to their coops. It must be eaten while warm; and, if they have also beer to drink, they will soon grow very fat. A mixture of oatmeal and treacle, combined till it crumbles, is said to form a food for chickens, of which they are so fond, and with which they thrive so rapidly, that at the end of two months they become as large as the generality of full-grown fowls fed in the common way.

Lord Orford's curious method of Feeding Carp in Ponds.

Make a gallon of barley meal, three pounds of chalk, and a sufficient quantity of fine clay, into a very stiff paste; put it into a net, and place it so as to hang about a foot from the bottom of the water. When the carp have sucked away all but the clay, supply them with more made up in the same manner; and, in three weeks or a month, they will be found exceedingly fat.

Dr. Fuller's Chemical Snuff for the Head-Ache, Palsy, and Drowsy Distempers.

Medicinal snuffs, or errhines, are chiefly to be used in the morning; but, if needful, at any other time also. "They draw," Dr. Fuller observes, "out of the head and nose, abundance of water, mucus, and viscid phlegm, and are pertinently prescribed against such illnesses of the head as are caused by tough clammy matter, and have been of long continuance and contumacious; such as gravative head-ache, palsy, and drowsy distempers." He particularly recommends, for these purposes, a snuff made in the following manner: Take half a scruple of turbith mineral, half a drachm of powdered liquorice, a scruple of nutmeg, and two drops of oil of rosemary; make them all into a fine powder, and snuff up into the nose a very small quantity. This is so wonderfully powerful, that it brings off thin lympha as if it raised a salivation through the nose, so plentifully and streamingly, that no person could have imagined who had never seen its effects. He advises, therefore, that it should not be often repeated, without snuffing up after it a little warm milk or oil, to prevent any soreness by fretting the membrane of the nostrils.

Speedy Remedy for a Bruised Eye.

Boil a handful of hyssop leaves in a little water, till they are quite tender: then put them up in linen, apply it hot to the eye, tie it on tightly at bed-time, and the eye will next day be well. This receipt is taken from a large and valuable collection that formerly belonged to the family of the Earl of Shaftesbury; and it is therein asserted, that "a man, who had his thigh terribly bruised by the kick of a horse, was cured in a few hours, only by a poultice of the leaves of hyssop, cut or minced very small, and beaten up with unsalted butter. Culpepper in his herbal asserts the same respecting the virtues of hyssop.

Stomach Plaster for a Cough.

Take bees' wax, Burgundy pitch, and rosin, each an ounce; melt them together in a clean pipkin, and then stir in three quarters of an ounce of common turpentine, and half an ounce of oil of mace. Spread it on a piece of sheep's leather, grate some nutmeg over the whole plaster, and apply it quite warm to the region of the stomach.

Oil of Brown Paper, for Burns.

Take a piece of the thickest coarse brown paper, and dip it in the best salad oil; then set the paper on the fire, and carefully preserve all the oil that drops for use. This is said to be an admirable remedy for all sorts of burns. Oil of writing paper, collected in a similar manner, is often recommended for the tooth-ache.

Liquid for removing Spots of Grease, Pitch, or Oil, from Woollen Cloth.

In a pint of spring water dissolve an ounce of pure pearl-ash; adding, to the solution, a lemon cut in small slices. This being properly mixed, and kept in a warm state for two days, the whole must be strained, and the clear liquid kept in a bottle for use. A little of this liquid being poured on the stained part, is said instantaneously to remove all spots of grease, pitch, or oil; and the moment they disappear, the cloth is to be washed in clear water.

Method of taking out Ink Spots from Woollen, Linen, and Silk.

To take spots of ink out of woollen, they must first be rubbed with a composition, consisting of the white of an egg, and a few drops of oil of vitriol, properly incorporated: next, immediately washed with pure water; and, lastly, have the parts smoothed, in the direction of the nap, with a piece of flannel or white woollen cloth. From linen, ink spots may be removed, by immediately dropping plentifully on them, while wet with the ink, the tallow from a lighted candle, and letting it remain on a few days before washing the linen: this is also said to take the stains of red-port out of linen. Ink spots on silk require to be well rubbed with the ashes of wormwood and strong distilled vinegar, and to be afterwards cleansed with soap-water. When ink is once dried on linen, the spot is to be taken out by rubbing it well with a piece of lemon, and then using a hot iron till the ink totally disappears. If a lemon be cut in half, the linen where spotted pressed down over it till the juice penetrates through and the hot iron then placed on the linen, the spot will immediately give way, and soon entirely vanish.

Ink Stains taken out of Mahogany.

PUT a few drops of spirit of sea-salt, or oil of vitriol, in a tea-spoonful of water, and touch the stain or spot with a feather; and, on the ink disappearing, rub it over with a rag wetted in cold water, or there will be a white mark not easily effaced.

Red Mixture for giving a fine Colour to Mahogany Furniture.

STAINS of ink being first removed by the method above described, wash the tables or other mahogany furniture with vinegar, and then rub them all over with a red mixture made in the following manner: Put into a pint of cold-drawn linseed oil four pennyworth of alkanet root, and two pennyworth of rose-pink; stir them well together in any earthen vessel, and let them remain all night, when the mixture, being again well stirred, will be immediately fit for use. When it has been left an hour on the furniture, it may be rubbed off till bright with linen cloths; and will soon have a beautiful colour, as well as a glossy appearance.

Mr. Jayne's Patent Method of preserving Eggs.

VARIOUS have been the expedients by which good housewives have endeavoured to preserve eggs. They have, in turns, been kept in salt, in flour, and in bran; they have been scalded in hot water, and deposited at the bottom of a cold running stream; they have been steeped in vinegar, and they have been bathed with oil. None of these expedients, however, seem to be universally approved, though each has had its respective advocates, and been warmly recommended to attention. In the year 1791, a patent was obtained by Mr. William Jayne, for his newly-invented composition calculated to preserve eggs. The specification of Mr. Jayne, whose patent expired of course in the year 1805, directs that, for preparing his composition, a Winchester bushel of quick or unslacked lime, two pounds of common salt, and half a pound of cream of tartar, should be incorporated with such a quantity of common water as may reduce the mixture to a state of consistence in which an egg will float with its top above the surface. In this liquid the eggs are to be constantly kept for use, and the patentee asserts, that they will thus certainly be preserved perfectly sound for at least two years.

Chinese Mode of rendering all Sorts of Cloth, and even Muslin, Water-Proof.

BY the following very simple process for making cloth water-proof, it is asserted that the Chinese render not only all the strongest cloths but even the most open muslins, impenetrable to the heaviest showers of rain; nor yet, as it is said, will this composition fill up the interstices of the finest lawn, or in the slightest degree injure the most brilliant colours. The composition to which these valuable qualities are imputed, is merely a solution of half an ounce of white wax in a pint of spirits of turpentine. In a sufficient quantity of the mixture, made with these materials, immerse the articles intended to be rendered water-proof, and then hang them in the open air till they become perfectly dry. This is all the process necessary for accomplishing so desirable a purpose; against which, however, may be objected, perhaps, the expense, and unpleasant scent, of the turpentine spirits: the latter objection may be remedied by using equal parts of spirits of wine and oil of wormwood, a mixture of which is said to dissipate the smell of turpentine; but the former, it is not to be denied, must necessarily be, at the same time, in some degree, augmented. It has lately been attempted, in England, to render the use of water-proof cloth general.

Beautiful newly-discovered Golden Yellow Dye, for Silks, Cotton, &c.

This fine, lively, and durable yellow dye, has recently been discovered by M. Lasteyrie, who thus describes the process by which it is obtained from the shaggy spunk, or boletus hirsutus of Linnæus; a species of mushroom, or fungus, growing chiefly on apple or walnut trees. This vegetable substance is replete with colouring matter, which must be expressed by pounding in a mortar: after which the liquid thus acquired is to be boiled about a quarter of an hour. Six pints of water may be well tinged for dying, by a single ounce of the expressed fluid. This being strained, the silk, cotton, &c. intended to be dyed, must be immersed and boiled in it for about fifteen or twenty minutes; when fine silk, in particular, if it be afterwards passed through soft soap water, will appear of a bright golden yellow hue, equal in lustre to that of the silk hitherto imported from China, at a great expense, for imitating gold embroidery. In short, every sort of stuff retains a fine yellow colour; but it is, of course, less bright on linen and cotton. Nor is the use of this vegetable substance confined to dying; since it has been ascertained that the yellow extract which it yields is applicable to the purposes of painting, both in oil and in water colours.

Curious Method of Breeding an innumerable Quantity of the beautiful Gold and Silver Fish.

The curious process by which this is to be easily effected, may be in general applied, on a larger scale, to the breeding, in equal profusion, most of our esculent fresh-water fish. It is, simply, as follows: Get a large deep cistern or vat, of any dimensions, but one of about four feet diameter, and nearly the same height or depth, will very well answer the purpose; then take a quantity of birch, or small faggot wood, which has been previously soaked some time in a stream, spring, or pond, so as to have lost all power of discolouring or giving any farther taste to fresh water, and lay this wood all along the bottom, to the thickness of about a foot, in some parts at least, having large stones on the top to keep it from rising or motion. Being thus certain that neither the vat nor the birch can spoil the water, nearly fill it with the best soft water from a river or pond such as there can be no doubt that fish will be able to live in. The vat, it is to be observed, must be placed in the open air, but not in a too cold or exposed situation; and the breeding is to commence in the spring, when the fish are full, and just ready to spawn. Choose, as breeders, four hard-roed or females, and only one soft-roed milcher or male. Put the five, with all possible care not to hurt them, into the vat; feeding them occasionally, by throwing in a few crumbs of bread, or some other trifling food, but in no other way disturbing them. When they appear quite thin, or shotten as it is termed, they must be quietly taken out with a small net, so as by no means to disturb the spawn, and entirely kept away; as they would, if allowed to remain, (such is the nature of these and most other fish,) soon devour the greatest part of the spawn and small fry, suffering little or none ever to reach maturity. The vat must not be disturbed during the whole summer; only, as the water decreases, a little fresh must from time to time be as gently as possible poured in, to supply the deficiency. In the course of the summer, the vivified roes will be hatched, and the water perceived swarming with a minute fry; fully sufficient to stock a large piece of water, if not devoured by other fish, or the several birds which make fish their prey. By this method, myriads of those beautiful fish may be easily bred; and, consequently, become very common. At present, it is true, though originally introduced from the East Indies, of which, as well as of China, the gold fish, or cyprinus auratus of Linnæus, is a native, it is still chiefly kept in glass globular vessels for ornament. It has, however, within these few years, been sufficiently ascertained, that these fishes thrive and propagate in ponds, or other reservoirs of water; where they are said to acquire a much larger growth, and come to greater perfection, than in the oriental countries.

Syrup of Red Cabbage, as prepared in France.

Cut and wash a large red cabbage, put it into a pot covered with water, and let it simmer three or four hours over a moderate fire, till there only remains about a pint of liquor; then strain it through a sieve, pressing the cabbage forcibly to get all the juice; let the liquor stand some hours to settle, and pour off the clear. Put a pound of Narbonne honey into a saucepan, over a stove, with a glass of water; and keep skimming it all the time it is boiling, till it be completely clarified. Then put in the cabbage juice, and make the whole boil to the consistence of a syrup; which is always to be known, by taking a little of it on one finger, and finding that, on its being rubbed against the next, it forms a thread which does not instantly break. This syrup is regarded in France as a most excellent fortifier of the breast. It is undoubtedly a good pectoral syrup, very pleasant, not at all expensive, and easily made. A decoction of red cabbage, even in England, by some eminent physicians, has been frequently recommended for softening acrimonious humours in disorders of the breast, and also in hoarseness.

Boluses for the Rheumatism and Contractions of the Joints

Bruise four cloves of garlic with two drachms of gum ammoniac and make them into six boluses with spring water. Take one every morning and evening, drinking plentifully of sassafras tea, at least twice a day, while using this medicine. This is said to be a most effectual remedy for the rheumatism, and equally good in contractions of the joints.

Pill for an Aching Hollow Tooth.

Take half a grain each of opium and yellow sub-sulphate of quicksilver, formerly called turpeth mineral; make them into a pill, and place it in the hollow of the tooth some hours before bed-time, with a small piece of wax over the top, when it is said never to fail effecting a complete cure. It was originally communicated, with many other medical receipts, by a learned physician at York.

Tea for the Gout.

Take the leaves of carduus benedictus, or the holy thistle, with a sufficient proportion of angelica leaves to make it palatable, but not much of either at a time, and drink half a pint of this infusion made like common tea, rather weak, constantly every morning for twelve months. This is said to have alone relieved several persons who were almost crippled with the gout. The leaves of the blessed thistle, in strong decoction, are generally agreed to be beneficial where there is a loss of appetite, or the stomach has been impaired by irregularities; and, whether an infusion be made in cold or warm water, it occasions, if drank freely, a copious perspiration, and greatly promotes the secretions. The dried leaf, which may be used for making the tea recommended, loses much of that forbidding flavour always possessed by the fresh plant; and which occasions it to be sometimes employed in strong decoctions, either as an emetic, or as the auxiliary of an emetic.

Infallible Powder for Shortness of Breath.

This excellent remedy for shortness of breath is particularly recommended to young ladies. The powder is thus directed to be made: Take an ounce each of carraway seeds and anniseeds, half an ounce of liquorice, a large nutmeg, an ounce of prepared steel and two ounces of double-refined sugar; reduce the whole into a very fine powder, and take as much as will lie on a shilling every morning fasting, and the same quantity at five in the afternoon. It will be requisite to use exercise while taking this medicine, which generally very soon effects a cure. Where any invincible prejudice against the use of steel exists in the mind, the medicine may be tried without it; it will even then frequently afford relief.

Excellent Wash for Numbed or Trembling Hands

These disagreeable complaints are said to be soon remedied by the very simple expedient of frequently washing the hands so affected in a strong decoction of wormwood and mustard seed; to be strained, and used when cold.

Mustard Whey, for a Palsy and Nervous Disorders.

TURN half a pint of boiling milk, by putting in a table-spoonful of made mustard. Strain the whey from the curd, through a sieve, and drink it in bed. This will give a generous and glowing warmth, the whey thus conveying the mustard into the constitution. Dr. Stephen Hales says, that he knew a woman, who had a great degree of numbness all over her, remarkably relieved with two doses only, and mentions several instances where it has done good in nervous cases, and in palsy, greatly abating the malady and prolonging life.

Ingenious French Vegetative Liquid for making Bulbous Roots flower beautifully in ornamental Glasses, without Earth, during the Winter Season.

DISSOLVE, gradually, in a glazed earthen or glass vessel, three ounces of saltpetre, one ounce of common salt, and half an ounce of salt of tartar, with a pint of rain water. When the solution is completed, add half an ounce of loaf sugar; filter the whole through a bag or blotting paper, and keep it bottled for use. Into each flower-glass, filled with rain or river water, are to be put eight or ten drops of this liquid. The glasses must be kept constantly full, and the water renewed every tenth or twelfth day at farthest; to which must always be added the requisite number of drops of the vegetative liquor. To ensure complete success, however, the glasses ought to stand on a mantle or chimney-piece where a fire is regularly kept in cold weather. The fibres of the roots must of course always imbibe the liquid; and, with proper management, a fine succession of flowers may be kept up during the most rigorous seasons; such as crocuses of different colours, tulips, hyacinths, snow-drops, &c.

Art of Extracting the finest Carmine Powder from Clippings of Scarlet Cloth.

THAT incomparable crimson colour, called carmine, which so beautifully participates in the most delicate tints of scarlet and of purple, is so very expensive, that miniature painters are often induced to substitute for carmine a composition of lake; by the following process, however, it is credibly asserted, that a better carmine may with certainty be manufactured than much of what is imported from France. Take five or six gallons of the purest water, and dissolve in it a sufficient quantity of pot-ash to make a strong ley. After having filtered the solution, put it in a brass pot, and boil in it a pound of the clean shreds or clippings of the finest scarlet broad cloth dyed in grain, till they have entirely lost their colour; then squeeze the shreds, and pass all the ley through a flannel bag. Dissolve two pounds of alum in a proper quantity of water, and add this solution to the ley; stir them well together, and the whole will become rather thick. It is then to be repassed through the flannel bag, and the liquor will run out clear; but, if it be at all tinged, it is again to be boiled, with the addition of a small quantity of dissolved alum, and passed through the bag a third time, when all the carmine will be left behind. Fresh water is then to be poured repeatedly into the bag, till all the alum is washed away: after which the colour must be dried. so as to prevent any dust from settling on it; and, being previously reduced to an impalpable powder, on glass or marble, it will be immediately fit for use.

Substitute for Verdigrease, in producing a fine Black Dye without Injury to Cloth, &c.

As verdigrease, though generally combined with logwood for dying black, is extremely apt to corrode the texture of the cloth, &c. the Society for the Encouragement of Arts, Manufactures, and Commerce, in the Adelphi, rewarded Mr. Cleg for his discovery of a substitute in dying that colour. For this purpose, equal parts of pot-ash, or any other strong alkaline salt, and vitriol of copper, are to be separately dissolved, and the two solutions gradually mixed. If the vitriol be sufficiently saturated, the water on the surface will become transparent on adding a few drops of the alkaline solution; but, if not, it will produce a blue colour, so that no pot-ash should be added till a complete saturation be effected. These proportions of vitriol and alkaline salt will be equivalent to a similar quantity of verdigrease; and, on being combined with decoctions of logwood, in the same manner as verdigrease, will impart a fine black dye, which is by no means prejudicial to the texture of cloth, hats, or other articles, so often rotted by pernicious black dyes.

Artificial Musk.

The mode of making artificial musk, which is often used in Germany for that expensive odorous drug, is simply as follows: Add, to one drachm of oil of amber, by small portions at a time, four times the quantity of nitrous acid, commonly called aqua-fortis; carefully stirring them together with a glass rod all the time, and continuing so to do till the whole be converted into a yellow resin, possessing the smell of musk in great perfection. It must, of course, be kept closely stopped up, like real musk; and may sometimes supply the place of that high-priced article, not forgetting the nature of its chief ingredient.

Wonderful but easy and effectual Method of rendering all Sorts of Paper Fire-Proof.

This astonishing effect is produced by a most simple process. It is only necessary, whether the paper be plain, written, or printed on, or even marbled, stained, on painted for hangings, to immerse it in a strong solution of alum-water, and then thoroughly dry it, when it will immediately become fire proof. This experiment is readily ascertained, by holding a slip of paper thus prepared over a candle. Some paper, however, will require to imbibe more of the solution than it may receive by a single immersion; in which case, the operation of dipping and drying must be repeated till such paper becomes fully saturated, when, it is positively asserted, neither the colour nor quality of the paper will be in the smallest degree affected; but that, on the contrary, both will be even improved.

Bellamy's Patent Methods of making Leather of all Sorts Water-Proof.

The patentee and inventor of these methods, Mr. John Bellamy, makes use of two compositions; which, according to his specification in the Patent Office, registered 1794, are as follow: A gallon each of nut and poppy oils are to be mixed with three gallons of linseed oil; or, one gallon of either nut or poppy oil may be added to three of that expressed from linseed; or, two gallons of linseed oil may be combined with a pint of nut oil and the like quantity of poppy oil. These ingredients, either in the above proportions, or such others as may be required by the nature of the oils, being mixed in an iron pot, are to be placed over a gentle fire; and to each gallon of oil must be added a pound of white copperas, sugar of lead, colcothar, or any other drying substance. When the whole has remained six or seven hours over such a degree of heat as it will bear without rising, till it become sufficiently dry, it is to be taken off, and suffered to cool: this first compound is then fit for use. The second compound, for the same purpose of rendering all kinds of leather water-proof, is thus directed to be made: Take a pound of gum resin, half a pound of pitch, and a quarter of a pound each of tar and turpentine; well mix these ingredients with one gallon of the oils prepared according to the first method, by gently heating the entire mass, and then increasing the fire till the whole be thoroughly incorporated. When the oils prepared according to the first method, or the gums according to the second, are sufficiently cool, either is to be rubbed into the leather with a brush dipped in the respective composition; and the thoroughly-impregnated leather being stretched on an even board, the superfluous matter is to be removed from its surface. Sole leather, and other thick substances, are to be first gently warmed: and, after being fully saturated with the composition, and properly dried in a warm place, they are ready for use.

Genuine Receipt for making the Invaluable Cordial Liquor called Vespetro, recommended by the king of France's Physicians at Montpellier.

This truly excellent and agreeable cordial, which comes thus sanctioned to the world, is recommended for all complaints in the stomach, indigestion, sickness, colic, obstructions, stitches of the side, spasms in the breast, diseases of the kidneys, strangury, gravel, oppression of the spleen, loathing, vertigo, rheumatism, shortness of breath, &c. The following are the genuine instructions for making it: Take a thick glass or stone bottle which will hold considerably more than two English quarts, and put in it two Paris pints, being equal to about two English quarts, of the best brandy; adding the following seeds, first grossly pounded in a mortar; two drachms of angelica seeds, one ounce of coriander seeds, and a large pinch of pugil each of fennel seeds and anniseeds. Then squeeze in the juice of two fresh lemons, putting in also their rinds; add a pound of loaf sugar; and, well shaking the bottle from time to time, let the whole infuse five days. After this, to render the liquor clearer, pass it through a cotton bag, or filtering paper, and bottle it up, carefully and closely corked. To be taken, a small cordial glass at a time, more or less frequently, according to circumstances. A table-spoonful taken four or five successive mornings, is said to kill the worms in children; and, on rubbing with that small quantity the nose and temples fasting, it is a preservative of the person so using it against the ill effects of damp or unwholesome air. In short, this liquor will abundantly satisfy all who may have occasion to use it; and a gentleman having been long afflicted with an hepatic flux, which gave him continual torment, the use of this liquor carried it off, and completely cured him.

Incomparable Method of Salting Meat, as adopted by the late Empress of Russia.

The following method of salting meat is asserted to have been used by the great empress Catharine, in her household establishment, with the utmost success: Boil together, over a gentle fire, six pounds of common salt, two pounds of powdered loaf sugar, three ounces of saltpetre, and three gallons of spring water. Carefully skim it while boiling; and, when quite cold, pour it over the meat, every part of which must be covered with the brine. In this pickle, it is said, the meat will not only keep for many months, but the hardest and toughest beef will thus be rendered as mellow and tender as the flesh of a young fowl; while either beef, pork, or even mutton, will have a fine flavour imparted by it. In warm weather, however, the blood must be expressed from the meat, and the whole well rubbed over with fine salt, before it is immersed in the liquor. Young pork should not be left longer than three or four days in this pickle, as it will then be quite sufficiently softened: but hams, intended for drying, may remain a fortnight before they are hung up; when they should be rubbed with pollard, and closely covered with paper bags, to prevent their being fly-blown. Though this pickle is, at first, somewhat more expensive than common brine, (as it may be again used, on being boiled with additional water and the other ingredients,) it is far from being, on the whole, importantly more dear; whilst it seems to promise advantages which most people would be happy to purchase at a much higher price.

Electuary for the Rheumatism, by Dr. Brookes.

Take conserve of orange peel, two ounces; cinnabar of antimony levigated, half an ounce; gum guiacum in powder, one ounce; Winter's bark in powder, three drachms; syrup of orange peel sufficient to make an electuary. The dose three drachms, morning and evening.

Art of making the best Black Ink Powder.

INFUSE a quarter of a pound of finely powdered nut galls in three pints of rain or river water; exposing it, occasionally well stirred, to a moderate degree of warmth for a few days, till the colouring matter seems fully extracted: then filter the solution into a vessel slightly covered, and place it in the open air for several weeks: when, on removing the mouldy skin from the top, which has gradually been formed, it must be carefully collected, have hot water poured over it, undergo another filtration, and then be evaporated to dryness. Thus will be produced a gray crystalline salt, called the acid salt of galls, and which is the essential basis of black ink. On triturating a single drachm of this salt with an equal quantity of vitriol of iron, and about a pennyweight of the driest gum arabic, a composition will be obtained which affords an excellent black ink, merely on being dissolved in warm water.

Genuine Syrup for Coughs, Spitting of Blood, &c

THIS excellent remedy for such frequently very alarming symptoms, cannot be made too public. "He must," says the learned and liberal Dr. Fuller, "be a mere stranger in physic, who is not acquainted with this most noble syrup, and how mightily it succours those who cough up blood." It is thus made: Take six ounces of comfrey roots, and twelve handsful of plantain leaves: cut and beat them well; strain out the juice; and, with an equal weight of sugar, boil it up to a syrup.

Vast advantages of Baking instead of Boiling Beet-Root.

THE beet-root too forcibly intrudes itself on the improved sagacity of mankind to be entirely neglected, as a source of cheap and salubrious food. The late Dr. Lettsom, some few years since, took uncommon pains to recommend a variety of one species of this genus, the German mangel-wurzel, or famine-root, under the appellation of the root of scarcity, or large white beet-root, as an article worthy of being universally cultivated. The time, however, seems not yet arrived for the full value of even the more attractive red species to be generally known and duly appreciated; so that his philanthropic design may be said to have hitherto failed. In speaking of the beet-root generally, the red beet-root, therefore, is to be considered as alone designated; and we are about to offer a few hints for bringing its modest and humble merits into a little more deserved estimation. The rich saccharine juice of the beet-root is, in a great degree, lost, and the root itself rendered, at once, less nutritious by the adventitious watery weakness which it is made to imbibe, as well as by parting with the native gelatinous syrup, of which it is thus forcibly deprived. It is, therefore, most strongly recommended to adopt the mode of baking beet-roots, instead of boiling them, for general use; when they will, unquestionably, be found to afford a very delicious and most wholesome food. This is not offered as an untried novelty: beet-roots are universally baked all over the continent of Europe; and, in Italy particularly, they are carried about, warm from the oven, twice a day, like hot loaves, &c. in London. They are there purchased by all ranks of people, and afford to many thousands, with bread and a little salt only, a very satisfactory meal.

Remedy for Wind in the Veins.

This state of the veins, though always visible on the slightest inspection, often escapes any notice, though it leads to many disorders. The following remedy may be taken with advantage whenever they appear in a suspicious state: Take equal quantities of powdered liquorice, carraway seeds, and sugar candy: to which add a third part of rhubarb, and the like quantity of cream of tartar, both finely pulverized. Of this mixture, take a tea-spoonful three or four times a day; either by itself, or in a glass of wine. It should be continued about a week; and, being gently laxative, it cools the blood, eases pains, and relieves and prevents many disorders.

Best Method of making Sage Cheese.

Take the tops of young red sage; and, having pressed the juice from them by beating in a mortar, do the same with the leaves of spinage, and then mix the two juices together. After putting the rennet to the milk, pour in some of this juice, regulating the quantity by the degree of colour and taste it is intended to give the cheese. As the curd appears, break it gently, and in an equal manner; then, emptying it into a cheese vat, let it be a little pressed, in order to make it eat mellow. Having stood for about seven hours, salt and turn it daily for four or five weeks, when it will be fit for the table. The spinage, besides improving the flavour and correcting the bitterness of the sage, will give it a much more pleasing colour than can be obtained from sage alone.

Syrup of Ginger.

An agreeable and moderately aromatic syrup, impregnated with the flavour and medicinal virtues of ginger, is thus prepared: Macerate an ounce and a half of beaten ginger in a quart of boiling water, closely covered up, for twenty-four hours: then, straining off the infusion, make it into a syrup, by adding at least two parts of fine loaf sugar, dissolved and boiled up in a hot water bath.

Wonderful Power of the Turkish Glue, or Armenian Cement, with the Art of making it.

The jewellers in Turkey, who are mostly Armenians, according to Mr. Eton, formerly a consul, and author of the Survey of the Turkish Empire, have a singular method of ornamenting watch-cases, &c. with diamonds and other precious stones, by simply gluing or cementing them. The stone is set in silver or gold, and the other part of the metal made flat to correspond with the part to which it is to be fixed; it is then warmed gently, and has the glue applied, which is so very strong, that the parts cemented never separate. This glue, which will strongly unite bits of glass, and even polished steel, and may of course be applied to a vast variety of useful purposes, is thus made: Dissolve five or six bits of gum mastich, each the size of a large pea, in as much spirits of wine as will suffice to render it liquid: and, in another vessel, dissolve as much isinglass, previously a little swelled or softened in water, though none of the water must be used, in French brandy or good rum, as will make a two-ounce phial of very strong glue: adding two small bits of gum galbanum, or ammoniacum, which must be rubbed or ground till they are dissolved. Then mix the whole with a sufficient heat. Keep the glue in a phial stopped close, and, when it is to be used, set the bottle in hot or boiling water. Mr. Eton observes, that some persons have, in England, prepared and sold this composition under the name of Armenian Cement; but it is much too thin, and the quantity of mastich in it too small: it must, this gentleman adds, be like strong carpenters' glue. This certainly is one of the most valuable known cements in the world. Nor is it at all improbable, that a plan, said to have been invented in France or Germany, for making up clothes, &c. by uniting cloth without sewing, in some attempt founded on the use of this very cement; with what ultimate success, we must leave time to develope. In the mean while, there can be no sort of doubt, that much may be effected by ingenious applications of so powerful an agent.

Valuable Secret in preparing Foil for Diamonds, and other precious Stones, as used by the Armenian Jewellers.

THE method of preparing the rich foils in which the Armenian jewellers set precious stones, particularly diamonds, to much advantage, and which, under roses or half-brilliants, is most remarkably beautiful, and not subject to tarnish, is generally kept as a great secret; and such foils, Mr. Eton assures us, sells at Constantinople for from half to three-quarters of a dollar each. The mode of preparing them is extremely simple. An agate is cut, and highly polished, of the shape desired; a cavity of about its own size is next formed in a block of lead, and over this cavity is placed a bit of tin, the thickness of strong brown paper, scraped very bright. The agate is then placed on the tin, over the cavity, and struck with a mallet; when the beautiful polish which the tin instantly receives, is scarcely to be imagined by those who have never seen it.

Easy method of Dying Cotton with Madder, as practised at Smyrna.

COTTON, at Smyrna, Mr. Eton tells us, is dyed with madder in the following manner: The cotton is boiled in common olive oil, and then in mild alkali; being thus cleaned, it will take the madder dye: and this is the fine colour so greatly admired in Smyrna cotton-yarn. "I have heard," adds this gentleman, "that the sum of five thousand pounds was given in England for this secret!" It is doubtless, a secret in preparing cottons, and perhaps other articles, for the reception of a particular dye, very well worth knowing

The Duchess of Marlborough's admirable Water for Thickening the Hair, and to prevent its falling off.

This most excellent water for the hair is produced in the following manner: Distil, as cool and slowly as possible, two pounds of honey, a handful of rosemary, and twelve handsful of the curlings or tendrils of grape-vines, infused in a gallon of new milk, from which about two quarts of the water will be obtained.

Celebrated French Worm Medicine for Dog

This medicine has the reputation of effectually killing and expelling the worms with which dogs are often so grievously tormented, and which, probably, may be one grand cause of their running mad. It is thus made: Take, for one dose, which generally proves sufficient, two drachms each of juice of wormwood, aloes, and staves-acre, the two last powdered as small as possible; with one drachm each of pounded burnt hartshorn and sulphur. Mix the whole together in nut oil, to the quantity of about half a glass, which must be given to the dog for a dose. If at all necessary, another dose may be given a day or two after.

Superior Use of the celebrated German Tinder, and great Importance of its being universally adopted.

On the continent of Europe, every traveller, sportsman, &c. carries constantly this tinder about him, which is conveniently portable, and resembles a piece of soft and very thick tanned leather, of elastic substance, and a sort of velvet surface on the upper part. It is, in fact, a large fungus, commonly called punk, which grows at the roots of old trees, where it spreads to a considerable size. This substance is dressed, hammered, and otherwise manufactured for the purpose, into this appearance, and, being dried, forms the true German tinder at all times ready for use, and far less liable to become damp than English tinder. The manner of using it is by tearing off a small bit, which will serve several times, and holding it at the edge of the flint, which is smote by the steel, instead of the steel by the flint. In this the Germans are so expert, and can so well rely on their tinder, that they will engage to light it at a single stroke, and, indeed, seldom fail to do so. The tinder being thus kindled, may be placed in a pipe of tobacco, or extinguished instantly between the finger and thumb, after lighting a match for this or any other purpose. It is always kept in a pouch or box, with a flint, steel, and short German matches; and few persons are much from home without carrying them constantly in their pockets. If the German tinder were to be manufactured in England, many poor persons might be employed in collecting the punk, which is now suffered to rot without utility; and, could it be brought entirely to prevent the destruction of rags for tinder, a quantity far exceeding what may be generally imagined, it might prove the means of greatly assisting the manufacture of paper.

To make a Powder, by which you may write with water.

Bruise to powder a handful of galls, half an ounce of vitriol, an ounce of gum arabic and gum sandrick. Mingle them finely sifted together, then rub your paper with a little of it laid upon cotton wool; and, having smoothed it, take water, and write upon the paper; then suffering it to dry, it will be black.

Turkish Method of Filtering Water by Ascension.

The process is this: They make two wells, from five to ten feet, or any other depth, at a small distance from each other, with a communication between the two at their bottoms. The separation is of clay well beaten, or other substances impenetrable by water. Both wells are then filled with sand and gravel. The opening of the well into which the water to be filtered runs, is made somewhat higher than that into which it is to ascend; nor does the sand of this latter approach the brim, where there is either sufficient room left for all the filtered water, or it is drawn off by a spout run into a vessel placed for that purpose. The greater the difference is between the height of the two wells, the faster the water filters; but the less it is, the better it operates, provided a sufficient quantity of water be supplied by it for the intended purpose. This, Mr. Eton observes, may be practised in a cask, tub, jar, or other vessel, and would be useful on board of ships: the water being conveyed to the bottom by a pipe, and the lower end having in it a sponge, or the pipe might be filled with coarse sand. It is evident, that all such particles as, by their gravity, are carried down in filtration by descent, will not rise with the water in filtration by ascension. From this account, it should seem, that the principle of filtration by ascent, considered as a new discovery by some ingenious Europeans, has been long known to the Turks.

Mr. Peacock's Patent Machine for Purifying and Filtering the foulest water.

The utility of filtering machines, in the different processes of brewing, distillery, and dying, as well as that of making bread, and all other domestic arts, is sufficiently obvious. The filtering machine of Mr. Peacock has been contrived and composed with a combination of skill and simplicity which is seldom witnessed. The turbid fluid is poured into a vessel, with layers of sifted gravel or small pebbles, in different gradations of size, at the botton, and connected somewhat like the Turkish filtering wells, with a similar vessel, with like strata or layers, in progressive degrees of fineness, through which the water, however foul, on its entrance into the first vessel, now rises clear and pure in this. Had Mr. Peacock, who is one of the first architects in the world, been a poor or a mercenary man, this invention might have obtained him a large fortune: but, being neither one nor the other, though this gentleman secured his right by patent, and he was only solicitous of its being adopted from philanthropic motives, and has probably lost more money than he has gained by the invention. When its use becomes duly appreciated, some future manufacturer of Mr. Peacock's filtering machines may probably reap the advantage. A specimen of his machine is deposited in Guildhall, London, and, though capable of yielding a constant and pure stream of three hundred gallons in twenty-four hours, it does not occupy more room than a common large drip or filtering stone, with all its accompanying apparatus: that nothing may be wanting to its perfection, it is easily cleansed, though seldom necessary, in the short space of a single minute. Nothing, therefore, is easier than for brewers, distillers, dyers, &c. who are so inclined, to have all their water filtered by means of Mr. Peacock's invention, which is capable of being extended to any magnitude, at an expense which cannot be the smallest object to the generality of persons concerned in those respective manufactories. This invention, could it be brought into general use, might be considered as a blessing to the nation. At sea, if the strata may be so fixed as not to be too much disturbed or deranged by the ship's motion, which seems very possible, the use of such a machine must be so great, that no vessel ought to sail without one. A little charcoal, from its antiseptic quality, might perhaps be introduced with advantage among the strata of gravel. The want of filtered water gives rise to more nephritic complaints than is imagined.

Management of Coffee in France.

Those who wish to have excellent coffee, in France, roast it every day as it is used: they even say, that it should be roasted, ground, infused, and drunk, in the space of two hours; and assert that, if these processes be longer in succeeding each other, the coffee loses much of that volatile spirit which constitutes all its agreeable flavour The quantity commonly used is an ounce to five cups of spring water, to produce four of good and clear coffee. In the mean time, it is usual to throw their coffee grounds into a vessel, boil them half an hour, and leave them to settle: this infusion so well serves for a third part of the coffee in powder, that in a coffee-pot of fourteen cups of pure spring water, which should have three ounces to be good, two ounces with this infusion will be of equal strength and goodness. The operation of boiling the grounds is performed, in large coffee-houses, five or six times every day. This is the common way of making coffee throughout France, where it is generally drank with sugar and cream; while, at different coffee-houses, and in particular families, vanilla, isinglass, and other ingredients, are also introduced, as they have lately been in England. The French, beside breakfasting often on coffee, usually drink two cups about half an hour after dinner, to hasten digestion, or abate the fumes of wine and liqueurs when they have been taken to exceed the bounds of necessity.

An invaluable, though cleanly and easily made Mixture, for effectually destroying those noisome Vermin Bugs.

Mix half a pint of spirits of turpentine and half a pint of best rectified spirits of wine in a strong bottle, and add in small pieces about half an ounce of camphire, which will dissolve in a few minutes. Shake the mixture well together; and, with a sponge or brush dipped in it, well wet the bed and furniture where the vermin breed. This will infallibly destroy both them and their nits, though they swarm. The dust, however, should be well brushed from the bedstead and furniture, to prevent, from such carelessness, any stain. If that precaution is attended to, there will be no danger of soiling the richest silk or damask.

On touching a live bug with only the tip of a pin put into the mixture, the insect will be instantly deprived of existence, and should any bugs happen to appear after using the mixture, it will only be from not wetting the linen, &c. of the bed; the foldings or linings of the curtains near the rings or the joints, or holes in and about the bed or head-board, in which places the vermin nestle and breed; so that those parts being well wetted with more of the mixture, which dries as fast as it is used, and pouring it into the joints and holes, where the sponge and brush cannot reach, it will never fail totally to destroy them.

The smell of this mixture, though powerful, is extremely wholesome, and to many persons very agreeable. It exhales, however, in two or three days.

Only one caution is necessary; but that is important. The mixture must be well shaken when used; but *never* applied by candlelight, lest the spirits, being attracted by the flare of the candle, might cause a conflagration.

Grand Ptisan, or Diet Drink of Health and Longevity, by a celebrated French Physician, who lived nearly a hundred and twenty years.

THE famous inventor of this admirable prolonger of human existence was Monsieur De Sainte Catharine; who, by taking it himself for a fortnight, three times a year, before winter, toward Easter, and during the greatest heats of summer, lived to the age of nearly an hundred and twenty years. This ptisan is pronounced useful to all sorts of persons: if they are ill, to cure them; if well, to preserve them in health. It is even good for infants; and, above all, excellent for old people. An infinitude of facts attest its wonderful effects. It is thus directed to be prepared: Take about a quart of the best-sifted and well-washed oats, and a small handful of wild succory roots newly drawn out of the earth; boil them gently in six quarts of river water for three-quarters of an hour, and then add half an ounce of crystal mineral, and three or four spoonsful of the best honey, or a quarter of a pound of it in weight. Let the whole now boil half an hour longer; then strain it through linen, put the liquid in an earthen vessel, and leave it covered to cool. For persons of a bilious habit, only half the quantity of honey should be used, as the sweetness has a tendency to increase the bile. Two good glasses of this ptisan should be drank every morning fasting, without eating any thing for some hours: and the same quantity three hours after dinner. This course must be continued for fourteen days, without bleeding or confinement, or taking broth, new-laid eggs, or any other particular diet, but in all respects living as usual. The weak and infirm need only take a single glass, and they will not fail to feel the good effect. It is natural that persons who are too gross and costive should commence with some previous purgative; after which this remedy will prove more efficacious. This ptisan is easy to take, and pleasant in its operations; not occasioning any griping pains or other disagreeable sensations: at the same time, it perfectly cleanses the reins, is very diuretic, greatly promotes expectoration; purges the brain; cleanses the lungs, the liver, and the spleen; expels putrid and malignant humours, all pain from the head, gravel, and even stone when newly formed; cures tertian and quartan agues, however inveterate; all colics and pleurisies; the itch, blotches, and other foul eruptions; and, in short, every kind of heaviness, lassitude, and general debility. It rouses the senses, clears the sight, excites appetite, and gives rest and sleep. It refreshes, feeds, and conveys perfect health; and even seems still sensibly operating, and doing good, for a month or two after it has been taken. It is, beside all this, very nourishing. Instead of weakening, as is the case with the greater part of other remedies, it absolutely strengthens: and, during the dog-days and greatest heats of summer, when medicines in general are subject to become dangerous, and even fatal, this is in fact more salutary than at any other season. It might, indeed, be taken every day without doing the smallest injury; the party taking care, during intensely cold weather, to keep constantly warm. To attain long life, it will perhaps be sufficient to take it for a fortnight once or twice in the year; if once only, during the great heats, as the best season for its use. This panegyric, however great, is translated almost verbatim from a most respectable French author. It is undoubtedly an excellent medicine.

Curious and Simple Manner of Keeping Apricots, Peaches, Nectarines, Plums, &c. and even Figs, fresh all the Year.

FOR this small but excellent article, we are indebted to no less a person than the celebrated Monsieur Lemery, one of the first chemists France ever produced: Beat well up together equal quantities of honey and common water, pour it into an earthen vessel, put in the fruits all freshly gathered, and cover them up quite close. When any of the fruit is taken out, wash it in cold water, and it is fit for immediate use.

Genuine Windsor Soap.

To make this famous soap for washing the hands, shaving, &c. nothing more is necessary, than to slice the best white soap as thin as possible, melt it in a stew-pan over a slow fire, scent it well with oil of carraway, and then pour it into a frame or mould made for that purpose, or a small drawer, adapted in size and form to the quantity. When it has stood three or four days in a dry situation, cut it into square pieces, and it is ready for use. By this simple mode, substituting any more favourite scent for that of carraway, all persons may suit themselves with a good perfumed soap at the most trifling expense. Shaving-boxes may be at once filled with the melted soap, instead of a mould.

Art of Dying or Staining Leather Gloves, to resemble the beautiful York Tan, Limerick Dye, &c.

THESE different pleasing hues of yellow brown or tan colour, are readily imparted to leather gloves by the following simple process: Steep saffron in boiling hot soft water for about twelve hours: then having slightly sewed up the tops of the gloves, to prevent the dye from staining the insides, wet them over with a sponge or soft brush dipped into the liquid. The quantity of saffron, as well as of water, will of course depend on how much dye may be wanted; and their relative proportions, or the depth of colour required. A common tea-cup will contain sufficient in quantity for a single pair of gloves.

Art of making Phosphoric Tapers or Matches.

IN a tubular piece of glass four inches long, and a single line only internal diameter, closed at one end, put a small bit of phosphorus; and pushing it to the extremity, introduce a taper covered slightly with wax, to fill up the rest of the tube, which must be hermetically sealed; when plunging the other end into boiling water, the phosphorus melts, and adheres to the taper or match. A line is usually marked on the glass with a flint, at about one-third the length of the tube, where it is to be broken when the taper is wanted for use; which being then briskly drawn out, will be found completely lighted by the phosphorus.

Easy Method of preparing Phosphoric Bottles.

HEAT a common glass phial, by fixing it in a ladleful of sand; then, putting in two or three minute bits of phosphorus, stir them about with a piece of red-hot iron wire, till the phosphorus is all spread over and adheres to the internal surface of the bottle, where it will form a reddish coating. When, by repeated introductions of the heated wire, this is completely effected, the bottle is to remain open a quarter of an hour, and then be corked for use. One end of a common match being put into a bottle thus prepared, on touching the phosphorus, and being suddenly drawn out, will be with certainty lighted. As there can be no particular danger of accidental fire from the use of these bottles; and, with reasonable care in using them, and keeping them closely stopped, a single bottle would last a considerable time, and might, were the demand general, be replenished at a most trifling expense: it may, possibly, in the hands of some ingenious and enterprising person, be finally made to supersede the tinder-box, that dreadful consumer of rags, and consequent enemy to the manufacture of paper. Phosphorus is one of those grand discoveries of modern times, the chief utilities of which seem to be reserved for a future and wiser age.

Specifications of Lord William Murray's Patent for extracting Starch from Horse Chesnuts.

The patent for this useful invention and discovery is dated March 8, 1796; of course the exclusive privilege of extracting starch from horse chesnuts in the following manner was confined to the patentee till the expiration of fourteen years. We shall present our curious readers with the mode of preparing this starch in his lordship's own words, extracted from the specification in the Patent Office: "I first take the horse chesnuts out of the outward green prickly husks; and then, either by hand, with a knife or other tool, or else with a mill adapted for that purpose, I very carefully pare off the brown rind: being particular not to leave the smallest speck, and to entirely eradicate the sprout or growth. I next take the nuts, and rasp, grate, or grind, them fine into water: either by hand, or by a mill adapted for that purpose. The pulp, which is thereby formed in that water, I wash as clean as possible through a coarse hair sieve; and then, again, through a still finer; constantly adding clean water, to prevent any starch from adhering to the pulp. The last process is, to put it, with a large quantity of water, about four gallons to a pound of starch, through a fine gauze, muslin, or lawn, so as entirely to clear it of all bran, or other impurities. As soon as it settles, I pour off the water, and then mix it up with clean; repeating this operation till it no longer imparts any green, yellow, or other colour, to the water. I then drain it off, till nearly dry; and set it to bake, either in the usual mode of baking starch, or else spread out before a brisk fire; being very attentive to stir it frequently, to prevent its horning; that is to say, turning to a paste or jelly, which, on being dried, turns hard like horn. The whole process should be conducted as quick as possible. The utility of this invention requires no comment Should it come into general use, not only a vast consumption of wheat flour must be saved; but, from the necessity of planting more chesnut trees, for the sake of a fruit hitherto considered as of no sort of value, much of that excellent and beautiful wood will be produced for the many purposes to which it is applicable.

Patent Potato Composition to be used instead of Yeast.

For this ingenious contrivance, which introduces potatos as a sort of leaven for making wheaten bread, a patent was obtained by the inventor, Mr. Richard Tillyer Blunt, in the year 1787; which, of course, is now expired. The following is the process for this purpose, as described by Mr. Blunt in his specification: To make a yeast gallon of this composition, such yeast gallon containing eight beer quarts, boil in common water eight pounds of potatos as for eating; bruise them perfectly smooth; and mix with them while warm, two ounces of honey, or any other sweet, and one beer quart of common yeast. For making bread, mix three beer pints of the above composition with a bushel of flour, using warm water in making the bread. The water .: be warmer in winter than in summer, and the co·nposition to be ·sed in a few hours after it is made: and, as soon as the sponge, or the mixture of the composition with the flour, begins to fall the first time, the bread should be made, and put in the oven.

Britannic Elastic Gum.

For the invention of this curious and useful composition, a patent was obtained, in the year 1781, by Mr. Albert Angel: who describes it, in his specification, as being very serviceable and useful in the several branches of portrait and house painting, by making the colours durable and free from peeling; as of great utility in gilding, painting, penciling, and staining of silks, calicos, &c. and in dressing silk, linen, and cotton, in the loom, instead of gum or paste, so as to strengthen the threads of the finest cottons; as excellent for beautifying and fixing the colours on paper, equal to that done in India; as of the greatest use for rendering the clay, or composition, used in modeling, sufficiently supple, and preventing its drying too fast; and, lastly, not less effectual in causing a transparency of colours fit for china and earthen ware, so as to stand baking or burning. This Britannic gum is stated to be prepared in the following very simple manner: Put into an iron kettle, and melt down together, till the mixture become this composition or elastic gum, a gallon of linseed or nut oil, a pound of yellow or bleached bees' wax, six pounds of glue or size, a quarter of a pound of verdigrease, a quarter of a pound of litharge, and two quarts of spring or rain water.

West India Bitters, or Anti-Bilious Drops.

The following is said to have been Tousaint's, late Emperor of Hayti, celebrated bitters, called by him anti-bilious drops, and used generally throughout the West India islands: Take three drachms of Seville orange peel; two drachms of gentian root; one drachm each of cardamoms, grains of paradise, and gallengals; half a drachm each of nutmeg and cloves; one scruple each of saffron and cochineal; and half a handful each of camomile flowers and Roman wormwood. Infuse the whole in two quarts of brandy, rum, or Madeira wine; and, after it has stood some time, pour off what is clear, and add to the ingredients a quart more of either liquor, though brandy is considered as best for the purpose. This, too, having remained a somewhat longer time, and been occasionally shaken, may be in like manner poured off for use. Two tea-spoonsful, or somewhat less, are directed to be taken, an hour before dinner, in half a glass of wine.

Oxymel of Garlic for Asthmatic Complaints, Rheumatism, &c.

N a general sense, oxymels are any compositions of honey and vinegar boiled to the consistence of a syrup. Simple oxymel, for example, is merely clarified honey melted in an equal weight of water, with the addition of as much vinegar as water, boiled to the consistence of a syrup, and even this, taken about half an ounce at a time, is said to attenuate gross hum··rs, carry away slimy matter, open old stoppages and obstructions of the lungs, and remove phlegm, with whatever else occasions shortness of breath. In the humid asthma, for promoting expectoration and the fluid secretions, &c. the oxymel of garlic seems to stand in still higher estimation with the faculty It is thus made: Boil, in a pint of vinegar, half an ounce of cleansed carraway and sweet fennel seeds, for about a quarter of an hour; then take it off the fire, slice in three ounces of garlic, and cover it closely up. As soon as it becomes cold, the liquor must be strained and expressed; and mixed, by the heat of a water bath, with a pound and a quarter of clarified honey, to a proper syrupy consistence. A tea-spoonful or two of this oxymel, taken occasionally, particularly night and morning, will scarcely ever fail of proving beneficial to all persons afflicted with an asthma. It is also frequently serviceable in rheumatic complaints, especially when assisted by warm embrocations.

The Honourable Mr. Charles Hamilton's Method of making Grape Wines, fully equal to Champaign and Old Hock, from the Fruit of his beautiful Vineyard at Pain's Hill, in Surry, England.

THE vineyard belonging to Pain's Hill, one of the finest country residences in the united kingdom, is situated on the south side of a gentle hill, the soil being gravelly sand. It is planted entirely with two sorts of Burgundy grapes: the Avernat, which is the most delicate and tender; and the miller's grape, originally so named from the powdered whiteness on the leaves in the spring, called in England the Black cluster or Burgundy grape. We shall give, in the Honourable Mr. Hamilton's own words, his valuable account of the process pursued, and its successful effect: "The first year I attempted to make wine in the usual way, by treading the grapes; then letting them ferment in the vat till all the husks and impurities formed a thick crust at the top, the boiling ceased, and the clear wine was drawn off from the bottom. This essay did not answer. The wine was so very harsh and austere, that I despaired of ever making red wine fit to drink; but, through that harshness, I perceived a flavour something like that of small French white wines, which made me hope I should succeed better with white wine. That experiment succeeded far beyond my most sanguine expectations, for, the very first year I made white wine, it nearly resembled the flavour of Champaign; and, in two or three years more, as the wine grew stronger, to my great amazement, my wine had a finer flavour than the best Champaign I ever tasted. The first running was as clear as spirits; the second running was œilde per drix, or partridge-eye colour; and both sparkled and creamed in the glass like Champaign. It would be endless to mention how many good judges of wine were deceived by my wine, and thought it superior to any Champaign they had ever drank. Even the Duke de Mirepoix preferred it to any other wine. But, such is the prejudice of some people against any thing of English growth, I generally found it most prudent not to declare where it grew till after they passed their verdict on it. The surest proof I can give of its excellence is, that I have sold it to wine merchants for fifty guineas a hogshead; and one wine merchant, to whom I sold five hundred pounds worth at one time, assured me he sold some of the best of it from seven shillings and sixpence to ten shillings per bottle. After many years experience, the best method I found of managing it was this: I let the grapes hang, till they had got all the maturity the season would give them; then they were carefully cut off with scissors, and brought home to the wine barn in small quantities to prevent their breaking or pressing one another. Then, they were all picked off the stalks, and all the mouldering or green ones discarded, before they were committed to the press; where they were all pressed in a few hours after they were gathered. Much would run from them, before the press squeezed them, from their own weight on one another. This running was as clear as water, and as sweet as syrup; and all of the first pressing, and part of the second, continued white: the other pressings grew reddish, and were not mixed with the best. As fast as the juice run from the press into a large receiver, it was put into the hogsheads, and closely bunged up. In a few hours, one would hear the fermentation begin; which would soon burst the casks, if not guarded again by hooping them strongly with iron, and securing them in strong wooden frames, and the heads with wedges. In the height of the fermentation, I have frequently seen the wine oozing through the pores of the staves. These hogsheads were left all the depth of winter in the cold barn, to have the benefit of the frost. When the fermentation was over, which was easily discovered by the cessation of the noise and oozing. (but, to be more certain, the pegging the cask showed when it would be quite clear,) then it was racked off into clean hogsheads, and carried to the vaults, before any warmth of weather could raise a second fermentation. In March the hogsheads were examined. If they were not quite fine, they were fined down with common fish glue or isinglass, in the usual manner; those which were fine of themselves were not fined down. All were bottled about the end of March; and, in about six weeks more, would be in perfect order for drinking, and would be in their prime for above one year: but, the second year, the flavour would abate; and would gradually decline, till it lost all flavour and sweetness. Some, that I kept sixteen years, became so like Old Hock, that it might pass for such to one who was not a perfect connoisseur. The only art I ever used to it was, putting three pounds of white sugar-candy to some of the hogsheads, when the wine was first tunned from the press; in order to conform to a rage that prevailed, to drink none but very sweet Champaign." In the astonishing success of this process, we see demonstrated how little assistance from art is required by nature, provided that little be judiciously applied.

Art of Extracting Spots of Grease, Tallow, Oil, &c. from Valuable Books, Prints, and Papers of all Sorts, without the smallest Injury to the Printing or Writing.

The frequency of such accidents as spot with grease valuable printed books, prints, ledgers, and other account books, as well as letters and writings of all descriptions, renders the method of restoring them to their pristine purity of appearance an article of no little importance. For this purpose, the following is the exact process: Having in readiness some common blotting paper, gently warm the spotted part of the book, or other article damaged by grease, tallow, or oil; and, as it melts, take up as much as possible, by repeated applications of fresh bits of the blotting paper. When no more can thus be imbibed, dip a small brush in the essential oil of well-rectified spirit of turpentine heated almost to a boiling state; and wet with it both sides of the paper, which should also be at the same time a little warm. This operation must be repeated till all the grease be extracted: when another brush, dipped in highly rectified spirit of wine, being passed over the same part, the spot or spots will entirely disappear, and the paper re-assume its original whiteness, without detriment of any sort to the paper, or any printed or written characters previously impressed thereon.

Blaikie's Patent Substitute for Gum, in thickening Colours for Calico Printers, &c.

This useful article is thus described by Mr. Francis Blaikie of Glasgow, the patentee, in his specification: The gum substitute, to thicken colours for linen and calico printing, and making up or furnishing printers' colour tubs, and which may also be applied to several other uses, is prepared by boiling any quantity of flax-seed in a sufficient quantity of water, till the whole substance be extracted; and, having strained it through a linen or woollen cloth, again boiling down the liquor to the consistence of a jelly. This is to be kept in a close vessel; and, for preservation, to have a little strong spirits put in, or some sweet oil poured on the top. It might, however, be preserved with bitters. The printer, in using this substitute, may either put a certain quantity into a gallon of colour, according to the nature of it, and the particular kind of work to be done, and regulate himself by trial, as is common in using gum, or reduce the substitute by boiling it in water to the consistence that may be found requisite.

French Method of Making Garlic Vinegar.

This, which is one of the favourite French vinegars, is thus simply made: Steep an ounce of garlic in two quarts of the best white-wine vinegar, with a nutmeg soaked and cut in bits, and about a dozen cloves.

Fine Tarragon Vinegar.

The peculiar and agreeable spicy warmth which this slightly-bitter herb, the Artemesia dracunculus of the Linnæan system, communicates to vinegar, makes it much used for that purpose, as well as in salads, soups, &c. throughout Europe. In Spain, and the south of France, it grows naturally to great perfection; and it flourishes in the soil of our English gardens, where it flowers in July, and produces ripe seeds in autumn. The best way of making tarragon vinegar is, by putting a quantity of the fresh leaves loosely into a jar, and then filling it up with vinegar to the height first occupied by the leaves; if, for example, the jar must be thus apparently filled, there will be still room enough for the proper quantity of vinegar. After it has thus remained two or three weeks, chiefly in the sun or other warm situation, it may be strained off, and passed through a cotton or flannel jelly-bag; and, if not sufficiently fine for putting up in bottles, is to be cleared in the usual way, either by means of isinglass or a little alum water. It is commonly kept in large bottles, which should be well corked, and placed in a dry situation. As tarragon is strongly recommended to be eaten with lettuce, this vinegar may in some measure supply the place of the herb: as a corrector of coldness, it is also advisable to be used with cucumbers, &c. The famous Evelyn says, that tarragon is not only highly cordial, but friendly to the head, heart, and liver, and a great corrector of the weakness of the ventricle.

Vinegar of Roses.

This fine and beautiful vinegar is made by pouring the best white wine vinegar into a jar or bottle loosely filled with rose leaves, and letting it remain and be treated exactly after the same manner as the tarragon; putting, however, into each bottle, a lump of refined sugar. Precisely in this way are also to be made vinegars of gilly-flowers, elder-flowers, &c.

Cheap and excellent Blue Colour for Ceilings, &c.

Boil, slowly, for three hours, a pound of blue vitriol, and half a pound of the best whiting, in about three quarts of water: stir it frequently while boiling, and also on taking it off the fire. When it has stood till quite cold, pour off the blue liquor; then mix the cake of colour with good size, and use it with a plasterer's brush in the same manner as white-wash, either for walls or ceilings.

Composition for cleaning Marble Hearths, Chimney Pieces, Alabaster, &c.

Mix finely pulverized pumice stone with verjuice, somewhat more than sufficient to cover it; and, after it has stood an hour or more, dip a sponge in the composition, rub it well over the marble or alabaster which requires cleaning, wash it off with warm water, and dry it with clean linen or cotton cloths.

Art of Manufacturing the fine Red and Yellow Morocco Leather, as practised in Crim Tartary.

The celebrated Tour of Mrs. Guthrie, in Taurida, or the Crimea, commonly called Crim Tartary, which was made by that lady in 1795 and 1796, furnishes the particulars of this interesting article. In the city of Karasubazar, Mrs. Guthrie informs us, there is an ancient manufactory of Morocco leather, where great quantity are prepared with the skins of the numerous flocks of Tauric goats. The process is thus described: After steeping the raw hides in cold water for twenty-four hours to free them from the blood and other impurities the fleshy parts are scraped off with proper instruments; when they are macerated for ten days in cold lime water, to loosen the hair, which is likewise scraped off as clean as possible. Being then soaked in cold common water for fifteen days, they are trod or worked under foot in a succession of fresh waters; till, at length, an admixture of dog's dung being added, they receive a second scraping, and are drained of their humidity. They next proceed to what they denominate feeding the skins, by steeping them four days in a cold infusion of wheat bran; and then in a decoction of twenty-eight pounds of honey to five pails of water, cooled to the temperature of milk from the cow. After remaining thus steeped the same period, they are put into a vessel with holes at the bottom, and pressed till all the liquid has escaped. Lastly, they are steeped, for another four days in a slight solution of salt and water, one pound only to five pails, when the leather is quite ready for the reception of the dye. A strong decoction of Artemisa annua, or southernwood, in the proportion of four pounds to ten pails of water, seems to be the basis of all the different colours which they give to the Morocco in the Taurida, Astracan, and the other cities formerly belonging to the Turkish empire, where the secret has till now remained. When a red colour is required, one pound of powdered cochineal is gradually stirred into ten pails of the fine yellow decoction of Artemisa, with five or six drachms of alum spread on the leather, in a proper vessel. They are next worked under foot, in an infusion of oak leaves in warm water, till they become supple and soft; when they are finished, by being rinsed in cold water, rubbed over with olive oil, and calendered with wooden rollers. Yellow Morocco leather is dyed with a stronger decoction of Artemisa, twenty pounds to fifteen pails of water; nothing being added, but two pounds of powdered alum, which is gradually introduced, by half a table spoonful at a time. Each skin is twice stained, previously to the final operations of oiling and calendering. It is also necessary to remark, that the skins are prepared in a somewhat different mode for the yellow Morocco leather, than for the red. Neither honey nor salt is used; but, instead of the decoction of honey, immediately after the skins are taken out of the wheat bran infusion, they are steeped two days in an infusion of oak leaves: after which, they are next rinsed in cold water, and thus made ready for staining yellow. Mrs. Guthrie candidly acknowledges, that the above is all the certain information which she has been able to obtain on this curious subject; as she could by no means depend on the vague reports which she had heard relative to the colouring matter added for staining the green and blue kinds. It may, however, be presumed, that the light, which this lady has thrown on the process of dying Morocco leather in general, will sufficiently guide our manufacturers to a judicious search after those particular but inferior objects, which yet remain undiscovered.

Turkish Rouge; or, Secret of the Seraglio for making an admirable Carmine.

INFUSE, for three or four days, in a bottle of the finest white wine vinegar, half a pound of Fernambourg Brasil wood, of a golden red colour, well pounded in a mortar. Boil them together half an hour; strain them through linen, and place the liquid again over the fire. In the mean time, having dissolved a quarter of a pound of alum in a pint of white wine vinegar, mix the two liquids, and stir them well together with a spatula. The scum which now arises, on being carefully taken off and gradually dried, will prove a most beautiful delicate, and perfectly inoffensive, rouge or carmine.

Purified Syrup of Molasses.

In many parts of the continent of Europe, a method has for some years been successfully practised, on a large scale, of divesting molasses, vulgarly called treacle, of its peculiar mawkish and unpleasant taste, so as to render it, for many purposes, little less useful and pleasant than sugar. Indeed, unless it be for cordials mixed with spices, or in domestic dishes where milk is an ingredient, it may very generally be substituted for sugar. The process for thus preparing it is sufficiently simple, and by no means expensive: Boil twelve pounds of molasses, with three pounds of coarsely-pounded charcoal, in six quarts of water, over a slow fire. After the mixture has been stirred together, and simmered for at least half an hour, decant it into a deep vessel; and, when the charcoal has subsided, pour off the liquid, and again place it over the fire, that the superfluous water may evaporate, and restore the syrup to about its original consistence. Thus refined, it will produce twelve pounds of a mild and good syrup, proper for use in many articles of food, &c.

Art of preparing a fine Red Lake from Dutch Madder.

The use of madder, in dying a fine red colour, and also as a first tint for several other shades, has long rendered it famous among dyers; and, by the following process, it will afford a permanent lake of a fine red, applicable to every purpose of painting: Dissolve two ounces of the purest alum in three quarts of distilled water previously boiled in a clean glazed vessel, and again set over the fire. Withdraw the solution as soon as it begins to simmer, and add to it two ounces of the best Dutch madder; then, boiling it up once or twice, remove it from the fire, and filter it through clean white paper. Let the liquor thus filtered stand all night to subside; and, next day, pour the clear fluid into the glazed vessel, heat it over the fire, and gradually add a strained solution of salt of tartar, till the madder be wholly precipitated. The mixture must now be again filtered, and boiling distilled water be poured on the red powder till the fluid no longer obtains a saline taste. Nothing more is now necessary, but to dry the lake, which will be of a deep red colour. If two parts of madder be used to one of alum, the shade will be still deeper; and, if one part of the latter article be added to four parts of the former, a beautiful rose colour will be produced.

Clarified Goose Grease.

Goose grease is a valuable but neglected article in most families; and, when properly clarified, forms a most delicate basis for man culinary purposes. This is easily effected by the following simple process: On drawing a goose, separate all the internal fat, and put it by in a basin. When the goose is roasted, carefully preserve the dripping separated from the gravy, &c. which is most effectually done on its getting quite cold. The sooner this is put in a saucepan, with the raw fat, accompanied by a small onion having three cloves stuck into it, the better. Being gently simmered, press it with a wooden spoon till the whole be melted; then, having well scummed it, pass it through a sieve, into a jar capable of containing whatever quantity is likely to be thus added during the season. A moderate use of this article will render many dishes inconceivably savoury, particularly rice, thick soups, force-meats, &c. It should be served out with a wooden spoon; and, if kept in a cool place, properly covered, will continue sweet and good the year round.

Composition for Restoring scorched Linen.

THE following composition will be found completely to restore linen which has been scorched in ironing, or by hanging too near the fire, &c. accidents that too frequently occur; and, hitherto, without any effectual remedy: Boil to a good consistency, in half a pint of vinegar, two ounces of fullers' earth, an ounce of hen's dung, half an ounce of cake soap, and the juice of two onions. Spread this composition over the whole of the damaged part; and, if the scorching were not quite through, and the threads actually consumed, after suffering it to dry on, and letting it receive a subsequent good washing or two, the place will appear full as white and perfect as any other part of the linen.

Easy French Method to prevent Bacon from becoming Rusty.

WHEN the bacon has been salted about a fortnight, put it in a box the size of the flitches or pieces to be preserved, on a good bedding of hay: and wrap each piece round entirely with hay, placing also a layer between every two flitches or pieces. The box must, of course, be closed, to keep out rats, &c. In this state, it will continue as good as at first, and without the possibility of getting rusty, for much longer than a year, as has frequently been experienced. It must, however, be kept in a place free from damp.

Best Saxon Blue.

MIX an ounce of the best powdered indigo with four ounces of oil of vitriol, in a glass body, and digest it for an hour with the heat of boiling water, frequently shaking the mixture. Then add three quarters of a pint of water; stir the whole well together; and, when cold, filter it. This produces a very rich deep blue colour; if wanted paler, more water must be added. The heat of boiling water, which is sufficient for this operation, can never spoil the colour. By previously digesting the indigo in a large quantity of spirit of wine, drying it, and then using it as above, a still finer blue may be produced; but this is not often judged necessary, except for very fine paintings.

The Reverend Mr. Cartwright's Account of the Wonderful Efficacy of Yeast in the Cure of Putrid Diseases.

The following account of the Reverend Mr. Cartwright's first discovery, and subsequent experience, of the good effects of administering yeast in putrid sore throats, fevers, &c. cannot be too generally made known :—" Several years ago," says this gentleman, for we shall transcribe verbatim his own highly interesting narrative, " I went to reside at Brampton, a very populous village near Chesterfield. I had not been there many months before a putrid fever broke out among us ; and, finding by far the greater number of my new parishioners much too poor to afford themselves medical assistance, I undertook, by the help of such books on the subject of medicine as were in my possession, to prescribe for them. I early attended a boy about fourteen years of age, who was attacked by this fever ; he had not been ill many days, before the symptoms were unequivocally putrid. I then administered bark, wine, and such other remedies as my books directed. My exertions, however, were of no avail : his disorder grew every day more untractable and malignant, so that I was in hourly expectation of his dissolution. Being under the absolute necessity of taking a journey, before I set off I went to see him, as I thought for the last time ; and I prepared his parents for the event of his death, which I considered as inevitable ; reconciling them, in the best manner I was able, to a loss which I knew they would feel severely. While I was in conversation on this distressing subject with his mother, I observed, in a corner of the room, a small tub of wort working. The sight brought to my recollection an experiment I had somewhere met with, of a piece of putrid meat being made sweet by suspending it over a tub of wort in the act of fermentation. The idea instantly flashed into my mind, that the yeast might correct the putrid nature of this disease : and I instantly gave him two large spoonsful, telling the mother, if she found her son better, to repeat this dose every three hours. I then set out on my journey. On my return, after a few days, I anxiously inquired about the boy, and was informed he had recovered. I could not repress my curiosity. Though I was greatly fatigued with my journey, and night was come on, I went directly to where he lived ; which was three miles off, in a wild part of the moors. The boy himself opened the door ; looked surprisingly well ; and told me, that he felt better from the instant he took the yeast. After I left Brampton, I lived in Leicestershire ; and, my parishioners being there few and opulent, I dropped entirely my medical character, and would not even prescribe for any of my own family. One of my domestics falling ill, accordingly the apothecary was sent for. The servant's complaint was a violent fever ; which, in its progress, became putrid. Having great reliance, and deservedly, on the apothecary's penetration and judgment, the man was left solely to his management. His disorder, however, kept daily gaining ground : till, at length, the apothecary considered him in very great danger. At last, finding every effort to be of service to him baffled, he told me, he considered it as a lost case ; for, in his opinion, the man could not survive four and twenty hours. On the apothecary thus giving him up, I determined to try the effects of yeast, and gave him two large tea-spoonsful. In fifteen minutes from taking it, his pulse, though still feeble, began to get composed and full; and, in thirty-two minutes from taking the yeast, he was able to get up from his bed, and walk in his room. At the expiration of the second hour, I gave him a basin of sago, with a good deal of lemon wine, and ginger in it, and he ate it with appetite. In another hour, I repeated the yeast; an hour afterward, I gave him the bark; and, the next hour, he had food. He had, next, another dose of yeast; and then went to bed, being nine o'clock. I went to him next morning, at six o'clock; when he told me he had had a good night, and was recovered. I, however, repeated his medicine, and he was able to go about his business as usual. A year after this, as I was riding past a detached farm-house at the outskirts of the village, I observed the farmer's daughter standing at the door apparently in great affliction. On inquiring into the cause of her distress, she told me her father was dying. I dismounted, and went into the house to see him. I found him in the last stage of a putrid fever; his tongue was black; his pulse was scarcely perceptible; and he lay stretched out, like a corpse, in a state of drowsy insensibility. I immediately procured some yeast; which I diluted with water, and poured down his throat. I then left him, with little hope of his recovery. I returned to him in about two hours; and found him sensible, and able to converse. I then gave him a dose of bark. He afterward took, at a proper interval, some refreshment. I continued with him till he repeated the yeast; and then left him, with directions how to proceed. I called on him the next morning at nine o'clock, and found him apparently well, walking in his garden. He was an old man, upwards of seventy. I have, since, administered the yeast to above fifty persons labouring under putrid fevers; and, what is singular, I have not lost one patient." Dr. Thornton, whose opportunities have been great, as superintending physician of the General Dispensary, including the poor of nine parishes in London, has made frequent trials of yeast. In St. Giles's, particularly, among the numerous poor of that crowded district, he administers, in putrid diseases, after cleansing the first passages, nothing else but two table spoonsful of yeast in some porter, every two hours; and, in about fifty successive cases, not a single patient died under this treatment. The following cases are selected, from this physician's successful practice, as peculiarly interesting. As Dr. Thornton was accidentally passing the shop of Mr. Burford, in Tottenham Court Road, he heard the shrieks of a mother, agonized at seeing her child apparently expire. These alarming screams renewed the struggles of the child; and the nurse was, at this moment, threatening to take away the child, that it might die in peace. The doctor immediately got down some tartar emetic, which quickly acted on the stomach; and, that operation ended, gave a dose of rhubarb, to clear also the intestines. He then ordered the child yeast and water every two hours, with wine and bark; and, in three days, the dying child was up and well The infection had spread to two other persons in the same house. With this, and another child, the putrid fever was attended by swelled glands, which had suppurated, and threatened mortification: with a robust servant girl, it took the form of a putrid sore throat. This girl also had an emetic, and afterward rhubarb, followed by yeast and water every two hours. The first effect of the yeast was that of rendering the pulse fuller, and diminishing it fifteen beats a minute: the blackness of her tongue soon began to assume a clean and a red appearance; and, without either bark or wine, she was speedily restored to health. In Husband-street, a very confined situation near Berwick-street, a malignant fever prevailed; which, within a fortnight, had swept away six persons from three houses only, when Dr. Thornton was called in, to the assistance of a mother, who lay in the same bed with her two children. She was delirious; and violently rejected both food and medicine, with which she was, consequently, obliged to be drenched. After an emetic and cathartic had been got down each, herself and children were all put on the same plan: that is, each was made to swallow, every three hours, two-thirds of a glass of fresh porter, with two table spoonsful of yeast, and the juice of half a lemon. The food given at intervals was the white of eggs, beat up with some sugar and water; the doctor judging that, as the white of eggs, even under the heat of a hen's body during incubation, does not corrupt, but actually serves as milk to the embryo in the shell, this was of all things least liable to putrefy. Strawberries, being in season, were also ordered; and, with this management alone, she and her little family all rapidly recovered. More testimonies might easily be added, and from several other respectable practitioners; but farther proofs seem unnecessary to establish the prodigious efficacy of yeast, in one of the most fatal class of maladies with which human nature is peculiarly subject to be afflicted. Where, indeed, is the family, which has not suffered by the dreadful ravages of some putrid disease, which, under Providence, a knowledge of this simple but potent emedy, and for which we are indebted to the Reverend Mr. Cartwright, might happily have prevented!

Admirable Cement, or Mortar, as made on the Cotswold Hills.

On the Cotswold Hills, in Gloucestershire, where lime is dear, and sand not to be had, an excellent mortar is prepared at a moderate price. Invention is seldom more successful than when it is prompted by necessity. The scrapings of the public roads over these hills, being levigated lime-stone, more or less impregnated with the dung and urine of the animals travelling on them, are found to be a most admirable basis for cement. The scrapings are often used for ordinary walls; and the general proportion, for even the best buildings, is not more than one part lime to three of scrapings. This mortar, of less than ten years standing, has been observed to possess a stone-like tenacity, much firmer than the common stone of the country: and, consequently, much harder than the stones from which either the basis or the lime was made. The method of preparing this powerful mortar, or cement, is simply by collecting the road scrapings, slacking the lime, and mixing them very thoroughly together; carefully picking out, as the mass is worked over, the stones or other foulnesses which may have been collected. For stone-work, this is quite sufficient; for brick-work, it might be necessary to pass the materials through a screen or sieve, previously to their being united, and made up into mortar. Similar scrapings may be collected, wherever lime stone is used as a material in making or repairing roads; this admirable mortar can, therefore, readily be prepared, in all such places, with very little trouble or expense.

Ancient British Liquor, called Bragget.

This once famous old British liquor is still made by a few respectable families, chiefly in Wales; from one of which we have been favoured with an admirable method of preparing it. The original Welsh name is bragod; from which has been formed that of bragget, or braggot, for it is found both ways in the few old dictionaries and other books where it occurs, and simply defined as a drink consisting of honey and spices. Were this correct, it could only be considered as the Welsh appellation of mead or metheglin; but, according to our information, bragget implies a combination of malt liquor with honey and spices, the best method of preparing which is as follows: Take after the rate of a gallon of water to a pound of honey, and stir it till the honey be melted. Then, adding half a handful each of rosemary tops, bay-leaves, sweet briar, angelica, balm, thyme, or other sweet herbs, with half an ounce of sliced ginger, and a little nutmeg, mace, cinnamon, and a few cloves, boil them gently together for nearly half an hour; scumming it well, till it looks tolerably clear. In the mean time, having prepared three gallons of the first runnings of strong ale, or sweet wort, mix the two liquids quite hot, with all the herbs and spices; and, stirring them together for some time over a fire, but without suffering them to boil, strain off the liquor, and set it to cool. When it becomes only the warmth of new milk, ferment it with good ale yeast; and, after it has properly worked, tun it up, and hang a bag of bruised spices in the barrel, where it is to remain all the time of drawing. It is generally drank from the cask; but may be bottled, like other liquors, any time after it has entirely ceased to hiss in the barrel. A weaker sort of bragget is sometimes prepared with the third runnings of the ale, a smaller proportion of honey, and the strained spices, &c. with a few herbs; the second runnings, in that case, being made the family These arrangements, however, and other obvious deviations, are made according to the taste or inclination of the respective parties.

Wonderful effect of Potato Liquid, in Cleaning Silk, Woollen, and Cotton Furniture or Apparel, &c. without Injury to the Texture or Colour.

For the communication of this valuable discovery to the Society for the Encouragement of Arts, Manufactures, and Commerce, in the Adelphi, February 4, 1805, Mrs. Morris obtained a premium of fifteen guineas from that truly honourable institution; in whose

Transactions of that year it is thus regularly described: Take raw potatoes, in the state they are taken out of the earth. Wash them well: then rub them on a grater, over a vessel of clean water, to a fine pulp; pass the liquid matter, through a coarse sieve, into another tub of clear water; let the mixture stand, till the fine white particles of the potatoes are precipitated; then pour the mucilaginous liquor from the fecula, and preserve this liquor for use. The article to be cleaned should be laid, on a linen cloth, on a table: and, having provided a clean sponge, dip the sponge in the potato liquor, and apply the sponge thus wet on the article to be cleaned; and rub it well on with repeated portions of the potato liquor, till the dirt is perfectly separated. Then wash the article in clean water several times, to remove the loose dirt. It may, afterward, be smoothed o dried. Two middle sized potatoes will be sufficient for a pint of water. The white fecula, which separates in making the mucilaginous liquor, will answer the purpose of tapioca: it will make a useful and nourishing food with soup or milk, or serve to make starch and hair powder. The coarse pulp, which does not pass the sieve, is of great use in cleaning worsted curtains, tapestry, carpets, or other coarse goods. The mucilaginous liquor of the potatoes will clean all sorts of silk, cotton, or woollen goods, without damaging the texture of the article or spoiling the colour. It is also useful in cleaning oil paintings, or furniture that is soiled. Dirty painted wainscots may be cleaned by wetting a sponge in the liquor, then dipping it in a little fine clean sand, and afterward rubbing the wainscot therewith. Various experiments were made by Mrs. Morris, in the presence of a committee, at the society's house; and the whole process, on fine and coarse goods of different fabrics, was performed to their entire satisfaction. This simple but very valuable discovery may certainly be applied to many other useful purposes, as well as those which are here particularly enumerated.

New method of Clearing Feathers from their Animal Oil.

The process for effecting this useful purpose, is thus described in the Transactions of the Adelphi Society, who rewarded Mrs. Richardson with a premium of twenty guineas for making the discovery: Take for every gallon of clear water, a pound of quick lime. Mix them well together; and, when the undissolved lime is precipitated in fine powder, pour off the clear lime-water for use, at the time it is wanted. Put the feathers to be cleaned in another tub, and add to them a sufficient quantity of the clear lime-water to cover the feathers about three inches when well immersed and stirred therein. The feathers, when thoroughly moistened, will sink down; and should remain in the lime-water three or four days: after which, the foul liquor should be separated from the feathers, by laying them on a sieve. The feathers should be afterward well washed in clean water, and dried on nets, the meshes being about the same firmness as those of cabbage nets. The feathers must, from time to time, be shaken on the nets; and, as they dry, they will fall through the meshes, and are to be collected for use. The admission of air will be serviceable in the drying, and the whole process may be completed in about three weeks. The feathers, after being thus prepared, will want nothing more than beating for use, either as beds, bolsters, pillows, or cushions. So effectual is this method, and so preferable to the old and common way of stoving or baking, that an eminent dealer having sent to the society some bags of foreign feathers, which retained their unpleasant smell after having been stoved the usual period of three days, Mrs. Richardson rendered them perfectly sweet and clean. This is a very important discovery; more particularly as the feathers, by not being hardened with heat, certainly require less beating.

Mr. Sebastian Grandi's Restoration or Discovery of the old Venetian Art of preparing Grounds for Painting on Pannels, Copper, or Canvas, &c.

This ingenious gentleman, having long had the honour of being employed by the most eminent professors of the fine arts in Italy and England, and assisted and improved the processes of preparing canvases and the pannels, seems to have discovered, as far as experience can prove, the manner of preparing either canvas, copper, or pannel, in the old Venetian stile; an art which has been long lost, and to which it is well known that Titian, Paul Veronese, Bassani, and other Venetian masters, owed much of the peculiar harmony, brightness, and durability, of their beautiful productions. Mr. Grandi having communicated, for the public benefit, his entire process of thus preparing pannels, canvas, &c. for artists; and also made other valuable communications with regard to the preparation of oils, colours, crayons, &c. for painting and drawing; was rewarded by the Honourable Society in the Adelphi for the encouragement of Arts, &c. with their elegant and honourary silver medal, as well as a pecuniary premium of twenty guineas. These, therefore, in perfect concert with the design of that liberal and truly patriotic institution, we shall contribute all in our power to make more generally known. Mr. Grandi's method of preparing pannels and canvases for painters is thus described: Break, grossly, the bones of sheep's trotters, and boil them in water till they are cleared from their grease, then putting them into a crucible, calcine them, and afterward grind them to powder. Dry some wheaten flour in a pan, over a slow fire; then make it into a thin paste, adding an equal quantity of the pulverized bone ashes, and grind the whole mass well together. This mixture forms the ground for the pannel. When the pannel has been well pumiced, some of the mixture or ground is to be well rubbed on a pumice stone, that it may be incorporated with the pannel: another coat of the composition is next applied, with a brush on the pannel, where it is suffered to dry, the surface being afterward rubbed over with sand paper. A thin coat of the composition is then applied with a brush; and, if a coloured ground be required, a coat or two more must be added, so as to complete the absorbent ground. When a pannel thus prepared is wanted to be painted on, it must be rubbed over with a coat of raw linseed or poppy oil, as drying oil would destroy the absorbent quality of the ground; and the painter's colours should also be mixed up with the purified oil for painting hereafter mentioned. Canvas grounds are prepared by giving them a thin coat of the composition, and afterward drying and pumicing them; then giving them a second coat, and, lastly, a coat of colouring matter along with the composition. The grounds thus prepared do not crack: they may be painted in a very short time after being laid; and, from their absorbent quality, allow the business to be proceeded in with greater facility and better effect than with those prepared in the usual mode. These valuable qualities have been sufficiently ascertained, and are liberally avowed, by Sir William Beechy and other Royal Academicians, whose names are added to Mr. Grandi's last communication.

Method of Purifying the Oil for mixing up Colours.

MAKE some of the bone-ashes into paste with a little water, so as to form a mass or ball. Put this ball into the fire, and make it red hot; then immerse it, for an hour, in a quantity of raw linseed oil sufficient to cover it. When cold, pour the oil into bottles; add to it a little of the bone-ashes; let it stand to settle; and, in a single day, it will be clear, and fit for use.

Preparation of White, Brown, Yellow, Red, Gray, and Blue Black Colours, which never Change, and may be used either in Oil or Water.

WHITE is made by calcining the bones of sheep's trotters in a clear open fire, till they become a perfect white, which will never change. BROWN is made from bones in a similar manner, only calcining from them in a crucible instead of an open fire. YELLOW, or masticot, by burning a piece of soft brick of a yellowish colour in the fire; grinding a quarter of a pound of flake white with every pound of brick: calcining them, as well as grinding them, together; and, afterward, washing the mixture to separate the sand, and letting the finer part gradually dry for use. RED, equal in beauty to Indian red, by calcining some of the pyrites usually found in coal pits. GRAY, by calcining together blue slate and bone ashes powdered, grinding them together, washing the texture, and gradually drying it. BLUE BLACK, by burning vine stalks within a close crucible and in a slow fire, till they become a perfect charcoal, which must be well ground for use.

Superior Crayons, of Permanent Colours, to be applied either in Water or Oil.

THESE crayons, produced also by Mr. Grandi, are of a quality superior to any heretofore in use; they are fixed, so as to prevent their rubbing off the paper when used, and may be applied in water or oil. This process of preparing the crayons is thus described:—They are made of bone-ash powder mixed with spermaceti, adding the colouring matters. The proper proportion is, three ounces of spermaceti to a pound of the powder; the spermaceti to be first dissolved in a pint of boiling water; then the white bone-ashes added; and the whole to be well ground together, with as much of the respective colouring matter as may be necessary for the shade of colour wanted. They are then to be rolled up in the proper form, and gradually dried on a board.

Preparation of White and Coloured Chalks.

If white chalk be required to work soft, add a quarter of a pound of whiting to a pound of the bone-ash powder; otherwise, the bone-ashes will answer alone. Coloured chalks are prepared by grinding the respective colouring matters with bone-ashes. These several communications, relative to the preparation of grounds, oil, colours, crayons, and chalks, for painters, were most respectably certified to the Society in the Adelphi, by Sir William Beechy, and the following other Royal Academicians, &c. Benjamin West, John Opie, Martin Archer Shee, James Northcote, Thomas Lawrence, Joseph Farrington, Richard Cosway, P. J. De Loutherbourg, Richard M. Paye, and Isaac Pocock, Esquires; who all confirm the good qualities of the pannels prepared by Mr. Grandi, and generally recommend his colours as useful and permanent. The materials are certainly extremely cheap, as well as easy to be procured, and none of the processes for preparation are at all difficult.

Syrup of Damask Roses.

The Edinburgh Dispensatory describes syrup of damask roses as an agreeable and mild purgative for children, in doses of from half to a whole table spoonful. It likewise mentions, that this syrup proves gently laxative to adults; and, with that intention, may be of service to costive habits. The method of preparing it, according to the London practice, is as follows:—Take seven ounces of the dried petals of the damask rose, six pounds of double-refined sugar, and four pints of boiling distilled water. Macerate the roses in the water for twelve hours, and then strain. Evaporate the strained liquor to two pints and a half; and add the sugar, that it may be made a syrup. In the Edinburgh practice, it is prepared thus:—Take one pound of the fresh petals of the damask rose, four pounds of boiling water, and three pounds of double-refined sugar. Macerate the roses in the water for twelve hours; then, to the strained infusion, add the sugar, and boil them to a syrup in the usual manner, as directed for syrup of clove gillyflowers, &c.

Syrup of Red Roses.

This, in the Edinburgh Dispensatory, is properly distinguished from the syrup of damask roses; being considered as mildly astringent, instead of gently laxative. It seems, however, principally valued on account of its beautiful red colour. The manner of preparing it is almost the same as the London method of making the syrup of damask roses, called simply syrup of roses:—Take seven ounces of the dried petals of red roses, six pounds of double-refined sugar, and five pounds of boiling water. Macerate the roses in the water for twelve hours; then boil a little, and strain the liquor: add to it the sugar, and boil again for a little, so as to form a syrup. There is, it must be confessed, a marked distinction between the London and Edinburgh methods of preparing syrup of roses, much in favour of the latter's superior discrimination: particularly, as the damask rose, besides differing essentially in its medicinal effect, has its odour almost destroyed by drying; while the red rose leaves or petals, on the contrary, are well known to gain increased fragrance when carefully dried.

Excellent Spruce Beer.

THE salubrity of spruce beer is universally acknowledged; and, notwithstanding its invincible terebinthine flavour, forms so refreshing and lively a summer drink, that it begins to be greatly used. It is, in fact, a powerful antiscorbutic: and, as it by no means offends the weakest stomach, whatever may be its effect on the palate, it is highly entitled to our attention. In situations where the green shoots and tops, &c. are easily obtained, it may be brewed immediately from them, instead of from the extract; which, however, is by no means to be commonly effected in England, where these trees are not remarkably numerous, and are always private property. The regular method of brewing spruce beer, as it is at present in the best manner prepared, and so highly admired for its excessive briskness, is as follows:—Pour eight gallons of cold water into a barrel: and then, boiling eight gallons more, put that in also; to this, add twelve pounds of molasses, with about half a pound of the essence of spruce; and, on its getting a little cooler, half a pint of good ale yeast. The whole being well stirred, or rolled in the barrel, must be left with the bung out for two or three days; after which, the liquor may be immediately bottled, well corked up, and packed in saw-dust or sand, when it will be ripe and fit for drink in a fortnight If spruce beer be made immediately from the branches or cones, they are required to be boiled for two hours; after which, the liquor is to be strained into a barrel, the molasses and yeast are to be added to the extract, and to be in all respects treated after the same manner. Spruce beer is best bottled in stone; and, from its volatile nature, the whole should be immediately drank when the bottle is once opened.

Blackman's celebrated Oil Colour Cakes for Artists.

THE following is the process, as described in the transactions of the Society of Arts:—Take four ounces of the clearest gum mastich, and a pint of spirits of turpentine; mix them together in a bottle, stirring them frequently till the mastich be dissolved. Where haste is required, some heat may be applied, but the solution is better when made cold. Let the colours be the best which can be procured; taking care that, by washing, &c. they are brought to the greatest possible degree of fineness. When the colours are dry, grind them on a hard close stone, for which purpose porphyry is best, in spirits of turpentine, adding a small quantity of the mastich varnish. Let the colours so ground become again dry; then prepare, in the following manner, the composition for forming them into cakes: procure some of the purest and whitest spermaceti; melt it, in a clean earthen vessel, over a gentle fire; and, when fluid, adding one third its weight of pure poppy oil, stir the whole well together. These things being in readiness, place over a frame or support the stone on which the colours were ground, with a charcoal fire to warm it beneath. This done, grind the colour fine with a muller, on the warm stone; after which, adding a sufficient quantity of the mixture of poppy oil and spermaceti, work the whole together with a muller to the proper consistence. Lastly, taking a piece of the fit size for the cake intended to be made, roll it into a ball, put it into a mould and press it, when the process will be complete. These cakes, on being wanted for use, must be rubbed down in poppy or other oil, or in a mixture of spirits of turpentine and oil, as may best suit the convenience or intention of the artist.

A curious and useful Glue.

Take an ounce of isinglass, beat it to shreds, and put it into a pint of brandy; when gradually dissolved, which it soon is with a gentle heat, strain the solution through a piece of fine muslin, and the glue will be obtained, which is to be kept in a glass closely stopped. On being dissolved, in a moderate heat, it is thin, transparent, and almost limpid. When used in the manner of common glue, it joins together the parts of wood stronger than the wood itself is united: so that the pieces thus joined will break in any other part sooner than where they are glued together. It is also remarkable, that, if saw-dust, or powdered wood, be made into a ball with this glue, the ball will prove solid and elastic; so that it may be turned and used as a bowl, without breaking. As the glue thus made with brandy will keep long without corrupting, it is by no means an improper form to preserve isinglass ready dissolved, for fining wines and other purposes. Another use of this curious glue is, that of its serving excellently for taking off impressions of medals or coins: thus, if a little of it, when melted, be poured thinly on a new guinea, &c. so as to cover the whole surface of the piece, and suffered so to remain a day or two, till it become thoroughly dry, it will appear hard and transparent, like a piece of Muscovy glass, with the impression of the guinea in intaglio, as it is denominated, on one side, and in relievo on the other. This glue dries into a very strong, tough, and transparent substance; not easily damaged by any thing but equeous moisture, which would soon dissolve it. This last reason renders it unfit for any use where it would be much exposed to wet or damp air. Common glue, dissolved with linseed oil, is admirably calculated to stand the weather; a secret little known by those who would be most benefited by its adoption.

Norfolk Milk Punch.

Steep the thin parings of seven lemons, and as many Seville oranges, in a pint of brandy, for three days. Then squeeze all the juice of these oranges and lemons into the brandy; and add three pints of rum, three pints more of brandy, and six pints of water. Grate a nutmeg into two quarts of milk; and, having made it boiling hot, pour it into the above ingredients, carefully keeping the whole well stirred till completely mixed; then add two pounds of fine loaf sugar, which must also be well stirred. Let the punch thus made stand twelve hours, then strain it through a flannel bag till it appear perfectly bright. It may, probably, require to be three or four times strained, according to the fineness or coarseness of the sugar, and other circumstances. When quite clear, this charming liquor is immediately fit to drink; or will keep, if bottled, any length of time, and in all climates.

Art of making the Curious Sympathetic Ink.

This curious ink has been long known in the world; but the manner of preparing it, and means of procuring the materials, as described in various chemical books, rendered the task too discouraging to be often attempted. By the following easy method, however, it is readily accomplishable:—Take an ounce and a half of zaffre, which may be obtained at any colour-shop, and put it into a glass vessel with a narrow and long neck, pouring over it an ounce measure of strong nitrous acid, diluted with five times the quantity of water. Keep it in a warm situation, but not too hot, for about ten or twelve hours, and then decant the clearest part of the liquor. Having so done, pour nearly as much more diluted nitrous acid on the remainder: which is to continue in the same situation, and for as long a time as before, and then be decanted and mixed with what was obtained by the first operation. This being done, dissolve in it two ounces of common salt, and the sympathetic ink is completely made. The property of this ink is, that the writing made with it, on common paper, is legible only while the paper is hot and dry; so that, by exposing it, alternately, to the ambient air, and to the heat of a fire or burning sun, whatever is written may be caused to appear and disappear at pleasure. The universal knowledge of this secret rather diminishes than increases the security of guilt in using it for any improper purpose; since detection is certain, from the moment suspicion takes place, by simply holding every letter or other doubtful paper to the fire, or in the warm rays of the sun.

Soft Sealing Wax, for Impressing Seals of Office, &c.

This sealing wax, which is seldom used for any other purpose than that of receiving the impressions of seals of office to charters, patents, proceedings in chancery, &c. is prepared, when to be used white, or rather uncoloured, by mixing half a pound of bees' wax, an ounce and a half of turpentine, and half an ounce of sweet oil; and carefully boiling them together, till the compound becomes of a fit consistency for moulding into rolls, cakes, or balls, for use. If colour be wanted, it is readily obtained by stirring into the melted mass about half an ounce of a proper pigment, as in making the red or other coloured hard sealing wax.

Capital Sugar Vinegar.

This useful article of domestic economy might easily be made in the poorest families:—To every quart of spring water put a quarter of a pound of the coarsest sugar; boil them together, and keep skimming the liquor as long as any scum rises. After pouring it into a tub or other vessel, let it stand till cool enough to work; and then place in it a toast spread with yeast, of a size proportioned to the quantity made. Let it ferment a day or two; then beat the yeast into it, put it into a cag or barrel with a piece of tile or slate over the bung-hole, and place it in a situation where it may best receive the heat of the sun. Make it in March, or the beginning of April, and it will be fit for use in July or August. If not sour enough, which can seldom happen when properly managed, let it stand a month longer before it be bottled off. It may be kept in stone or glass bottles. During the time of making, it must never be disturbed, after the first week or ten days; and though, in very fine weather, the bung-hole would be best left open all day, as it might be fatal to leave it open a single night, or exposed to any sudden rain, the greatest caution will in that case be necessary. Previously to its being bottled, it may be drawn off into a fresh cask; and, if it fill a large barrel, a handful of shred isinglass may be thrown in, or less in proportion to the quantity: this, after it has stood a few days, will render the vinegar fine, when it may be drawn off, or bottled, for use. This sugar vinegar, though very strong, may be used in pickling for sea-store or exportation, without being at all lowered; but for pickles to be eaten in England it will bear mixing with at least an equal quantity of cold spring water. There are few pickles for which this vinegar need ever be boiled. Without boiling, it will keep walnuts very finely, even for the East or West Indies; but then, as remarked in general of pickles for foreign use, it must be unmixed with water. If much vinegar be made, so as to require expensive casks, the outsides should always be painted, for the sake of preserving them from the influence of the weather, during so many months of exposure to sun and rain.

Excellent Embrocation for the Hooping-Cough.

All the dreadful consequences of the chin or hooping cough, and its commonly tedious duration, may be obviated and shortened by the following admirable remedy:—Mix well together half an ounce each of spirit of hartshorn and oil of amber; with which plentifully anoint the palms of the hands, the pit of the stomach, the soles of the feet, the arm-pits, and the back bone, every morning and evening for a month, suffering no water to come near the parts thus anointed, though the fingers and backs of the hands may be wiped with a damp cloth. It should be rubbed in near the fire, and care naturally used to prevent afterwards taking cold. It is best to make only the above quantity at a time; because, by frequently opening the bottle, much of the virtue will be lost. It should, by rights, be kept in a glass-stopper bottle. Indeed, the hartshorn is always thus kept by the faculty; and where it forms so large a part of the mixture, the necessity of preventing its effluvia from escaping is equally great. These precautions taken, and the other directions followed, its use will seldom fail to be attended with the most complete success; frequently in a much shorter time than it is judged prudent to advise its being continued, as it can never possibly do the smallest injury even to the tenderest infants.

Speedy Cure for a Sprain.

Take a large spoonful of honey, the same quantity of salt, and the white of an egg: beat the whole up together incessantly for two hours; then let it stand an hour, and anoint the place sprained with the oil which will be produced, keeping the part well rolled with a good bandage. This is said generally to have enabled persons with sprained ankles, frequently more tediously cured than even a broken limb, and often leaving a perpetual weakness in the joint, to walk in twenty-four hours, entirely free from pain.

Singular and simple manner of preserving Apples from the effects of frost in North America.

Apples being produced almost abundantly in North America, and forming an article of chief necessity in almost every family, the greatest care is constantly taken to protect them from frost at the earliest commencement of the winter season; it being well known, that apples, if left unprotected, are inevitably destroyed by the first frost which occurs. This desirable object, during their long and severe winters, is said to be completely effected, by only throwing over them a thin linen cloth before the approach of frost, when the fruit is never injured, how severe soever the winter may happen to prove. Yet apples are there usually kept in a small apartment, immediately beneath the roof of the house, which is particularly appropriated to that purpose, and where there is never any fire. This is a fact so well known, that the Americans are astonished it should appear at all wonderful: and they have some reason to be so, when it is considered that, throughout Germany, the same method of preserving fruit is universally practised; from whence probably it made its way to North America. It appears that linen cloth only is used for this purpose; woollen cloth, in particular, having been experienced to prove ineffectual. There seems abundant reason to believe, that even potatoes might be protected from frost by some such simple expedient. This, also, like the preceding article, to which the principle seems so very analogous, merits high consideration; and for the same important reason, its capability of conducing to the universal benefit of mankind, and the numerous animals under our protection.

Cure for Chilblains.

If, before any inflammation take place, the feet or hands affected are well washed morning and evening with hot water, or even with cold water on going to bed, it will generally stop their progress;

especially if warm socks or gloves be constantly worn: but, when they are actually inflamed, dip a four times folded rag into a mixture composed of four ounces of spirits of wine and camphor, and one ounce of Venice treacle; which must be tied every night on the chilblains till they quite disappear. With these precautions, they will seldom or never be found to ulcerate; or, as it is commonly called, to break: when this happens, dissolve an ounce of common turpentine in the yolk of an egg, and mix it up into a balsam, with half an ounce of lamp black, or even soot, and a drachm of oil or spirits of turpentine. Spread this balsam on a plegit of lint large enough entirely to cover the ulcer, tie it on with warm cloths over the part affected; and renew the dressings every morning and evening, which will speedily effect a cure. Soft leather socks, if worn before the first approach of winter, in October at farthest, and never suffered to get wet or hard, will generally preserve from chilblains even those who are most subject to be troubled with them.

Delicate Cream Cheese.

Take to every quart of new milk a gill of cream, make the mixture slightly warm, and put into it as little rennet as may be necessary just to turn it. The curd being come, to use the language of the dairy, lay a cloth on the vat or mould, which may be the bottom of a sieve, but should be the exact size of the intended cheese; then, cutting out the curd with a skimming dish, fill up the mould, turn the cloth over it, and leave it to drain. As the curd drains and settles, keep filling in more with a gentle pressure, till all the whey is out, and there is sufficient substance for the cheese. It must be then turned into a dry cloth, and pressed with a moderate weight, not exceeding two pounds. At night, it is to be turned into a clean cloth; and, the next morning, very slightly sprinkled with fine salt: after which, if sufficiently dry, it may be laid on a bed of fresh nettle, strawberry, or ash leaves; covered over with more; and, being shifted and turned twice a day, having the leaves occasionally renewed, will, in less than a fortnight, be sufficiently ripened for eating. If expedition be desirable, the maturity of the cheese may be considerably hastened by keeping it in a warm place, between two pewter dishes, and giving it a fresh bed and covering of leaves every day.

INDEX TO

THE NEW FAMILY RECEIPT-BOOK.

	Page		Page
German method of Clarifying and Preserving Fresh Butter	3	Lozenges for the Heart-burn	4
Queen Elizabeth's Cordial Electuary	ib.	Decoction for the Stone and Gravel	5
Genuine Friar's Balsam	4	Instant relief for a pain of the Bowels	ib.
		The true Daffy's Elixir	ib.

	Page
Infallible remedy for the Ague	5
Bayley's Patent Cakes for Liquid Blacking	6
Incomparable Fumigation, or Vapour for a Sore Throat	ib.
To make Fine Red Ink	7
Method of Polishing Rusty Steel	ib.
A fine Balsamic Elixir for Coughs and Consumptions	ib.
Admiral Gascoigne's Tincture of Rheubarb	ib.
German Cure for a Consumption	8
Easy and effectual Cure for Wens	ib.
Genuine Lozenges for the Piles	ib.
Easy method of cleaning Paper Hangings	9
Sir John Hill's Specific for the Scurvy	ib.
Russian method to preserve Green Peas for Winter	10
Admirable wash for the Hair	ib.
Fine Raspberry Vinegar	11
Genuine Turlington's Balsam	ib.
Cephalic Snuff	ib.
An excellent and cheap Composition for Weather Boarding, &c.	ib.
Incomparable Liquid for changing the Colour of the Hair	12
Dutch method of extracting beautiful Colours from Flowers	ib.
Excellent remedy for the Dropsy	13
Another powerful remedy for the Dropsy	ib.
Of the fining of Malt Liquors	ib.
To make Elderberry Beer	14
An easy method of Drying Currants in Bunches	ib.
Dr. Stoughton's celebrated Stomachic Elixir	ib.
Cure for a Pimpled Face	ib.
Curious method of separating Gold or Silver from Lace	15
Permanent Red .. k for marking Linen	15
Portable Balls for taking out Spots from Clothes	ib.
Art of preparing a newly-discovered Permanent Green Pigment both for Oil and Water Colours	ib.
Stewed Oysters in French Rolls	16
Dr. Anderson's admirable improvement of Salting Butter	ib.
Method of Fattening Chickens	17
Lord Orford's curious method of feeding Carp in Ponds	ib.
Dr. Fuller's Chemical Snuff for the Head Ache, Palsy, and Drowsy Distempers	ib.
Speedy remedy for a Bruised Eye	ib.
Stomach Plaster for a Cough	18
Oil of Brown Paper for Burns	ib.
Liquid for removing Spots of Grease, Pitch, or Oil from Cloth	ib.
To take out Ink Spots from Woollen, Linen, and Silk	ib.
Ink Stains taken out of Mahogany Furniture	19
Red Mixture for giving a fine Colour to Mahogany Furniture	ib.
Mr. Jayne's Patent method of preserving Eggs	ib.
Chinese mode of rendering Cloth, and even Muslin, Waterproof	ib.
Beautiful newly-discovered Golden Yellow Dye	20
Curious method of Breeding Gold and Silver Fish	ib.
Syrup of Red Cabbage, as prepared in France	21
Boluses for the Rheumatism and Contractions of the Joints	22

	Page
Pill for an Aching Hollow Tooth	22
Tea for the Gout	ib.
Infallible Powder for Shortness of Breath	ib.
Excellent Wash for Numbed or Trembling Hands	ib.
Mustard Whey for a Palsy and Nervous Disorders	23
Ingenious French Liquid for making Bulbous Roots flower beautifully in the Winter Season	ib.
Art of Extracting the finest Carmine Powder from Clippings of Scarlet Cloth	ib.
Substitute for Verdigris in producing a fine Black Dye without injury to Cloth	24
Artificial Musk	ib.
Wonderful, but easy and effectual method of rendering all sorts of Paper Fireproof	ib.
Bellamy's Patent methods of making Leather of all Sorts Waterproof	25
Genuine Receipt for making the Invaluable Cordial Liquor called Vespetro, recommended by the king of France's Physicians	ib.
Incomparable method of Salting Meat, as adopted by the late Empress of Russia	26
Electuary for the Rheumatism	ib.
Art of making the best Black Ink Powder	27
Genuine Syrup for Coughs, Spitting of Blood, &c.	ib.
Vast advantages of Baking instead of Boiling Beet-Root	ib.
Remedy for Wind in the Veins	28
Best method of making Sage Cheese	ib.
Syrup of Ginger	ib.
Wonderful Power of the Turkish Glue, with the Art of making it	ib
Valuable Secret in preparing Foil for Diamonds	29
Easy method of Dying Cotton with Madder	ib.
Admirable Water for Thickening the Hair, and to prevent its falling off	30
Celebrated French Worm Medicine for Dogs	ib.
Use of the celebrated German Tinder, and its great Importance	ib.
To make a Powder, by which you may write with water	31
Turkish method of Filtering Water by Ascension.	ib.
Patent Machine for Purifying the foulest water	ib.
Management of Coffee in France	32
An invaluable Mixture, for effectually destroying Bugs	ib.
Grand Ptisan, or Diet Drink of Health and Longevity, by a celebrated French Physician	33
Curious and simple manner of keeping Apricots, Peaches, Plums, &c. fresh all the Year	34
Genuine Windsor Soap	ib.
Art of Dying or Staining Leather Gloves, to resemble the beautiful York Tan, Limerick Dye, &c.	35
Art of making Phosphoric Tapers or Matches	ib.
Easy method of making Phosphoric Bottles	ib
Specifications of Lord William Murray's Patent for extracting Starch from Horse Chesnuts	36
Patent Potato Composition to be used instead of Yeast	ib.
Britannic Elastic Gum	37

Page

West India Bitters, or Anti-Bilious Drops 37
Oxymel of Garlic for Asthmatic complaints, Rheumatism, &c. ib.
Method of making Grape Wines, fully equal to Champaign and old Hock 38
Art of Extracting Spots of Grease, Tallow, Oil, &c. from Valuable Books, Prints, and Papers of all sorts, without injury to the Printing or Writing 39
Blaikie's Patent Substitute for Gum, in thickening Colours for Calico Printers, &c. 40
French method of making Garlic Vinegar ib.
Fine Tarragon Vinegar ib.
Vinegar of Roses 41
Excellent Blue Colour for Ceilings, &c. ib.
Composition for cleaning Marble Hearths, Chimney Pieces, Alabaster, &c. ib.
Turkish Rouge; or admirable Carmine 42
Purified Syrup of Molasses 43
Art of Preparing a fine Red Lake from Dutch Madder ib.
Clarified Goose Grease ib.
Composition for Restoring Scorched Linen 44
Easy method to prevent Bacon from becoming Rusty ib.
Best Saxon Blue ib.
Wonderful efficacy of Yeast in the cure of Putrid Diseases 45
Admirable Cement, or Mortar 47
Ancient British Liquor, called Bragget 48
Wonderful effect of Po ato Liquid, in cleaning Silk Woollen, and Cotton Furniture or Apparel, &c. without injury to the Texture or Colour 48
Method of clearing Feathers from their Animal Oil 49
Sebastian Grandi's Restoration or Discovery of the old Venetian Art of preparing Grounds for Painting on Pannels, Copper, or Canvas, &c. 50
Method of Purifying the Oil for mixing up Colours 51
Preparation of White, Brown, Yellow, Red, Gray, and Blue Black Colours, which never change, and may be used either in Oil or Water ib.
Superior Crayons of permanent Colours, to be applied either in Water or Oil ib.
Preparation of White and Coloured Chalks 52
Syrup of Damask Roses ib.
Syrup of Red Roses ib.
Excellent Spruce Beer 53
Blackman's celebrated Oil Colour Cakes for Artists ib
A curious and useful Glue 54
Norfolk Milk Punch ib.
Art of making the Curious Sympathetic Ink 55
Soft Sealing Wax, for Impressing Seals of Office, &c. ib.
Capital Sugar Vinegar 56
Excellent Embrocation for the Hooping-Cough ib.
Speedy Cure for a Sprain 57
Singular and simple manner of preserving Apples from the effects of frost in North America ib.
Cure for Chilblains ib.
Delicate Cream Cheese 58

INDEX

TO

ART OF COOKING, ETC.

CHAPTER I.

SOUPS and BROTHS.

	Page
Soup Vermicelli	12
Do. white	13
A-la-Reine	ib.
Cressy	14
Transparent	ib.
Almond	15
Sante, or Gravy	ib.
and Bouille	16
Ox Cheek	ib.
Macaroni	17
Calf's Head	ib.
Peas	18
White Peas	ib.
Green Peas	ib.
Onion	19
Milk	ib.
Milk, with Onions	20
Rice	ib.
Rice, or Potage du Ris	21
Scotch Barley Broth	ib.
Lorraine	ib.
Maigre	22
Giblet	23
Hodge Podge	ib.
Cow Heel	ib.
White	24
Gravy	ib.
Spring	25
Hare	ib.
Partridge	ib.
Cray Fish	26
Eel	ib.
Oyster	ib.
Mutton Broth	27
Beef Broth	ib.
Beef Drink	28
Beef Broth to keep	28
Veal Broth	ib.
Chicken Broth	ib.
Spring Broth	29
Plum Porridge to keep	ib.
Mock Turtle Soup	ib.
Portable Soup	30

CHAPTER II.

SECTION 1.

BOILING MEAT.

To dress a Calf's Head	33
Grass Lamb	ib.
A Ham	ib.
Do. another way	ib.
Ham a-la-Braise	34
Tongues	ib.
Neat's Tongue	ib.
Leg of Mutton	ib.
Lamb's Head	35
Do. another way	ib.
Leg of Lamb	36
A Haunch, or Neck of Venison	ib.
Pickled Pork	ib.
Pig's Pettitoes	37

SECTION 2.

BOILING POULTRY.

Turkeys	37
Chickens	38
Fowls	39
Rabbits and Ducks	ib.
Pigeons	40
Geese	ib.
Partridges	ib.
Pheasants	41
Snipes or Woodcocks	ib

SECTION 3.

BOILING FISH.

	Page
Turbot	42
Do. another way	ib.
Turbot en Maigre	43
Salmon	ib.
Do. whole for a large company	ib.
Cod's Head	ib.
Whole Cod	44
Salt Cod	45
Cod Sounds	ib.
Soles	ib.
Trout	46
Pike	ib.
Carp	47
Mullets	ib.
Mackarel	ib.
Mackarel a-la-Bourgeoise	48
Herrings	ib.
Flounders, Plaice, Perch, and Dabs	ib.
Eels	49
Sturgeon	ib.
Turtle	ib.
Court Bouillon	51

CHAPTER III.

SECTION 1.

ROASTING IN GENERAL.

BUTCHER'S MEAT.

Beef	53
Mutton and Lamb	ib.
Haunch of Mutton dressed like Venison	54
A Fore-quarter of Lamb	ib.
Tongues and Udders	ib.
Veal	ib.
Pork	55
Sucking Pigs	56
Calf's Head	57
Ham, or Gammon of Bacon	58

SECTION 2.

ROASTING POULTRY.

	Page
Turkeys	58
Fowls	59
Chickens	ib.
[illegible] een Geese	60
A Stubble Goose	60
Ducks	ib.
Pigeons	61
Larks	ib.
Rabbits	ib.

SECTION 3.

ROASTING GAME

Pheasants and Partridges	62
Woodcocks or Snipes	63
Hares	ib.
Venison	64

SECTION 4.

ROASTING FISH.

To roast Sturgeon	64
Roasted en Gras	ib.
Lobsters	ib.

CHAPTER IV.

SECTION 1.

BAKING.

BUTCHER'S MEAT.

Rump of Beef a-la-Braise	65
Calf's Head	ib.
Pigs	66
A Bullock's or Calf's Heart	ib

SECTION 2.

BAKING FISH.

Cod's Head	67
Salmon	ib.
Carp	68
Eels and Lampreys	ib.
Herrings	69
Turbot	ib.
Pike, with forcemeat	70
Mackarel	ib.

CHAPTER V.

BROILING.

SECTION 1.

Beef Steaks	71
Mutton Steaks	72
Pork Chops	ib.
Ox Palates	ib.
Chickens	73
Pigeons	ib.

Section 2.

BROILING FISH.

	Page
resh Salmon	74
Dried Salmon	ib.
Cod	ib.
Crimped do.	75
Cod Sounds	ib.
Trout	ib.
Mackarel	76
a-la-Maitre d'Hotel	ib.
Haddocks and Whitings	ib.
Eels	77
pitch-cocked	ib.
Herrings	ib.

CHAPTER VI.

Section 1.

FRYING.

BUTCHER'S MEAT.

Venison	78
Veal Cutlets	ib.
Neck or Loin of Lamb	79
Sweetbreads	ib.
Calf's Brains	ib.
Beef Steaks	80
Ox Tongues	ib.
Ox Feet, or Cow-Heel	ib.
Tripe	ib.
Sausages	81
Chickens	ib.
Artichoke Bottoms	ib.
Celery	ib.
Potatoes	82

Section 2.

FRYING FISH

Turbot	82
Carp	83
Tench	ib.
Soles	84
Smelts	ib.
Eels	ib.
Lampreys	85
Mullets	ib.
Herrings	ib.
Oysters	ib.

CHAPTER VII.

Section 1.

STEWING.

BUTCHER'S MEAT.

	Page
Fillet of Veal	86
Breast of Veal	ib.
Knuckle of Veal	ib.
Neck of Veal	87
Calf's Head	ib.
Liver	88
Rump of Beef	ib.
Beef Steaks	ib.
Goblets	ib.
Neat's Tongue	89
To dress Ox Palates	ib.
Ox Palates forced	ib.
To Marinade Ox Palates	90

Section 2.

STEWING POULTRY.

Turkey en Pain	90
Fowls	ib.
Chickens	91
Goose Giblets	ib.
Ducks	ib.
with Green Peas	92
Pigeons	ib.
Pheasants	ib.
Partridges	93
Cucumbers	ib.
Peas and Lettuce	94

Section 3.

STEWING FISH.

Carp and Tench	94
Barbel	95
Small Barbel	ib.
Trout	ib.
Pike	ib.
A Fricandeau of Pike	96
Cod	ib.
Soles, Plaice, and Flounders	ib.
Lampreys and Eels	ib.
Prawns, Shrimps, and Cray-Fish	97
Oysters	ib.
Scolloped	98
Muscles	

CHAPTER VIII.

SECTION 1.

HASHING AND MINCING.

BUTCHER'S MEAT.

	Page
Calf's Head	98
Veal Minced	100
Mutton Hashed	ib.

SECTION 2.

HASHING POULTRY AND GAME.

Turkeys	100
another way	101
Fowls	ib.
Chickens	ib.
Partridges or Woodcocks	ib.
Wild Ducks	102
Hares	ib.
Hare Jugged	ib.
Venison	103

CHAPTER IX.

SECTION 1.

FRICASSEEING.

BUTCHER'S MEAT, POULTRY, &c.

Neat's Tongue	103
Sweetbreads White	ib.
Calf's Feet a-la-Carmagot	104
Tripe	ib.
Chickens	ib.
Rabbits White	105
Brown	ib.

SECTION 2.

FRICASSEEING FISH, &c.

Cod Sounds	105
Soles	106
Eels	ib.
Flounders	107
Skate or Thornback	ib.
Oysters	108
Eggs	ib.
Eggs with Onions and Mushrooms	ib.
Mushrooms	ib.
Skirrits	109
Artichoke Bottoms	ib.

CHAPTER X.

SECTION 1.

RAGOOS.

BUTCHER'S MEAT.

	Page
Breast of Veal	109
Neck of Veal	110
Sweetbreads Brown	ib.
Calf's Feet	111
Pig's Feet and Ears	ib.
Fore-quarter of House Lamb	ib.
Beef	112
Mutton	ib.

SECTION 2.

RAGOOS OF POULTRY, VEGETABLES, &c.

A Goose	113
Livers of Poultry	ib.
Oysters	114
Muscles	ib.
Mushrooms	115
Artichoke Bottoms	ib.
Asparagus	ib.
Cucumbers	116
another way	ib.
Cauliflowers	ib.
French Beans	ib.
Endive or Succory	117
Cabbage Force-Maigre	118
Asparagus forced in French Rolls	ib.
Peas François	ib.

CHAPTER XI.

GRAVIES, CULLISES, AND OTHER SAUCES.

Gravies	119
A very rich Gravy	ib.
Brown Gravy	120
Sauce Italian	ib.
Piquante	ib.
A Cullis for all sorts of Ragoos and rich Sauces	121
A Family Cullis	ib.
A White do.	ib

Page
A Cullis for Fish 122
Ham Sauce ib.
Essence of Ham 123
Sauce for Lamb ib.
Sauce for any kind of Roast Meat ib.
A White Sauce ib.
Sauce for most kinds of Fish 124
Nonpareil ib.
Sauce a-la-Menehou ib.
Egg Sauce ib.
Bread Sauce ib.
Anchovy Sauce 125
Shrimp Sauce ib.
Oyster Sauce ib.
To melt Butter ib.
Caper Sauce 126
Shalot Sauce ib.
Lemon Sauce for boiled Fowls ib.
Gooseberry Sauce ib.
Fennel Sauce ib.
Mint Sauce ib.
A relishing Sauce ib.
To crisp Parsley ib.
Sauce for Wild Ducks, Teal, &c. 127
Pontiff Sauce ib.
Aspic Sauce ib.
Forcemeat Balls ib.
Lemon Pickle 128

CHAPTER XII.
MADE DISHES.
SECTION 1.
BUTCHER'S MEAT.

Bombarded Veal 128
Fricandeau of Veal 129
Veal Olives ib.
Grenadines of Veal 30
Veal Cutlets en Papilotes ib.
Porcupine of a Breast of Veal ib.
Fricandeau of Veal a-la-Bourgeois 131
Calf's Head Surprise ib.
Calf's Pluck 132
Loin of Veal en Epigram ib.
Pillow of Veal 133
Shoulder of Veal a-la-Piedmontoise ib.

Page
Sweetbreads of Veal a-la-Dauphine 134
Sweetbreads en Gordineere ib.
Sweetbreads a-la-daub 135
Scotch Collops ib.
Beef Collops 136
Beef a-la-daub ib.
Beef Tremblent 137
Beef Kidneys a-la-Bourgeois ib.
Beef a-la-mode ib.
Beef a-la-Royal 138
Beef Olives ib.
Bouille Beef 139
Sirloin of Beef en Epigram ib.
The inside of a Sirloin of Beef forced 140
A Round of Beef forced ib.
Beef Steaks rolled 141
Beef Rump en Matelotte ib.
Beef Escarlot 142
Tongue and Udder forced ib.
Tripe a-la-Kilkenny ib.
Harrico of Mutton ib.
Shoulder of Mutton surprised 143
To dress Umbles of Deer ib.
Mutton Kebobbed ib.
Leg of Mutton a-la-haut Gout 144
Leg of Mutton roasted with Oysters ib.
Shoulder of Mutton en Epigram ib
Sheep's Rumps and Kidneys ib.
Mutton Rumps a-la Braise 145
Mutton Chops in Disguise ib.
A Shoulder of Mutton called Hen and Chickens 146
A Quarter of Lamb forced ib.
Lamb's Bits ib.
Lamb a-la-Bechamel 147
Lamb Chops en Casarole ib.
Barbacued Pig ib.
A Pig au Pere Duillet 148
A Pig Matelotte 148
Sheep's Trotters en Gratten 149

SECTION 2.
MADE DISHES OF POULTRY, &c.

Turkey a-la-daub 149
in a hurry 150

	Page
Fowls a-la-Braise	150
forced	151
marinaded	ib.
Chickens Chiringrate	ib.
a-la-Braise	152
in savoury Jelly	153
and Tongues	ib.
Pullets a-la-Sainte Menehout	ib.
Ducks a-la-Braise	154
a-la-Mode	ib.
a-la-Françoise	155
A Goose a-la-Mode	ib.
marinaded	156
Pigeons Compote	ib.
French Pupton of Pigeons	157
Pigeons a- la-Braise	ib.
au Poise	ib.
Fricandeau of Pigeons	158
Pigeons a-la-Daub	ib.
a-la-Soussel	159
in a Hole	ib.
Jugged Pigeons	ib.
Partridges a-la-Braise	160
Pheasants a-la-Braise	ib.
Snipes or Woodcocks, in Surtout	161
Snipes, with Purslain Leaves	ib.
Larks a-la-Françoise	162
Florendine Hares	ib.
Rabbits	163
Jugged Hare	ib.
Rabbits Surprised	ib.
Rabbits en Casserole	164
Macaroni	ib.
Amulets	ib.
of Asparagus	165
Oyster Loaves	ib.
Mushroom Loaves	ib.
Eggs in Surtout	ib.
and Broccoli	ib.
Spinach and Eggs	166
To make Ramekins	ib.

CHAPTER XIII.

VEGETABLES AND ROOTS.

	Page
Asparagus	167
Artichokes	ib.
Broccoli	167
Cauliflowers	168
Green Peas	ib.
Windsor Beans	169
Kidney do.	ib.
Spinach	ib.
Cabbages	ib.
Turnips	170
Carrots	ib
Parsnips	ib.
Potatoes	ib.
Scolloped	171
Hops	ib.

CHAPTER XIV.

SECTION 1.

BOILED PUDDINGS.

Bread Pudding	171
Batter do.	173
Custard do.	ib.
Quaking do.	ib.
Sago do.	174
Marrow do.	ib.
Biscuit do.	ib.
Almond do.	ib.
Tansy do.	ib.
another way	175
Herb do.	ib.
Spinach do.	ib.
Cream do.	176
Hunting do.	ib.
Steak do.	ib.
Calf's Foot do.	177
Prune do.	ib.
Plum do.	ib.
Hasty do.	ib.
Oatmeal do.	178
Suet do.	ib.
Veal Suet do.	ib.
Cabbage do.	ib.
A Spoonful do.	179
White Puddings in Skins	ib.
Apple do.	ib.
Apple Dumplings	ib.
Suet do.	180
Raspberry do	ib.
Yeast do.	ib.

	Page
Norfolk Dumplings	180
Hard do.	181
Potato Pudding	ib.
Black do.	ib.

SECTION 2.

BAKED PUDDINGS.

Vermicelli Pudding	182
Sweetmeat do.	ib.
Orange do.	ib.
Lemon do.	183
Almond do.	ib.
Rice do.	184
Millet do.	ib.
Oat do.	ib.
Transparent do.	185
French Barley do.	ib.
Lady Sunderland's do.	ib.
Citron do.	186
Chesnut do.	ib.
Quince do.	ib.
Cowslip do.	187
Cheese-curd do.	ib.
Apple do.	ib.
New-Market do.	ib.
A Grateful do.	188
Carrot do.	ib.
Yorkshire do.	ib.

CHAPTER XV.

SECTION 1.

PIES.

MEAT PIES.

Beef Steak Pie	190
Mutton do.	ib.
A Mutton Pie a-la-Perigord	191
Veal do.	ib.
A Rich Veal do.	ib.
Lamb or Veal do. in high taste	ib.
Venison Pasty	192
Olive Pie	ib.
Calf's Head do.	193
Feet do.	ib.
Sweetbread do.	194
Chesnire Pork do.	ib.
Devonsnire Squab do	ib

SECTION 2.

PIES made of POULTRY &c.

	Page
A Plain Goose Pie	195
Duck do.	ib.
Pigeon do.	196
Chicken do.	ib.
another way	ib.
Partridge do.	197
Hare do.	ib.
Rabbit do.	ib.
another way	198
Fine Patties	ib.
To make any sort of Timbale	199

SECTION 3.

FRUIT PIES.

Apple Pie	199
Tart	200
Cherry Pie	ib.
Mince Pies	201
Another Method of making Mince Pies	ib.
To make Mincemeat	202
Orange and Lemon Tarts	ib.
Tart de Moi	ib.
Artichoke Pie	203
Vermicelli do.	ib.

SECTION 4.

FISH PIES.

Eel Pie	203
Turbot do.	204
Sole do.	ib.
Flounder do.	ib.
Carp do.	205
Tench do.	ib.
Trout do.	ib.
Salmon do.	206
Herring do.	ib.
Lobster do.	ib.

CHAPTER XVI.

PANCAKES and FRITTERS.

Pancakes	207
Cream Pancakes	ib.
Rice do.	ib.

	Page
Pink-coloured Pancakes	208
Clary do.	ib.
Plain Fritters	ib.
Apple Fritters	209
Water Fritters	ib.
White Fritters	ib.
Hasty Fritters	ib.
Fritters Royal	210
Tansy Fritters	ib.
Rice do.	ib.
Chicken do.	211
Bilboquet do.	ib.
Orange do.	ib.
Strawberry do.	212
Do. another way	ib.
Raspberry Fritters	ib.
Currant do.	ib.
German do.	213
Almond Fraze	ib.

CHAPTER XVII.

Section 1.

TARTS AND PUFFS.

Raspberry Tart	214
Green Almond Tart	ib.
Angelica Tarts	215
Rhubarb Tarts	ib.
Spinach Tarts	ib.
Petit Patties	216
Orange Tarts	ib.
Chocolate Tarts	ib.

Section 2.

PUFFS, &c.

Sugar Puffs	217
Lemon Puffs	ib.
Almond Puffs	ib.
Chocolate Puffs	ib.
Curd Puffs	218
Wafers	ib.

CHAPTER XVIII.

Section 1.

CHEESECAKES AND CUSTARDS.

	Page
Cheesecakes	218
Common Cheesecakes	219
Fine Cheesecakes	219
Bread Cheesecakes	220
Rice Cheesecakes	ib.
Almond Cheesecakes	ib.
Do. another way	ib.
Lemon Cheesecakes	221
Citron Cheesecakes	ib.

Section 2.

CUSTARDS

Plain Custards	221
Do. another way	222
Baked Custards	ib.
Rice Custards	ib.
Almond Custards	ib.
Lemon Custards	ib
Orange Custards	223

CHAPTER XIX.

CAKES, BISCUITS, &c.

A Common Cake	224
A rich Seed Cake	ib.
A Pound Cake plain	ib.
Cream Cakes	ib.
Wedding or Christening Cake	225
Rice Cakes	ib.
Gingerbread Cakes	ib.
Bath Cakes or Buns	226
Shrewsbury Cakes	ib.
Portugal Cakes	ib.
Saffron Cakes	ib.
Prussian Cakes	227
Queen Cakes	ib.
Almond Cakes	ib.
Little Plum Cakes	228
Ratifia Cakes	ib.
Apricot Cakes	ib.
Orange Cakes	229
Lemon Cakes	ib.
Currant Cakes	ib.
Whigs	230
Common Biscuits	ib.
Sponge Biscuits	ib.
Spanish Biscuits	ib.
Drop Biscuits	231
Lemon Biscuits	ib.
Macaroons	ib.

	Page
Green Caps	231
Black Caps	232
Snow Balls	ib.

CHAPTER XX.

Section 1.

THE ART OF CONFECTIONARY.

The Method of preparing Sugars and Colours	233
Smooth or Candy Suga	ib.
Bloom Sugar	ib.
Feathered do.	ib.
Crackled do.	ib.
Carmel do.	ib.
Red Colour do.	235
Blue do.	ib.
Yellow do.	ib.
Green do	ib.
Devices in Sugar	ib.
Sugar of Roses in various figures	236

Section 2.

CREAMS AND JAMS.

Orange Cream	236
Lemon do.	ib.
Hartshorn do.	237
Burnt do.	ib,
— another way	ib.
Blanched do.	ib.
Cream a-la-Franchipane	238
Whipt Cream	ib.
Spanish do.	ib.
Steeple do.	ib.
Barley do.	239
Pistachio do.	ib.
Tea do.	ib.
Coffee do.	ib.
Chocolate do.	240
— another way	ib.
Pompadour do.	ib.
Ratifia do.	ib.
Raspberry de.	241
Ice do.	ib.
Various Fruit, Custard Ices, &c.	241
Raspberry Jam	242
Strawberry do.	ib.
Apricot do.	ib.
Gooseberry do.	ib.
Black Currant do.	243
Iceings for Cakes or various Articles in Confectionary	ib.
Do. another way	ib.

Section 3.

JELLIES and SYLLABUBS.

Calf's Feet Jelly	243
Hartshorn do.	244
Orange do.	245
Blanc Mange	ib.
Jaunmange	246
Black Currant Jelly	ib.
Riband do.	247
Savoury do.	ib.
Common Syllabubs	248
Whipt do.	ib.
Solid do.	ib.
Lemon do.	ib.
Everlasting do.	249
A Hedgehog	ib.
Flummery	250
French do.	ib.
Green Melon in Flummery	251
Solomon's Temple in do.	ib.

Section 4.

PRESERVING FRUIT, &c.

Apricots	252
Peaches	ib.
Quinces	253
Barberries	ib.
Pine Apples	254
Grapes	ib.
Morello Cherries	255
Green Codlins	ib.
Golden Pippins	ib.
Green-Gage Plums	256
Oranges	ib.
Raspberries	257
Strawberries	ib.

	Page
Currants in Bunches	258
Gooseberries	259
Do. in imitation of Hops	ib.
Damsons	260
Walnuts	261
Cucumbers	262

SECTION 5.

DRYING AND CANDYING.

Dried Apricots	263
Peaches	ib.
Candied Angelica	264
Green-Gage Plums dried	ib.
Dried Cherries	ib.
Damsons	265
Candied Cassia	ib.
Lemon and Orange Peels Candied	ib.
Candied Ginger	ib.
Horehound	266
Almond Cake, or Gateau Noga	ib.
Candied Rhubarb Cakes	ib.
Compote of Crude Orange	267
of Apples	ib.
of Pears	ib.
of Quinces	ib.
Orange Chips	ib.
Marmalade	268
Apricot do.	ib.
Quince do.	ib.
Transparent do.	269
Burnt Almonds	ib.
Raspberry Paste	ib.
Currant do.	270
Gooseberry do.	ib.

SECTION 6.

ORNAMENTS IN CONFECTIONARY.

ARTIFICIAL FRUIT.

A Dish of Snow	271
Moonshine	ib.
Floating Island	272
Desert Island	273
Chinese Temple	ib.

CHAPTER XXI

PICKLING.

	Page
Mangoes	274
Girkins	275
Cucumbers	276
in Slices	ib.
To keep Cucumbers	277
Walnuts	ib.
Red Cabbage	280
Onions	ib.
Kidney, or French Beans	281
Barberries	ib.
Beet Roots	282
Radish Pods	ib.
Cauliflowers	ib.
Artichokes	283
Nasturtiums	ib.
Mushrooms	ib.
Mushroom Catsup	284
Powder	ib.
Walnut Catsup	ib.
Indian Pickle	285
Asparagus	ib.
Parsley Pickled Green	286
Peaches	ib.
Golden Pippins	287
Grapes	ib.
Red Currants	288
Caveach or Pickled Mackarel	ib.
Smelts	289
Oysters	ib.
Anchovies	290
Ox Palates	ib.

CHAPTER XXII.

COLLARING

VENISON.

Breast of Veal	292
Breast of Mutton	ib.
Beef	293
Calf's Head	294
Pig	ib.
Eels	295
Mackarel	ib.
Salmon	ib

CHAPTER XXIII.

Section 1.

POTTING MEAT and POULTRY.

	Page
Venison	296
Hares	297
Marble Veal	ib.
Tongues	ib.
Geese and Fowls	298
Beef	ib.
Pigeons	299
Woodcocks	ib.

Section 2.

FISH.

Salmon	300
Lobster	301

CHAPTER XXIV

CURING of various Kinds of MEATS, &c.

Hams	302
Do. various	303
Bacon	ib.
Mutton Hams	304
Beef do.	ib.
Neat's Tongue	305
Hung Beef	ib.
Hunting do.	306
Pickled Pork	ib.
Mock Brawn	307
Turkey Soused	ib.
To make fine Sausages	308
Oxford Sausages	ib.

CHAPTER XXV.

To keep Green Peas till Christmas	309
To keep Gooseberries	ib.
To keep Mushrooms	310
To bottle Damsons	ib.

CHAPTER XXVI.

POSSETS and GRUELS.

	Page
Sack Possets	311
Wine Posset	312
Ale Posset	ib.
Orange Posset	312
White Caudle	ib.
Brown Caudle	ib.
White Wine Whey	313
Water Gruel	ib
Barley Gruel	ib
Orgeat Paste	ib.

CHAPTER XXVII.

MADE WINES, &c.

Raisin Wine	314
An excellent Wine	ib.
Currant Wine	315
Gooseberry Wine	ib.
Mulberry Wine	316
Raspberry Wine	ib.
Damson Wine	ib.
Orange Wine	317
Lemon Wine	ib.
Grape Wine	318
Cherry Wine	ib.
Elder Wine	319
Apricot Wine	ib.
Quince Wine	ib.
Blackberry Wine	320
Turnip Wine	ib.
Birch Wine	321
Rose Wine	ib.
Ginger Wine	322
Balm Wine	ib.
Mead Wine	ib.
Raspberry Brandy	323
Orange Brandy	ib.
Lemon Brandy	324
Black Cherry Brandy	ib.

CHAPTER XXVIII.

CORDIAL WATERS.

Rose Water	324
Lavender Water	325
Peppermint Water	ib.
Surfeit Water	ib.

CHAPTER XXIX.

Section 1.

THE ART OF BREWING.

On the Copper, &c.	326

Section 2. Page

Vessels for Brewing 327

Section 3.

The Mash-tub, Penstaff, &c. 329

Section 4.

Of the proper time of Brewing 331

Section 5.

Water proper for Brewing 332

Section 6.

The Quality of the Malt and Hops 334

Section 7.

The process of Brewing 336

Section 8.

The proper Management of Malt Liquors 341

Section 9. Page

Of Bottling Malt Liquors 343

To Preserve Yeast 345

CHAPTER XXX.

DIRECTIONS for TRUSSING POULTRY, &c.

Turkeys 346

Fowls 348

Chickens ib.

Geese 349

Pigeons ib.

Wild Fowl 350

Pheasants and Partridges ib.

Woodcocks and Snipes 351

Larks ib.

Hares ib.

Rabbits 352

www.ingramcontent.com/pod-product-compliance
Lightning Source LLC
Chambersburg PA
CBHW032301280326
41932CB00009B/646